Teacher's

WorldView 3

SERIES EDITOR: MICHAEL ROST

Ellen Kisslinger

WorldView Teacher's Edition 3

Authorized adaptation from the United Kingdom edition entitled *Language to Go*, First Edition, published by Pearson Education Limited publishing under its Longman imprint.
Copyright © 2002 by Pearson Education Limited

All rights reserved.
No part of this publication may be reproduced, stored in a retrieval system, or transmitted in any form or by any means, electronic, mechanical, photocopying, recording, or otherwise, without the prior permission of the publisher.

American English adaptation published by Pearson Education, Inc.
Copyright © 2005.

Pearson Education, 10 Bank Street, White Plains, NY 10606

Editorial director: Pamela Fishman
Project manager: Irene Frankel
Senior development editors: Robin Longshaw, José Antonio Méndez
Vice president, director of design and production: Rhea Banker
Executive managing editor: Linda Moser
Associate managing editor: Mike Kemper
Production editor: Sasha Kintzler
Art director: Elizabeth Carlson
Vice president, director of international marketing: Bruno Paul
Senior manufacturing buyer: Edie Pullman
Cover design: Elizabeth Carlson
Text design: Elizabeth Carlson and Word and Image Design
Photo research: Aerin Csigay
Text composition: TSI Graphics
Text font: 8.5/11pt Utopia

ISBN: 0-13-184009-6

Printed in the United States of America
3 4 5 6 7 8 9 10–BAM–09 08

Text Credits

Page 21, Good To See You. Words and music by Neil Young. © 1998 Silver Fiddle Music. All rights reserved. Used by permission of Warner Bros. Publications. 59, My Way. Words by Paul Anka, music by Jacques Revaux and Claude François. Copyright 1967 Société des Nouvelles Editions Eddie Barclay, Paris, France. Copyright for the U.S.A. and Canada © 1969 Management Agency & Music Publishing, Inc. (BMI) All rights reserved. Used by permission. 97, You've Got a Friend. Words and music by Carole King. © 1971 (Renewed 1999) Colgems-EMI Music Inc. All rights reserved. International copyright secured. Used by permission. 135, If I Could Turn Back Time. Words and music by Diane Warren. ©1989 Realsongs (ASCAP). All rights reserved. Used by permission.

Illustration Credits

Steve Attoe, pp. 5, 66, 102, 106; Paul McCusker, 38, 81; Stephen Quinlan, 20, 96.

Photo Credits

Page 2, David Lees/Getty Images; 4, Robert Frerck/Odyssey; 6, *(top)* ImageState/International Stock, *(bottom)* Omni Photo Communications Inc./Index Stock Imagery, 10, *(A)* Seth Resnick/Stock, Boston Inc./ PictureQuest, *(B)* James Marshall/Corbis, *(C)* Robert Holmes/Corbis, *(D)* Dorota & Mariusz Jarymowicz/Dorling Kindersley Media Library; 12, Yang Liu/Corbis; 13, Getty Images; 15, Stone/Ben Edwards; 18, Spencer Grant/PhotoEdit; 20, Justin Sullivan/Getty Images; 24, Peter Cade/Getty Images; 26, *(left)* Frank Spooner Pictures/Gamma, *(middle)* Britstock-IFA/Wirth, *(right)* South American Pictures/Tony Morrison; 28, The Image Bank/Romilly Lockyer; 29, Andrew Shennan/Getty Images; 30, *(left)* Mary Kate Denny/PhotoEdit, *(right)* Tony Arruza/Getty Images; 31, Larry Gatz/Getty Images; 33, Paul Steel/Corbis; 34, Associated Press, AP/Chris Pizzello; 35, Image State/AGE Fotostock; 36, Siegfried Tauqueur/eStock Photo/PictureQuest; 42, Bob Krist/Corbis; 44, *(top)* Creatas/Creatas/PictureQuest, *(bottom)* First Light; 48, *(left)* IPC, *(right)* Trevor Clifford; 50, *(left)* Abode, *(right)* Abode; 53, *(top)* Associated Press/Simon Thong, *(bottom)* Trevor Clifford; 54, Klaus Lahnstein/Getty Images; 56, Bruce Leighty/Index Stock Imagery; 58, Neal Preston/Corbis; 60, Stone/Jake Rais; 61, *(left)* Corbis Stock Market/Paul Barton, *(right)* Corbis Stock Market/Larry Williams; 64, *(A)* Pictor International, *(B)* The Image Bank/Donata Pizzi, *(C)* Powerstock Zefa, *(G)* Powerstock Zefa, *(H)* Telegraph Colour Library/Ian D. Cartwight; 65, *(D)* Stone/G.D.T., *(E)* Stone/Christopher Bissell, *(F)* The Image Bank/Daniel E. Arsenault Photography; 68, Trevor Clifford; 69, Trevor Clifford; 71, Erlanson Productions/Getty Images; 72, *(left)* Howard Huang/Getty Images, *(left bottom)* Getty Images, *(right)* Zefa Visual Media - Germany/Index Stock Imagery, *(middle)* Michael Keller/Corbis, *(bottom right)* Thomas Del Brase/Getty Images; 73, Corbis Images/PictureQuest; 75, *(left)* Pictor International, *(middle)* Powerstock Zefa/Benelux Press, *(right)* ActionPlus/Neale Haynes; 76, Professional Sport/ImageState-Pictor/PictureQuest; 77, *(left)* Magnum/Peter Marlow, *(right)* Magnum/Peter Marlow; 78, ThinkStock LLC/Index Stock Imagery; 82, *(top left)* Junko Kimura/Getty Images, *(top right)* Terry McCormick/Getty Images, *(bottom)* Steve Mason/Photodisc/PictureQuest; 84, Adam Smith/Getty Images; 86, *(background)* Powerstock Zefa, *(left)* World Pictures, *(A-H)* Trevor Clifford; 88, Glen Allison/Getty Images; 90, *(top right)* Columbia/Sony/The Kobal Collection, *(bottom right)* Stephane Cardinale/Corbis, *(left)* Dreamworks LLC/The Kobal Collection; 92, Digital Vision /Getty Images; 95, Trevor Clifford; 96, Neal Preston/Corbis; 98, *(top right)* Images.com/Corbis, *(bottom left)* Randy Faris/Corbis; 99, ins. attribution for Mona Lisa, 103, *(left)* Stuart McClymont /Getty Images; 104, Bettmann/Corbis; 105, Bettmann/Corbis; 107, Gareth Boden; 108, Corbis Images/PictureQuest; 112, Stewart Cohen/Index Stock Imagery; 113, *(left)* Michael Keller/Corbis, *(right)* ITStock Int'l/eStock Photo/PictureQuest; 117, Mark Hunt/Index Stock Imagery; 120, *(top)* Corbis Stock Market/Peter Beek, *(bottom)* Corbis Stock Market/Jon Feingersh; 121, *(right)* Telegraph Picture Library/M. Krasowitz; 123, William Thomas Cain/Getty Images; 126, Digital Vision/Getty Images; 128, Superstock; 130, Digital Vision/Getty Images; 133, *(left)* Bill Bachmann/PhotoEdit, *(middle left)* Richard Klune/Corbis, *(middle right)* Jonathan Nourok/PhotoEdit, *(right)* Forest Johnson/Corbis; 135, Robert Mora/Getty Images.

Acknowledgments

The authors and series editor wish to acknowledge with gratitude the following reviewers, consultants, and piloters for their thoughtful contributions to the development of *WorldView*.
BRAZIL: São Paulo: Sérgio Gabriel, **FMU/Cultura Inglesa, Jundiaí;** Heloísa Helena Medeiros Ramos, **Kiddy and Teen;** Zaina Nunes, Márcia Mathias Pinto, Angelita Goulvea Quevedo, **Pontifícia Universidade Católica;** Rosa Laquimia Souza, **FMU-FIAM;** Élcio Camilo Alves de Souza, **Associação Alumni;** Maria Antonieta Gagliardi, Marie Adele Ryan, **Centro Britânico;** Chris Ritchie, **Sevenidiomas;** Joacyr Oliveira, Debora Schisler, **FMU;** Maria Thereza Garrelhas Gentil, **Colégio Mackenzie;** Carlos Renato Lopes, **Uni-Santana;** Yara M. Bannwart Rago, Jacqueline Zilberman, **Instituto King's Cross;** Vera Lúcia Cardoso Berk, **Talkative Idioms Center;** Ana Paula Hoepers, **Instituto Winners;** Carlos C.S. de Celis, Daniel Martins Neto, **CEL-LEP;** Maria Carmen Castellani, **União Cultural Brasil Estados Unidos;** Kátia Martins P. de Moraes Leme, **Colégio Pueri Domus;** Luciene Martins Farias, **Aliança Brasil Estados Unidos;** Neide Aparecida Silva, **Cultura Inglesa;** Áurea Shinto, **Santos:** Maria Lúcia Bastos, **Instituto Four Seasons. Curitiba:** Marila de Carvalho Hanech. **COLOMBIA: Bogota:** Sergio Monguí, Rafael Díaz Morales, **Universidad de la Salle;** Yecid Ortega Páez, Yojanna Ruiz G., **Universidad Javeriana;** Merry García Metzger, **Universidad Minuto de Dios;** Maria Caterina Barbosa, **Coninglés;** Nelson Martínez R., **Asesorías Académicas;** Eduardo Martínez, Stella Lozano Vega, **Universidad Santo Tomás de Aquino;** Kenneth McIntyre, **ABC English Institute.**
JAPAN: Tokyo: Peter Bellars, **Obirin University;** Michael Kenning, **Takushoku University;** Martin Meldrum, **Takushoku University;** Carol Ann Moritz, **New International School;** Mary Sandkamp, **Musashi Sakai;** Dan Thompson, **Yachiyo Chiba-ken/American Language Institute;** Carol Vaughn, **Kanto Kokusai High School. Osaka:** Lance Burrows, **Osaka Prefecture Settsu High School;** Bonnie Carpenter, **Mukogawa Joshi Daigaku/ Hannan Daigaku;** Josh Glaser, Richard Roy, **Human International University/Osaka Jogakuin Junior College;** Gregg Kennerly, **Osaka YMCA;** Ted Ostis, **Otemon University;** Chris Page, **ECC Language Institute;** Leon Pinsky, **Kwansei Gakuin University;** Chris Ruddenklau, **Kinki University;** John Smith, **Osaka International University. Saitama:** Marie Cosgrove, **Surugadai University. Kobe:** Donna Fujimoto, **Kobe University of Commerce. KOREA: Seoul:** Adrienne Edwards-Daugherty, Min Hee Kang, James Kirkmeyer, Paula Reynolds, Warren Weappa, Matthew Williams, **YBM ELS Shinchon;** Brian Cook, Jack Scott, Russell Tandy, **Hanseoung College. MEXICO: Mexico City:** Alberto Hern, **Instituto Anglo Americano de Idiomas;** Eugenia Carbonell, **Universidad Interamericana;** Cecilia Rey Gutiérrez, María del Rosario Escalada Ruiz, **Universidad Motolinia;** Raquel Márquez Colin, **Universidad St. John's;** Francisco Castillo, Carlos René Malacara Ramos, **CELE – UNAM/Mascarones;** Belem Saint Martin, **Preparatoria ISEC;** María Guadalupe Aguirre Hernández, **Comunidad Educativa Montessori;** Isel Vargas Ruelas, Patricia Contreras, **Centro Universitario Oparin;** Gabriela Juárez Hernández, Arturo Vergara Esteban Juan, **English Fast Center;** Jesús Armando Martínez Salgado, **Preparatoria Leon Tolstoi;** Regina Peña Martínez, **Centro Escolar Anahuac;** Guadalupe Buenrostro, **Colegio Partenon;** Rosendo Rivera Sánchez, **Colegio Anglo Español;** María Rosario Hernández Reyes, **Escuela Preparatoria Monte Albán;** Fernanda Cruzado, **Instituto Tecnológico del Sur;** Janet Harris M., **Colegio Anglo Español;** Rosalba Pérez Contreras, **Centro Lingüístico Empresarial. Ecatepec:** Diana Patricia Ordaz García, **Comunidad Educativa Montessori;** Leticia Ricart P., **Colegio Holandés;** Samuel Hernández B. **Instituto Cultural Renacimiento. Tlalpan:** Ana María Cortés, **Centro Educativo José P. Cacho. San Luis Potosi:** Sigi Orta Hernández, María de Guadalupe Barrientos J., **Instituto Hispano Inglés;** Antonieta Raya Z., **Instituto Potosino;** Gloria Carpizo, **Seminario Mayor Arquidiocesano de San Luis Potosí;** Susana Prieto Noyola, Silvia Yolanda Ortiz Romo **Universidad Politécnica de San Luis Potosí;** Rosa Arrendondo Flores, **Instituto Potosino/Universidad Champagnat;** María Cristina Carmillo, María Carmen García Leos, **Departamento Universitario de Inglés, UASLP;** María Gloria Candia Castro, **Universidad Tecnológica SLP;** Bertha Guadalupe Garza Treviño, **Centro de Idiomas, UASLP. Guadalajara:** Nancy Patricia Gómez Ley, **Escuela Técnica Palmares;** Gabriela Michel Vázquez, **Colegio Cervantes Costa Rica;** Abraham Barbosa Martínez, **Colegio Enrique de Osso;** Ana Cristina Plascencia Haro, Joaquín Limón Ramos, **Centro Educativo Tlaquepaque III;** Lucía Huerta Cervantes, Paulina Cervantes Fernández, Audrey Lizaola López, **Colegio Enrique de Osso,** Rocío de Miguel, **Colegio La Paz;** Jim Nixon, **Colegio Cervantes Costa Rica;** Hilda Delgado Parga, **Colegio D'Monaco;** Claudia Rodríguez, **English Key. León:** Laura Montes de la Serna, **Colegio Británico A.C.;** Antoinette Marie Hernández, **"The Place 4U2 Learn" Language School;** Delia Zavala Torres, Verónica Medellín Urbina, **EPCA Sur;** María Eugenia Gutiérrez Mena, Ana Paulina Suárez Cervantes, **Universidad la Salle;** Herlinda Rodríguez Hernández, **Instituto Mundo Verde,** María Rosario Torres Neri, **Instituto Jassa. Aguascalientes:** María Dolores Jiménez Chávez, **ECA – Universidad Autónoma de Aguascalientes;** María Aguirre Hernández, **ECA – Proyecto Start;** Fernando Xavier Goúrey O., **UAA – IEA "Keep On";** Felisia Guadalupe García Ruiz, **Universidad Tecnológica;** Margarita Zapiain B, Martha Ayala de la Concordia, Fernando Xavier Gomez Orenday, **Universidad Autónoma de Aguascalientes;** Gloria Aguirre Hernández, **Escuela de la Ciudad de Aguascalientes;** Hector Arturo Moreno Diaz, **Universidad Bonaterra.**

Contents

Scope and Sequence		vi
Introduction		x

Teaching Notes

Unit 1	Nice to see you again	T2
Unit 2	Why women iron	T6
Unit 3	Living in luxury	T10
Unit 4	Allergic reactions	T14
Review 1		T18
World of Music 1		T20
Unit 5	A typical day	T22
Unit 6	It's absolutely true!	T26
Unit 7	Eating out	T30
Unit 8	It's a deal!	T34
Review 2		T38
Unit 9	The river	T40
Unit 10	On the other hand	T44
Unit 11	Trading spaces	T48
Unit 12	A soccer fan's website	T52
Review 3		T56
World of Music 2		T58
Unit 13	Green card	T60
Unit 14	What's that noise?	T64
Unit 15	Mumbai Soap	T68
Unit 16	The message behind the ad	T72
Review 4		T76
Unit 17	Willpower	T78
Unit 18	Wave of the future	T82
Unit 19	Made in the U.S.A.	T86
Unit 20	At the movies	T90
Review 5		T94
World of Music 3		T96
Unit 21	How polite are you?	T98
Unit 22	The art of crime	T102
Unit 23	A balanced life	T106
Unit 24	Digital age	T110
Review 6		T114
Unit 25	Arranged marriages	T116
Unit 26	Money matters	T120
Unit 27	Less is more	T124
Unit 28	Celebrate	T128
Review 7		T132
World of Music 4		T134

Information for pair and group work	136
Grammar reference	143
Vocabulary	151
Student Book Audioscript	T154
Workbook Audioscript	T172
Workbook Answer Key	T178
Pronunciation Table	T188

Scope and Sequence

UNIT	TITLE	VOCABULARY	LISTENING/READING
UNIT 1 Page 2	Nice to see you again	Parts of a conversation	Listening: Three people talking about what is happening in their lives
UNIT 2 Page 6	Why women iron	Adjectives to describe a person's character	Reading: A review of a book about differences between men and women
UNIT 3 Page 10	Living in luxury	Numbers; hotel facilities	Listening: A conversation about making a reservation for a hotel room
UNIT 4 Page 14	Allergic reactions	Medical symptoms	Reading: A newspaper article about allergies
Review 1 (Units 1–4) Page 18			
World of Music 1 Page 20			
UNIT 5 Page 22	A typical day	Verb and noun combinations	Listening: An interview with a man who has an unusual job
UNIT 6 Page 26	It's absolutely true!	Adjectives and intensifiers	Listening: A conversation about Carnaval in Rio de Janeiro, Brazil
UNIT 7 Page 30	Eating out	Adjectives to describe restaurants and food	Reading: A restaurant review
UNIT 8 Page 34	It's a deal!	Verb and noun combinations	Reading: An article about prenuptial agreements
Review 2 (Units 5–8) Page 38			
UNIT 9 Page 40	The river	Phrasal verbs related to tourism	Listening: A conversation between a travel agent and tourist about a river tour
UNIT 10 Page 44	On the other hand	Levels of difficulty	Reading: An article on some differences between left- and right-handed people Listening: Two people talking about being left-handed
UNIT 11 Page 48	Trading spaces	Furniture	Reading: A summary of a TV program episode Listening: People on a TV program reacting to changes in their living room
UNIT 12 Page 52	A soccer fan's website	Time expressions with *in*, *on*, *at*, or no preposition	Reading: A soccer fan's web page and travel plans Listening: A conversation about travel arrangements
Review 3 (Units 9–12) Page 56			
World of Music 2 Page 58			
UNIT 13 Page 60	Green card	Immigration	Reading: An immigration officer's interview notes Listening: An immigration officer's interview
UNIT 14 Page 64	What's that noise?	Sounds people make	Listening: A radio phone-in contest

GRAMMAR FOCUS	PRONUNCIATION	SPEAKING	WRITING
Present continuous for extended present	Stress on important words in sentences	Making small talk	Write a letter describing what is happening in your life
Comparative adjectives; *as . . . as*	Weak forms: *as, than*	Making comparisons	Compare a man and a woman (or a boy and a girl) you know well
Review: simple present statements and questions	Stress in numbers in *–teen* and *-ty*	Describing places	Write a postcard describing a luxury hotel
Adjectives ending in *-ed* and *-ing*	*-ed* adjective endings	Describing how you feel	Describe a bad cold or allergy and what you did to feel better
Subject and object questions	Locating the focus word in questions and answers	Asking questions	Write an email telling about your typical day
Review: simple past vs. past continuous	Number of syllables and stress in words	Telling stories	Write a true story about something that happened to you
too, enough	Schwa /ə/ in weak syllables, as in *po<u>lite</u>*	Describing and giving opinions about food and restaurants	Write a note explaining what menu items to choose and avoid at a restaurant
Modals: *have to/don't have to, must, can't* for obligation and prohibition	*Have to* ("hafta") and *has to* ("hasta") in rapid speech	Expressing obligation, no obligation, and prohibition	Write an informal agreement about rules and obligations
Simple present and present continuous for future	Linking in phrasal verbs	Describing plans for a trip	Write an email telling a friend about plans for a tour
Modal verbs for ability	*can/can't* and *could/couldn't*	Describing abilities and challenges	Describe things you could and couldn't do with your non-dominant hand
Present perfect for indefinite past	Different pronunciations of letter *a*	Talking about changes you can see	Write a letter describing recent changes in your home or life
Modals: *may, might, could* for possibility	Weak forms: prepositions	Talking about possible future arrangements	Write an email telling a friend about possible future plans
Review: present perfect with *for* and *since*	Strong and weak forms of *have* and *has*; contracted *has*	Talking about how long you have done something	Write a report drawing conclusions from two interviews
Modals: *must be, might be, can't be* for deduction	Reduced /t/ in *might be, can't be,* and *must be*	Making deductions	Describe what someone does at a job without naming the job

UNIT	TITLE	VOCABULARY	LISTENING/READING
UNIT 15 Page 68	Mumbai Soap	Topics for TV soap operas	Reading: Summaries of three parts of a TV soap opera
UNIT 16 Page 72	The message behind the ad	Adjectives used in advertisements	Reading: An article giving people's reactions to TV ads Listening: A interview with an advertising executive about creating different TV ads
Review 4 (Units 13-16) Page 76			
UNIT 17 Page 78	Willpower	Reading: A quiz to evaluate willpower	Verbs + gerund; verbs + infinitive to express opinion
UNIT 18 Page 82	Wave of the future	Words related to new trends	Listening: A conversation about a woman's unusual job and how she does it
UNIT 19 Page 86	Made in the U.S.A.	Materials; possessions	Listening: Tourists talking about items in a shop on Fisherman's Wharf
UNIT 20 Page 90	At the movies	Types of movies	Listening: An interview with an author of a book about movie facts
Review 5 (Units 17-20) Page 94			
World of Music 3 Page 96			
UNIT 21 Page 98	How polite are you?	Phrasal verbs with *turn*, *switch*, *go*	Reading: A quiz to evaluate responses to annoying situations
UNIT 22 Page 102	The art of crime	Words related to crime	Listening: A story about the theft of a famous painting
UNIT 23 Page 106	A balanced life	Expressions with *take*	Listening: Two people discussing exercise
UNIT 24 Page 110	Digital age	Technical equipment	Reading: An article about digital TV
Review 6 (Units 21-24) Page 114			
UNIT 25 Page 116	Arranged marriages	Wedding party; expressions with *get*	Listening: Two friends discussing a movie about arranged marriages
UNIT 26 Page 120	Money matters	Money and banks	Reading: A web page for an online banking service
UNIT 27 Page 124	Less is more	*Waste, use, spend, save* + noun	Listening: An interview with an author who gives advice on how to find balance in life
UNIT 28 Page 128	Celebrate	Words related to parties	Reading: An ad for a contest to celebrate a magazine's 100th edition

Review 7 (Units 25-28) Page 132

World of Music 4 Page 134

Information for pair and group work Page 136

Grammar reference Page 143

Vocabulary Page 151

GRAMMAR FOCUS	PRONUNCIATION	SPEAKING	WRITING
will/won't for future	Contractions with *will*	Predicting the future	Predict an episode of a soap opera, a news story, or the result of a sports event
Future real conditional (*If* + simple present + *will*)	Intonation in future real conditional sentences	Talking about future possibilities	Propose ideas for an advertisement to sell a product
Verbs + gerund; verbs + infinitive	Weak forms of *to* in infinitives; blended "wanna" for *want to*	Talking about changing habits	Write a letter describing recent changes in your work or personal life
used to and *would*	Blended pronunciation of *used to* ("useta")	Comparing past and present trends	Compare your lifestyle with that of your parents when they were your age
Passive (simple present)	Syllabic consonants (*cotton*, *metal*) with no vowel sound	Describing where things come from	Describe a special item you bought on a trip or that someone gave you
so, too, neither, (not) either	Number of syllables and word stress patterns	Talking about favorite movies	Describe what kinds of movies you and a friend or relative like and don't like
Modals: *Could you, Would you, Would you mind . . . ?* for polite requests	Weak forms and linking: *could you, would you*	Making or responding to requests	Describe an annoying situation and what you did about it
Passive (simple past)	Stress and rhythm in passive sentences	Describing a crime	Write a newspaper article about a real or imaginary crime
Review: verbs for likes/dislikes followed by gerund and/or infinitive	Consonant clusters (*stand*, *play*, *sports*)	Discussing work and after-work activities	Write an email about your efforts to balance work and play
Relative clauses with *that, which, who, where*	Stress in nouns and noun phrases	Describing people, places, and things	Describe different kinds of technical equipment you would like to have
It's + adjective/noun + infinitive to express opinion	Different pronunciations of /t/ linked to a following word	Talking about relationships	Write an email giving advice about a marriage problem
Verbs with two objects	Weak pronunciation of object pronouns	Talking about money	Write a letter explaining how you would spend one million dollars
Review: *should/shouldn't, could, ought to* for advice	Reduced forms of *should/could/ought to*	Giving advice	Write a letter giving advice to a friend or relative about a problem
Present unreal conditional (*If* + simple past + *would* + verb)	Contracted and weak forms of *would* in rapid speech	Talking about imaginary situations	Write an invitation to a party

WorldView
An introduction to the course
by Michael Rost

Welcome to *WorldView*, a four-level English course for adults and young adults. *WorldView* builds fluency by letting students explore and talk about a wide range of compelling topics presented from an international perspective. *Worldview*'s trademark two-page lesson design, with clear and attainable language goals, ensures that students feel a sense of accomplishment and increased self-confidence in every class.

WorldView's approach to language learning follows a simple and proven **M.A.P.**:

☆ **M**otivate learning through stimulating content and achievable learning goals

☆ **A**nchor language production with strong, focused language presentations

☆ **P**ersonalize learning through engaging and communicative speaking activities

Course components

- **Student Book with Student Audio CD**
- The **Student Book** contains 28, four-page units, seven Review Units (one after every four units), four World of Music Units, Information for pair and group work, a Vocabulary list, and a Grammar reference section.
- The **Student Audio CD** includes tracks for all pronunciation exercises and listening extracts (or reading extracts, in selected units) in the *Student Book*. The *Student Audio CD* can be used with the *Student Book* for self-study and also coordinates with the *Workbook* listening and pronunciation exercises.
- The interleaved **Teacher's Edition** provides step-by-step procedures and exercise answer keys for each activity in the *Student Book* as well as a wealth of teacher support: unit Warm-ups, Optional Activities, Extensions, Culture Notes, Background Information, Teaching Tips, Wrap-ups, and extensive Language Notes. In addition, the *Teacher's Edition* includes a Course Orientation Guide, Audio Scripts, and the *Workbook* Answer Key.
- The **Workbook** has 28, three-page units that correspond to each of the *Student Book* units. The *Workbook* provides abundant review and practice activities for vocabulary, grammar, listening, and pronunciation (listening and pronunciation exercises are done in conjunction with the *Student Audio CD*). In addition, the *Workbook* includes self-quizzes after every four units. A Learning Strategies section at the beginning of the *Workbook* helps students to be active learners.
- The **Class Audio Program** is available in either CD or cassette format and contains all the recorded material for in-class use.
- The **Teacher's Resource Book** (with **Testing Audio CD** and **TestGen Software**) has three sections of reproducible material: extra communication activities for in-class use, model writing passages for each *Student Book* writing assignment, and a complete testing program: seven quizzes and two tests, along with scoring guides and answer keys. Also included are an audio CD and an easy-to-use TestGen software CD for customizing the tests.
- For each level of the course, the **WorldView** Video presents seven, five-minute authentic video segments connected to *Student Book* topics. Notes to the Teacher are available in the *Video* package, and Student Activity Sheets can be downloaded from the *WorldView* Companion Website.
- The **WorldView** Companion Website (www.longman.com/worldview) provides a variety of teaching support and includes Video Activity Sheets and supplemental reading material.

Unit contents

Each of the 28 units in *WorldView* has seven closely linked sections:

- **Getting started:** a communicative opening exercise that introduces target vocabulary
- **Listening/Reading:** a functional conversation or thematic passage that introduces target grammar
- **Grammar focus:** an exercise sequence that allows students to focus on the grammar point that has been introduced in the reading and listening extracts and to solidify their learning
- **Pronunciation:** stress, rhythm, and intonation practice based on the target vocabulary and grammar
- **Speaking:** an interactive speaking task focused on student production of target vocabulary, grammar, and functional language
- **Writing:** a personalized writing activity that stimulates student production of target vocabulary and grammar
- **Conversation to go**: a concise reminder of the functional language introduced in each unit

Course length

With its flexible format and course components, *WorldView* responds to a variety of course needs. *WorldView* is suitable for 70 to 90 hours of classroom instruction. Each unit can be easily expanded by using bonus activities from the *Teacher's Edition*, reproducible activities available in the *Teacher's Resource Book*, linked lessons from the *WorldView Video* program, and supplementary reading assignments in the *WorldView Companion Website*.

The *WorldView Student Book with Student Audio CD* and the *Workbook* are also available in split editions.

Teaching Principles in *WorldView*

WorldView approaches language learning from a belief in three fundamental principles: motivate, anchor, and personalize.

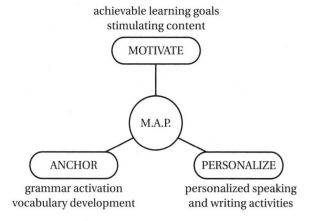

Motivate

Motivate learning through stimulating content and achievable learning goals

At all levels of proficiency, language students learn better when they are given stimulating content and activities. The topics chosen for *WorldView* are international in scope, compelling, and engaging, and the activities designed around them promote student participation and active learning.

Each unit in *WorldView* is made up of 2, two-page lessons that set clear, achievable goals. By working through short, goal-oriented activities—for vocabulary, listening, reading, grammar, pronunciation, speaking, and writing—students feel both a sense of accomplishment and increased self-confidence.

Anchor

Anchor language production with strong, focused language presentations of vocabulary and grammar

Anchoring knowledge—planting it firmly—is the basis for systematic progress in language learning. *WorldView* features a strong vocabulary and grammar syllabus that anchors each unit.

Vocabulary is presented in various formats in the *Getting started* section of each unit, allowing students to gain mastery of specific lexical sets. Students interact with the new words in a series of activities before they encounter them in reading or listening texts.

Grammar is introduced in the listening and reading texts so that students are first exposed to the grammar receptively. Students are then given examples of the target structure to study, with their attention directed to specific aspects of the language. They then complete grammar charts, which allows them to focus on the way the language works. Once they have worked with the grammar examples and charts, students use the grammar in structured exercises to help the new grammar concepts take root.

Personalize

Personalize learning through engaging and communicative speaking and writing activities

In every *WorldView* unit, the central goal is fluent self-expression. This goal is achieved through a careful sequence of activities, each building toward personalized speaking and writing tasks.

Personalization is the basis for making language learning memorable—and enjoyable. *WorldView* provides opportunities for students to personalize what they learn throughout the unit: *Getting started* elicits students' ideas; the *Reading* and *Listening* sections draw out students' views and opinions; and the *Speaking* and *Writing* sections allow students to express their own thoughts, plans, preferences, and experiences.

The *WorldView* Teaching Plan

Teaching from *WorldView* is easy because each unit of the *Student Book* is based on a carefully planned flow of activities. Each four-page unit is designed as a complete instructional cycle that focuses on all key language areas—vocabulary, grammar, and pronunciation—and links the skills of listening, speaking, reading, and writing in an integrated, reinforcing fashion. Within each unit are two lessons: Lesson A builds comprehension, and Lesson B builds fluency.

The two lessons include the following:

- **Getting started:** Designed to get students interacting from the start, this opening activity introduces and contextualizes the target vocabulary of the unit. Vocabulary sets are always semantically related and include useful expressions and collocations. *Getting started* allows you to check what students already know and to teach words and phrases that may not be familiar. As students learn the meaning and pronunciation of the words and expressions, engaging follow-up activities encourage them to use and extend their new vocabulary.

- **Listening** or **Reading:** This section presents a realistic listening extract—conversations, interviews, talk shows, etc.—or an authentically based reading passage, such as a magazine article, an ad, or a website—that is related to the unit theme. Each high-interest listening or reading passage incorporates the target vocabulary and models the grammar in context. In keeping with principles of authenticity, the listening extracts are recorded at natural speed and the reading selections contain idiomatic expressions beyond the students' production capacity. Students are not expected to understand every word of the passages; rather, students are given multiple opportunities to work with the same passage for different purposes, which serves to deepen their comprehension skills and their confidence in dealing with authentic language.

- **Grammar focus:** In this pivotal section of the unit, students work with practical examples of the target structures—all previously featured in the Reading or Listening extracts—and notice the rules for themselves. Students get actively involved in grammar discovery, an approach that anchors their learning of the language. Once students have formulated the grammar rules, they use the target grammar in contextualized practice exercises. An enhanced Grammar Reference section for each unit is included at the back of the book so students have full grammar paradigms and explanations at their fingertips.
- **Pronunciation:** Brief pronunciation activities in every unit target word and sentence stress, rhythm, intonation, linking, and problematic sounds through clear, contextualized examples based on the target vocabulary or grammar of the unit. The pronunciation activity prepares the students for the upcoming speaking activity by providing useful models for communication.
- **Speaking:** This interactive task builds upon the Listening or Reading theme and incorporates the target vocabulary, grammar, and pronunciation, giving students the opportunity to use this language creatively to build fluency. Students are encouraged to share opinions, exchange information about themselves, and discuss ideas with their classmates.
- **Writing:** The final activity in each unit encourages further personal expression by students, who are directed to write about their own ideas and experiences in a guided, communicative assignment. This activity, which may be done in class or as homework, encourages personalized writing that can be shared with the class as an idea exchange, and be used by the teacher as evidence of the students' control of targeted grammar and vocabulary.
- **Conversation to go:** A brief conversation to remind students of the key communicative function and grammar appears at the end of each unit. Students can act out the conversation, or extend it to create their own "conversations to go."

Review Units

Review Units appear after every four units to help both students and teachers to revisit key presentations. Review Units incorporate an audio model (found in the *Class Audio Program*) to give students another opportunity to use the language of each unit in a productive, engaging speaking activity. The Review Units can be used as reinforcement or for an assessment of students' progress.

World of Music Units

Four World of Music units in each *Student Book* build a stimulating class activity around a popular song, using music from the past few decades. Structured as selective listening activities, the World of Music units encourage students to activate vocabulary and grammar before they listen, and conclude with a sing-along option (contained in the *Class Audio Program*).

Teaching Tips

You will find a range of Teaching Tips in this *Teacher's Edition* to give you specific suggestions for adding learning value to individual activities in the *WorldView Student Book*. The specific tips revolve around the following general teaching principles: **keep your class active, extend your students' learning strategies, make it easy for students to participate,** and **help students with specific skills**. These principles are demonstrated below, with general suggestions that can be implemented throughout the *WorldView* course.

- **Keep your class active**
  - Make sure students participate actively. The key is finding the right balance between "teacher-fronted" instruction and "student-centered" instruction. In communicative classes, it is important to direct your instruction time toward brief demonstrations and explanations, support for tasks, and feedback. Aim to maximize the time that students use the language.
  - Vary the groups. Most activities call for students to work with a partner or in a small group. Try various groupings of students. Working with new partners can often inject new energy into the class and help the class develop a larger sense of community. Particularly if you have students of mixed levels, it will be important to try different groupings so that students have an opportunity to work with partners of differing levels.
  - When possible, offer students alternate ways of doing an activity. You will find suggestions in the unit notes in this *Teacher's Edition* as well as on the *WorldView* companion website.
- **Extend students' learning**
  - Look for opportunities to introduce learning strategies. (You can consult the list of strategies at the beginning of the *WorldView Workbook*, or look through the Teaching Tips in the *Teacher's Edition*.) Take advantage of the times in class—for example, when a student needs to ask a clarification question—to call students' attention to a particular strategy. If you introduce and reinforce learning strategies on a regular basis, you will encourage learning beyond the classroom.
  - Provide at-home assignments for students. Giving sufficient homework is important to reinforce in-class learning. Homework can easily be assigned from the *Workbook*, and additional homework ideas are given in the *Teacher's Edition*. Spend just a short time in each class checking homework, having students work in pairs and small groups to compare answers. Take notice of how students have done, and provide brief mini-lessons to address any common errors.
  - Monitor your students' progress and provide feedback to them, verbally and through regular quizzes and tests.

- **Make it easy for students to participate in class**
  - Aim to create a comfortable environment in the classroom. You want your students to feel relaxed enough to talk to you and to each other in English. Students who feel relaxed will be more likely to take risks in their language learning and will gain confidence more rapidly.
  - Insure that each student has an opportunity to contribute ideas, opinions, and experiences in every class meeting. One way to do so is by fully utilizing the steps in activities that encourage comparing ideas and sharing answers, as well as by having students work in pairs and small groups.
  - Let the students do the talking. In communicative classes, it is important that students have ample time to talk, to each other in pairs and small groups, and to the whole class. Don't be too eager to correct. Generally, it is best to respond to meaning first in communication activities. Let the students know when you understand their ideas and when you don't. When they know you are interested in their ideas and not just their English ability, they will become more relaxed.
  - Keep your classroom activities in English. Although it is natural for you and your students to use their first language from time to time, aim to keep all classroom activities in English, including your instructions. Teach clarification expressions (such as "Could you say that again?") and information questions ("Whose turn is it now?") that will help your students stay in English. Make agreements with the students about when their first language can be used in class. The consistent use of English in the classroom will eventually make the classroom more comfortable for your students.

- **Help students with specific skills**

  Although most students will make progress through the use of models, participation in classroom activities, and feedback on their classwork and homework, many students will need specific help with one or more skills.

  - **Help students become better listeners**

    The recordings in *WorldView* are at natural speed, and students need to be reassured that they can do the listening activities successfully without understanding every word. Listening ability develops gradually by having students work with the same listening material in a number of ways. The listening exercises in *WorldView* use both "bottom up" and "top down" methods. *Bottom-up processing* refers to hearing the exact words and grammatical structures that the speaker uses, even if these are reduced or ellipted. Bottom-up activities include dictation (full dictation or cloze dictation), pre-teaching of vocabulary and structures used in a listening extract, and targeted listening for a specific item. *Top-down processing* refers to using expectations in order to infer what the speaker means, even if the speaker's message is incomplete or unclear. Top-down activities include selective listening for given information, answering questions (and guessing unknown answers), and summarizing.

    Another listening skill that students need to develop is interactive listening, which is the ability to understand live conversation, give feedback, ask for clarification, and respond in real time. This aspect of listening can improve dramatically through the guided interaction tasks (like information gaps) provided in *WorldView*, especially if supplemented with instruction on how to give feedback (such as using comprehension signals like "Oh" and "Um-hmm") and ask clarification questions (such as "What do you mean?").

  - **Help students improve their pronunciation**

    Pronunciation is an important skill and most students can make and sustain improvements in their pronunciation with a concerted effort. Most students can improve their pronunciation both on a segmental level (the individual sounds of words) and on a suprasegmental level (the overriding rhythm and intonation of a whole utterance).

    The majority of pronunciation exercises in *WorldView* focus on the suprasegmentals because this is the area of pronunciation that most influences communication. Encourage your students to work through these lessons carefully and to practice with the *WorldView Student Audio CD*.

    In addition, provide focused feedback to students. When you really don't understand a student because of a pronunciation problem, ask him or her to repeat it so you do understand—and then point out the pronunciation issue for him or her to work on in the future. (For individual sounds of words, see the Pronunciation table on page T188.) Focused feedback helps students identify a small number of pronunciation points that will truly boost their speaking ability.

  - **Help students develop fluency**

    Most students want to become fluent speakers of English, the essence of which is staying focused and assuring that their communicative goal is reached. As students begin to accomplish communicative goals, they will begin to speak more smoothly and effortlessly.

    There are three specific ways of developing fluency in communication tasks, all of which have been incorporated into *WorldView*. The first way is *pre-task planning*. This means having an overview of the communication task in advance, knowing how the procedures work, and what the outcome will be. This kind of planning allows for an internal rehearsal of the communication process, which generally improves fluency. The second way is to *preview vocabulary* that is needed in the task. Knowing what vocabulary to use in advance is like having stepping stones through the task, and this obviously increases the smoothness of the communication. The third way to improve fluency is *authentic repetition*. Communicative tasks that involve real personal information and ideas can be done again with new partners, without a feeling of mechanical repetition. Having students repeat tasks with new partners, or recycling tasks later in the course, or using parallel tasks (as is done in the *WorldView* Review Units) will all help students gain genuine fluency.

- **Help students become better writers**

    The most direct way to help students become better writers is to give them ample opportunities for extended, communicative writing. In addition to helping learners consolidate their learning of grammar and vocabulary, writing provides an avenue for creativity and self-expression that many learners value.

    A few simple guidelines can help your class get the most out of writing tasks:

    Have students write multiple drafts and revisions of an assignment whenever possible. In the first draft of an assignment, encourage them to write freely and not worry about mistakes. Give at least one round of feedback before students produce the "final product."

    Use models of the completed writing assignment (from the *Teacher's Resource Book*) to provide your students with a "macrostructure" for their work. Models can motivate students to raise their expectations and provide guidance for homework assignments.

    Give feedback on content as well as form. Because students are writing for a communicative purpose, it is important to let them know what they have communicated to their audience.

    Be selective when offering corrections. For most writing assignments, you will not want to correct every error. Concentrate on those that get in the way of communication.

    Present a simple "key" or code for corrections (like *v* for vocabulary problem, *t* for verb tense problem). This will enable you to respond more quickly to students' writing.

    Have your students keep all their written work and create a portfolio. Review the students' portfolio at the end of the course. This will build confidence for your students and give you a sense of satisfaction as well!

    If time allows, have students share their writing in class with a partner. Partners can give feedback on specific aspects of the writing—for example, on the content, the organization, or the choice of words.

- **Correcting errors**

    In both meaning-focused and form-focused activities, students will make errors, and many errors will seem to persist. Your attitude and approach to feedback and error correction should be related to the purpose of the activity and what you think your students are ready to learn.

    One error-correction method is to note commonly occurring errors in the class and give a short presentation for the whole class at the end of an activity. For instance, you may note frequent errors in verb tenses during one speaking activity, and provide a short review of the problematic points before going on to the next activity. This focused feedback, provided at regular times during the flow of classroom activities, seems to be more effective for most learners than simply being corrected for every grammatical error they make.

    Another method that works well is *recasting* an utterance that has contained an error. For instance, a student may say, "Yesterday, I don't come to class," and you recast it as, "Oh, you didn't come to class yesterday?" In this process, it is important for the student to "notice" the error and then restate the correct utterance, as in, "Right. I didn't come to class yesterday." This process is effective because the student has the opportunity to self-correct an error that is still in short-term memory.

    When students notice and recast their own errors, they are more likely to remember the correction. For instance, you might ask students to look at their own writing assignment and circle all uses of a particular tense and then to rewrite any parts with errors that they notice. Or you may ask students to make their own audio recording of a short conversation or speech and then transcribe exactly what they said in one column and make grammatical improvements in another column.

How to Get the Most From This *Teacher's Edition*

In each of the interleaved units of this *Teacher's Edition*, you'll find notes for how to proceed with each exercise, as well as answer keys, if appropriate. You will also find the following types of teaching ideas and information:

(Lesson A) Warm-up: a brief activity to get the students involved in the topic of the unit at its outset

(Lesson B) Warm-up: a brief activity recommended for when time has passed between doing Lesson A and B. Since Lesson B begins with the *Grammar focus* section, and the grammar has been modeled in the Listening or Reading done in Lesson A, this activity involves playing the audio for the Listening (or Reading, which has been recorded for this purpose), so that students can hear the grammar in context before they begin their work on the grammar.

Vocabulary Preview: a brief, optional activity that allows you to pre-teach the vocabulary students will interact with in the *Getting started* section of the unit

Extension: an additional activity for students to do after they've finished a student book activity, as time allows

Option: an alternative way you can have students do a particular activity

FYI: information that you may find useful but that is *not* intended for the students to know

Culture Note: information that will help students understand the cultural context of the language or content

Background Information: factual information about people, places, and events that you may want students to know

Language Note: information for students about how English works, including information about the grammar, functions, pronunciation, and similar topics.

Teaching Tip: a tactic that will help students get the most out of an activity, such as specific conversation management strategies, listening strategies, reading strategies, and so on.

Note: additional information that doesn't fit into any other category

Follow-up: an activity based on what you find when you are circulating and noticing how students are doing on specific tasks

Wrap-up: a whole-class activity that brings closure to a pair or group activity

Cross-references

The unit notes also provide cross-references to the following:

TRB *Teacher's Resource Book*, Reproducible Activities

TRB *Teacher's Resource Book*, Writing models

📖 *Workbook* practice material for homework*

📖 *Workbook* self-quizzes

🌐 Companion Website, www.longman.com/worldview, supplementary reading material

📼 Video

*****Note:** If you are not using the *Workbook*, an additional homework assignment is suggested for students to do with the *Student Audio CD*.

At the back of the *Teacher's Edition*, we've included the **Audioscripts** for the *Student Book* (Class Audio Program) and the audio scripts for the *Workbook* (Student Audio CD). The **Answer Key to the *Workbook* exercises** follows the audioscripts.

We would like to thank and officially acknowledge Sharon Goldstein for all her consulting, writing, and editorial work on the pronunciation exercises in the *Student Book*s and *Teacher's Editions*.

We are grateful to the following Pearson Longman editors for their invaluable assistance on this project:

John Barnes	Bill Preston
Nancy Blodgett	Julie Schmidt
Wendy Long	Debbie Sistino
Marc Oliver	Paula Van Ells

UNIT 1

Nice to see you again

Vocabulary Parts of a conversation
Grammar Present continuous for the extended present
Speaking Making small talk

Lesson A

Getting started

1 **PAIRS.** When we meet someone for the first time, we often make "small talk." What topics do you think are appropriate for small talk?

| the other person's appearance | politics | sports |
| your health | your love life | your salary | the weather |

2 Match the sentences to the conversation functions in the box.

Conversation functions
a. greeting
b. introducing
c. complimenting
d. making conversation (small talk)
e. ending a conversation

1. A: I'd like you to meet my friend, Ana. _b_
   B: _Hi. Nice to meet you._

2. A: See you soon! Say hello to your family for me! ___
   B: _____

3. A: Wonderful dinner! Everything was delicious. ___
   B: _____

4. A: Hi, how are you doing? ___
   B: _____

5. A: It's a beautiful day, isn't it? ___
   B: _____

3 **PAIRS.** Read the responses below. Write the best response under each sentence in Exercise 2.

Yeah! I'm so glad it stopped raining.   Great. How about you?
~~Hi. Nice to meet you.~~   OK, thanks. Bye!
Thanks! I'm glad you enjoyed it.

4 🎧 Listen and check your answers.

2

Nice to see you again

UNIT 1

OBJECTIVES

Students will:
- activate vocabulary related to greetings and small talk
- use the present continuous for extended present
- practice English rhythm, putting stress on only the important words in sentences

LANGUAGE NOTES

- Greetings can be very informal (*Hey, what's up?*), informal (*Hi, how are you doing?*), or more formal (*Hello, how are you?*). More formal expressions are generally used when meeting someone for the first time, when meeting older people, or in business situations.
- Make sure students use *nice to meet you* when meeting someone for the first time, and not *nice to see you*, which is used between people who already know each other.

WARM-UP: GREETINGS

- Write the following on the board: *to greet someone*. Elicit from students different ways to say hello in English. (*Hey. Hi. How's it going? Hey, what's up? Hello. Hi, how are you doing? Hello, how are you?*)
- Ask students to identify which of the greetings on the board are used when you already know someone (*Hey. Hi. How's it going? Hey, what's up?*) and which are used when you first meet someone (*Hello, how are you?*).
- Set a time limit of 3 minutes. Have students walk around the room and greet as many people as they can. Students should also introduce themselves if they are meeting someone for the first time.

Getting started

OPTION: VOCABULARY PREVIEW

- Have students study the words and phrases in Exercise 1.
- Form groups of 3. Explain the task: Students brainstorm the meaning of the words and phrases. Set a time limit of 4 minutes. Walk around the room, helping as needed.
- Call on students for their definitions.
- Go over any vocabulary or topics that students don't understand.

Exercise ❶

- Ask students to look at the topics in the box. Explain that when we meet someone for the first time, we usually try to pick something to talk about that will get a conversation started easily. Ask students what they usually talk about when they first meet someone.

- Pair students. Explain the task: Students decide which of the topics are appropriate for small talk with someone they have just met. Explain that the topics of conversation for small talk vary culturally.
- Set a time limit of 5 minutes. While students are working, walk around the room, helping as needed.
- Have pairs work in small groups to check their answers.
- Go over the answers with the class. Discuss their reasons for deciding a topic was inappropriate.

Answer key
Appropriate topic: the weather

Exercise ❷

- Ask students to look at the conversation functions in the box. Explain these are the of parts of a conversation.
- Pair students. Explain the task: Students decide the conversation functions. Go over the first sentence.
- Set a time limit of 3 minutes. Walk around the room, helping as needed.
- Go over the answers with the class.

Answer key
1. introducing   b
2. ending a conversation   e
3. complimenting   c
4. greeting   a
5. making conversation (small talk)   d

Exercise ❸

- Pair students. Explain the task: Students decide the best response for each sentence. Go over the example.
- Set a time limit of 3 minutes. Walk around the room, helping as needed.
- Do not go over the answers until after Exercise 4.

Exercise ❹

- 🎧 Play the audio for students to check their answers.
- 🎧 Play the audio again: Students listen and repeat.
- Go over the answers with the class.

Answer key
1. Hi. Nice to meet you.
2. OK, thanks. Bye!
3. Thanks! I'm glad you enjoyed it.
4. Great. How about you?
5. Yeah! I'm so glad it stopped raining!

EXTENSION

Form pairs. Have students role-play the conversations from Exercise 2.

Teacher's Notes — Lesson A

Listening

Teaching Tip! Making predictions

Asking students to make predictions is a useful way to preteach vocabulary, grammar, or concepts. Guide students to rely on context clues in photographs or text as a basis for their predictions.

Exercise 5

- Have students look at the photograph. Ask questions such as *Where are they? What are they doing? Do you think they know each other?*
- Pair students. Explain the task: Students read the topics in the box and predict which three topics Sue, Bernardo, and Tom will talk about.
- Go over the answers with the class.

> **Answer key**
>
> If students think the people in the photo know each other from before, they might talk about:
> the weather   job or school   his or her appearance
>
> If students think the people in the photo are meeting for the first time, they might talk about:
> the weather   job or school   why they're there

Exercise 6

- Explain the task: Students listen to the conversation and check (✓) the topics Sue, Bernardo, and Tom talk about.
- 🎧 Play the audio.
- Have pairs check their answers.
- 🎧 Play the audio one more time so that students can confirm their answers.
- Go over the answers with the class. Ask them if their predictions were correct.

> **Answer key**
>
> his or her appearance (Tom's, Sue's)
> the weather (in California)
> jobs (Tom's, Sue's)
> school (Sue's)

Exercise 7

- Have students read the sentences before listening to focus on what to listen for.
- 🎧 Play the audio again. Tell students to listen for the answers, and to decide if each statement is true or false.
- Have students work in pairs to check their answers.
- 🎧 Play the audio again, if needed, so that students can confirm their answers.
- Go over the answers with the class. Ask students how they knew which phrases or sentences were false.

> **Answer key**
>
> 1. T   5. T
> 2. F   6. F
> 3. T   7. T
> 4. T

🌐 Please go to www.longman.com/worldview for additional in-class model conversation practice and supplementary reading practice.

HOMEWORK

- 📖 For homework, assign *Workbook* page 12, Vocabulary Exercises 1, 2, and 3, and page 14, Listening Exercises 6 and 7.

Listening

5 **PAIRS.** Look at the photo of Bernardo, Sue, and Tom. Predict which three topics they'll talk about and circle them.

a death in the family	his or her appearance	cost of his or her clothes
last night's TV programs	school	someone's health
soccer/baseball scores	their jobs	their love lives
their salaries	the weather	why they're there

6 Listen to Bernardo, Sue, and Tom's conversation. Which topics do they talk about? Check (✓) the topics in the box above. Were your predictions correct?

7 Listen again and write *T* (true) or *F* (false) after each statement.

1. Sue is surprised to see Tom. T
2. Bernardo and Tom know each other.
3. Tom is Canadian.
4. Sue and Tom worked together.
5. Sue is taking courses for her master's degree.
6. Tom is working in California.
7. Tom wants to see Sue again.

Grammar focus

1 Look at the examples. Which ones use the present continuous? Put a check (✓) next to them.

> How **are** you **doing**?
> The sun always **seems** to shine here.
> I**'m visiting** an old friend.
> I **love** the weather in San Diego.

2 Look at the examples again. Underline the correct words to complete the rules in the chart.

Present continuous for the extended present
Use the present continuous to talk about **temporary / permanent** situations.
The present continuous is **usually / not usually** used with non-action verbs (for example, *be, know, like*).

Grammar Reference page 143

3 Underline the correct form of the verb in each sentence.

1. I **do / am doing** fine, thank you. How are you?
2. We **take / are taking** a class together this semester. We **see / are seeing** each other every day.
3. I **study / am studying** English for my trip to the U.S. I always **have / am having** a lot of homework!
4. Josefa **thinks / is thinking** about taking an accounting class. She **likes / is liking** math.
5. I know I **seem / 'm seeming** tired. I **don't sleep / 'm not sleeping** much these days.
6. My brother **lives / is living** at home until he finds an apartment.
7. They **take / 're taking** web design classes at the university. They **want / are wanting** to change careers.
8. Kyung-hee **looks / is looking** for a house near her job. She **spends / is spending** two hours commuting each way.

Grammar focus

LANGUAGE NOTES

- The present continuous, also known as the present progressive, can be used to talk about what is happening right now (*She is reading a book*) or an extended, temporary situation (*He is working in London this year*).
- The simple present is used to talk about what generally happens (*She [usually] spends too much money*) or general truths (*Water freezes at 0° C*).
- Non-action verbs aren't usually used in the present continuous. These include emotions such as *love* or *like*; perceptions, such as *feel, hear, taste, look,* and *seem*; and mental states such as *remember* and *know*.

WARM-UP

Note: Skip this warm-up if you're doing this lesson (Lesson B) during the same class period as Lesson A.

- Books closed. Tell students they are going to listen to the conversation between Sue, Bernardo, and Tom that they heard in the Listening section.
- Write the following questions on the board, and ask students to listen and decide which ones they hear: *What are you doing in San Diego? How are you doing? Are you still working in New York? Are you still working as a project manager?*
- 🎧 Play the audio for Lesson A, Exercise 6.
- Ask students which questions they heard. *(the first two)*
- Ask: *Where is Sue working now?* Elicit: *She is working at West Coast Advertising.*

Exercise ❶

- Have students look at the examples and study the boldfaced words.
- Ask students to focus on the first two examples.
- Elicit from students that the first sentence uses the present continuous, and the second uses the simple present.
- Ask students to look at the next two examples. Elicit from students that the sentences use the present continuous and the simple present, respectively.

Teaching Tip! Non-action verbs

Write on the board *do* and *visit* in one column, and *seem* and *love* in another column. Elicit from students the difference between the columns (*do* and *visit* are "action" verbs—they imply some movement; *seem* and *love* are "non-action" verbs). Read these words to the class and have them tell you which column they go in: *run, like, want, work, study, have.* (action—*run, work, study*; non-action—*like, want, have*)

Exercise ❷

- Have students study the examples again.
- Tell them to underline the information that completes the rules about the present continuous.
- Have students check their answers with a partner.
- Go over the answers with the class.
- Refer students to Grammar Reference page 143, as needed.

Answer key
temporary   not usually

Exercise ❸

- Ask students to look at the sentences. Explain the task: Students underline the correct form of the verb in each sentence. Go over the first sentence.
- Set a time limit of 5 minutes. Walk around the room, helping as needed.
- Have students work in pairs to check their answers.
- Go over the answers with the class. Call on different students to read each sentence aloud.

Answer key

1. am doing
2. are taking; see
3. am studying; have
4. is thinking; likes
5. seem; 'm not sleeping
6. is living
7. 're taking; want
8. is looking; spends

Pronunciation

Exercise 4

- Explain that in English, some syllables are longer and stronger and other syllables are shorter and weaker.
- 🎧 Play the audio. Ask students to listen to the rhythm. You can highlight the rhythm by tapping out the strong beats.
- Tell students that important words in a sentence are stressed. These words are longer and clearer.
- 🎧 Play the audio again. Ask students to notice the important words, shown in red.
- If your students all speak the same language, you can compare its rhythm with the rhythm of English, especially if all syllables tend to be about the same length in the students' language.

Exercise 5

- 🎧 Have students listen to the audio for Exercise 4. Stop the audio after each line and have students repeat it chorally.
- Tap out the beat to reinforce the rhythm of the sentences (see below). Encourage students to make stressed vowels long.

   <u>How</u> are you <u>doing</u>?
   <u>Great</u>! <u>What</u> about <u>you</u>?

   So, <u>how</u> do you <u>like</u> <u>California</u>?
   It's <u>great</u>. I <u>love</u> the <u>weath</u>er here.

   It was <u>good</u> to <u>see</u> you again.
   <u>Why</u> don't you <u>give</u> me a <u>call</u>?

- Ask a few individual pairs of students to say the questions and answers and check their pronunciation.

Speaking

Teaching Tip! Asking follow-up questions

Encourage students to keep the conversation going by asking follow-up questions. Model exchanges: A: *I'm living in an apartment.* B: *Where?* // A: *I'm looking for a teaching job.* B: *What do you want to teach?*

Exercise 6

- Pair students. Tell them they are at a party. Student A's name is Pat; Student B's name is Alex. Explain that they haven't seen each other for a long time. They talk about what is happening in their lives.
- Tell Student A to turn to page 136 and Student B to turn to page 138. They should not look at each other's cues. They will take turns asking and answering questions about their lives. Give the students a minute to go over the information.
- With a student, model the greeting. Take Alex's part.

   Pat: I haven't seen you in a long time. How are you?
   Alex: I'm fine, thanks, really busy! I'm acting in a play right now.

- Elicit ideas on questions Pat might ask. Examples include: *Where? What's the name of the play?*
- Set a time limit of 10 minutes for the students to complete the conversation. Walk around, helping with vocabulary as needed.

> **WRAP-UP**
>
> Call on students to share with the class what they learned about their partners.

TRB For additional interactive grammar practice, have students do the reproducible activity for this unit in the *Teacher's Resource Book*.

Writing

Exercise 7

- Assign the writing task for class work or homework. Before students start the letter, ask them to first think about what's happening and write simple notes. Prompt them with questions such as *Where are you working? What are you doing for fun? Where are you living?*
- **TRB** Optionally, give students a copy of the model of a letter (see the *Teacher's Resource Book,* Writing Models). Ask them to read the model and notice the different parts of the letter and the punctuation used.
- If students don't have the model, write the first few sentences of the letter on the board. Make sure they understand the organization and punctuation.

   Dear Tracy,
   I'm sorry I haven't written sooner, but I've been really busy. I'm on vacation this week so . . .

- If the assignment is done in class, ask several volunteers to read their letters to the class.

For suggestions on how to give feedback on writing, see page xiv of this *Teacher's Edition*.

CONVERSATION TO GO

- As the students leave class, have them read the dialogue.
- Tell students that *hang out* (or just *hang*) means to spend time somewhere or with someone.

HOMEWORK

- 📖 Assign *Workbook* page 16, Grammar Exercises 3 and 4, and page 17, Pronunciation Exercises 7 and 8.
- 💿 If students do not have the *WorldView Workbook*, assign listening homework from the Student CD. Write on the board:

   Track 2
   Why does Sue have to leave?

- 🎧 Tell students to listen to the audio and write their answer. Have them bring it to the next class. (*She has to meet her mother.*)

Pronunciation

4 🎧 Listen to the rhythm in these sentences. Notice that the important words are stressed. These words are longer and clearer than the other words.

How are you **do**ing?   **Great! What** about **you**?

So, **how** do you **like** Cali**for**nia?   It's **great**. I **love** the **weath**er here.

It was **good** to **see** you again.   **Why** don't you **give** me a **call**?

5 🎧 Listen again and repeat.

Speaking

6 *PAIRS.* You're at a party. You haven't seen each other in a long time. Talk about what's happening in your lives.

Student A, look at page 136. Student B, look at page 138.

A: I haven't seen you in a long time. How are you?
B: I'm fine, thanks, really busy! I'm . . .

Writing

7 Write a letter to a friend. Describe what's happening in your life. For example, are you taking any new classes? Are you living in the same place or someplace new? Use the present continuous.

CONVERSATION TO GO

A: What **are** you **doing** these days?
B: Oh, nothing. **I'm** just **hanging out**.

UNIT 2

Why women iron

Vocabulary Adjectives to describe a person's character
Grammar Comparative adjectives; as . . . as
Speaking Making comparisons

Lesson A

Getting started

1 **PAIRS.** Use the words in the box to complete the sentences.

aggressive	cooperative	competitive	emotional
~~hardworking~~	messy	noisy	talkative

1. Ben is very _hardworking_. He studies every night.
2. My brother is very _____. He never cleans his room.
3. Marcelo never says anything, but his sister is the opposite. She's very _____.
4. Could you please help? You're not being very _____.
5. Emilia is very _____. She always wants to win.
6. Jack is always getting into fights. He's very _____.
7. I couldn't hear the movie. The people in front of me were too _____.
8. I always cry at weddings. I'm very _____.

2 🎧 Listen and check your answers.

3 **PAIRS.** Describe the people in the photos. Use some adjectives from Exercise 1.

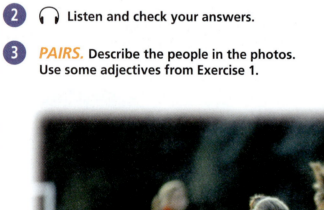

Why women iron

UNIT 2

Teacher's Notes — Lesson A

OBJECTIVES

Students will:
- activate vocabulary related to describing character and behavioral traits
- use comparative adjectives and *as . . . as*
- practice listening for and saying the weak forms of the words *as* and *than*

> **WARM-UP: WHO DRIVES WELL?**
> - Tell students this unit is about character traits and some differences between men and women. Elicit ideas from students about what the unit title means. If necessary, explain that *iron* is a verb here, and pantomime *ironing clothes*.
> - Pair students. Ask students to think about common beliefs about men and women. Give a few prompts such as *drive, cook, play soccer, decorate a house . . .* and have students say things such as *M/W drive well, W/M don't; M/W are usually good soccer players; W/M like to cook*.
> - Set a time limit of 2 minutes. Tell students to think of as many differences as possible, and not debate the ideas now. Remind students to listen carefully because they may have to report to the class what their partner says. Walk around the room, helping with vocabulary as needed.
> - Call on a few students to report about what their partners said.

Getting started

OPTION: VOCABULARY PREVIEW

- Write these descriptions (but not the answers, in parentheses) on the board: *like to talk* (talkative); *work well with others* (cooperative); *are very forceful* (aggressive); *determined to win* (competitive); *show their feelings* (emotional); *make a lot of noise* (noisy); *put a lot of effort into their work* (hardworking); *not organized* (messy).
- Pair students. Ask them to match the descriptions with the adjectives in the box.
- Set a time limit of 3 minutes. Tell students to match the easy definitions first (*talkative, noisy*). Walk around the room, helping as needed.
- Call on a few pairs to report on their work.
- Go over the answers with the class.

Exercise 1

- Pair students. Ask them to look at the words in the box. Explain the task: Students complete the sentences. Go over the first sentence.
- Set a time limit of 3 minutes. Walk around the room, helping as needed.

Exercise 2

- 🎧 Play the audio for students to check their answers.
- Go over the answers with the class.
- 🎧 Play the audio again, as needed.

> **Answer key**
> 1. hardworking
> 2. messy
> 3. talkative
> 4. cooperative
> 5. competitive
> 6. aggressive
> 7. noisy
> 8. emotional

Exercise 3

- Pair students. Have them look at the photographs. Explain the task: Students use adjectives from Exercise 1 to describe the people in the photographs. Encourage students to give reasons for the adjectives they choose, and to use any other vocabulary they know as well.
- Set a time limit of 5 minutes. Walk around the room, helping as needed.
- Have pairs form small groups. Set a time limit of 2 minutes to exchange their ideas.
- Go over the answers with the class. Check that they understand the words by asking them to say why they chose them (e.g., *I think the girls are competitive because they are playing hard*).

> **Answer key**
> Answers may vary; encourage students to give reasons. Students might say that the soccer players are *hardworking, cooperative, aggressive,* and *competitive*, and that the family is *talkative, hardworking, messy,* and *cooperative*.

> **EXTENSION**
> - Form groups of 3. Have students take turns saying which of the adjectives in the box applies to them.
> - Set a time limit of 3 minutes. Encourage students to qualify their statements if they need to (e.g., *I'm very competitive when I play sports, because I like winning. But I'm not competitive in my personal life*). Tell students to ask and answer follow-up questions, and to pay attention to what other students say because they may have to report back to the class.
> - If time allows, call on a few students to report about what other students have said (e.g., *Jonathan is very competitive when he plays sports, but not in his personal life*).

T6

Reading

Teaching Tip! Controversial topics

The topic of this unit might provoke some debate about gender roles and appropriate behavior. The purpose here is to teach students vocabulary needed to describe behavior, not to promote a particular point of view. To ensure that everyone is comfortable contributing to the discussion, it is important that the teacher not be seen as taking one side or the other. That is why it's important to ask students to give reasons for their adjective choices.

Exercise 4

- Pair students. Have them look at the chart. Explain the task: Students decide which of the adjectives from Exercise 1 usually describe men or women, and write the adjectives in the chart. Emphasize that this is a discussion and that there are NO correct answers.
- Set a time limit of 3 minutes. Walk around the room, helping as needed.
- Ask several pairs to share their answers with the class. Give students the prompt *We think (men) are . . . because . . .*

Answer key

Answers can vary, but may include:
Men: aggressive, competitive, messy, noisy, hardworking
Women: cooperative, emotional, hardworking, talkative, noisy

Teaching Tip! Encouraging students to read for a specific purpose

Good readers use different approaches to reading depending on their purpose for reading a particular passage or text. In this exercise, encourage students to focus on one question: *Do the authors of the book agree with you?* Tell students to keep the adjectives from Exercise 4 in mind as they read the article. Encourage students to take brief notes as they read.

Exercise 5

- Verify that students understand that a book review is a critique (opinion) or an analysis of a book. They are often found in newspapers or on bookstore websites. Find out if students ever read book reviews, and if so, where.
- Explain the task: Students read the book review and decide if the authors of the book being reviewed agree with their answers to Exercise 4. Read aloud the title, *Why Men Don't Iron,* and briefly elicit ideas about what the book might be about.
- Set a time limit of 5 minutes for students to read the review.
- Ask students if the authors of the book agree with them. Have them explain why.

Teaching Tip! Reading for specific information

When reading to find specific information, students should scan for key words that are related to the information they need. Have students read the questions before they read the article again. By pre-reading the questions, students will activate words and ideas that will help them focus on the important information in the text.

Exercise 6

- Pair students. Explain the task: Students reread the book review, and discuss the questions in the book. Encourage students to underline important information or take notes as they read.
- Set a time limit of 5 minutes for students to read the review and answer the questions. Remind them to answer questions 1–3 according to the information in the book review, not their opinions.

Answer key

1. Some differences include: boys are usually messier, more competitive, and noisier than girls; girls are often better students, more hardworking, and more talkative than boys.
2. Many people believe that society teaches these differences. The Moirs believe that men and women are born with these differences.
3. Many people think modern men should cook, take care of the children, be more cooperative, and be less aggressive.
4. Answers will vary.

Exercise 7

- Have pairs form small groups to compare answers and share ideas.
- Ask students to present their answers to the class. Remind students to give reasons.
- Check to see if there is any vocabulary students don't understand.

EXTENSION

- Form groups of 3. Set a time limit of 4 minutes. Explain the task: Students pick two activities that either men or women did not do in the past, but are doing now. Students should describe how and analyze why the roles and attitudes surrounding these activities have changed.
- Have a few groups share one of the specific activities and analysis with the class.

Please go to www.longman.com/worldview for additional in-class model conversation practice.

HOMEWORK

- For homework, assign *Workbook* page 15, Vocabulary Exercises 1 and 2, and page 17, Listening Exercises 5 and 6.

Reading

4 **PAIRS.** Which adjectives from Exercise 1 do you think usually describe men? Women?

Men	Women
messy	

5 Read the book review. Do the authors of the book *Why Men Don't Iron* agree with you?

Why Men Don't Iron
by Ann and Bill Moir

BOOK OF THE WEEK

Why do women cry more than men? Why do so many men like sports? In their book *Why Men Don't Iron* Ann and Bill Moir answer these questions—and more.

According to the Moirs, the differences between boys and girls are obvious from a very early age. At school, boys are usually messier and more competitive than girls; boys like to win! But girls are often better students. They're more hardworking than boys, and they do more homework. Girls may be more talkative than boys, but boys are noisier. Some doctors believe that baby girls are stronger than baby boys. But by school age, girls aren't as strong as boys.

Why? Does society—our family, friends, and teachers—change us?

A lot of people believe that society teaches boys and girls to behave differently. They say that as adults we can change this. The "new man" should cook, take care of the children, and be more cooperative and less aggressive. He should be neater, more emotional, and a better listener. But are these changes possible? Can men be as emotional as women, for example?

In their book, Ann and Bill Moir say "no." They say that men are more aggressive, more competitive, and messier than women because they are *born* that way. And society can't change their behavior.

6 Read the book review again and answer the questions.

1. What are some differences between the behavior of boys and girls?
2. What do many people believe about these differences? What do the Moirs believe?
3. What do many people think modern men should do?
4. What do you think? Are men and women born with different behaviors or do they learn them?

7 **PAIRS.** Compare your answers.

Lesson B

Grammar focus

1 Study the examples of comparative adjectives and equatives ([*not*] *as* + adjective + *as*).

Boys are **stronger than** girls.	=	Girls aren't **as strong as** boys.
Boys are more **competitive than** girls.	=	Girls aren't **as competitive as** boys.
Boys and girls are both sensitive.	=	Boys are **as sensitive as** girls.

2 Look at the examples again. Match the rule in the chart with the correct information.

Comparative adjectives and equatives (*as* + adjective + *as*)	
To form comparatives of one-syllable adjectives (e.g., *strong*), _____	a. use *more . . . than*.
To form comparatives of adjectives with two or more syllables (e.g., *tired, talkative, competitive*), _____	b. use the adjective, not the comparative.
In comparative sentences with (*not*) *as . . . as*, _____	c. add *-er* (*than*).
NOTE: Irregular comparatives: good → **better than** / bad → **worse than**	

Grammar Reference page 143

3 Rewrite the sentences so that they have the same meaning.

1. Women aren't as messy as men. Men are <u>messier than women</u> .
2. Boys are faster than girls. Girls aren't _____.
3. Girls aren't as noisy as boys. Boys are _____.
4. Men aren't as talkative as women. Women are _____.
5. Men aren't as emotional as women. Women are _____.
6. Women aren't as tall as men. Men are _____.
7. Both girls and boys are hardworking. Boys are _____.
8. Boys are better than girls at soccer. Girls aren't _____.

Pronunciation

4 🎧 Listen to these sentences from Exercise 1. Notice the short, weak pronunciation of *as* and *than*.

5 🎧 Listen again and repeat.

6 **PAIRS.** Say a sentence from Exercise 3. Your partner says the sentence that has the same meaning. Take turns.

A: *Women aren't as tall as men.*
B: *Men are taller than women.*

Grammar focus

> **LANGUAGE NOTES**
> - The comparative form is used to show the differences or similarities between people, places, or things.
> - One way to form the comparative is to add *-er*. Spelling may change: *thin/thinner; lazy/lazier.*
> - Most adjectives with two or more syllables form comparatives with *more* or *less: more exciting, less dangerous.*
> - *As . . . as* can show both similarities and differences: *He is as tall as his brother. / He isn't as tall as his sister.*

> **WARM-UP**
>
> Note: Skip this warm-up if you're doing this lesson (Lesson B) during the same class period as Lesson A.
> - Tell students they are going to listen to the book review of *Why Men Don't Iron* that they read in the Reading section.
> - On the board, make a chart with three columns. At the top of the left-hand column write *-er*. At the top of the middle column write *more . . . than* and *less . . . than*. At the top of the right-hand column write *irregular*. Ask students to copy the chart. Tell students to listen for adjectives used to describe boys and girls and fill in their charts.
> - 🎧 Students listen to the review.
> - Ask students which adjectives they heard (*messier, more competitive, better, more hardworking, more talkative, noisier, stronger, more cooperative, less aggressive, neater, more emotional*). Write the adjectives in the chart on the board.

Exercise ❶

- Have students look at the examples and study the boldfaced words.
- Ask students to focus on the first pair of sentences. Point out that the meaning of the two sentences is the same. Elicit how the grammar is different: the order is reversed and the negative is used in the *as . . . as* form.
- Ask students to look at the rest of the sentences. Help with vocabulary if needed.

Exercise ❷

- Have students study the examples again.
- Explain the task in the first part of this excercise. Students complete the rules in the box.
- Have students check answers in pairs.
- Go over the answers with the class.
- Point out the **note** in the chart on the irregular comparatives *good/**better than*** and *bad/**worse than**.*
- Refer students to Grammar Reference page 143, as needed.

Answer key	c	a	b

Exercise ❸

- Explain the task. Students will rewrite the sentences so that they have the same meaning. Go over the first sentence.
- Have students complete the exercise individually. Set a time limit of 5–8 minutes.
- Have students work in pairs to check their answers.
- Go over the answers with the class.

> **Answer key**
> 1. messier than women
> 2. as fast as boys
> 3. more noisy than girls
> 4. more talkative than men
> 5. more emotional than men
> 6. taller than women
> 7. as hardworking as girls
> 8. as good as boys at soccer

Teaching Tip! Keeping students involved

An important part of classroom management is keeping students involved in class activities. One way to do this is to say the sentence *before* calling on a student.

Pronunciation

Exercise ❹

- Explain that some words in English, such as comparatives, have a strong pronunciation and a weak one. Tell them the weak pronunciation is more common.
- Ask students to look at the examples for Lesson B, Exercise 1 and listen to the audio.
- 🎧 Play the audio and have students listen. Ask them to notice the weak pronunciation of *as* and *than*.
- You can also contrast the strong and weak pronunciations of *as* and *than* words by saying each word, first by itself and then in a sentence.

Exercise ❺

- 🎧 Play the audio. Stop the audio after each line and have students repeat it chorally.
- Ask a few individual students to repeat to check their pronunciation.
- Encourage students to link the words together in the comparative phrases and to stress the adjective; for example: *as **strong** as* /ə/, ***strong**er than* /ə/.
- Students may have difficulty with the /ð/ sound in *than*. You can demonstrate the position of the tongue between the upper and lower teeth, lightly touching the top teeth.

Exercise ❻

- Explain the task: One student chooses a sentence in Exercise 3 and says it. The other student says the sentence that has the same meaning.
- Pair students. Set a time limit of 2–3 minutes.
- Walk around the room, helping as needed.

Speaking

Teaching Tip! Expressing point of view

Sometimes in conversation we want to make sure others understand we are presenting something as an opinion, not a fact. Explain that there are some expressions we can use to "soften" how we state an opinion. Remind them they can use simple phrases like *I think . . . , in my opinion,* or *it seems to me.*

Exercise 7

- Have students look at their book and present the questionnaire, checking that students understand vocabulary.
- Explain the task: Students complete the questionnaire using their own ideas.
- Set a time limit of 5 minutes. Walk around the room, helping as needed.

Exercise 8

- Form groups of 3, preferably mixed male and female. Have them compare answers and discuss any differences in opinions, being sure to give reasons.
- Remind students of some phrases they can use to express polite disagreement. Examples: *I really don't agree; I have to disagree; Sorry, but I don't really agree because . . .*
- Tell students to listen carefully so they can report to the class about the opinions in their group.

WRAP-UP

Call on a few students to report about their group's discussion. Optionally, ask with a show of hands: *Who agrees (that women are more romantic)?* Encourage students to give reasons.

TRB For additional interactive grammar practice, have students do the reproducible activity for this unit in the *Teacher's Resource Book.*

Writing

Exercise 9

- Assign the writing task for class work or homework.
- **TRB** Optionally give students a copy of the model (see the *Teacher's Resource Book,* Writing Models). Ask them to read the model and notice the comparative adjectives that are used. Additionally, remind them of some of the vocabulary from this unit they might use (*hardworking, romantic, competitive,* and so on).
- If students do not have the model, write the following on the board:

    My Aunt Agnes and Uncle Fred are a wonderful couple. They live in the suburbs in a small house with a huge garden. They get along really well, and . . .

    Walk around the room to make sure students understand the task.

- If the assignment is done in class, have students read their work aloud as time permits.

For suggestions on how to give feedback on writing, see page xiv of this *Teacher's Edition.*

CONVERSATION TO GO

- As the students leave class, have them read the dialogue.
- Optionally, ask students to read the short dialogue in pairs, switching parts.

HOMEWORK

- Assign *Workbook* page 16, Grammar Exercises 3 and 4, and page 17, Pronunciation Exercises 7 and 8.
- If students do not have the *WorldView Workbook,* assign listening homework from the Student CD. Write on the board:

    Track 4
    According to the authors, can society change men's and women's behavior?

- Tell students to listen to the audio and write their answer. Have students bring it to the next class. (*No, they are born that way.*)

Speaking

7 **BEFORE YOU SPEAK.** What do you think about the personalities and behavior of women and men in general? Add one more question. Then complete the questionnaire.

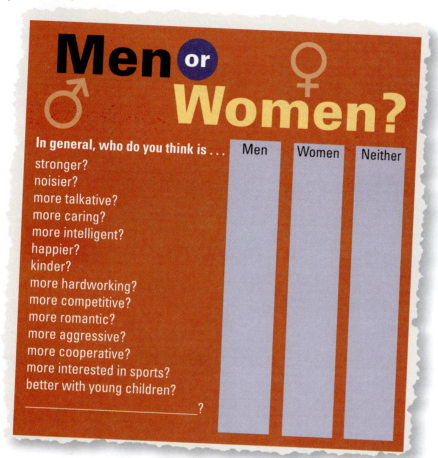

8 **GROUPS OF 3.** Compare your answers. Talk about any differences in your opinions.

A: *I think men are stronger than women.*
B: *I think they're stronger physically, but I think women are stronger . . .*

Writing

9 Think of a man and a woman (or a girl and a boy) you know well. Write a short paragraph comparing them. Use comparative adjectives and *as* + adjective + *as*.

CONVERSATION TO GO

A: He's **stronger** and **more aggressive than** me.
B: But he isn't **as fast as** you!

UNIT 3

Living in luxury

Vocabulary Numbers; hotel facilities
Grammar Review: Simple present statements and questions
Speaking Describing places

Lesson A

Getting started

1. **PAIRS.** Which of these facilities and services can you see in the photos?

a baby-sitting service	ballrooms	a business center
cafés	casinos	conference rooms
a fitness center	guest rooms	a limousine service
a lobby	restaurants	a sauna
a swimming pool	tennis courts	a video arcade

2. Check (✓) the facilities and services that you think the Four Seasons Hotels offer.

3. 🎧 Listen and check your answers. Then listen and repeat.

4. **PAIRS.** Which of the facilities and services in Exercise 1 are the most important to you? Why?

10

Living in luxury

UNIT 3

OBJECTIVES

Students will:

- activate vocabulary related to hotel facilities and numbers
- review the simple present in statements and questions
- practice stress in numbers ending in *-teen* and *-ty*

WARM-UP: A NICE PLACE TO STAY

- Write the following on the board: *living in luxury*. Elicit from students or explain that this phrase is used to describe someone's lifestyle and that it usually means that someone has a lot of money.
- Form groups of 3. Have students think about what their definition of *living in luxury* is when they think about their lives. Ask them what they would need to create their own luxury life (*more money, long vacations, a swimming pool, a maid, a car*, etc.).
- Call on a few students to share their answers and write their ideas on the board. Explain any words that students don't know.

OPTION: VOCABULARY PREVIEW

- Explain the task: Students associate an activity with the place where it usually takes place.
- Write the words from the box on the board.
- Tell students you are going to say an activity, and they say where it takes place. Give an example: *This is where you exercise.* (fitness center)
- Read through the list of activities below. Have students say the correct place.

  Exercise. *(fitness center)*
  Have a business meeting. *(conference room)*
  Check in. *(lobby)*
  Have coffee. *(café)*
  Dance. *(ballroom)*
  Make photocopies. *(business center)*
  Relax. *(sauna)*
  Eat. *(restaurant)*
  Swim. *(swimming pool)*
  Go to the airport. *(limousine service)*

Exercise ❶

- Ask students to look at the photographs of a Four Seasons hotel. Ask them to describe what they see. For now, focus on the objects, the furniture, and specific characteristics that make the hotel feel luxurious.
- Have students work in pairs to identify which of the facilities listed they can see in the photos. Present the first facility listed *(a baby-sitting service)*.

- Set a time limit of 3 minutes. Walk around the room, helping as needed.
- Go over the answers with the class.

Answer key

A. guest room   C. restaurant
B. conference room   D. lobby

Exercise ❷

- Tell students to think of the facilities and services a Four Seasons hotel might offer.
- Explain the task: Students work individually to check (✓) their choices.
- Have students work in pairs to compare answers. Wait until they have done Exercise 3 to go over the answers.

Exercise ❸

- Explain the task: Students listen to a description of some of the services and facilities at Four Seasons hotels, and check their predictions.
- 🎧 Play the audio as students check their answers.
- 🎧 Play the audio again, pausing for students to repeat.
- Check answers with the class.

Answer key

All words but *video arcade* and *casino* are checked.

Exercise ❹

- Explain the task: Students discuss which facilities in Exercise 1 are most important. Give examples of different types of guests and have students say which services such guests would think are important. For example, ask, *Which facilities might be most important to a family with young children?* (a baby-sitting service).
- Pair students. Have them decide which of the services and facilities are important to them and why. Set a time limit of 5 minutes. Remind students to give reasons for their choices.
- Walk around the room, helping as needed.
- Have two pairs work together to compare their choices.

EXTENSION

Take a class survey of the most important hotel facilities. Tell students to imagine they are traveling for pleasure, and to name the two most important hotel services or facilities to him or her. Have a student volunteer keep a tally on the board.

Teacher's Notes — Lesson A

T10

Listening

> **LANGUAGE NOTES**
> - Numbers such as 1,500 are read as *one thousand, five hundred*, or *fifteen hundred* in more colloquial speech.
> - With large numbers, *and* is said before the last two numbers in some regions: *2,345 = two thousand, three hundred, AND forty-five*; *2004 = two thousand AND four*. In more formal English, *and* is not commonly used other than with dollars and cents ($12.50 = *twelve dollars and fifty cents*).

Exercise 5

- Tell students they are going to practice listening to numbers as a warm-up to listening to a conversation about a Four Seasons hotel. Students listen and circle the numbers they hear.
- 🎧 Play the audio as students listen and circle the correct numbers.
- 🎧 Play the audio again so that students can confirm their answers.
- Go over the answers with the class.

Answer key

58	715	14,850	140,000
218	850	13,000	16,000,000
560	1,217		

Exercise 6

- Explain the task: Students listen to the conversation and answer the questions. Ask students to read the questions. Elicit ideas about who is having the conversation. Encourage students to predict who it might be *(someone making a reservation and a hotel employee)*.
- 🎧 Play the audio. If needed, play the audio again.
- Go over the answers with the class.
- Optionally, play the recording one more time so that students can confirm their answers.

Answer key

1. 58
2. 14,850
3. 26,000
4. $1,300
5. $550

Pronunciation

Exercise 7

- Explain that when numbers ending in *-teen* and *-ty* are said by themselves, their stress is different. Give examples *(seventeen, seventy)*.
- 🎧 Play the audio and have students listen. Then play the audio again and have students repeat the numbers chorally.

- You may want to point out that the *t* in *eighty* and *forty* sounds like a quick /d/.
- Optionally, say different *-teen* and *-ty* numbers at random. Ask students to identify the numbers by saying the numerals used to write them (e.g., *eight-zero* or *one-eight*).

Exercise 8

- Explain that there isn't always a difference in stress between *-teen* and *-ty* numbers. When another word comes right after a *-teen* number, stress in the *-teen* number moves to the first syllable.
- 🎧 Play the audio and have students listen. Then play the audio again and have students repeat the phrases chorally.
- Ask a few individual students to repeat and check their pronunciation.

Exercise 9

- Explain the task: Students listen and circle the numbers they hear in the ad.
- 🎧 Play the audio. Students listen and circle the correct numbers.
- 🎧 Play the audio again so that students can confirm their answers.

Exercise 10

- Form pairs. Explain the task: Students compare answers by saying the numbers, without looking at each other's books. Model the language students can use if they are not sure what number their partner said. For example: *Did you say one–three or three–zero?*
- Optionally, students can take turns saying the sentences in pairs. Student A says a sentence, choosing a number to say. Student B says which number Student A used.

Answer key

1. 13 2. 218 3. 30 4. 9,650 5. 15

> **WRAP-UP**
> - Ask the class, *How much money would you pay per night to stay at a hotel?* Call on a number of students and write their answers on the board.
> - Call on a few students and ask for their opinions. Tell students they may use expressions such as *I'd (I would) never pay . . . , I think it's worth paying that if . . .*

💻 Please go to www.longman.com/worldview for additional in-class model conversation practice and supplementary reading practice.

HOMEWORK

- 📖 For homework, assign *Workbook* page 18, Vocabulary Exercise 1, and page 20, Listening Exercises 4 and 5.

Listening

5 🎧 Listen and circle the numbers you hear.

58	218	385	560
715	719	850	1,217
9,650	13,000	14,850	
140,000		16,000,000	

6 🎧 Listen to the conversation and answer the questions.

1. About how many Four Seasons hotels are there in the world?
2. About how many rooms does the Four Seasons hotel chain have?
3. How many employees does the Four Seasons chain have?
4. How much does a premier suite cost per night?
5. How much does a deluxe double room cost per night?

Pronunciation

7 🎧 Listen. Notice the difference in stress between numbers ending in *-teen* and *-ty*.

eighty   eigh**teen**   **for**ty   four**teen**   **six**ty   six**teen**

8 🎧 Listen. Now notice how the stress changes when a *-teen* number comes before another word. Then listen again and repeat.

eighty **rooms**   **eigh**teen **rooms**

forty **dol**lars   **four**teen **dol**lars

sixty **miles**   **six**teen **miles**

9 🎧 Listen to the ad and circle the correct number in each sentence.

1. The hotel is **13 / 30** minutes from the airport.
2. It has **218 / 280** guest rooms.
3. There are **13 / 30** guest suites with balconies.
4. The hotel has **9,615 / 9,650** square feet for dining and dancing.
5. There are **15 / 50** conference rooms.

10 **PAIRS.** Compare your answers.

Grammar focus

1 Look at the examples. Complete the sentences with the auxiliaries *do, does, don't,* or *doesn't.*

> (+) The premier suite **has** a view of the ocean.
> We want to reserve a suite.
>
> (−) A double deluxe room _____ **cost** as much as the suite.
> We _____ **need** an absolutely perfect suite.
>
> (?) _____ the guest rooms **have** Internet connections?
> How much _____ dinner **cost**?

2 Look at the examples again. Complete the rules in the chart.

> **Simple present statements**
>
> Add _____ to the base form of the verb if the subject is *he, she,* or *it* in affirmative statements.
>
> Use a form of the auxiliary _____ for negative statements and questions.

Grammar Reference page 143

3 Complete the conversation with the simple present of the verbs in parentheses.

A: You're at the Four Seasons? What's it like? **(1)** <u>Do you have</u> **(you/have)** a room with a balcony?

B: We **(2)** _____ **(not have)** a balcony, but we **(3)** _____ **(have)** a spectacular ocean view.

A: **(4)** _____ **(your room/have)** a TV?

B: Of course. It **(5)** _____ **(get)** over 100 channels.

A: **(6)** _____ **(the hotel/have)** a swimming pool?

B: Yes, but we **(7)** _____ **(prefer)** the beach.

A: Where **(8)** _____ **(you/eat)**?

B: Usually at a fancy restaurant at the hotel. The waiters are very polite and the food **(9)** _____ **(taste)** great.

A: That sounds wonderful. How much **(10)** _____ **(everything/cost)**?

B: The rooms **(11)** _____ **(cost)** over $500, and dinner is usually over $100.

A: That's expensive!

B: It is, but I **(12)** _____ **(not care)**. It's our honeymoon, after all!

Grammar focus

> **LANGUAGE NOTES**
> - *Yes/No* questions are formed with *do* (*Do you prefer smoking or nonsmoking?*) or *does* (*Does the room have a refrigerator?*).
> - Short answers to *Yes/No* questions do not require the full verb form.
>   *Do you have room service? Yes, we do/No, we don't.*
>   *Does the concierge work in the evenings? Yes, he does/No, he doesn't.*

> **WARM-UP**
> **Note: Skip this warm-up if you're doing this lesson (Lesson B) during the same class period as Lesson A.**
> - Books closed. Tell students they are going to listen again to the conversation about the Four Seasons hotels that they heard in the Listening section.
> - Tell students to listen for questions that use *does*.
> - 🎧 Play the audio for Lesson A, Exercise 6.
> - Ask students what questions they heard (*And how much does the premiere suite cost? Does it have an ocean view?*).

Exercise ❶

- Have students look at the first two example sentences.
- Elicit the following from students:
  Has is the third-person singular of *have*. Third-person singular in verbs is different from other forms.
  The forms of auxiliary *do* are used for negative sentences and questions. *Does* is the third-person singular of *do*.
  Don't is the contracted form of *do not*, and *doesn't* is the contracted form of *does not*.
- Explain the symbols: + means affirmative, – means negative, and ? means question.
- Have students work to individually complete the examples.
- Have students check their answers with a partner.
- Go over the answers with the class.

> **Answer key**
>
> (–) doesn't   (?) Do
>   don't   does

Exercise ❷

- Have students study the examples again.
- Tell students to complete the rules in the chart.
- Have students compare their answers with a partner.
- Go over the answers with the class.
- Ask a few questions to elicit the key points about the grammar, for example: *What is the difference between affirmative sentences and questions or negative sentences?* (They need do/does, don't/doesn't.) *What's the first word in a Yes/No question?* (Do/Does)
- Refer students to Grammar Reference page 143, as needed.

> **Answer key**
>
> s   do

Exercise ❸

- Tell students to complete the conversation with the simple present of the verbs in parentheses. Go over the completed first line together. Remind students to look at the punctuation and context to help them decide their answers.
- Set a time limit of 3 minutes. Students work individually. Walk around the room, helping as needed.
- Ask students to check their answers in pairs.
- Go over the answers with the class.

> **Answer key**
>
> 1. Do you have   7. prefer
> 2. don't have   8. do you eat
> 3. have   9. tastes
> 4. Does your room   10. does everything cost
> 5. gets   11. cost
> 6. Does the hotel have 12. don't care

> **WRAP-UP**
> Have students practice the conversation in pairs.

Speaking

 **Stating preferences**

Point out to students that there are a number of ways we can state a preference, for example, *I like Hotel Monaco the best* or *I'd rather stay at Hotel Monaco*. Review the expressions: *I prefer a hotel with ..., I'd rather stay at ... because, I like ... better because ...*

Exercise 4

- Pair students. Tell them they are going on a business trip together. They need to decide which hotel to stay at, the Delta Hotel or the Marina Hotel.
- Tell Student A to stay on this *Student Book* page, and Student B to turn to page 136. They should not look at each other's books. Students will take turns asking and answering questions about the facilities and services of the two hotels. The hotels cost the same. Together, they need to choose one of the hotels.
- With a student, model the exchange in the book.

    A: How many rooms does the Delta Hotel have?
    B: It has 32 rooms. Does the Marina offer free airport transportation?

- Remind students to take turns and to follow the model, whenever possible.
- Set a time limit of 10 minutes for the students to complete the conversation. Walk around the room, helping as needed.

Exercise 5

- Check which pairs chose the Marina, and which chose the Delta. Combine two pairs to form groups of 4. If possible, group a Marina pair with a Delta pair, so they can discuss and disagree.
- Have students in each pair take turns speaking about their results. Set a time limit of 5 minutes. While students work, monitor their discussions and check that they give reasons for which hotel they chose.

> **WRAP-UP**
>
> Conclude by calling on students to share with the class which hotel they chose and why.

EXTENSION

- Form groups of 4. Tell them to describe their ideal hotel. This can be a hotel they have visited, or they can use their imagination. Other members of the group ask questions about the hotel's services and facilities. Encourage students to use the appropriate form of *do* in their questions and answers.
- Set a time limit of 3 minutes. Walk around the room, helping as needed.

TRB For additional interactive grammar practice, have students do the reproducible activity for this unit in the *Teacher's Resource Book*.

Writing

Exercise 6

- Assign the writing task for class work or homework.
- Optionally, give students a copy of the model of a postcard (see the *Teacher's Resource Book*, Writing Models). Ask them to read the model and notice the verbs used.
- If students don't have the model, write the following on the board:

    Dear Pam,
    Hi from Barcelona! I'm here in Spain for a convention—attending a lot of interesting meetings, and ...

- Make sure the students understand the organization and punctuation of a postcard. Walk around to make sure they understand the task.
- If the assignment is done in class, ask several volunteers to read their postcards to the class. Tell the other students to listen carefully and ask questions.

For suggestions on how to give feedback on writing, see page xiv of this *Teacher's Edition*.

CONVERSATION TO GO

- As the students leave class, have them read the dialogue.
- Optionally, read aloud together, emphasizing the simple present verbs. Demonstrate rising intonation on the question.
- Have pairs of students take turns asking and answering a *Yes/No* question about a hotel they both know, for example, *Does the Continental have a swimming pool? / No, it doesn't, but it has a wonderful gym.*

HOMEWORK

- 📖 Assign *Workbook* page 19, Grammar Exercises 2 and 3, and page 20, Pronunciation Exercises 6, 7, and 8.
- 💿 If students do not have the *WorldView Workbook*, assign listening homework from the Student CD. Write on the board:

    Track 6
    Which room did the customer reserve?

- 🎧 Tell students to listen to the audio and write the answer. Have them bring it to the next class. (*deluxe double room*)

Speaking

4 **PAIRS.** You're going on a business trip together. Decide which hotel to stay at, the Delta Hotel or the Marina Hotel. Student A, look at this page. Student B, look at page 136.

Read the brochure. Then take turns asking and answering questions about the facilities and services at your partner's hotel. Both hotels cost $115 per night. Together, choose one of the hotels.

A: How many rooms does the Delta Hotel have?
B: It has 32 rooms. Does the Marina offer free airport transportation?

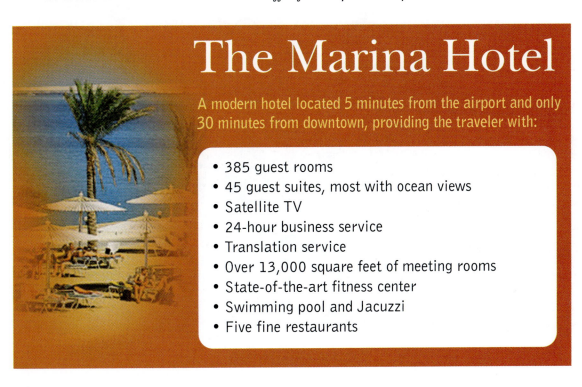

The Marina Hotel

A modern hotel located 5 minutes from the airport and only 30 minutes from downtown, providing the traveler with:

- 385 guest rooms
- 45 guest suites, most with ocean views
- Satellite TV
- 24-hour business service
- Translation service
- Over 13,000 square feet of meeting rooms
- State-of-the-art fitness center
- Swimming pool and Jacuzzi
- Five fine restaurants

5 **GROUPS OF 4.** Talk about your results. Which hotel did you choose? Why?

Writing

6 You are staying at a luxury hotel. Write a postcard to a friend. Describe your hotel. Use the simple present.

CONVERSATION TO GO

A: **Does** the hotel **have** a fitness center?
B: I **don't know**. But it **has** a nice sauna!

UNIT 4

Allergic reactions

Vocabulary Medical symptoms
Grammar Adjectives ending in -ed and -ing
Speaking Describing how you feel

Lesson A

Getting started

1 **PAIRS.** Match the following symptoms with the people in the picture.

1. a headache __D__
2. a sore throat _____
3. a rash _____
4. a cold _____
5. a backache _____
6. a stomachache _____
7. an earache _____

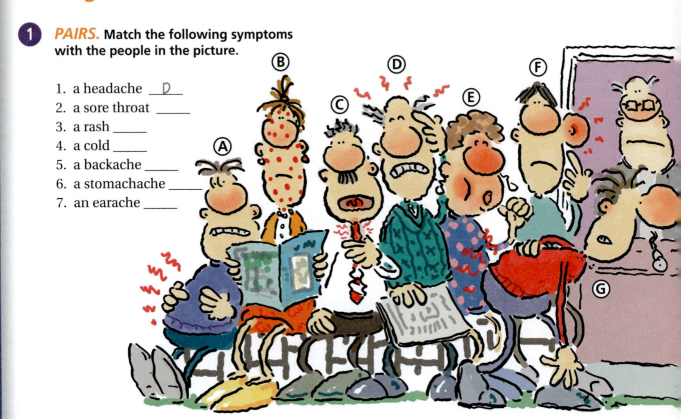

2 🎧 Listen and check your answers. Then listen and repeat.

3 **PAIRS.** What advice would you give each person in the picture? Take turns beginning the conversation. Use a symptom from Exercise 1 and some advice from the list below.

A: What's the matter?
B: I have a stomachache.
A: Sorry to hear that. You should take it easy. Don't eat anything spicy or oily.

- Don't carry heavy things.
- Have a cup of tea with honey and lemon.
- Sit quietly and try to relax.
- Don't eat anything spicy or oily.
- Take lots of Vitamin C and get plenty of rest.
- Try not to scratch it.
- Don't go swimming.

14

Allergic reactions

UNIT 4

OBJECTIVES

Students will:
- activate vocabulary related to medical symptoms
- use adjectives ending in -ed and -ing
- practice listening for and saying -ed adjective endings

> **WARM-UP: WHAT WAS THE MATTER?**
> - Write the following on the board: *What was the matter? What did you do?* Ask students to think about a time when they didn't feel well. Call on a student to answer the questions and write the student's answers in the columns: *What was the matter?* I had a bad headache. *What did you do?* I took two aspirin and then took a nap.
> - Form groups of 3. Set a time limit of 2 minutes. Have students take turns asking each other the questions and giving personal examples.
> - Call on a few students to report on a group member.

Getting started

OPTION: VOCABULARY PREVIEW

Preteach the vocabulary items in the Getting started section with brief pantomimes of the symptoms in the list.

- Focus on the words with the *-ache* suffix first. Pantomime *headache* and elicit *headache* from students. Write *headache* on the board, and remind students that the *ch* has the sound /k/ instead of its usual /tʃ/ sound.
- Continue with *ear* and elicit *earache* from students. Complete the list with *backache* and *stomachache*.
- Point to your throat and elicit *sore throat* and then pantomime *cold* (sneeze) and *rash* (scratch an arm).

> *LANGUAGE NOTE*
>
> Students are often challenged by when to use *ache* and when to use *sore*. The best way for students to learn the different ailments is as lexical items in groups (i.e., which ones go with *sore*, and which ones go with *ache*).

Exercise ❶

- Ask students to look at the people in the picture. Explain that the people are waiting in line at a doctor's office. Each one has a different problem. Ask students to read the symptoms listed in the book *(a headache, etc.)*.
- Explain the task: Students work in pairs to match the symptoms with the people in the picture. Go over the first symptom together, *a headache, D.*
- Set a time limit of 3 minutes. While students are working, walk around the room, helping as needed.

Exercise ❷

- 🎧 Play the audio and tell students to listen and check their answers from Exercise 1.
- 🎧 Play the audio again and have students repeat.
- Go over the answers with the class and encourage students to use complete sentences, for example, *a headache, D. He has a headache.*

> **Answer key**
> 1. a headache D
> 2. a sore throat C
> 3. a rash B
> 4. a cold E
> 5. a backache G
> 6. a stomachache A
> 7. an earache F

Exercise ❸

- Tell students we often offer advice when we're talking to someone who isn't feeling well. On the board, write a few common symptoms and popular remedies, for example: *I have a sore throat. / You should gargle with salt water.*
- Pair students. Explain the task: Students give advice to each person in the picture. They take turns beginning the conversation using the model in the book.
- Go over the example in the book.
- Students work in pairs to make conversations.
- Call on various pairs to present to the class.

> **Answer key**
> Answers may vary. Possible answers include:
> *Don't carry heavy things. (a backache)*
> *Have a cup of tea with honey and lemon. (a sore throat, a cold)*
> *Sit quietly and try to relax. (a backache, a headache, a cold)*
> *Don't eat anything spicy or oily. (a stomachache)*
> *Take lots of Vitamin C and get plenty of rest. (a sore throat, a cold)*
> *Try not to scratch it. (a rash)*
> *Don't go swimming. (an earache)*

> **EXTENSION**
>
> Do a chain conversation with the whole class. Model the conversation by asking Student A *What's the matter, (Alex)?* Student A responds (*I have a . . .*). Offer advice (*You should/n't . . .*). Then call on Student A to ask another Student (B) *What's the matter, (Pam)?* If time permits, continue in this way with several students.

Teacher's Notes — Lesson A

T14

Reading

Exercise 4

- Have students look at the drawings of some causes of allergic reactions. Help students identify them. Elicit what students know about other causes of allergic reactions.
- Pair students. Explain the task: Students ask each other about any allergies that they have. Set a time limit of 3 minutes.
- Call on students to say if they or their partners have allergies, and if so, what the symptoms are. Take a poll of the class to see how many people have allergies.

Exercise 5

- Hold up your book and point to the picture of Doctor Monica. Elicit who Doctor Monica is, and what a helpline is (*a telephone number you can call if you need special advice or information*). Explain that a doctor who is "on call" is a doctor who is available to give medical advice (or treatment, in a hospital setting).
- Explain the task: Students read Doctor Monica's article about allergies and answer the questions. Have students read the questions first. Remind students that they will read the article twice, and this time they should read just to find out how each person felt.
- Set a time limit of 2 minutes. Students should practice reading quickly for general understanding, and then answer the questions. Monitor their work.
- Go over answers with the class by asking the question *Which person was (annoyed)?*

> **Answer key**
> Sarah was depressed.
> Fabio was annoyed.
> Silvia was embarrassed.

Exercise 6

- Tell students to read the article again and to pay attention to what symptoms each patient had. Set a time limit of 5 minutes.
- Students work individually to read the article and complete the chart. Walk around the room, helping as needed.
- Have students work in pairs to check their answers.
- Go over answers with the class. Have students summarize the information in complete sentences: *Fabio was allergic to pollen. His symptoms were . . .*

> **Answer key**
>
> | Allergic to | Symptons |
> |---|---|
> | pollen | sore throat; itchy, red eyes |
> | animals | rash; red, sore eyes |
> | chocolate | headaches |

EXTENSION

- Form pairs. Ask students to read the article again. Have students summarize each patient's case: describe the symptoms, say what the patient is allergic to and what causes the problem, and the solution. For example: *Fabio had a sore throat and itchy, red eyes. He's allergic to pollen from trees and plants. He should stay inside more during the spring and the summer.*
- You may want to write the following information on the board for students to refer to during the activity:

  Symptoms
  Allergic to _____ because of/from the _____
  He/she should _____.

Please go to www.longman.com/worldview for additional in-class model conversation practice.

HOMEWORK

- For homework, assign *Workbook* page 21, Vocabulary Exercises 1 and 2, and page 23, Listening Exercises 5 and 6.

Reading

4 **PAIRS.** Discuss these questions.

Do you or your friends have allergies?
What are some of the symptoms?

5 Read Doctor Monica's article about allergies and answer the questions. Which person was:

1. depressed?
2. annoyed?
3. embarrassed?

This week: **Allergy Alert**

Doctor Monica on Call

Allergies are very common and are considered medical conditions. About 40% of the population now shows symptoms of some sort of allergy. Allergies can be very frightening. In the worst case, an allergic reaction can cause death.

Allergies are so common that it's surprising that more people aren't aware of them. Recently a young man named Fabio came into my office complaining of a sore throat and itchy, red eyes. He thought he had a cold. Fabio loves to play sports, and he found it annoying that every time he went outdoors to play sports, his cold got worse. In fact, he did not have a cold at all. Fabio was allergic to the pollen from trees and plants.

A young university student, Silvia, came in the other day to talk about her allergy to animals. Her parents have dogs and cats, and, whenever she's home during school vacation, she gets a rash on her neck and her eyes become red and sore. She said it was embarrassing. Everyone thinks she is crying!

Another patient, Sarah, came to see me about her terrible headaches. She said it was depressing to think that she might have to live with headaches all the time. I found out that Sarah ate a chocolate bar every day. I told her she might be allergic to chocolate. She stopped eating chocolate for two weeks and came back to see me—headache-free.

6 Read the article again. What symptoms did each patient have? Complete the chart.

Name	Allergic to	Symptoms
Fabio	pollen	
Silvia	animals	
Sarah	chocolate	

Grammar focus

1 Study the examples of adjectives ending in *-ed* and *-ing*.

> Fabio is **annoyed**. Having allergies is **annoying**.
> Silvia is **embarrassed**. Her red, itchy eyes are **embarrassing**.

2 Look at the examples again. Underline the correct information to complete the rules in the chart.

Adjectives ending in *-ed* and *-ing*
Adjectives that end in **-ed / -ing** describe how you feel.
Adjectives that end in **-ed / -ing** describe what or who makes you feel this way.

Grammar Reference page 143

3 Underline the correct adjectives in each conversation.

1. A: I'm really **surprised / surprising**. I never get colds and now I have one.
   B: It's not **surprised / surprising**. You have a stressful job.
2. A: This rash is really **frustrated / frustrating**. I can't seem to get rid of it.
   B: If you're **frustrated / frustrating**, you should go see a doctor.
3. A: I've just read an **interested / interesting** article on allergies. It says lots of them are caused by pollution.
   B: I know. Politicians should be more **interested / interesting** in the problem.
4. A: I was **shocked / shocking** to hear he's in the hospital.
   B: And nobody in the family has gone to visit. It's **shocked / shocking**.
5. A: She used to hate doctors. Her visits to the doctor were always so **frightened / frightening** to her.
   B: Well, she's not **frightened / frightening** any more. She is a doctor.

Pronunciation

4 🎧 Listen to the adjectives. Notice the pronunciation of the *-ed* ending. Write each adjective in the correct sound group. What is the difference between the two sound groups?

relaxed / bored	excited
tired	disappointed

5 🎧 Listen and check your answers. Then listen again and repeat.

6 *PAIRS.* Practice the conversations in Exercise 3.

Grammar focus

WARM-UP

Note: Skip this warm-up if you're doing this lesson (Lesson B) during the same class period as Lesson A.

- Books closed. Tell students they are going to listen to the article *Doctor Monica on Call* that they read in the Reading section.
- Write on the board *It was . . .* Tell students to listen for the phrase used to describe Fabio, Sarah, and Silvia's situation.
- Students listen to the article.
- Write *Fabio, Sarah,* and *Silvia* on the board. Point to one name at a time. Students say the phrase: *It was annoying/embarrassing/depressing.*
- Write the sentence pairs on the board: *Fabio was annoyed/It was annoying,* and so on.

LANGUAGE NOTE

It is very common for students to confuse the use of adjectives ending in *-ed* (how you feel) with those ending in *-ing* (who or what makes you feel that way), e.g., *The movie was frightening/I felt frightened.* One way to help understand an error such as ~~I am boring~~ is to ask: *Did you make someone else feel bored, or did you feel bored?*

Exercise 1

- Have students look at the examples and study the boldfaced words.
- Elicit that the words in boldface are adjectives.
- Ask students what they notice about the adjectives in the box (some end in *-ed,* others end in *-ing*).

Exercise 2

- Have students study the examples again.
- Ask individual students: *How does Fabio feel? (He's annoyed.) What makes him feel that way? (Allergies.)*
- Students work individually to complete the rules by underlining the correct information in each sentence.
- Go over the rules with the class.
- Refer students to Grammar Reference page 143.

Answer key -ed, -ing

Exercise 3

- Explain the task: Students underline the correct adjectives in each conversation. Go over the first sentence. Explain that the correct answer here is *I'm really surprised* because <u>I feel surprised</u>. Contrast this with the next sentence in which the situation <u>is not surprising to me</u> *(It's not surprising).*
- Have students complete the exercise individually. Set a time limit of 5 minutes.
- In pairs, have students check their answers.
- Go over answers with the class: call on pairs to read aloud.

Answer key

1. A: surprised   B: surprising
2. A: frustrating   B: frustrated
3. A: interesting   B: interested
4. A: shocked   B: shocking
5. A: frightening   B: frightened

WRAP-UP

- Write three headings on the board: *boring, depressing, annoying.*
- Call on individual students and ask, *What's boring? (A rainy Sunday.) How do you feel when that happens? (Bored.)* Ask other students questions about depressing and annoying situations.

Pronunciation

Exercise 4

- Explain that the *-ed* ending sounds different in the three adjectives at the top of the table. Ask students to listen to the sound of the *-ed* ending in these words.
- 🎧 Have students listen to the first three words on the audio: *relaxed, bored, excited.*
- Tell students they are going to listen to more adjectives. Ask them to listen to the sound of the *-ed* ending and write the adjective in the correct group.
- 🎧 Stop the audio after the first adjective *(tired)* and check that students understand what to do. Then play the audio to the end while students complete the table.

Exercise 5

- Tell students to listen and check their answers.
- 🎧 Play the audio as students listen only. The words on the audio are grouped according to the pronunciation of the *-ed* ending.

Answer key

relax<u>ed</u> / bor<u>ed</u>		excit<u>ed</u>
tired	shocked	disappointed
depressed	frightened	frustrated
annoyed	embarrassed	interested
surprised		

The difference is that *-ed* doesn't add an extra syllable to the left column, but it does to the right.

Exercise 6

- Explain the task: Students work in pairs to practice the conversations in Exercise 3.
- Pair students. Set a time limit of 2 minutes. Walk around the room, helping as needed.
- Call on pairs to present to the class.
- Optionally, encourage students to continue the conversations with at least one follow-up question.

Speaking

Teaching Tip! Giving and receiving advice

The verb *should* is often used to give advice. Remind students of other expressions they can use to offer advice such as: *You ought to . . . , You need to . . . , Why don't you . . . , I recommend that you . . .* In addition, there are ways to thank someone for advice, such as *Thanks for the advice. I'll try that.* OR *That sounds like a good idea, but (I don't have time to rest).* The expression *You'd better . . .* is used only rarely, when there is a serious consequence involved (*You'd better go to the doctor right now before that wound gets infected*).

Exercise 7

- Pair students. Explain the task: Student A is a patient and Student B is a doctor.
- Tell Student A to turn to page 137, and Student B to stay on this page. They should not look at each other's books. Student A will arrive at the doctor's office. Student B will ask questions to find out what the problem is, and write notes on the notepad. Student B will then offer Student A two pieces of advice.
- Set a time limit of 1 minute to read over the situations and choose one. Remind Student A to read the directions at the top of the page carefully and to use *-ed* adjectives (*I feel tired*).
- Set a time limit of 3 minutes for the students to complete the conversation. Walk around the room, helping as needed.

> **WRAP-UP**
>
> Ask a few pairs to summarize their conversations for the class. Student B summarizes the problem, and Student A the advice given by Student B.

EXTENSION

Have students switch roles and role-play a different allergy or medical problem.

TRB For additional interactive grammar practice, have students do the reproducible activity for this unit in the *Teacher's Resource Book*.

Writing

Exercise 8

- Assign the writing task for class work or homework. Go over the directions, making sure students understand their paragraph should include how they felt, what they did to get better, and the advice they received. If necessary, allow students to write about another illness or physical problem.
- **TRB** Optionally, give students a copy of the model (see the *Teacher's Resource Book*, Writing Models). Ask them to read the model and notice the adjectives ending in *-ed* and *-ing*.

- If students do not have the model, write the following on the board:

    I'll never forget the night I had a really terrifying allergic reaction to something I ate. I was at a nice restaurant with my friend . . .

    Walk around the room to make sure students understand the task.

- If the assignment is done in class, have students exchange papers and read each other's work as time permits.

For suggestions on how to give feedback on writing, see page xiv of this *Teacher's Edition*.

CONVERSATION TO GO

- As the students leave class, have them read the dialogue. Ask students what the situation is (*a psychiatrist's office*).
- Optionally, divide the class into two parts and read aloud together chorally.

HOMEWORK

- Assign *Workbook* page 22, Grammar Exercises 3 and 4, and page 23, Pronunciation Exercises 7 and 8. Assign *Workbook* Self-quiz Units 1–4.
- If students do not have the *WorldView Workbook*, assign listening homework from the Student CD. Write on the board:

    Track 10
    Which patient was complaining about headaches?

- Tell students to listen to the audio and write their answer. Have them bring it to the next class. (*Sarah*)

BEFORE NEXT CLASS

Have students review the material they have studied in these four units:

Unit no.	Review Grammar	Listen to Student CD	Study Grammar Reference
1	present continuous	Track 2	Page 143
2	comparative adjectives	Track 4	Page 143
3	simple present	Track 6	Page 143
4	adjectives ending in *-ed* and *-ing*	Track 10	Page 143

FOR NEXT CLASS

TRB Make copies of Quiz 1 in the *Teacher's Resource Book*.

Speaking

7 **PAIRS.** Student A, look at page 137. Student B, look at this page.

You're a doctor. When your patient arrives, ask several questions to find out what the problem is. Write notes below. Offer two pieces of advice.

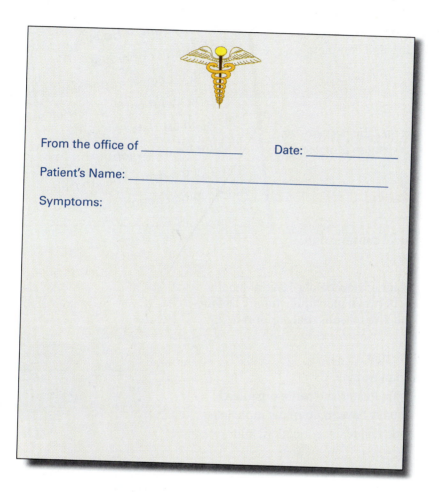

From the office of _____   Date: _____
Patient's Name: _____
Symptoms:

Writing

8 Think about the worst cold or allergy that you've ever had. Did you receive any good advice from anyone? Write a paragraph about how you felt and what you did to feel better. Use adjectives ending in *-ing* and *-ed*.

CONVERSATION TO GO

A: Life is really **depressing**.
B: Of course you're **depressed**. I'm very expensive.

Review 1 — Units 1–4

Unit 1 Nice to see you again

1. 🎧 Listen to the model conversation.

2. Talk to your classmates and complete the chart.

3. Report to the class.

   Paul is changing his diet. He isn't eating bread or pasta. He's trying to lose weight.

Find someone who is . . .
- changing his or her diet
- looking for a new apartment (or house)
- thinking about getting married soon
- taking an art class
- looking for a new job
- going to the gym or health club
- not sleeping enough

Name _____

Unit 2 Why women iron

4. 🎧 Listen to the model conversation.

5. **PAIRS.** Read your point of view below. Have a debate about the differences between men and women. Defend your point of view and give reasons that support it.

   Student A, you believe that . . .
   - men are stronger than women.
   - in general, women are neater and more organized than men. (They usually have to do many more jobs, including housework, childcare, education, and outside work.)

   Student B, you believe that . . .
   - overall, women are stronger than men. (Men are often physically more powerful, but women have greater endurance and also can handle pain better.)
   - men are neater and more organized than women.

6. **GROUPS OF 4.** Discuss your true feelings about differences between men and women. Who do you think is neater, more organized, stronger, more hardworking, or more emotional?

Review 1: Units 1–4

📼 You may wish to use the video for Units 1–4 at this point. For video activity worksheets, go to www.longman.com/worldview.

Unit 1: Nice to see you again

OBJECTIVE

Grammar: focus on using the present continuous to talk about the extended present

Exercise 1

- Explain the task: Students listen to the model conversation.
- 🎧 Play the audio.
- 🎧 Play the audio again, and then have the students repeat the conversation.

Exercise 2

- Explain the task: Students try to find someone who is doing each of the activities listed in the chart. When they find someone, they fill in the name.
- Write on the board the sentence starter: *Are you . . . ?* and the responses, *Yes, I am/No, I'm not.*
- Tell students that they should use the present continuous form to ask and answer questions. Remind students that the present continuous for duration (extended present) is used for situations happening "these days," but not necessarily at the exact time of speaking.
- Set a time limit of 10 minutes. While students are working, walk around the room, helping as needed.

Exercise 3

- Tell students they will report to the class what they found out about their classmates.
- Go over the example.
- Call on individual students to report to the class about their classmates. Set a time limit of 3 minutes.

> **WRAP-UP**
>
> - Do a question-and-answer chain with the class.
> - Have the students use the information in their charts from Exercise 2. Tell them to answer in complete sentences. Example: Ask the class *Who is looking for a new apartment? (Lee is).*
> - Then, ask a student (Juan) a new question. (Juan) answers, using his chart. Have (Juan) call on another student with a different question, who uses his or her chart to answer.

Unit 2: Why women iron

OBJECTIVE

Grammar: focus on using comparative adjectives and *as . . . as*

Exercise 4

- Explain the task: Students listen to the model conversation.
- 🎧 Play the audio.
- 🎧 Play the audio again, and then have the students repeat the conversation.

Exercise 5

- Form pairs. Assign roles: Student A and Student B for each pair.
- Explain the task: Students read their point of view, which they will then present to their partner and give reasons.
- Write on the board the phrases: *In my opinion,* and *Really? Why do you think that . . .*
- Give students 2 minutes to read their parts and organize their ideas. Encourage students to take brief notes on their reasons.
- Set a time limit of 5 minutes for students to debate their ideas. Walk around the room, helping as needed.

Exercise 6

- Have pairs work with another pair to form groups of 4.
- Explain the task: Ask students to discuss their own ideas about differences between men and women. Prompt them by asking *Who is neater, more organized,* and so on. Encourage them to give reasons.

> **WRAP-UP**
>
> Ask each group if they reached any agreement on who is neater, more organized, etc. For consolidation, write each comparative adjective on the board as you ask the question. For example, write *neater*, then ask *Group (1), who is neater, men or women?*; write *more hardworking,* and then ask *Group (2), who is more hardworking?*

T18

Unit 3: Living in luxury

OBJECTIVE

Grammar: focus on reviewing the simple present in statements and questions

Exercise 7

- Explain the task: Students listen to the model conversation.
- 🎧 Play the audio. Then write on the board: *Could you tell me a little bit about the hotel? / Sure. What would you like to know?* and *Do you offer . . . ?*
- 🎧 Play the audio again, and have the students repeat the conversation.

Exercise 8

- Form pairs. Assign roles: Student A and Student B for each pair.
- Explain the task: Tell the students they are going on vacation, and they need to make hotel reservations. They are each going to call a hotel. Explain that when Student A calls the Super Seven, Student B is an employee of the hotel. When Student B calls the Drake Hotel, Student A is an employee there.
- Tell the Student A's to go to page 141 to read the features of the Drake Hotel, and the Student B's to go to page 138 to read the features of the Super Seven.
- Set a time limit of 8 minutes. Have pairs call and ask questions about each hotel's facilities and services. Walk around the room, helping as needed.

Exercise 9

- Explain the task: Students discuss which hotel they would prefer to stay at, and why. Set a time limit of 2 minutes.
- Call on a few pairs to say which hotel they prefer. Encourage them to give reasons.

> **WRAP-UP**
>
> - Do a question-and-answer exchange with the class. Explain the task: Students compare the Super Seven and the Drake Hotel.
> - Tell students to answer using comparative adjectives. Example questions: *Which hotel has more rooms? Which hotel is more expensive? Do you think the Super Seven is closer to the airport? Which hotel has a better restaurant?*

Unit 4: Allergic reactions

OBJECTIVE

Grammar: focus on using adjectives ending in -ed and -ing

Exercise 10

- Form groups of 4. Explain the task: Students play the board game.
- Tell students the rules: Students toss a coin. If it lands on heads, they move ahead one space; if it's tails, two spaces. When they land on a space, they say a sentence using the word. If the sentence is correct, they stay. If it isn't correct, they move back one space.
- Demonstrate tossing the coin, and then taking a turn. Be sure students understand *heads* and *tails*.
- Make sure each group has a coin to use.

Exercise 11

- Explain the task: Students listen to the model conversation and then play the game.
- 🎧 Play the audio.
- 🎧 Play the audio again, and have the students repeat the conversation.
- Set a time limit of 10 minutes for students to play the game. Walk around the room, helping as needed.

> **WRAP-UP**
>
> - Write five adjectives on the board, such as *bored, excited, interested, exciting, boring*. Tell students to work in pairs to say sentences using each of the adjectives. Tell students to raise their hands as soon as they finish.
> - Then, ask the pair that finished first to say their sentences for the class. Have the rest of the class listen and check if the sentences are correct.

Unit 3 Living in luxury

7 🎧 Listen to the model conversation.

8 **PAIRS.** You are going on a vacation and need to make hotel reservations. Call and ask questions about the hotel's facilities and services. Student A, look at page 141. Student B, look at page 138.

9 Which hotel would you prefer staying at? Why?

Unit 4 Allergic reactions

10 **GROUPS OF 4.** Take turns. Toss a coin (one side = move ahead one space, the other side = move ahead two spaces). When you land on a space, say a sentence with the word. If your sentence is correct, stay there. If not, move back one space.

11 🎧 Listen to the model conversation and play the game.

World of Music 1

Good to See You
Neil Young

Vocabulary

1 Match the pictures with the phrases.

endless highway __

good to see you __

suitcase in the hallway __

passing on solid line __

Neil Young has been a member of several rock and roll "super-groups"—Buffalo Springfield; Crosby, Stills, Nash & Young; and Crazy Horse. A son of the Canadian prairie, Young's music reflects a sense of country solitude and independence.

Listening

2 **PAIRS.** Listen to the song. Is the singer happy or sad? Why?

World of Music 1

OBJECTIVES

- introduce Neil Young's song, "Good to See You"
- vocabulary: personal relationships
- express personal interpretation of a song

BACKGROUND INFORMATION

Neil Young began his musical career as a "coffee-house folkie" performing traditional songs, though he quickly began writing his own pieces. Some of his most famous songs include "Cinnamon Girl," "Down by the River," "Comes a Time," "Southern Man," and "Tonight's the Night."

WARM-UP

- Books closed. Ask: *How do you feel when you get home after a long trip?* (Possible answers: *I'm tired, I'm happy to see my family.*)
- Ask students if they have ever been on a long trip. What did they do first when they got home?
- Tell the class they are going to listen to a song about seeing someone special after a long trip. Tell them to think about being away from home as they listen to the song.

Reading

- Tell students to read the information about Neil Young. Tell them they are going to listen to one of Neil Young's best-known songs, "Good to See You." Ask them if they know the song, or if they have heard of it. Encourage the class to hum or sing parts of the song that they know.
- Ask: *Which bands did Neil Young play with?* (*He played with Buffalo Springfield; Crosby, Stills, Nash & Young; and Crazy Horse.*) Ask: *What kind of person do you think Neil Young is? Explain your answer.* (*He is probably very independent, because his music reflects independence.*)
- Ask them what they know about Neil Young. (*He was raised in Canada, and has been a performer in three very important groups. He is still making music today.*) For the titles of other Neil Young songs, see the background information, above.

Vocabulary

Exercise 1

- Have students look at the pictures. Explain the task: Students match the pictures and the phrases. Tell students they may use the pictures more than once.
- Set a time limit of 3 minutes.
- Have students work in pairs to check their answers. Walk around the room, helping as needed.
- Go over the answers with the class.

Answer key

endless highway: B
good to see you: A
suitcase in the hall: C
passing on a solid line: B

Listening

Exercise 2

- Pair students. Explain the task: Students listen to the song and then decide if the singer is happy or sad, and give reasons.
- Ask students to look at the pictures again and predict whether the singer is happy or sad. Encourage them to point out details that support their opinions (e.g., *I think he is happy because of how they are looking at each other*).
- 🎧 Play the song as students listen.
- 🎧 Play the song again. Tell students to take brief notes on lyrics that show it is happy or sad.
- Set a time limit of 5 minutes for students to discuss the song. Walk around the room, helping as needed.
- Conclude by asking pairs to share their opinions with the class. Remind them to give reasons for their opinions.

Answer key

The singer is happy, because the chorus of the song is "good to see you."

Exercise 3

- Explain the task: Students listen to the song again. They write 1, 2, 3, or 4 in front of each line of the lyrics to put them in the correct order. Hold up your book and point to 1 and 2 by the first two lines.
- 🎧 Play the song.
- 🎧 Play the song again for the students to confirm their answers.
- Do not go over the answers with the class until they have completed Exercise 4.

Exercise 4

- Form pairs. Have pairs check their answers.
- Go over the answers with the class. One way to do this is to call on individual students to read the lyrics aloud in the correct order.

> **Answer key**
>
> [full audio of song: © 2000 Neil Young, from "Silver and Gold," Reprise Records]
>
> **Good to See You**
> Good to see you
> Good to see you again
> Good to see your face again
> Good to see you
>
> _2_ I'm the footsteps on your floor
> _1_ I'm the suitcase in your hallway
> _4_ I feel like I know what my life is for
> _3_ When I'm looking down on you
>
> Good to see you
> Good to see you again
> Good to see your face again
> Good to see you
>
> _4_ I feel like making up for lost time
> _3_ Now at last I'm home to you
> _2_ I've passed on the solid line
> _1_ I've been down on the endless highway
>
> Good to see you
> Good to see you again
> Good to see your face again
> It's good to see you

Speaking

Exercise 5

- Form groups of 3. Explain the task: Students discuss the questions. Have students read the questions, or read them aloud for the class.
- Set a time limit of 10 minutes. Remind students to explain their opinions and give examples. Encourage students to take notes on their discussions.
- Conclude by calling on groups to share their ideas with the class. Find out if there is general agreement about the song: *Do most of you like it? Why or Why not?*

> **EXTENSION**
>
> Encourage students to interpret or explain specific lines of the song, for example, "I'm the footsteps on your floor."

> **OPTION**
>
> Play the song and have the students sing along at the end of the class. Play again as time permits.

3 🎧 Listen to the song again. The lines of the verses are not in the correct order. Write *1, 2, 3,* and *4* in front of each line to put them in the correct order.

Good to See You

Good to see you
Good to see you again
Good to see your face again
Good to see you

___ I feel like making up for lost time
___ Now at last I'm home to you
___ I've passed on the solid line
___ I've been down on the endless highway

_2_ I'm the footsteps on your floor
_1_ I'm the suitcase in your hallway
___ I feel like I know what my life is for
___ When I'm looking down on you

Good to see you
Good to see you again
Good to see your face again
It's good to see you

Good to see you
Good to see you again
Good to see your face again
Good to see you

4 **PAIRS.** Compare your answers.

Speaking

5 **GROUPS OF 3.** Discuss these questions.

What do you like about this song?
The words? The music? The idea?
Do you think a simple song with lyrics that repeat is powerful and effective or repetitive and boring?

UNIT 5

A typical day

Vocabulary Verb and noun combinations
Grammar Subject and object questions
Speaking Asking questions

Lesson A

Getting started

1 Match the verbs in the box with the nouns in the word webs.

| deliver | hire | make | pay |
| send | spend | take | take out |

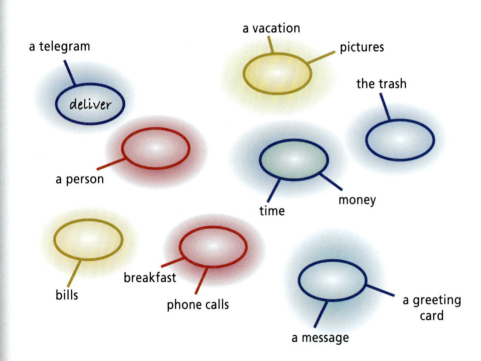

- a telegram — deliver
- a person
- bills
- breakfast
- phone calls
- a vacation
- pictures
- the trash
- time
- money
- a message
- a greeting card

2 **PAIRS.** Compare your answers.

3 **PAIRS.** Make five true sentences about yourself. Use verb and noun combinations from Exercise 1. Take turns saying your sentences to your partner.

A: I like to spend time with my friends on the weekend.
B: Me, too. But I only get time to go out with them on Sunday afternoons.

A typical day

UNIT 5

Teacher's Notes — Lesson A

OBJECTIVES
Students will:
- activate vocabulary related to daily tasks
- use subject and object questions
- practice listening for the focus word (the most important word) in questions and answers

WARM-UP: TODAY
- Tell students this unit is about activities people do each day. Explain that "a typical day" refers to what someone usually does in a day.
- Have students think about the activities they do every day, and give a personal example: *I take the train to work every day.*
- Form groups of 4. Set a time limit of 2 minutes. Students greet each other and talk about what they do each day. Each person must say at least two activities.
- Call on a few students to report about one of their partners.

Getting started

LANGUAGE NOTES
- Explain that in British English *hire* means *to rent*, while in American English, it means *to give a job to someone*.
- Review the habitual present tense, which is used to talk about what someone does in a typical day (*I wake up at 6:00 A.M., I take a shower, I go to the office at 8:30*).

OPTION: VOCABULARY PREVIEW
- Ask the class, *What's one thing people often send?* Elicit *a letter, a card.* Ask, *What's something people often deliver?* Elicit *a pizza, groceries.*
- Continue with *make (breakfast, money)*, and *pay (bills)*.
- Point out that *when you send something, someone else takes it for you;* but *when you deliver something, you take it yourself.*
- Have students work in pairs to think of other examples for *send, deliver, make,* and *pay.*

Exercise ❶
- Ask students to look at the words in the box. Explain the task: Students write the verbs in the box next to the associated words in the web. Present the example. Explain that the words in the web are the objects of the verbs (that is, the verb affects the word in some way). You may want to do more than one item together to make sure students understand the concept of verb-object word order.
- Set a time limit of 5 minutes. While students are working, walk around the room, helping as needed.
- Do not go over the answers with the class until they have completed Exercise 2.

Exercise ❷
- Have students work in pairs to check their answers.
- Go over the answers with the class.

Answer key
deliver	a telegram
hire	a person
make	breakfast, phone calls
pay	bills
send	a message, a greeting card
spend	time, money
take	a vacation, pictures
take out	the trash

Exercise ❸
- Explain the task: Students make five true statements about themselves using verb-object combinations from Exercise 1. Go over the example. Review words of frequency if needed: *always, often, usually, sometimes,* as in *I often spend time with my friends.*
- Set a time limit of 3 minutes. Walk around the room, helping as needed.
- Pair students. Ask them to take turns reading their questions and to make follow-up comments on their partner's sentences.

WRAP-UP
Call on a few students to share with the class what their partners do on a regular basis. Encourage students to use some of the verb-object combinations in Exercise 1. If time permits, you may want to poll the whole class.

Listening

Teaching Tip! Using illustrations

Using visual aids such as illustrations activates vocabulary related to a given topic, and helps students understand audio. Have students spend some time looking at the picture of the party scene and discussing their observations. Prompt them by holding up your book, pointing to the illustration and asking questions: *Where are they? What is (he) doing?*

Exercise 4

- Form groups of 3. Explain the task: Students take turns telling one another about one of the topics in the list. Check understanding of the word *memorable* by asking students what other similar words they know in English (*remember, memory*). Help them understand that a *memorable party* is one that they remember for a special reason.
- Go over the example in the book. Tell students they must listen carefully and be ready to ask a follow-up question, such as *Oh, really, where was it?* or continue with a statement about themselves, such as *Really? I had an unusual job, too.*
- Set a time limit of 5 minutes. Walk around the room, helping as needed. Make sure students ask follow-up questions and give comments to keep the conversation going.
- Ask students to say what their unusual jobs were. Take a poll of the class to find out which job seems the most unusual, and why.

Exercise 5

- Have students look at the picture of the party scene again. Tell them to listen to the interview with Ron, and then find Ron and his wife in the picture.
- 🎧 Play the audio.
- Ask students to point to Ron and his wife in the picture. Ask them to describe Ron and what he and his wife are doing.
- 🎧 Play the audio again, as needed.

> **Answer key**
>
> Ron is the man with the flowers and his wife is behind him (in the red shirt) taking a picture.

Exercise 6

- Explain the task: Students listen to the conversation again and answer the questions.
- 🎧 Have students read the questions, and then play the audio.
- 🎧 Play the audio again. Students confirm their answers.

Exercise 7

- Have students work with a partner to check their answers.
- Go over the answers with the class.

> **Answer key**
>
> 1. Ron delivers singing telegrams.
> 2. fifty dollars
> 3. the agency (Say It with a Song)
> 4. the agency
> 5. She buys flowers and takes a picture.

🌐 Please go to www.longman.com/worldview for additional in-class model conversation practice and supplmental reading practice.

HOMEWORK

- 📖 For homework, assign *Workbook* page 26, Vocabulary Exercises 1 and 2, and page 28, Listening Exercises 4 and 5.

Listening

4 **GROUPS OF 3.** Tell one another about one of the following:
- an unusual job you (or someone you know) had
- a memorable party you had or you went to
- a special present you gave or received

A: *My cousin had an unusual job once. He was a bodyguard for a famous singer.*
B: *Really? Who?*

5 🎧 Listen to the interview with Ron. Can you find Ron and his wife in the picture?

6 🎧 Listen again and answer the questions.
1. What is Ron's job?
2. How much does a singing telegram cost?
3. Who should people call if they want to send a singing telegram?
4. Who pays Ron?
5. What does Ron's wife do to help?

7 **PAIRS.** Compare your answers.

Lesson A

Grammar focus

1 Study the examples of subject and object questions.

Subject	Verb	Object
The agency	pays	Ron.
a) **Who** pays Ron? The agency.		b) **Who** does the agency *pay*? Ron.

2 Look at the examples again. Complete the blanks in the chart with *subject* or *object*.

Subject and object questions using the present simple

In example question a), *who* refers to the _____ of the sentence.
In example question b), *who* refers to the _____ of the sentence.
Use the auxiliary *do/does* in _____ questions.

NOTE: Object questions can ask about the object of a preposition (for example, *with, for, to...*): **Who does** Ron **go** to the parties **with**? His wife.

Grammar Reference page 144

3 Complete the subject and object questions with *who* and the appropriate form of the verbs in parentheses.

A: (1) __Who gets up__ (get up) first in your house?
B: Usually I do.
A: And (2) _____ (you/have) breakfast with?
B: We all have breakfast together.
A: (3) _____ (use) the Internet the most in your house?
B: My younger brother.
A: (4) _____ (make) the most phone calls?
B: I do, I think.
A: (5) _____ (you/call) the most?
B: My friend Judith.
A: (6) _____ (you/spend) more time with, your friends or your family?
B: My friends, I think.
A: And (7) _____ (spend) the most time in the house?
B: Not me. That's for sure.

Grammar focus

LANGUAGE NOTE

The agency pays Ron is a simple subject + verb + object sentence. In the sentence *Who pays Ron?*, *Who* is the subject (it substitutes for *The agency*). In *Who does the agency pay?*, *Who* is the object (it substitutes for *Ron*).

In conversation, *Who does he go with?* is typically used instead of the more formal *With whom does he go?* To help students understand the more common spoken usage, ask the class: *Who goes dancing on Saturdays? (I do.)* Then ask, *Who do you go with? (With my friends.) Who* in subject position can also be practiced with other questions, such as *Who likes rock? / Who likes sports?*

Although all the examples in this unit are in the simple present, the rules for subject and object questions are the same for other tenses.

WARM-UP

Note: Skip this warm-up if you're doing this lesson (Lesson B) during the same class period as Lesson A.

- Books closed. Tell students they are going to listen again to the interview with Ron that they heard in the Listening section.
- Tell students to think about what Ron does and who he works for.
- 🎧 Play the audio for Lesson A, Exercise 5.
- Ask students what Ron does (*He delivers singing telegrams*), and who he works for (*an agency*).
- Ask students if they remember what his wife does. (*She buys flowers and takes a picture.*)

Teaching Tip! Teaching grammar concepts

Students sometimes have trouble understanding certain grammatical concepts. *Who* in subject and object position may be especially difficult to understand. A brief explanation, or "recipe" may be helpful: Use <u>who</u> alone to ask about the person that did the action. Use <u>who + do / does</u> to ask about the person that received the action.

Exercise ❶

- Have students look at the examples and study the boldfaced words.
- Ask students to compare each question with the sentence *The agency pays Ron*.
- Write on the board, *Bob likes Mary*. Ask students to come up with a question for the answer *Bob* (*Who likes Mary?*). Write *Mary* on the board and ask for the appropriate question (*Who does Bob like?*).

Exercise ❷

- Have students study the examples again.
- Explain the task: Students complete the rules in the box by filling in the blanks with *subject* or *object*.
- Have students check their answers in pairs.
- Go over the answers with the class.
- Point out the note on objects of prepositions at the bottom of the chart. Point out that the complete answer would be *Ron goes to the parties with his wife*. In questions, the preposition can be placed at the end of the sentence.
- Refer students to Grammar Reference page 144, as needed.

Answer key

subject   object   object

Exercise ❸

- Ask students to look at the conversations. Explain the task: Students complete the subject and object questions with *who* and the appropriate form of the verbs in parentheses. Go over the first question with the class.
- Set a time limit of 5 minutes. Walk around the room, helping as needed.
- Have students work in pairs to check their answers.
- Go over the answers with the class.

Answer key

1. Who gets up
2. who do you have
3. Who uses
4. Who makes
5. Who do you call
6. Who do you spend
7. who spends

EXTENSION

Pair students. Have them ask and answer the questions in Exercise 3, substituting their own information. Encourage them to ask their own questions as well, using vocabulary from previous units. Walk around the room, helping as needed.

Pronunciation

Exercise 4

- Explain that in English, intonation changes in order to make the most important word in each sentence stand out. This word is called the focus word.
- 🎧 Play the audio and have students listen. Ask them to notice the way the most important word in the question and answer stands out.
- Tell students that the focus word stands out because (1) the word is stressed, and the vowel is long and clear and (2) the voice changes pitch on this word.

Exercise 5

- Explain the task: Students circle the focus word in each question and answer.
- 🎧 Play the audio. Walk around the room, helping as needed.
- Don't go over the answers with the class until they have completed Exercise 6.

> **Answer key**
> 1. shopping; father
> 2. cooking; mother
> 3. bills; parents
> 4. trash; brother

Exercise 6

- 🎧 Play the audio and have students repeat chorally.
- You can use gestures (such as raising your hand and then dropping it) to show how the intonation rises on the focus word and then falls. All the questions and answers here end with falling intonation.
- 🎧 Play the audio again.
- Have students work in pairs to check their answers.
- Ask a few individual pairs of students to repeat the questions and answers and check their pronunciation.
- Encourage students to make the focus word stand out. Make sure that the voice rises on this word and that the vowel is long and clear.

Speaking

Teaching Tip! Routine activities

Students don't always focus on which verb tense is most appropriate when they are speaking. Remind students to use the present tense for habitual activities, such as routines: *I wake up at 6:00 A.M.*

Exercise 7

- Hold up your book and point to the colored notebook page. Tell students to complete the sentences to make true statements about their lives. Explain that they have to fill it in with people's names, for example, *my brother, my friend Kate*.
- Students work individually. Walk around the room, helping as needed.

Exercise 8

- Pair students. Explain the task: Students take turns asking and answering questions about their partner's routines. Go over the example in the book.
- Set a time limit of 8 minutes. Encourage students to take notes on their partner's answers so that they can compare their routines later. Walk around the room, helping as needed.

> **WRAP-UP**
> Call on students to share with the class what they learned about their partners. You may want to provide a model first: *Both Ana and I make breakfast at home in the mornings. / I make my breakfast in the morning, but Ana eats her breakfast out.*

TRB For additional interactive grammar practice, have students do the reproducible activity for this unit in the *Teacher's Resource Book*.

Writing

Exercise 9

- Assign the writing task for class work or homework.
- **TRB** Optionally, give students a copy of the writing model (see the *Teacher's Resource Book*, Writing Models). Ask them to read the model and notice the simple present verbs.
- If students don't have the model, write the following on the board:

    Hi, Adam! How have you been? Who are you playing soccer with now that I'm gone? I have good news! I found a job . . .

    Walk around the room to make sure they understand the task and what to include in the email.
- If the assignment is done in class, have students exchange papers and read each other's work.

For suggestions on how to give feedback on writing, see page xiv of this *Teacher's Edition*.

CONVERSATION TO GO

- As the students leave class, have them practice the conversation. Remind students to emphasize the pronunciation of the questions.
- Optionally, call on individual students and ask, *Who uses the telephone the most in your house?*

HOMEWORK

- 📖 Assign *Workbook* page 27, Grammar Exercise 3, and page 28, Pronunciation Exercises 6 and 7.
- 🎧 If students do not have the *WorldView Workbook*, assign listening homework from the Student CD. Write on the board:

    Track 12
    Who takes pictures while Ron sings?

- 🎧 Tell students to listen to the audio and write their answer. Have them bring it to the next class. (*his wife, Mary*)

Pronunciation

4 🎧 Listen. Notice the way the focus word (the most important word) in each sentence stands out. The voice goes up on this word, and the vowel sound is long and clear.

Who gets up **first** in your house?   Usually **I** do.

5 🎧 Listen. Circle the focus word in each sentence.

1. A: Who does the shopping in your house?   B: Usually my father.
2. A: Who does the cooking?   B: My mother does.
3. A: Who pays the bills?   B: My parents both do.
4. A: Who takes out the trash?   B: My older brother.

6 🎧 Listen again and repeat. Check your answers.

Speaking

7 **BEFORE YOU SPEAK.** Complete the sentences to make true statements about your life.

1. _____ make(s) breakfast in my house.
2. _____ pay(s) the bills every month.
3. Sometimes I help _____ at home.
4. I usually have lunch with _____.
5. Sometimes I meet _____ after work/school.
6. _____ go(es) out for dinner with me once in a while.

8 **PAIRS.** Take turns asking and answering questions about your partner's routines.

A: Who makes breakfast in your house?
B: My roommate makes coffee, but then we usually buy something to eat on the corner.

Writing

9 Write an email to a friend overseas telling about your typical day. Include a few questions about your friend's daily life. Use the simple present and subject and object questions.

CONVERSATION TO GO

A: **Who uses** the telephone the most in your house?
B: My daughter.
A: **Who does** she **call**?
B: Everyone!

UNIT 6

It's absolutely true!

Vocabulary Adjectives and intensifiers
Grammar Review: simple past vs. past continuous
Speaking Telling stories

Lesson A

Getting started

1 **PAIRS.** Match the adjectives that are similar in meaning.

1. bad _a_	2. big ___	a. awful	b. boiling
3. cold ___	4. crowded ___	c. enormous	d. exhausted
5. good ___	6. hot ___	e. fantastic	f. fascinating
7. interesting ___	8. tired ___	g. freezing	h. packed

2 Complete the conversation with pairs of adjectives from Exercise 1.

A: Was the trip really **(1)** _interesting_?
B: Yes, it was absolutely **(2)** _fascinating_! I had a great time.
A: Was it very **(3)** _____ in Rio?
B: It was absolutely **(4)** _____! Even at night the temperature was over 100°F.
A: Lucky you! The weather here was really **(5)** _____. It was only 25°F.
B: Yeah, I heard it was really **(6)** _____ here.
A: Were the streets very **(7)** _____?
B: Yes, they were really **(8)** _____. I've never seen so many people in my life.
A: Was the music really **(9)** _____?
B: Even better! It was absolutely **(10)** _____! I danced all night long.
A: Were you very **(11)** _____ when you got back to the hotel?
B: Yes, I was really **(12)** _____. I just wanted to sleep.

26

It's absolutely true!

UNIT 6

Teacher's Notes — Lesson A

OBJECTIVES

Students will:
- activate vocabulary related to describing situations
- use adjectives and intensifiers and the simple vs. past continuous
- practice listening for and saying the number of syllables and the stress in adjectives

WARM-UP: ONE TIME . . .

- Tell students this unit is about telling stories and describing experiences. Explain to students that sometimes when we describe a great or unusual experience, the listener might respond *Oh, you didn't really do that!* Write the sentence on the board.
- Ask students to brainstorm other ways to express disbelief and write them on the board. *(I don't believe it! That can't be true! Really? Are you serious?)*
- Explain that the speaker's response could be *Yes, it's really true* or *I'm serious.*
- Form groups of 3. Set a time limit of 3 minutes. Have students take turns sharing a story or experience that was great or unusual. (Encourage students to keep it short.) The other group members should respond with disbelief using the examples on the board.
- Tell students they are going to learn adjectives for telling stories and describing experiences.

Getting started

LANGUAGE NOTE

Most common intensifiers are adverbs, such as *very* or *really*: *It's very hot* or *It's really hot!* Exercise 1 asks students to pair adjectives that are similar in meaning. One of the words in the pair has a more intense meaning than the other, for example: *big/enormous.*

OPTION: VOCABULARY PREVIEW

- Assign each of the adjectives in the box on the right to eight volunteers, but don't tell other students which adjective each student has. Make sure that the volunteers know the meaning of their adjectives.
- Have each student act out his or her adjective. The other students try to guess the adjective. Write the words on the board.
- As a follow-up, ask the class to name a place, thing, or situation associated with each of the adjectives; for example: *awful—getting sick, enormous—an elephant, fantastic—going out with friends, freezing—the South Pole, boiling—coffee or tea, exhausted—after playing a soccer game, fascinating— a trip to China, packed—the bus.*

Exercise 1

- Pair students. Ask them to look at the words in the boxes.
- Explain the task: Students find the adjectives in each box that are similar in meaning. Go over the example: *bad / awful.* Point out that *bad = very awful.*
- Set a time limit of 3 minutes. While students are working, walk around the room, helping as needed.
- Have each pair work with another pair to check answers.
- Go over the answers with the class.

Answer key

1. a   3. g   5. e   7. f
2. c   4. h   6. b   8. d

Exercise 2

- Explain the task: Students work individually to complete the conversation using pairs of adjectives from Exercise 1 for each exchange. Tell students that the first adjective of each pair comes from the box on the left. Encourage students to use the context of the conversation to decide on the appropriate pairs of adjectives.
- Set a time limit of 5 minutes. Walk around the room, helping as needed.
- Don't go over the answers with the class until they have completed Exercise 3.

Exercise 3

- Pair students. Have them check their answers.
- Go over answers with the class.

Answer key

1. interesting   5. cold   9. good
2. fascinating 6. freezing 10. fantastic
3. hot   7. crowded   11. tired
4. boiling   8. packed   12. exhausted

Exercise 4

- Tell students to look at the adjectives in Exercise 2 again and notice how *very, absolutely,* and *really* are used.
- Pair students. Explain the task: Students use *very, absolutely,* or *really* to complete the rules.
- Set a time limit of 2 minutes. Encourage students to refer back to Exercise 2 to help them complete the rules.
- Have two pairs form groups to compare rules.
- Go over the answers with the class.

Answer key

1. absolutely   2. very   3. really

T26

Teacher's Notes — Lesson A

Pronunciation

Exercise 5

- Explain that the circles in the table show the number of syllables. The big circles represent the syllables with the main stress.
- Go over the example words. Count out the syllables of the words on your fingers: *hot, awful*.
- Elicit the correct stress in *awful*: **aw**ful. Mark the stress with large and small circles.
- Explain the task: Students listen to each word, count the number of syllables, listen for the stressed syllable, and write the word in the correct stress group.
- 🎧 Play the audio and have students listen. Stop the audio after each item to give students time to write.

Exercise 6

- 🎧 Play the audio. Have students listen and check their answers to Exercise 5.
- 🎧 Play the audio again. Have students repeat chorally.
- Ask a few individual students to repeat the words.
- Encourage students to make the vowel in the stressed syllable sound long.
- Note that *interesting* has three syllables; the first *e* is usually silent: *int(e)resting*.

Answer key

●	● ●	● ● ●	● ● ●	● ● ● ●
hot	awful	fantastic	interesting	fascinating
cold	freezing	enormous		
packed	crowded	exhausted		
bad	boiling			
big				
good				
tired				

Exercise 7

- Pair students. Have them practice saying the completed conversations in Exercise 2.
- Walk around the room, helping as needed.

Listening

CULTURE NOTE

Carnaval is a four-day celebration that takes place all over Brazil, although many people associate it with Rio de Janeiro. It's usually in February or March. During those four days, the country stops normal activity while people dance, wear costumes, and have fun.

Exercise 8

- Form groups of 3. Ask students to look at the photos of Carnaval in Rio de Janeiro. Ask questions that will focus them on the content, such as *Who do you see? What are they wearing? What are they doing?*
- Explain the task: Students describe the photos, using some of the adjectives and intensifiers from Exercises 1 and 4.
- Go over the examples in the book and set a time limit of 5 minutes. Walk around the room, helping as needed.
- Call on a few students to describe what they see using the adjectives and intensifiers.

Exercise 9

- Explain the task: Students listen and check (✓) the vocabulary and intensifiers in Exercise 1 that they hear.
- 🎧 Play the audio. Walk around the room, helping as needed.
- Go over the answers with the class.

Answer key

very	enormous	packed
hot	really	tired
absolutely	awful	exhausted
boiling	crowded	fantastic

Teaching Tip! Listening for specific information

In Exercise 10, students listen for specific information about Sara's trip. A useful strategy here is for students to read the statements before listening. This will help them focus on the information they need.

Exercise 10

- Have students look at the statements.
- 🎧 Play the audio again. Encourage students to listen and to make brief notes as they hear the relevant information. If needed, play the audio again.
- Tell students to work individually to rewrite the false sentences with the correct information.
- Have students work in pairs to check their answers.
- Go over the answers with the class.

Answer key

1. F—*on vacation*   3. T   5. T
2. F—*February*   4. T   6. F—*300,000*

🌐 Please go to www.longman.com/worldview for additional in-class model conversation practice and supplementary reading practice.

HOMEWORK

- 📖 For homework, assign *Workbook* page 29, Vocabulary Exercises 1 and 2, and page 31, Listening Exercises 5 and 6.

3 **PAIRS. Compare your answers.**

4 **PAIRS. Use *very*, *absolutely*, and *really* to complete the rules.**

Use the intensifier _____ only with extreme adjectives (like *boiling*).
Use the intensifier _____ only with ordinary adjectives (like *hot*).
Use the intensifier _____ with either kind of adjective.

Pronunciation

5 🎧 **Listen to the adjectives from Exercise 1. Notice the number of syllables and the stress. Write each word in the correct group.**

●	● ○	○ ● ○	● ○ ○	● ○ ○ ○
hot	awful			

6 🎧 **Listen and check your answers. Then listen again and repeat.**

7 **PAIRS. Practice the conversations in Exercise 2.**

Listening

8 **GROUPS OF 3. Describe the photos of Carnaval in Rio de Janeiro, Brazil. Use some of the adjectives and intensifiers from Exercises 1 and 4.**

A: *It's really crowded.*
B: *It looks fascinating!*

9 🎧 **Listen to Sara talk about her visit to Carnaval. Check (✓) the adjectives in Exercise 1 that you hear.**

10 🎧 **Listen again and write *T* (true) or *F* (false) after each statement. If the statement is false, write the correct information.**

1. Sara went to Rio on a ~~business trip.~~ F—on vacation
2. Sara was in Rio in January.
3. It was raining when she arrived.
4. They were thinking of canceling Carnaval because of the rain.
5. When the rain stopped, Carnaval started.
6. An audience of 70,000 tourists was waiting in the Sambadrome.

Lesson B

6

Grammar focus

1 Look at the examples of the simple past and past continuous tenses. Underline the verbs in the simple past. Circle the verbs in the past continuous.

> Sara **was visiting** Rio.
> It **was raining** when she **arrived**.
> They **were thinking** of canceling Carnaval because of the rain.
> The weather **changed** and the rain **stopped**.

2 Look at the examples again. Complete the rules with *the simple past* or *the past continuous*.

Simple past vs. past continuous
Use _____ for a situation over a period of time in the past. It often helps set the context in a story.
Use _____ for an action or event that was completed in the past.
Use _____ when a longer action or event was interrupted by an action or event in the simple past.

Grammar Reference page 144

3 Complete each sentence with the correct form of the verb in parentheses. Use the simple past or past continuous.

I went to the Caribbean on vacation this past February. I __was standing__ in the lobby
                                                                    1. (stand)
of my hotel when I ____saw____ this tall, good-looking guy in jeans and a T-shirt.
                    2. (see)
He _____ familiar, and I _____ at him, trying to remember how
     3. (look)   4. (stare)
I knew him. Then I _____ that other people around me _____
                    5. (notice)   6. (look)
at him, too. I _____ that he was Keanu Reeves, the actor!
               7. (realize)

The other day, I _____ down the street when I _____
                   8. (walk)   9. (see)
some money on the sidewalk. I _____ anyone nearby, so I _____
                                10. (not see)   11. (pick)
up the money: six $50 bills! As I _____ to decide what to do, a young woman
                                   12. (try)
_____ up the street. She _____ the sidewalk for something, so I
 13. (come)   14. (search)
_____ her what she _____ for. She said, "I just lost $300!"
 15. (ask)   16. (look)

28

Grammar focus

LANGUAGE NOTES

- The past continuous is used to talk about an action that was in progress in the past: *What were you doing on Saturday? I was skiing with some friends.*
- *When* is used with the simple past to talk about an interrupting action: *He was sleeping when the phone rang. While* is used with the past continuous for the action that was interrupted: *While he was sleeping, the phone rang.*
- *While* is also used with the past continuous to talk about two actions in progress at the same time in the past: *While Jose was cooking dinner, Maria was driving home.*

WARM-UP

Note: Skip this warm-up if you're doing this lesson (Lesson B) during the same class period as Lesson A.

- Books closed. Tell students they are going to listen again to the conversation between Sara and her friend about her visit to Brazil that they heard in the Listening section.
- Tell students to think about the time period Sara and her friend are talking about: is it the past, the present, or the future?
- 🎧 Play the audio for Lesson A, Exercise 9.
- Ask students what the time period is (answer: *the past*).
- Ask students to write down as many verbs as they can while they listen to the conversation (possible answers: *went, was, was raining, was getting, changed, stopped, started, were*).

Exercise ❶

- Have students look at the examples and study the boldfaced words.
- Explain the task: Students underline the simple past verbs, and circle the past continuous verbs.
- Have students check their answers with a partner.
- Go over the answers with the class.

Answer key

simple past:
arrived, changed, stopped

past continuous:
was visiting, was raining, were thinking

Exercise ❷

- Have students study the examples again.
- Tell students to complete the rules in the box by writing *simple past* or *past continuous*.
- Have students check answers in pairs.
- Go over the answers with the class.
- Refer students to Grammar Reference page 144, as needed.

Answer key

1. past continuous
2. simple past
3. past continuous

Exercise ❸

- Explain the task: Students will complete each sentence with the correct form of the verb in parentheses. Ask students to look at the example. Ask why *was standing* is used in the first blank and *saw* in the second (because "I" was doing something when something else happened). This can be demonstrated on the board by drawing a horizontal line as you read the example *I was standing...*, then draw a vertical line through it when you say *I saw* to show that the action was interrupted.
- Have students complete the exercise individually. Set a time limit of 5 minutes.
- Pair students. Have them check their answers.
- Go over the answers with the class.

Answer key

1. was standing
2. saw
3. looked
4. was staring
5. noticed
6. were looking
7. realized
8. was walking
9. saw
10. didn't see
11. picked up
12. was trying
13. came
14. was searching
15. asked
16. was looking

WRAP-UP

Have students work with a partner to practice reading the paragraph aloud.

Speaking

Teaching Tip! Storytelling

The main purpose of this activity is for students to practice using the vocabulary of the unit and the simple and past continuous. If students are uncomfortable telling a true story about themselves, encourage them to make up a story instead. They should still use the first person "I."

Exercise 4

- Explain the task: Students tell a true story about something they have done. Have them read the ideas for possible stories to tell. Tell them that they can also make up a story, if they prefer. Tell students to write notes about the time, place, and situation. Hold up your book and show the notepaper on the page.
- Set a time limit of 8 minutes. Walk around the room, helping as needed.

Exercise 5

- Pair students. Explain the task: Students tell their partners their stories. Encourage students to listen carefully as they may have to report to the class on their partner's story.
- Have students read the example in the book before they begin. Set a time limit of 5 minutes.
- Walk around the room, helping as needed.

> **WRAP-UP**
>
> Call on a few students to tell their partner's story.

TRB For additional interactive grammar practice, have students do the reproducible activity for this unit in the *Teacher's Resource Book*.

Writing

Exercise 6

- Assign the writing task for class work or homework.
- **TRB** Optionally, give students a copy of the model (see the *Teacher's Resource Book*, Writing Models). Ask them to read the model and notice the verb forms that are used. Additionally, remind them of some of the vocabulary from this unit they might use (*crowded, interesting, fascinating, really, very, absolutely,* and so on).
- If students don't have the model, write the following on the board:

    I had a great experience a couple of years ago. My family and I were on vacation, and we were staying at...

    Walk around the room to make sure they understand the task.
- If done in class, have a few students read their work aloud as time permits.

For suggestions on how to give feedback on writing, see page xiv of this *Teacher's Edition*.

CONVERSATION TO GO

- As the students leave class, have them read the dialogue.
- Optionally, ask students in pairs to read the dialogue, switching parts.

HOMEWORK

- Assign *Workbook* page 30, Grammar Exercises 3 and 4, and page 31, Pronunciation Exercises 7, 8, and 9.
- If students do not have the *WorldView Workbook*, assign listening homework from the Student CD. Write on the board:

    Track 16
    How many dancers were in the Carnaval parade?

- Tell students to listen to the audio and write their answer. Have them bring it to the next class. (*over 70,000*)

Speaking

4 **BEFORE YOU SPEAK.** Think of a true story about yourself. Write notes about the time, place, and what happened.

Possible stories:
- You did something very dangerous.
- You met a famous person.
- You had an accident.
- You went to an unusual place.
- You found something interesting.
- You fell in love.

5 **PAIRS.** Tell your partner your story.

Last year I went bungee jumping in the Rocky Mountains . . .

Writing

6 Think of a story about yourself. (You can use the story you told in Exercise 5.) Write the story and describe what happened. Use the simple past, past continuous, and intensifiers from this unit.

CONVERSATION TO GO

A: We **saw** each other when we **were walking** down the street.
B: **Did** she **look** good?
A: Good? She **looked absolutely fantastic**!

Lesson B

UNIT 7

Eating out

Vocabulary Adjectives to describe restaurants and food
Grammar too, enough
Speaking Describing and giving opinions about food and restaurants

Lesson A

Getting started

1 Write the words from the box in the chart.

bland	~~casual~~	courteous	elegant	formal	greasy
healthful	hot	indifferent	low-fat	nutritious	polite
romantic	rude	salty	sour	spicy	sweet

Type of restaurant	Food flavor	Nutritional value	Service
casual			

2 🎧 Listen and check your answers.

3 **PAIRS.** Discuss the restaurants in the photos and the foods you see. Use as many adjectives from Exercise 1 as you can. Which restaurants and foods do you like?

A: This looks like a nice restaurant. It's very elegant.
B: It's nice, but I prefer more casual places, like this one.
A: What about the food? What's your favorite type of food?

30

Eating out

UNIT 7

OBJECTIVES

Students will:
- activate vocabulary related to describing restaurants and food
- use adjectives with *too* and *enough* and *enough* + noun
- practice listening for and saying the reduced vowel /ə/

> **WARM-UP: DO YOU WANT TO EAT OUT TONIGHT?**
> - Tell students this unit is about restaurants and food. Explain that "eating out" refers to going to a restaurant to eat.
> - Pair students. Have them talk about special occasions on which they eat out. Give an example, if needed. (*We always eat out / go out to eat on my birthday. / We always eat out / go out to eat on Friday nights.*)
> - Ask a few students to say when their partners eat out.

Getting started

> *LANGUAGE NOTE*
>
> Remind students that adjectives formed from nouns ending in *-e* that add *-y* typically drop the final *-e*. Examples from this unit include: *spice/spicy* and *grease/greasy*.

OPTION: VOCABULARY PREVIEW

- Form groups of 3. Have students study the words in Exercise 1.
- Set a time limit of 4 minutes. Ask students to make pairs of synonyms (words that have similar meanings) and antonyms (words that have opposite meanings). Write some examples on the board. Synonym pairs: *hot/spicy, healthful/nutritious/low-fat, formal/elegant, polite/courteous*. Antonym pairs: *bland/spicy, sweet/sour, greasy/low-fat, casual/formal, rude/polite*.
- Go over the answers. Explain any words students don't understand.
- Optionally, ask students for examples of some of the words. *Sweet: cake, chocolate. Spicy: food dishes with hot pepper. A casual restaurant: McDonald's. An elegant restaurant:* (name a restaurant in your area).

Exercise 1

- Have students look at the words listed above the chart. Ask them if they notice anything about the words *salty, spicy, greasy*. (They end in *-y*.) Then have students read the categories in the chart. Check that students understand that *nutritional value* shows how good a food is for people's health. Ask if there are any new words they don't understand.
- Explain the task: Students write the words in the correct column in the chart. Go over the example.
- Set a time limit of 5 minutes. While students are working, walk around the room, helping as needed.

Exercise 2

- Tell students they are going to listen to check their answers to Exercise 1.
- 🎧 Play the audio.
- 🎧 Play the audio again, as needed, for students to confirm their answers.
- Have students work in pairs to compare charts.
- Go over answers with the class.

> **Answer key**
>
> Type of restaurant: casual, elegant, formal, romantic
> Food flavor: bland, hot, salty, sour, spicy, sweet
> Nutritional value: greasy, healthful, low-fat, nutritious
> Service: courteous, indifferent, polite, rude

Teaching Tip! Showing agreement or disagreement

It's important to show agreement or disagreement politely. Some common phrases used to show agreement are: *I agree; I see what you mean; I think so, too*. Remind students they can show disagreement with: *I don't think so; It's OK, but I . . . ; Not me, I prefer . . .*

Exercise 3

- Pair students. Ask them to look at the photos of restaurants. Explain the task: Students use the adjectives from Exercise 1 to discuss the restaurants and foods in the photos. Encourage students to say which restaurants and foods they like and why.
- Go over the example with the class. Set a time limit of 5 minutes. Walk around the room, helping as needed.
- After 5 minutes, call on a few students to say a few sentences about which restaurants and foods they like and why. Check that they understand the words in the chart by asking questions about their choices (e.g., *Why do you think this restaurant is elegant?*).

EXTENSION

- Have students work in groups of 3 or 4 to discuss food they usually eat and the types of restaurants they go to.
- Set a time limit of 3 minutes. Tell students to take turns asking and answering questions such as *Do you usually go to formal restaurants, or do you prefer casual places? Do you like spicy or hot foods? Which ones?*

Teacher's Notes — Lesson A

Teacher's Notes — Lesson A

Pronunciation

Exercise 4

- Tell students they are going to listen to some adjectives from Exercise 1. Ask them to notice the sound of the vowels shown in blue.
- 🎧 Play the audio and have students listen.
- Ask students if the vowels shown in blue sound very different from each other. (They don't; these vowels all sound more or less the same.)
- Elicit or point out the different ways this sound is spelled here: cas*u*al, nutri*tio*us, health*fu*l, indiffer*e*nt.
- Tell students that this sound is the most common one for vowels in weak (unstressed) syllables. To make it easy to talk about this sound, tell students it is called *schwa*.

Exercise 5

- 🎧 Play the audio. Ask students to repeat each word chorally. Then ask individual students to repeat the words.
- Check students' pronunciation, focusing on the correct stress and the pronunciation of the weak vowels. If necessary, remind students to make the stressed vowels long and the weak vowels short.
- Note that *favorite* is usually pronounced as two syllables; the *o* is silent.

Exercise 6

- Explain the task: Students listen to the words and underline the vowels pronounced as the short, unstressed vowel /ə/.
- Use one of the words from Exercise 4 as an example. Model the pronunciation and write the word on the board, underlining the vowels pronounced as /ə/.
- 🎧 Play the audio. Have students listen and complete the task individually.

Exercise 7

- 🎧 Have students listen to the audio and repeat each word chorally.
- Ask some individual students to repeat the words and check their pronunciation.
- 🎧 Have students listen to the audio again and check their answers to Exercise 6.
- Go over the answers with the class.

Reading

> **LANGUAGE NOTES**
> - *Service* in a restaurant refers to how waiters and others treat the customers. The *decor* includes the furniture and decorations of a place.
> - *Calamari* is the Italian word for squid.

Exercise 8

- Form groups of 3. Tell students to think about their favorite restaurant. Give students a few minutes to make notes about why they like it. Remind students to use some of the vocabulary from Exercise 1.
- Set a time limit of 5 minutes and tell students to take turns talking about their favorite restaurant. Encourage students to ask their partners follow-up questions (e.g., *What do you like about it? What kind of food do they serve?*).
- Walk around the room, helping as needed.
- Call on a few students to talk about their restaurant.

Exercise 9

- Tell students this is a review of the Palm Restaurant. Have students look at the chart. Explain that this review will talk about the decor, service, and food. Check understanding of *service* and *decor* by giving examples of each. (See Language Notes.)
- Explain the task: Students read the review, and then decide if it is favorable or not and mark their charts.
- Set a time limit of 3 minutes.
- Check answers. Then ask students if they have any questions about the vocabulary.

> **Answer key**
> Decor: favorable   Service: favorable   Food: negative

Exercise 10

- Pair students. Have them look at the questions before they read the restaurant review again. Tell students to listen carefully to their partner's answer to question 3.
- Students read the review again and answer the questions. Walk around the room, helping as needed.
- Go over the answers with the class. Call on a few students to report about their partner's answer to question 3.

> **Answer key**
> 1. It is huge and complicated.
> 2. He/She didn't like the appetizers very much.
> 3. Answers will vary.

EXTENSION

- Have students prepare a questionnaire with four questions about restaurants and types of food.
- Set a time limit of 5 minutes. Have students walk around the room and ask their questions. Tell students they should start their questions with *Do you like . . . ?* If they find someone who answers *yes*, they should write the person's name down.
- After 5 minutes, form groups of 3. Have students compare their questions and the names they have on their questionnaire.

Please go to www.longman.com/worldview for additional in-clas model conversation practice.

HOMEWORK

- 📖 For homework, assign *Workbook* page 32, Vocabulary Exercises 1 and 2, and page 34, Listening Exercises 5 and 6.

Pronunciation

4 🎧 Listen. Notice the pronunciation of the vowels shown in blue. They all have the short, unclear sound /ə/. Most weak syllables have this vowel sound.

casual   nutritious   healthful   indifferent

5 🎧 Listen again and repeat.

6 🎧 Now listen to these words. Underline the vowels that have the short, unclear sound /ə/.

polite   formal   elegant   courteous

7 🎧 Listen again and repeat. Check your answers.

Reading

8 **GROUPS OF 3.** What is your favorite restaurant? Why?

9 Read the restaurant review. Is the review of the decor, service, and food favorable or negative?

	Favorable	Negative
Decor		
Service		
Food		

10 **PAIRS.** Read the review again and answer the questions.

1. What is wrong with the main menu at the Palm?
2. What did the reviewer think of the appetizers?
3. Would you go to this restaurant after reading the review? Why or why not?

The Palm Restaurant

350 PALM Boulevard

The Palm Restaurant is an old-time favorite with tons of character. The restaurant's spacious, discreetly decorated, and elegant dining room is quiet enough for a business meeting at lunch and also an ideal place for a romantic dinner. If you can, get a table facing the bay.

The employees are courteous and knowledgeable. "You were here last week, right?" a waitress asked me one evening, with a smile of recognition. The chef occasionally walks through the dining room greeting customers.

The Palm serves international cuisine, with varied daily specials. Unfortunately, the menu is already huge and the additional specials make it too complicated for my taste. I ordered from the appetizer menu, which is large enough.

I liked the chicken in a sweet and sour sauce. We sampled the "hot stuff" Mexican appetizers, but they were a little too spicy for some of my guests. The stuffed mushrooms weren't cooked enough, and the fried calamari was too greasy.

As for desserts, there is not enough variety on the dessert menu, but it includes an acceptable cheesecake and a not-so-bad double chocolate cake. The pear in the mixed fruit wasn't ripe enough, making dessert the least appealing part of a less-than-fantastic menu.

Lesson A

Grammar focus

1 Study the examples with *enough/not enough* and *too*.

> This room is **quiet enough** for a business meeting.
> The appetizer was **too spicy** for some people.
> There is**n't enough variety** in the dessert menu.

2 Look at the examples again. Underline the correct information to complete the rules in the chart.

> **(not) enough and too**
> The adjective goes **before / after** *too*.
> The adjective goes **before / after** *enough*.
> The noun goes **before / after** *enough*.

Grammar Reference page 144

3 Complete the conversation. Use the words in parentheses with *too* or *enough*.

Beth: Nice restaurant! But it was ___too loud___ to have a conversation there.
1. (loud)

Mike: Yeah, on weekends it's usually _____ for a quiet dinner.
2. (busy)

Beth: Anyway, I had a great time.

Mike: Me, too, although I always find the place a little uncomfortable. There isn't _____ between the tables.
3. (space)

Beth: Stop complaining! There was _____ for two more people at our table. And the waiters were great.
4. (room)

Mike: Yes, they were very courteous, but a bit _____ for my taste.
5. (formal)

Beth: They're just polite. You're _____ .
6. (demanding)

Mike: That's not true! I'm easy to please.

Beth: Really? The last time we went to a restaurant you complained all night long. You went on and on: "The soup isn't _____ , the coffee is
7. (hot)
_____ , they don't have _____ to choose from."
8. (bitter)   9. (desserts)

Mike: I never complain about your cooking!

Beth: No, I guess you don't! Maybe I should open a restaurant and call it "_____ for Mike!"
10. (good)

Grammar focus

WARM-UP

Note: Skip this warm-up if you're doing this lesson (Lesson B) during the same class period as Lesson A.

- Books closed. Tell students they are going to listen to the review of the Palm Restaurant that they read in the Reading section.
- Write *enough* and *too* on the board. Tell students to listen for combinations of adjectives or nouns + *too/enough*. Write examples on the board: *large enough; enough variety; too spicy*. Tell students to write down examples they hear.
- 🎧 Play the audio. Ask students to take notes as they listen. Play it again, as needed, for students to check their work.
- Ask students what adjective combinations they heard and write their answers on the board. (Possible answers: *the dining room is quiet enough, the menu is too complicated, large enough, too spicy, mushrooms weren't cooked enough, calamari was too greasy*.)

LANGUAGE NOTES

- Some students confuse *very* and *too*: *This soup is very good*, but not *This soup is too good*. However, *This soup is not too good* (meaning not very good) is acceptable. Another very common mistake is, *I like it too much*. Remind students that *very much* usually expresses a positive feeling (*I like it very much*), whereas *too much* usually expresses a less positive feeling; for example, *He talks too much*.
- Similarly, if someone didn't like the food in a restaurant, the comment might be *the food is very bad*, not *the food is too bad*.

Exercise ❶

- Have students look at the examples and study the boldfaced words.
- Ask students to focus on the words in boldface that appear next to *too* or *enough*.
- Optionally, ask students to underline the adjectives and circle the nouns in boldface that appear next to *too* and *enough*.

Exercise ❷

- Have students study the examples again.
- Explain the task: Students look at the examples and underline the correct information to complete the rules.
- Have students work in pairs to check their answers.
- Go over the answers with the class.
- Refer students to Grammar Reference page 144, as needed.

Answer key

after   before   after

EXTENSION

- Have students interchange *too* and *enough* in the examples in Exercise 1, when possible: *too quiet, spicy enough, enough variety* (no change is possible).
- Additionally, write *salty, polite, sour* on the board and call on individual students to combine those adjectives with *too* and *enough* (*too salty, salty enough; too polite, polite enough; too sour, sour enough*).

Exercise ❸

- Explain the task: Students complete the conversation using the words in parentheses and *too* or *enough*. Go over the example.
- Have students complete the exercise individually. Set a time limit of 5 minutes. Walk around the room, helping as needed.
- Have students work in pairs to check their answers.
- Go over the answers with the class. Then, have students read the conversations in pairs.

Answer key

1. too loud
2. too busy
3. enough space
4. enough room
5. too formal
6. too demanding
7. hot enough
8. too bitter
9. enough desserts
10. good enough

Speaking

Exercise 4

- Pair students. Tell them they have eaten at a casual Italian restaurant where they live. They both had salad and pizza.
- Tell Student A to look at this page and Student B to turn to page 136. They should not look at each other's books. They will take turns describing the food. Give the students a minute to go over the information.
- Go over the example in the book. Point out that Student A says *"Really?"* to show disagreement, then offers a different opinion. Tell students to listen carefully to their partner.
- Set a time limit of 5 minutes. Walk around the room, helping as needed.
- Call on a number of students and ask if they would eat at the restaurant again and why.

Exercise 5

- Combine two pairs to make groups of 4.
- Explain the task: Students choose a restaurant or café near their school and say what they like about it and why. Have one person take notes. This will make it easier later for them to report their discussion to the class.
- Set a time limit of 5 minutes. Walk around the room, helping as needed.

> **WRAP-UP**
> Call on a few students to report about their group.

TRB For additional interactive grammar practice, have students do the reproducible activity for this unit in the *Teacher's Resource Book*.

Writing

Exercise 6

- Assign the writing task for class work or homework. Make sure students understand that their note should include what not to eat and why.
- **TRB** Optionally, give students a copy of the model (see the *Teacher's Resource Book*, Writing Models). Ask them to read the model and notice the adjectives that are used. Remind them to use some of the vocabulary from this unit.
- If students don't have the model, write the following few on the board:

    David–
    I hear you're planning to go to Alexander's. It's an
    elegant restaurant, and it has a beautiful view . . . .

    Walk around the room to make sure students understand the task.

- If the assignment is done in class, have a few students read their work aloud as time permits.

For suggestions on how to give feedback on writing, see page xiv of this *Teacher's Edition*.

CONVERSATION TO GO

- As the students leave class, have them read the dialogue.
- Optionally, call on pairs of students and ask them to improvise an exchange about restaurants using *too* and/or *enough*, for example: *The restaurant on the corner is too expensive. / I agree. And they don't have enough waiters, so the food is always late.*

HOMEWORK

- Assign *Workbook* page 33, Grammar Exercises 3 and 4, and page 34, Pronunciation Exercises 7 and 8.
- If students do not have the *WorldView Workbook*, assign listening homework from the Student CD. Write on the board:

    Track 19
    What is the worst part of the restaurant's menu?

- Tell students to listen to the audio and write their answer. Have them bring it to the next class. (*the desserts*)

Speaking

4 **PAIRS.** Role-play. You just ate dinner at a new casual Italian restaurant in your city or town. You both had salad and pizza. Student A, look at this page. Student B, look at page 136.

Student A, your impressions of the restaurant include:

- a relaxed informal atmosphere
- a nice place for families with kids
- friendly waiters
- great pizza, not too spicy, plenty of cheese on top
- good salad, very fresh, but dressing not sweet enough, too much vinegar
- good selection of drinks
- a little too expensive

With your partner, decide if you would go back to this restaurant again.

A: I thought the salad was really fresh.
B: Yes, but I didn't like the dressing. I thought it was too sweet.
A: Really? I didn't think it was sweet enough. It seemed sour to me.

5 **GROUPS OF 4.** Think of a restaurant or café near your school. What do you like about the place? Why?

Writing

6 A friend from out of town is planning to go to a restaurant where some of the menu items are good and some aren't so good. Write a note telling him or her what to avoid and why.

CONVERSATION TO GO

A: This place is **too crowded**!
B: You're right. There are**n't enough restaurants** around here.

UNIT 8

It's a deal!

Vocabulary Verb + noun combinations
Grammar Modals: *have to/don't have to*, *must*, and *can't* for obligation and prohibition
Speaking Expressing obligation, no obligation, and prohibition

Lesson A

Getting started

1 **PAIRS.** Match the columns to make logical sentences.

1. When people are under stress, they may *lose* _e_
2. Nowadays, both men and women *do* ___
3. Before they get married, celebrities often *make* ___
4. The way to protect your possessions is to *have* ___
5. People should be responsible and *take care of* ___
6. When you marry someone, you actually *sign* ___
7. It's good to know how your spouse will *react to* ___
8. At weddings, most couples *exchange* ___

a. *the housework.*
b. *problems.*
c. *their financial obligations.*
d. *prenuptial agreements.*
e. *their temper.*
f. *wedding rings.*
g. *a contract.*
h. *some kind of insurance.*

2 🎧 Listen and check your answers.

3 **PAIRS.** Use the expressions in italics in Exercise 1 to make sentences about yourself or people you know.

I never lose my temper at work, but I often do at home and with friends.

34

It's a deal!

UNIT 8

OBJECTIVES

Students will:

- activate vocabulary related to weddings and other social agreements
- use modals: *have to/don't have to, must/must not, can't*
- practice listening for and saying *have to* and *has to* in connected speech

WARM-UP: GETTING MARRIED

- Tell students this unit is about marriage and agreements that people make, especially prenuptial agreements. Explain that *"It's a deal!"* means *"We have an agreement!"*
- Form groups of 3. Ask students to discuss what they think is the most important thing in a successful marriage, and what they think married couples argue about the most.
- Set a time limit of 2 minutes. Students take turns telling each other their opinions about marriage.
- Call on a few students to report to the class.

Getting started

OPTION: VOCABULARY PREVIEW

- Write the words in parentheses on the board. Read the italicized explanations below to the students and ask them to match them with the words on the board.
- *Tendency to get angry* (temper)
- *Work you do to take care of the house, such as washing the dishes or cleaning* (housework)
- *Legal agreement between two people or two companies* (contract)
- *Having to do with money* (financial)
- *Happening before the wedding* (prenuptial)
- *Agreement with a company in which you pay a fee and the company pays the costs if anything bad happens* (insurance)
- *Difficulty, trouble* (problems)
- *Jewelry worn to show that someone is married* (wedding ring)

Exercise 1

- Pair students. Explain the task: Students match the columns to make logical sentences. Explain that they need to find the verb and noun combinations that go together best. Go over the example with the class.
- If necessary, you can also do the second sentence as a whole class activity (*both men and women do the housework*).
- Set a time limit of 5 minutes. While students are working, walk around the room, helping as needed.

Teaching Tip! Using context to understand new vocabulary

A number of the vocabulary items in this unit may be new to the students. Encourage them to use the context to help them understand the meaning. For example, students can associate *stress/lose their temper* or they can match *Before (they get married)* with *prenuptial* if they know that *pre* means *before*.

Exercise 2

- Tell students to listen and check their answers.
- 🎧 Play the audio. Play again as needed.
- Go over the answers with the class. Have students use complete sentences.
- Optionally, discuss the context clues they used: for example, for question 3, *pre* means *before*, and a good guess is that *nuptial* means *marriage*.

Answer key

1. e. their temper
2. a. the housework
3. d. prenuptial agreements
4. h. some kind of insurance
5. c. their financial obligations
6. g. a contract
7. b. problems
8. f. wedding rings

Exercise 3

- Form new pairs. Explain the task: Students use the expressions in Exercise 1 to make sentences about themselves or people they know.
- Go over the example.
- Set a time limit of 3 minutes. Have students make at least three sentences each.
- Call on students to present their sentences to the class.

WRAP-UP

Take a class poll. Tell students to raise their hands if they can answer *yes* to these questions:

Do you do the housework in your house?
Who signed a contract last year?
How many people in class wear a wedding ring?
Who has car insurance?

Teacher's Notes — Lesson A

T34

Teacher's Notes — Lesson A

Reading

BACKGROUND INFORMATION

A prenuptial agreement is a contract that both husband- and wife-to-be sign before they get married. Usually, a prenuptial agreement is signed by people who are wealthy; however, some couples do it for other reasons. For example, a person may have large debts from school, and his or her future spouse wants to be protected from having to pay those debts if the marriage fails.

Michael Douglas and Catherine Zeta-Jones, and Jennifer Aniston and Brad Pitt are examples of famous Hollywood couples who made prenuptial agreements before they got married.

Exercise 4

- Pair students. Present the situations in the book. Explain the task: Students discuss which of the situations they would be in without a signed agreement (a contract). Tell students to give reasons.
- Set a time limit of 7 minutes for their discussion. Walk around the room, helping as needed.
- Take a poll of the class to find out which situations they would do without a signed agreement.

EXTENSION

Ask students to summarize the pros and cons of having a signed agreement. Write some of the ideas in a chart on the board.

Exercise 5

- Hold up your book and read the title, "Legal Terms of Endearment." You might want to explain that *endearment* means *something someone says or does to show affection* and that here it is being used sarcastically because the article is about making a contract to financially protect the husband- and wife-to-be.
- Point to the photos on the previous page. Ask students to identify who the couples are (answer: *Catherine Zeta-Jones and Michael Douglas, and Brad Pitt and Jennifer Aniston*), and what they know about them (*They are movie stars in Hollywood*).
- Explain the task: Students read the article and answer the questions. Have students read the questions first. Encourage students to take brief notes to help them complete the task.
- Tell students they will read the article twice. The first time, they should read quickly to get just the main ideas. Set a time limit of 3 minutes.
- Walk around the room, helping as needed.
- The second time students read, they should go more slowly to find the answers to the questions. Set a time limit of 6 minutes.
- Walk around the room, helping as needed.
- Have students work with a partner to check their answers.
- Go over answers with the class.

Answer key
1. to protect themselves financially
2. people's responsibilities and obligations before they get married
3. At first Bruce didn't want to talk about it. Then he lost his temper and thought Susan didn't trust him.
4. Bruce has to do all the housework and cook dinner, and Susan has to pay the bills. If they get divorced, Bruce can't ask Susan for any money.

Exercise 6

- Form groups of 3 to discuss the questions in the book. Each student must answer every question. Remind students of phrases they can use to express their opinions. Write on the board, *I think . . . , It seems to me that . . .* If needed, point out other words that students can use, such as *reasonable, (un)fair, (un)necessary,* or *ridiculous*.
- Set a time limit of 6 minutes and have students take turns sharing their opinions. Tell students to listen carefully to their partners' opinions, and take notes, if they wish.

EXTENSION

Call on a few students to report about their partners.

Please go to www.longman.com/worldview for additional in-class model conversation practice.

HOMEWORK

- For homework, assign *Workbook* page 35, Vocabulary Exercises 1 and 2, and page 37, Listening Exercises 5 and 6.

Reading

4 **PAIRS.** Which of these would you do without a signed agreement? Why?

- start a business with a friend
- buy a car from a relative
- marry a person you have known for five years
- share an apartment with a close friend

5 Read the article about prenuptial agreements. Answer these questions.

1. What is the main reason Hollywood stars make prenuptial agreements?
2. What can prenuptial agreements help make clear?
3. How did Bruce react when Susan asked for a prenuptial agreement?
4. What agreement did Bruce and Susan make?

Legal Terms of Endearment

THESE DAYS, IT SEEMS LIKE Hollywood stars must sign a prenuptial agreement before they exchange wedding rings. The most common reason stars sign these legal contracts is to protect themselves financially in case the marriage ends in divorce. Before Michael Douglas married Catherine Zeta-Jones, they signed a "prenup." If their marriage ends, he must give her $1.5 million for every year they were married. Similar agreements are common among movie stars and very wealthy people.

But times are changing. Prenuptial agreements aren't just for entertainers or millionaires anymore. They can help clarify financial obligations and other responsibilities in any marriage. Bruce Collins and Susan Taylor live in Dayton, Ohio. He is a math teacher, and she is a lawyer. Susan makes a lot more money than Bruce, and Bruce has more free time. So what's in their prenuptial agreement? They agreed that Bruce has to do all the housework and cook dinner. Susan has to pay the bills. And if they get divorced, Bruce can't ask Susan for any money.

"When I first mentioned the prenuptial agreement, he refused to even talk about it. When I insisted, he even lost his temper and accused me of not trusting him," Susan said. "Finally, we reached an agreement because Bruce understood that we're both sensible people. And sensible people have life insurance, car insurance, and homeowner's insurance. So why shouldn't they have marriage insurance?"

6 **GROUPS OF 3.** Discuss these questions.

Do you like the idea of prenuptial agreements? Why?
What do you think of the agreement between Michael Douglas and Catherine Zeta-Jones?
What do you think of the agreement between Bruce and Susan?

Grammar focus

1 Study the examples of *have to*, *don't have to*, *must*, and *can't*.

> Susan **has to** pay the bills.
> You **don't have to** do any housework.
> Hollywood stars **must** sign prenuptial agreements.
> Bruce **can't** ask Susan for money.

2 Look at the examples again. Complete the chart using *have to*, *don't have to*, *must*, and *can't*.

Modals of obligation, no obligation, and prohibition
Use _____ and _____ to say that something is necessary or required. (obligation)
Use _____ to say that something is not necessary. (no obligation)
Use _____ to say *don't do this*. (prohibition)

Grammar Reference page 144

3 Complete the sentences with *have to*, *don't have to*, *must*, or *can't*. More than one answer is possible in some cases.

1. You can get married quickly in Las Vegas. After you get the license, you _don't have to_ wait to get married.
2. The bride and groom _____ sign the marriage certificate. If they don't sign it, the certificate isn't legal.
3. When you get married, many people believe that you _____ put your spouse above friends and relatives.
4. In most states in the U.S., you_____ get married until you are 18 years old, unless you have your parents' permission.
5. The state of Mississippi has a different law: you _____ be at least 21 years old to get married, unless you have your parents' permission.
6. In some states, you _____ have two witnesses when you get married. In other states, you only need one witness.
7. Before people can get married in the U.S., they _____ apply for a marriage license.
8. In most states, the couple needs to have a blood test. But they _____ have one if they get married in Nevada.

Grammar focus

> **LANGUAGE NOTES**
> - In American English, *must* expresses strong obligation (*You must attend the meeting*) and *can't* commonly expresses prohibition (*You can't miss the meeting*).
> - *Have to* expresses less strong obligation, and *don't have to* implies choice (*You don't have to come, but we'd like you to*).
> - In a neutral information question, *have to* is typically used (*Do we have to attend the meeting?*).
> - *Do (you) have to* is used rather than *must* to show disapproval (*Do you have to make so much noise?*).

> **WARM-UP**
> Note: Skip this warm-up if you're doing this lesson (Lesson B) during the same class period as Lesson A.
> - Books closed. Tell students they are going to listen to the audio of the article "Legal Terms of Endearment."
> - Tell students to think about how the prenuptial agreement shows what the couple agrees to. What verbs express this?
> - 🎧 Play the audio.
> - Ask students to write down the verb forms that show what Michael Douglas, Bruce Collins, or Susan Taylor must do (*must, has to*).
> - Call on individual students to say what each of them *must* do or *has to* do.

Exercise ❶

- Have students look at the examples and study the boldfaced words.
- Ask students which sentences express obligation (first and fourth), which sentence expresses prohibition (third), and which sentence expresses choice (second).
- Point out that *can* and *must* have the same form in all persons: *I can't/he can't, I must/he must*.

Exercise ❷

- Have students look at the examples again.
- Explain the task: Students complete the rules in the box with *have to, don't have to, must,* and *can't*.
- Have students work in pairs to check their answers.
- Go over the answers with the class.
- Refer students to Grammar Reference page 144, as needed.

> **Answer key**
> must/have to   don't have to   can't

> **LANGUAGE NOTE**
> Point out to the students that the word *spouse* is used for either husband or wife. The phrasal verb *to put (your spouse) above* means to consider (your spouse) first. It can be used in other contexts as well (e.g., *She puts her job above everything*). A *witness* here means someone who is there at the marriage ceremony. A *marriage license* is a legal document that allows two people to get married. A *marriage certificate* is a legal document that states two people are married.

Exercise ❸

- Explain the task: Students complete the sentences with the correct form of *(don't) have to, must,* or *can't*. More than one answer is possible in some cases.
- Have students complete the exercise individually. Set a time limit of 5 minutes.
- Pair students to check their answers. Ask them to read the sentences aloud.
- Go over the answers with the class.

> **Answer key**
> 1. don't have to   4. can't   7. have to/must
> 2. must/have to   5. must/have to   8. don't have to
> 3. must/have to   6. must/have to

> **EXTENSION**
> Do a chain conversation with the whole class. Model the conversation by asking Student A *What do you have to do tonight, (Alex)?* Student A responds (*I have to . . .*). Then call on Student A to ask another student (B), *What do you have to do, (Pam)?* If time permits, continue in this way with several students.

Pronunciation

Exercise ❹

- 🎧 Play the audio and have students listen. Ask them to notice the way the words are blended together in *have to* and *has to*.
- Point out the weak pronunciation of *to*: /tə/.
- Say the words in *have + to* and *has + to* separately and then in the blended forms "hafta" and "hasta" to highlight the way they sound different. Use the respellings "hafta" and "hasta" to illustrate.
- Point out the different pronunciations of *have* in *Do they have to* /hæftə/ *have* /hæv/ *an agreement?*

Exercise ❺

- 🎧 Play the audio. Stop after each item to allow students to repeat chorally.
- Ask a few individual students to repeat the sentences and check their pronunciation.
- Encourage students to pronounce the words in *have to* and *has to* together as if they were a single word and to stress the first syllable. Putting stress on the first syllable will help them produce the weak form of *to*.

T36

Speaking

Exercise 6

- Pair students. Tell them they are going to share an apartment. They don't know each other very well. They need to work out the details of their agreement.
- Hold up your book and point to the notebook page. Tell students to take notes here.
- Tell Student A to turn to page 139, and Student B to turn to page 141. They should not look at each other's books. Tell them to pay attention to three things: what they are like, what they want their roommate to agree to, and what they both finally agree to. (**Note:** Student A is a very neat person who likes to go to bed early. Student B is not neat, and likes to go to bed late and sleep late.)
- Give students 2 minutes to read over their information individually. Walk around the room, helping as needed.
- Set a time limit of 6 minutes for the students to work out their agreements together. Walk around the room, helping as needed.

Exercise 7

- Combine two pairs to form groups of 4.
- Have students in each pair take turns talking about their agreements. Encourage students to summarize what they wanted, as well as what they finally agreed to. Tell students to listen carefully to find out if the other pair is satisfied.

> **WRAP-UP**
> Take a poll of the class to find out how many pairs are satisfied with the agreement they reached.

TRB For additional interactive grammar practice, have students do the reproducible activity for this unit in the *Teacher's Resource Book*.

Writing

Exercise 8

- Assign the writing task for class work or homework. Go over the directions, making sure students understand the difference between an informal agreement and a legal contract. (An informal agreement states the rules and obligations, but it isn't legal.)
- **TRB** Optionally, give students a copy of the model (see the *Teacher's Resource Book*, Writing Models). Ask them to read the model and notice the modals of obligation and prohibition that are used. Remind students to use some of the vocabulary from this unit.
- If students don't have the model, write the following on the board:

    This agreement is made on October 12 between the neighbors of West Valley. We all want our town to be safe so we agree on the following rules . . .

    Walk around the room to make sure students understand the task.

- If the assignment is done in class, have a few students read aloud as time permits.

For suggestions on how to give feedback on writing, see page xiv of this *Teacher's Edition*.

CONVERSATION TO GO

- As the students leave class, have them read the dialogue.
- Optionally, have pairs of students talk about something they can't do in class (e.g., *arrive late, play music, talk on the phone*), and something they don't have to do (e.g., *be in class ten minutes before the teacher arrives, be quiet all the time*).

HOMEWORK

- For homework, assign *Workbook* page 36, Grammar Exercises 3 and 4, and page 37, Pronunciation Exercises 7 and 8. Assign *Workbook* Self-quiz Units 5–8.
- If students do not have the *WorldView Workbook*, assign listening homework from the Student CD. Write on the board:

    Track 20
    Who makes more money, Susan or Bruce?

- Tell students to listen to the audio and write their answer. Have them bring it to the next class. (*Susan*)

BEFORE NEXT CLASS

Have students review the material they have studied in these four units:

Unit no.	Review Grammar	Listen to Student CD	Study Grammar Reference
5	subject and object questions	Track 12	Page 144
6	adjectives/intesifiers; simple *versus* past continuous	Track 16	Page 144
7	adjectives with *too* and *enough*	Track 19	Page 144
8	modals: *have to/don't have to, must/must not, can't*	Track 20	Page 144

FOR NEXT CLASS

TRB Make copies of Quiz 2 in the *Teacher's Resource Book*.

Pronunciation

4 🎧 Listen. Notice the pronunciation of *have to* ("hafta") and *has to* ("hasta").

have to
    They have to see a lawyer.
    He doesn't have to sign the agreement.
    Do they have to have an agreement?

has to
    Bruce has to do the housework.
    Susan has to pay the bills.
    Who has to do the cooking?

5 🎧 Listen again and repeat.

Speaking

6 *PAIRS.* You're going to share an apartment with someone you don't know very well. Student A, look at page 139. Student B, look at page 141. Take notes on the details of your agreement.

You don't have to go to bed early, but you have to be quiet if you're up after ten, so you can't play loud music then.

Agreement between _____ and _____

I have to:

I don't have to:

I can't:

He or she has to:

He or she doesn't have to:

He or she can't:

7 *GROUPS OF 4.* Tell one another about your agreements. Is everyone satisfied?

Writing

8 What are the rules and obligations of the neighbors in your community or of the students in your school? Write an informal agreement explaining these rules and obligations. Use modals of obligation, no obligation, and prohibition.

CONVERSATION TO GO

A: Shh! We **can't** make noise after ten.
B: I know, but we **don't have to** whisper!

Review 2: Units 5–8

Unit 5 A typical day

1 🎧 Listen to the model conversation and look at the pictures on the game board.

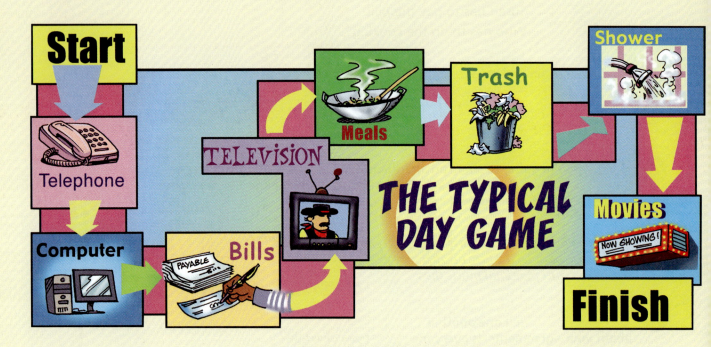

2 **GROUPS OF 4.** Take turns. Toss a coin (one side = move ahead one space, the other side = move ahead two spaces). When you land on a space with a picture, ask your partner two questions about the topic. Your partner answers your questions. If your questions are correct, stay there. If not, move back one space. The winner is the first player to reach the end.

Unit 6 It's absolutely true!

3 🎧 Listen to the model conversation.

4 **GROUPS OF 3.** Read these sentences from the beginning of a story. Write at least two more sentences each to make the story complete.

> Barbara was walking her dog one day when suddenly it started raining. The weather was absolutely awful! She didn't know what to do, so she took an umbrella that was leaning against a car.

5 Read your story to the class. Decide whose story is the funniest, the strangest, or the most exciting.

Review 2: Units 5–8

🎞️ You may wish to use the video for Units 5–8 at this point.
For video activity worksheets, go to www.longman.com/worldview.

Unit 5: A typical day

OBJECTIVE

Grammar: focus on using subject and object questions

Exercise 1

- Explain the task: Students listen to the model conversations as they look at the pictures on the game board.
- 🎧 Play the audio.
- 🎧 Tell students to listen carefully to the questions. Then, play the audio again.
- Ask students what questions they heard. (*Who makes the most telephone calls in your house? Who does she call? Do you have a computer at home? Who uses it the most? Who pays the bills in your house? What's your most expensive bill?*)

Exercise 2

- Form groups of 4. Explain the task: Students play the board game. Tell students the rules: Students toss a coin. If it lands on heads, they move ahead one space, and on tails, they move two spaces. When they land on a space with a picture, they ask a member of their group two questions about the topic. If the questions are correct, they stay. If they aren't correct, they move back one space. The winner is the first player to reach the end.
- Demonstrate tossing a coin, and then taking a turn.
- Make sure each group has a coin to use.
- Set a time limit of 12 minutes. While students are working, walk around the room, helping as needed.

> **WRAP-UP**
> - Have the students each write down three activities they do in a typical day.
> - Call on individual students to ask another student about one of these activities. For example, say a student's name (Ana). (Ana) asks a question: *Who wakes up first at your house?*
> - Then, (Ana) calls on another student (Alex). (Alex) answers, using true information. Set a time limit of 3 minutes.

Unit 6: It's absolutely true!

OBJECTIVE

Grammar: focus on using adjectives and intensifiers and the simple past vs. past continuous

Exercise 3

- Explain the task: Students listen to the model of a story based on the sentences in Exercise 4.
- 🎧 Play the audio.
- 🎧 Have students read the sentences in Exercise 4. Then, play the audio again.

Exercise 4

- Form groups of 3.
- Explain the task: Students read the sentences from the story, and then add more sentences to complete the story. Tell them that each member of their group should contribute at least two sentences.
- Have each group choose one person to write down their ideas. Suggest that they also choose one person to lead the discussion and make sure everyone contributes.
- Set a time limit of 10 minutes. Walk around the room, helping as needed.

Exercise 5

- Explain the task: Groups present their stories to the class.
- Take a poll and have the students decide whose story is the funniest, the strangest, or the most exciting.

> **WRAP-UP**
> - Have each group of 3 work with another group.
> - Students take turns asking each other questions about their stories. Example: *Where was Barbara? What happened? What did she do next? Then what happened?*
> - As students take turns, a new story will be formed. Set a time limit of 3 minutes.

T38

Unit 7: Eating out

> **OBJECTIVE**

Grammar: focus on using adjectives with *too* and *enough*

Exercise 6

- Explain the task: Students listen to the model conversation. Tell them the conversation is about Alice's Restaurant and The Blue Lantern. Ask them to listen for what the speakers like and dislike about each restaurant.
- 🎧 Play the audio. Make a two-column chart on the board with the names of the restaurants at the top. Underneath each name, write + and –. Then elicit from the students what the speakers like (+) and dislike (–) about the restaurants. Write their responses in the appropriate column.
- 🎧 Play the audio again, as needed, and have students add more ideas to the chart. Set a time limit of 7 minutes.

Exercise 7

- Form pairs. Assign roles: Student A and Student B for each pair.
- Explain the task: Students are going out to dinner. They will discuss local restaurants and choose a place to have dinner together.
- Tell the students to read the description for their assigned role, Student A or B.
- Set a time limit of 5 minutes for pairs to discuss the restaurants, what they want to eat and how much they want to spend, and then to decide where to go. Walk around the room, helping as needed.

> **WRAP-UP**
>
> - Ask several pairs which restaurant they decided to go to. Encourage students to give their reasons.
> - For extra challenge, ask students to consider creative solutions; for example, Student A decides to pay for Student B's dinner this time, and Student B promises to pay the next time when he or she has more money. Set a time limit of 3 minutes.

Unit 8: It's a deal!

> **OBJECTIVE**

Grammar: focus on using modals: *have to/don't have to, must/must not, can't*

Exercise 8

- Explain the task: Students listen to the model conversation.
- 🎧 Play the audio. Then write on the board: *have to*.
- 🎧 Tell students to listen for sentences with *have to*. Then play the audio again.
- Ask the students, *What does Molly have to do tonight?* Write: *She has to . . .* and elicit from the students what she has to do (*do laundry, pay the bills, do homework*).

Exercise 9

- Form pairs. Assign roles: Student A and Student B for each pair.
- Explain the task: Students role-play the two situations. Tell them to use *have to* and *don't have to* in their role-plays.
- Give students 2 minutes to read their parts and prepare for the role-plays. Encourage students to take brief notes on their ideas. Verify that students understand each situation by asking a few questions. Examples: *Student A, why do you call B? Why can't you ask your rich relative?* and so on.
- Set a time limit of 5 minutes. Walk around the room, helping as needed.

> **WRAP-UP**
>
> - Have students work in pairs. Ask them to tell each other at least three things they *have to/don't have to/can't* do this week.
> - Call on individual students to report on their partner's activities (*Tony has to take a driving exam*).

Unit 7 Eating out

6 🎧 Listen to the model conversation.

7 **PAIRS.** You are going out to dinner together. Talk to your partner and decide which restaurant you will go to.

Student A: You're a vegetarian. You have a lot of money, and you like fancy restaurants. You like spicy food from other countries. Think of a few restaurants near your school.

Student B: You like meat, but not fish or vegetables. You like American food. You don't have much money right now, so dinner has to cost less than $10.00.

Unit 8 It's a deal!

8 🎧 Listen to the model conversation.

9 **PAIRS.** Role-play the following situations.

Student A:

Situation 1. Call Student B and invite him or her to go with you to a great movie tonight.

Situation 2. Listen to Student B's request. Ask him about his rich relative. Tell him you'll have to see a lawyer and sign a contract before you can agree.

Student B:

Situation 1. Listen to Student A's invitation. You have a lot of things to do tonight: cook dinner, do housework, do the laundry, pay the bills, wash your hair, and get to bed early because you have to meet with your boss before work tomorrow.

Situation 2. Call Student A and ask him or her to lend you $10,000 to start a new business. You have a rich relative, but you can't ask him because he's on a world cruise. You have to have the money next week.

UNIT 9

The river

Vocabulary Phrasal verbs related to tourism
Grammar Simple present and present continuous for future
Speaking Describing plans for a trip

Lesson A

Getting started

1 Match the phrasal verbs in bold with the correct definitions.

Phrasal verbs	Definitions
1. They **headed out** at 6:30 in the morning. _g_	a. take someone to different parts of a new place to point out what is important or interesting
2. My friends **put** me **up** for two nights. ___	b. stopped working (used with machines)
3. She **got off** the bus at the last stop. ___	c. left a plane, train, boat, etc.
4. The car **broke down**, so I called the mechanic. ___	d. began a trip at a particular place
5. The train stopped briefly, and then **went on** to the next station. ___	e. continued traveling after a stop
6. We **started off** on High Street. ___	f. let someone stay in your home for a short time
7. We hired a tour guide to **show** us **around** London. ___	g. left at a specified time to go someplace or do something

2 **PAIRS.** Take turns describing an interesting trip you have taken (for example, a school trip, a weekend away, or a vacation). Use some of the phrasal verbs in Exercise 1.

Last summer, my family and I went camping. We headed out at six on a Friday morning . . .

40

The river

UNIT 9

OBJECTIVES

Students will:
- activate vocabulary related to tourism
- use verb tenses for schedules and plans
- practice stress and linking sounds together in phrasal verbs

WARM-UP: DREAM TRIP

- Tell students that this unit is about travel and tourism. Explain that the river in the title is the River Thames /temz/ in London.
- Pair students. Have them talk about a place they dream about visiting, and give a personal example, *I'd like to visit New Zealand because I've seen pictures of it. It looks beautiful and . . .*
- Set a time limit of 3 minutes. Tell each student to say where they would like to travel to and why. On the board, write *Where* and *Why*. Tell students to listen carefully because they may have to report to the class about their partner's dream trips.
- Call on a few students to report about their partner's "dream trip."

Getting started

FYI

Phrasal verbs can be divided into three different types.

- **Intransitive phrasal verbs** (no direct object is needed). Examples: *head out, break down, go on, start off*. Intransitive phrasal verbs are all inseparable by definition—there is no particle or object to split.
- **Inseparable phrasal verbs** are transitive (a direct object is needed) and the particle cannot be separated from the verb. Example: *get off (something)*. Note: *get off* can also be intransitive, as in *He got off at Main Street*. (All phrasal verbs with more than one particle, such as *run out of*, are inseparable.)
- **Separable phrasal verbs** are transitive (a direct object is needed) but the particle is separated from the verb by the object. Examples: *put (someone) up, show (someone) around*.

OPTION: VOCABULARY PREVIEW

- Pair students. Have students choose which words are closest in meaning to the phrasal verbs in Exercise 1. You can read them the choices out loud or you may want to write them on the board: **head out**: leave/stay; **put someone up**: someone visits and leaves/someone visits and stays overnight; **get off**: enter/exit; **break down**: something works/something doesn't work; **go on**: continue/stop; **start off**: begin/end; **show around**: ask someone to leave/give someone a tour.

- Go over the answers with the class. Answer any questions students have about the vocabulary.

Teaching Tip! Phrasal verbs

Phrasal verbs can be difficult for students to learn, and may require memorization. Since this is a vocabulary exercise, it is best to focus on the phrasal verbs presented here as only vocabulary items. *WorldView 4*, Units 23 and 27, deal with the grammar of phrasal verbs.

Exercise 1

- Ask students to look at the sentences. Ask them what is special about the verbs in color (they are phrasal verbs). Explain that phrasal verbs are made up of two parts, the verb and a particle. The particle looks like a preposition, but it is part of the verb phrase and it changes the meaning of the verb. (**Note:** Avoid going into a more complex discussion of the grammar of phrasal verbs.)
- Explain the task: Students match phrasal verbs to definitions. Go over the first sentence and definition.
- Set a time limit of 3 minutes. Walk around the room, helping as needed.
- Have students work in pairs to check their answers.
- Go over the answers with the class.

Answer key

1. g	3. c	5. e	7. a
2. f	4. b	6. d	

LANGUAGE NOTES

- *Went on*, meaning *continued*, can be used in other contexts as well: *He went on with his work/his trip/his plan to climb Mt. Everest.*
- *Start off*, meaning *begin*, can also be used in other contexts: *We started off dinner with appetizers. We started off our vacation with a trip to the beach.*

Exercise 2

- Tell students to think of an interesting trip they've taken. Give students a chance to make a few notes. They can also talk about an imaginary trip.
- Pair students. Set a time limit of 5 minutes. Remind students to use the phrasal verbs in Exercise 1.
- Walk around the room, helping as needed. Encourage students to ask their partners questions about their trips.

WRAP-UP

Call on individual students to say a few sentences about their trips using the phrasal verbs.

Teacher's Notes — Lesson A

T40

Teacher's Notes — Lesson A

Listening

BACKGROUND INFORMATION

The River Thames: the most important river in England, it runs through southern England for about 340 km (210 miles) and empties into the North Sea just east of London. (**Note:** In American English, the name of the river generally precedes the word *river*, as in the *Mississippi River*.)

Kingston: a busy, attractive shopping and residential area in south London.

Richmond: an area of southwest London that includes Hampton Court, a sixteenth-century palace and gardens; Kew /kyu/ Gardens, famous botanical gardens; and Richmond Park, a very large park.

The Houses of Parliament /pɑrləmənt/: also known as the Palace of Westminster, is the home of the British government.

Big Ben: a famous clock in a 320-foot-high clock tower named after its largest bell, weighing over thirteen tons.

Harrods Department Store: world-famous department store in the Knightsbridge area of London.

Shakespeare's Globe Theatre: a twentieth century replica of Shakespeare's original theater in London.

St. Paul's Cathedral: built between 1665 and 1710, its dome is the largest in the world.

Tate /teɪt/ **Modern:** a London art museum showing modern art.

The Tower of London: a fortress dating from the eleventh century and a former home to kings and queens of England; now a museum and tourist attraction. It includes the castle, prison, royal mint, and a zoo, and is the home of the famous Crown Jewels.

Tower Bridge: opened in 1894, it is now a symbol of London. Visitors can climb the towers and view the Thames River from 140 feet above on glass-sided walkways.

Trafalgar Square: a famous London square, known as the location of the National Gallery.

Exercise 3

- Have students look at the map of the River Thames. Elicit what students know about any of the places shown on the map. Many students, even if they have never been to England, will have heard about the Wimbledon tennis tournament, Harrods Department Store, Big Ben (part of the Houses of Parliament), or the Tower Bridge (next to the Tower of London). Provide additional information as needed.
- Pair students. Have them ask each other the questions in the book. Set a time limit of 5 minutes.
- Call on students to say which places they would like to visit.

Exercise 4

- Explain the task: Students identify the places the tourist will visit. Hold up your book and show the students that the tour will start from the west (off the map on the left side of the page).
- 🎧 Play the audio. Students check (✓) the places on the map that are mentioned.
- 🎧 Play the audio one more time so that students can confirm their answers.
- Go over the answers with the class.

Answer key

Hampton Court
Richmond Park
The Houses of Parliament
Tate Modern
Shakespeare's Globe Theatre
Tower Bridge

(**Note:** Kew Gardens is mentioned in the audio, but it is NOT on the map.)

Exercise 5

- Explain the task: Students listen and answer the questions. Before playing the audio, have students look at the questions. or read them aloud with the class.
- 🎧 Play the audio. Encourage students to listen for the answers, and to make brief notes. If needed, play the audio again.
- Have students work in pairs to check their answers.
- Go over the answers with the class.

Answer key

1. 9:00 (Monday morning)
2. 10:30
3. meeting a friend for dinner / spending the night at a friend's home
4. going to the theater

EXTENSION

Take a poll of the class. Ask students if they prefer touring on their own or going on an organized tour when they visit a new city.

🌐 Please go to www.longman.com/worldview for additional in-class model conversation practice and supplementary reading practice.

HOMEWORK

- 📖 For homework, assign *Workbook* page 40, Vocabulary Exercises 1 and 2, and page 42, Listening Exercises 5 and 6.

Listening

3 **PAIRS.** Look at the map of the River Thames in London. Discuss these questions.

Which places would you like to visit?
When you visit a new place, do you like having someone show you around, or do you like to explore on your own? Why?

4 🎧 Listen to the conversation between a tourist and a travel agent. Check (✓) the places on the map that they mention.

5 🎧 Listen again and answer the questions.

1. What time does the tour start on the first day?
2. What time do they get off at Hampton Court?
3. What is the tourist doing the first evening?
4. What is the tourist doing the second evening?

Grammar focus

1 Look at the examples of the simple present and present continuous tenses. Write *simple present* or *present continuous* next to each one.

a. The tour **starts** at nine on Monday.
b. I**'m meeting** a friend for dinner.
c. What time **does** the boat **head out**?
d. I**'m going** to the theater tonight.

2 Look at the examples again. Underline the correct information to complete the rules in the chart. Then match the examples with the rules.

Simple present and present continuous for future
Use the **simple present / present continuous** to talk about schedules, timetables, and events on the calendar in the future. Example sentences __ and __.
Use the **simple present / present continuous** to talk about personal plans in the future. Example sentences __ and __.

Grammar Reference page 145

3 Complete the sentences with the correct form of the simple present or present continuous for the future.

1. The tour ___starts off___ (start off) at Washington Square Park.
2. The movie _____ (begin) at seven tonight.
3. What _____ (you/do) this evening?
4. The semester _____ (end) on June 15.
5. Mike _____ (come) to see us tomorrow morning.
6. Where _____ (they/go) on vacation this summer?
7. I _____ (work) until four tomorrow.

Pronunciation

4 🎧 Listen to the phrasal verbs. Notice how a consonant or vowel sound at the end of a word is linked to a vowel sound at the beginning of the next word.

head out	When does the boat head out?
get off	We get off at Hampton Court.
show ͫ us around	A guide will show us around.
go ͫ on	Then we go on to the park.
putting me ʸ up	A friend is putting me up.

5 🎧 Listen again and repeat.

Grammar focus

> **LANGUAGE NOTES**
> - For most statements about the future, *be going to* or *will* are commonly used.
> - The simple present can also be used to refer to future actions, but only if these actions are part of a schedule or events on the calendar (*The train arrives at 6:04*). The simple present for future events is often used with verbs like *open, begin, start, finish, end, arrive, depart,* and *return*.
> - The present continuous is often used when we have already made arrangements for a personal plan (*We're having dinner with the Elliotts tonight*). The present continuous for personal plans is often used with verbs like *go, come, stay, see, meet,* and *work*.

> **WARM-UP**
>
> Note: Skip this warm-up if you're doing this lesson (Lesson B) during the same class period as Lesson A.
>
> - Books closed. Tell students they are going to listen again to the conversation between the travel agent and the tourist that they heard in the Listening section. Ask them to pay attention to cues that tell what time period they are talking about.
> - 🎧 Play the audio for Lesson A, Exercise 4.
> - Ask, *Are the agent and tourist talking about the past, the present, or the future?* (*the future*)
> - 🎧 Play the audio again. Ask the students to write down verb forms as they listen. Write a few of these on the board.

Exercise ❶

- Have students look at the four sentences and write *simple present* or *present continuous* next to each one.
- Have students work with a partner to check their answers.
- Go over the answers with the class.

> **Answer key**
>
> a. simple present c. simple present
> b. present continuous d. present continuous

Exercise ❷

- Tell students to complete the rules and write the letters of the sentences that illustrate each one.
- Have students work with a partner to check their answers.
- Go over the answers with the class.
- Refer students to Grammar Reference page 145, as needed.

> **Answer key**
>
> simple present; example sentences a and c
> present continuous; example sentences b and d

Exercise ❸

- Ask students to look at the example. Ask students why the present continuous is correct in *I'm working until 4:00 tomorrow*. (*because it's about a personal plan in the future*)
- Have students complete the exercise individually. Set a time limit of 3 minutes.
- Have students work with a partner to check their answers.
- Go over the answers with the class.

> **Answer key**
>
> 1. starts off   5. is coming
> 2. begins   6. are they going
> 3. are you doing   7. 'm working
> 4. ends

Pronunciation

Exercise ❹

- Explain that in English, words in a phrase are usually linked together. It can be hard to hear where one word ends and another begins.
- Choose two or three examples to demonstrate. Say the words in each phrase separately. Then say the words together, to show the way they sound different in connected speech. You can emphasize the linking by writing each phrase on the board as a single word: *headout; getoff*.
- 🎧 Play the audio and have students listen to the linking of the sounds.

Exercise ❺

- 🎧 Play the audio and have students repeat each item chorally.
- Ask a few individual students to repeat the sentences and check their pronunciation.
- Make sure that students do not stop their breath, adding a glottal stop, before the vowel sound at the beginning of the linked words.

Speaking

Teaching Tip! Clarification questions

Students should be comfortable asking each other for clarification in English. Remind them when they start Exercise 6 that when they don't understand something their partner says, they can use simple clarification expressions like: *I'm sorry. What did you say? / Can you repeat that?*

Exercise 6

- Pair students. Tell them they are taking a trip together to Washington, D.C. They each have some information about their travel arrangements.
- Tell Student A to turn to page 137 and Student B to turn to page 139. They should not look at each other's books. They will take turns asking and answering questions to fill in the missing information on their itineraries. Give the students 1 minute to go over their information.
- Call on one pair of students to model the first question:
    A: What airline are we on?
    B: We're on Jet Airways.
- Set a time limit of 10 minutes for the students to complete the task. Walk around the room, helping as needed.
- Go over the answers with the class.

> **Answer key**
> **FLIGHT INFORMATION**
>
> Airline: Ticket/class:
> Jet Airways   business class
>
> **to Washington, D.C.**   **from Washington, D.C.**
> Day/date: Day/date:
> Friday, April 19   Sunday, April 21
> Time departs: Time departs:
> 7:00 A.M.   4:00 P.M.
> Time arrives: Time arrives:
> 12:00 noon   9:00 P.M.
>
> **HOTEL INFORMATION**
> The Wellington Hotel
> (*Located 5 blocks from the White House*)
> Arrival date: Check-in time:
> Friday, April 19   1:00 P.M.
> Departure date: Check-out time:
> Sunday, April 21   11:00 A.M.
> Free airport transfers

Exercise 7

- Have students work with the same partner as in Exercise 6.
- Tell students to look at the brochure. They will see a list of places/restaurants in Washington, D.C.
- Have them plan their weekend. Provide an example, *On Saturday, at eight, let's have breakfast at the coffee shop near the hotel. / Okay, that's a good idea.* OR *I don't know. How about . . . ?* (Note: You may want to write phrases like these for suggesting, agreeing, and disagreeing on the board.)

> **WRAP-UP**
> Tell students to take notes in the planner on the *Student Book* page. They should plan activities for the morning, afternoon, and evening of both days.

Exercise 8

- Combine two pairs to form groups of 4.
- Explain the task: Students find out if the other pair is doing the same thing at the same time as they are. Go over the example in the book. Be sure the students notice the use of the present continuous.
- Set a time limit of 5 minutes. Have students in each pair take turns speaking about their plans.

TRB For additional interactive grammar practice, have students do the reproducible activity for this unit in the *Teacher's Resource Book*.

Writing

Exercise 9

- Assign the writing task for class work or homework.
- **TRB** Optionally, give students a copy of the model (see the *Teacher's Resource Book*, Writing Models). Ask them to read the model and notice what tenses are used. Remind them to use some of the vocabulary from this unit.
- If students don't have the model, write the following on the board:

    Hi, Andrew!
    Next week, Mariano and I are going to Iguazu Falls.
    We're heading out in the morning, on . . .

    Walk around the room to make sure students understand the task.

- If the assignment is done in class, have students exchange their letters as time permits.

For suggestions on how to give feedback on writing, see page xiv of this *Teacher's Edition*.

CONVERSATION TO GO

- As the students leave class, have them read the dialogue.
- Optionally, have students ask and answer questions about when the next class starts.

HOMEWORK

- 📖 For homework, assign *Workbook* page 41, Grammar Exercises 3 and 4, and page 42, Pronunciation Exercises 7 and 8.
- 💿 If students do not have the *WorldView Workbook*, assign listening homework from the Student CD. Write on the board:

    Track 22
    Where does the tour go after Hampton Court?

- 🎧 Tell students to listen to the audio and write their answer. Have them bring it to the next class. (*Richmond Park and Kew Gardens*)

Speaking

6 **PAIRS.** Imagine you're taking a weekend trip together to Washington, D.C. Student A, look at page 137. Student B, look at page 139.

7 **PAIRS.** Look at the brochure about Washington, D.C. Use the information to plan your weekend. Include places to go, places to eat, and the times for each activity. Take notes for both Saturday and Sunday.

A: OK, on Saturday, do you want to go dancing or go to dinner somewhere?
B: Let's do both. Let's eat dinner at about 7:30 at Star of Siam and then go to the Black Cat Club.

WASHINGTON, D.C.: Weekend activities

PLACES TO VISIT
- The U.S. Capitol Building
- The Lincoln Memorial
- The Washington Monument
- The National Air and Space Museum
- The National Zoo
- The National Museum of Art

TOURS
- D.C. Heritage Walking Tour (3 hours)
- Canal Boat Ride on the Chesapeake Canal (1 hour)
- Bus Tour of Washington (1½ hours)
- White House Tour (1½ hours)

RESTAURANTS
- Pizzeria Paradiso (Italian food)
- Five Guys (American food)
- Restaurant Nora (Organic/natural food)
- Star of Siam (Thai food)

NIGHTLIFE
- Alvin Ailey American Dance Theatre at the Kennedy Center
- Opera at Constitution Hall
- Blues (music) at the Zoo Bar Café
- Dancing at the Black Cat Club

8 **GROUPS OF 4.** Tell each other what you're planning to do on Saturday and Sunday. Find out if you are doing any of the same things at the same time.

On Saturday, we're heading out early and having a quick breakfast near our hotel. Then we're taking a walking tour. At about 12:00, we're having lunch at ...

Writing

9 You want a friend to join you on your trip. Write an email telling your friend about your plans. Use the simple present and present continuous for future.

CONVERSATION TO GO

A: What time **does** the tour **start**?
B: It **starts** at 9:00, but we**'re meeting** at 8:30. Don't be late!

UNIT 10

On the other hand

Vocabulary Levels of difficulty
Grammar Modal verbs for ability
Speaking Describing abilities and challenges

Lesson A

Getting started

1 **PAIRS.** Write the expressions from the box in the correct columns.

a piece of cake	challenging	complicated	doable
hard	impossible	manageable	no trouble
simple	straightforward	tough	

It was . . .

Easy	OK	Difficult
a piece of cake	doable	challenging

2 Listen and check your answers. Then listen and repeat.

3 **PAIRS.** Discuss how you felt when you first learned to do three of these things. Use the expressions in Exercise 1.

| drive a car | program a VCR | ride a bicycle |
| speak English | take care of a baby | use the Internet |

A: How did you feel when you first learned to drive a car?
B: It was impossible at the beginning, but then it became manageable.

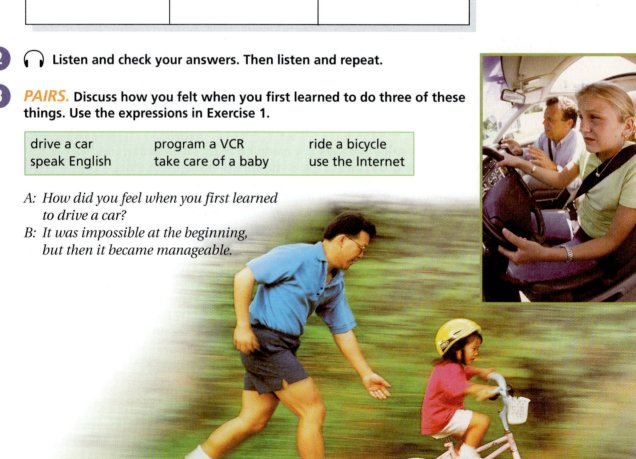

On the other hand

UNIT 10

OBJECTIVES

Students will:
- activate vocabulary related to abilities and challenges
- use modals for ability: *can/could, be able to, manage to*
- practice listening for and saying *can/can't* and *could/couldn't*

WARM-UP: ABILITIES

- Tell students this unit is about abilities, and that they will discuss being left-handed versus right-handed, and also talk about other challenges people have.
- Form groups of 3. Ask students to each think of one thing that is difficult for them to do. Give a personal example, such as *I think it is difficult to draw pictures, especially pictures of people.*
- Set a time limit of 3 minutes. Students discuss and compare their ideas.
- Call on a few students to report to the class.

Getting started

LANGUAGE NOTE

For vocabulary development, point out that one meaning of the ending *-able* is "capable of" and that it can be added to many verbs to make an adjective. Examples: *doable* (can be done), *washable* (can be washed), *manageable* (can be managed), *drinkable* (can be drunk).

OPTION: VOCABULARY PREVIEW

- In pairs. Ask students to study the words in Exercise 1. Encourage students to work out their meaning, and teach each other the adjectives they know.
- Go over any words the class doesn't know. Give examples: *complicated: Working on electronic equipment is so complicated. There are so many pieces and if you don't put them in the right place, the machine won't work!*

Exercise ❶

- Have students look at the expressions above the chart.
- Pair students. Explain the task: Students write the expressions in the correct column in the chart. They need to read each word and decide if it means *easy, OK,* or *difficult.* Go over the examples. As an example, explain that *a piece of cake* is an idiomatic expression that means *extremely easy.*
- Set a time limit of 5 minutes. While students are working, walk around the room, helping as needed.
- Do not go over the answers with the class until they have completed Exercise 2.

Exercise ❷

- 🎧 Tell students to listen and check their answers. Play the audio.
- 🎧 Play the audio again and have the students repeat.
- Go over the answers with the class.

Answer key	
easy:	a piece of cake, no trouble, simple, straightforward
OK:	doable, manageable
difficult:	challenging, complicated, hard, impossible, tough

Exercise ❸

- Form new pairs. Explain the task: Students use the expressions in Exercise 1 to say how they felt when they first learned to do the activities listed.
- Go over the example.
- Set a time limit of 3 minutes. Walk around the room, helping as needed.
- Call on individual students to present their sentences to the class.

WRAP-UP

For a note of humor, call on individual students and ask, *How did you find this vocabulary section? Was it challenging, doable, or was it a piece of cake?* Encourage students to use words from Exercise 1 in their responses.

EXTENSION

Form pairs. Students take turns quizzing each other on the words in Exercise 1. Remind students not to look in their books. Student A says *doable,* Student B says another word that has the same meaning: *OK, manageable, straightforward.* Then Student B says a word and Student A says one of the words with the same meaning.

Reading

> **LANGUAGE NOTE**
> The word *ambidextrous* comes from the Greek *ambi* (both) and *dexter* (right-hand). It means being skillful with both hands.

Exercise 4

- Pair students. Have them read the questions.
- Say, *I'm right-handed* (or *left-handed*, if that's the case), and point to a student in the class who writes with the opposite hand, and say (*Alex*) *is left- (right-) handed*. To verify that students understand the terms, act out writing with your right hand and say *right-handed*, repeat with the left hand and say *left-handed*, then switch hands back and forth and say *ambidextrous*. Point out that the terms *rightie* and *leftie* are also used.
- Set a time limit of 2 minutes for students to discuss the questions. Walk around the room, helping as needed.
- Call on a few students to answer the questions.

> **EXTENSION**
> Take a poll of the class to find out who is left-handed, who is right-handed, and who is ambidextrous. If someone is ambidextrous, ask for a writing sample on the board. Alternatively, ask ambidextrous students to tell the class what they can do with either hand.

Exercise 5

- Hold up your book and read the title, *Can Lefties Do it Right?* Ask students what *right* means here (*correctly*). Ask them to predict from the title what the article is about.
- Explain the task: Students read the article and answer the questions. Remind students to read the questions first.
- Set a time limit of 7 minutes. Suggest that students read the article twice. The first time, they read quickly to get just the main ideas. The second time, they should read more slowly to find the answers to the questions.
- Walk around the room, helping as needed.
- Have students work with a partner to check their answers.
- Go over answers with the class.

> **Answer key**
> 1. Left-handed people—because they are forced to use things originally designed for right-handed people.
> 2. It allows people to *easily* use things that are designed for right-handed people.

> **WRAP-UP**
> Ask the class: *Is there a connection between being left-handed and being successful? Why do you think so?* Encourage students to give examples to support their reasons.

Listening

Exercise 6

- Explain the task: Students listen to Mike and Juliana talk about being left-handed, and check (✓) in their books the things Mike and Juliana mention.
- 🎧 Play the audio of the first part of the conversation.
- 🎧 Play the audio again. Students confirm their answers.
- Go over the answers with the class.

> **Answer key**
> writing, drawing, kicking

Exercise 7

- Have students look at the pictures of the ability tests that Mike and Juliana did. Explain that they did the tests with their right hands. Elicit ideas about how hard Mike and Juliana probably thought the tests were.
- Explain the task: Students listen to the rest of the conversation to find out how hard each test was, and write M or J next to each result.
- 🎧 Play the audio. Play it again for students to confirm their answers.
- Have students work in pairs to check their answers.
- Go over answers with the class.

> **Answer key**
> throwing the ball:
> M   pretty easy
> J   a piece of cake
> writing:
> M   not too difficult
> J   really challenging
> using scissors:
> J   more manageable with right
> M   more straightforward with right
> drawing:
> M   pretty simple
> J   complicated

> **EXTENSION**
> Form pairs. Have students practice saying complete sentences with the answers from Exercise 6. You may want to write examples on the board. *It was pretty easy. It wasn't too difficult.*

🌐 Please go to www.longman.com/worldview for additional in-class model conversation practice.

HOMEWORK

- 📖 For homework, assign *Workbook* page 43, Vocabulary Exercises 1 and 2, and page 45, Listening Exercises 5 and 6.

Reading

4 **PAIRS.** Discuss these questions.

Do you know anyone who is left-handed?
Do you know anyone who is ambidextrous?
Are most people you know righties or lefties?

5 Read the article and answer the questions.

1. Who uses the "other" hand more often, lefties or righties? Why?
2. What is the advantage of being ambidextrous over being left-handed?

Can Lefties Do It Right?

Leonardo da Vinci, Marilyn Monroe, Paul McCartney, Pelé, Bill Gates . . . what do all these people have in common? They are all left-handed!

Being left-handed means that you find it more straightforward to do things with your left hand than with your right. It may also mean that you prefer to use your left foot or left eye (for example, with a camera).

Depending on how you define it, between 10% and 30% of people are left-handed. But most left-handers use their right hand for at least some things —like shaking hands.

Some people can do things with both hands equally well. Being ambidextrous is a big advantage over being a lefty, because we live in a world designed for right-handed people. Tools, sports equipment, and many musical instruments are designed for people who are right-handed.

If you are a lefty, take heart. Many famous lefties have risen above these challenges and succeeded, as Leonardo, Marilyn, Paul, Pelé, and Bill have shown.

Listening

6 Mike and Juliana are talking about being left-handed. Listen to the first part of their conversation. Check (✓) the things they mention.

___ writing   ___ cutting   ___ drawing   ___ kicking

7 Look at the pictures of the ability tests that Mike and Juliana did with their right hands. Listen to the rest of their conversation. How hard was each test? Write *M* for Mike or *J* for Juliana next to each result.

___ pretty easy   ___ not too difficult   ___ more manageable with right   ___ pretty simple
___ a piece of cake   ___ really challenging   ___ more straightforward with right   ___ complicated

Lesson A

10

Grammar focus

1 Study the examples of modals of ability.

She **can** play the piano really well. I **couldn't** cook until I got married. He **could** play chess when he was four. He **was able to** use a computer when he was five.	I was surprised that I **was able to** win that race. I **managed to** get an A in math. We **didn't manage to** get tickets to the opera. They **weren't able to** make reservations.

2 Look at the examples again. Complete the rules in the chart using *can (not), could (not), (not) be able to*, or *(not) manage to*.

Modals of ability: *can, could, be able to, manage to*
Use _____ to talk about ability in the present.
Use _____ or _____ to talk about a permanent ability in the past.
Use _____ or _____ (but not *could*) to talk about something that was possible at a specific time in the past.
Use _____ or _____ or _____ to talk about something that was not possible at a specific time in the past.

Grammar Reference page 145

3 Complete the sentences using the correct form of *can, could, be able to*, or *manage to*. Use each form at least once. Some sentences have more than one correct answer.

1. The homework was difficult, but in the end I __managed to__ do it.
2. Sara broke her leg last year, but she _____ walk just fine now.
3. Kyoko missed the train to the airport, but she _____ get a bus and arrived just in time for her flight.
4. When I was four, I _____ read all by myself.
5. I _____ save enough money for a new car, so I bought a used one.
6. My writing has improved, so I _____ pass the English test.
7. I took dance lessons this spring. Now I _____ dance to salsa music.
8. Tom locked his keys in the car with the keys inside, but he _____ open the door anyway.
9. Kim _____ fix her computer, so she called a technician.
10. I _____ tie my shoes until I was eight years old.

Grammar focus

> **LANGUAGE NOTES**
>
> Remind students that *can* and *could* have one form *(I/He/They can play tennis)*, while *be able to* changes for different subjects and tenses. *(I am able to go. He isn't able to go. They aren't able to go.)*
>
> Review how to form questions with modals of ability:
>
> - Questions formed with *can* ask about ability in the present: *Can you play tennis?*
> - A question about ability in the past usually includes a time marker: *Could you play tennis when you were in high school?*
> - Questions with *be able to* change according to subject and tense: *Are you/Were you able to look over the report? Is she/Was she able to look over the report?*
> - Questions with *manage* do not change with the subject: *Did he/she/you/they manage to get the tickets?*

> **WARM-UP**
>
> **Note:** Skip this warm-up if you're doing this lesson (Lesson B) during the same class period as Lesson A.
>
> - Books closed. Tell students they are going to listen again to the conversation between Mike and Juliana from Lesson A, Exercise 7.
> - Write these questions on the board. Do not write the words in parentheses.
>
>   *What does Juliana say about the ball test?*
>   (*I managed to throw the ball OK.*)
>
>   *What does Juliana say about the writing test?*
>   (*I couldn't do it at all.*)
>
>   *What does Juliana say about Mike's writing test?*
>   (*I can read it fine.*)
>
> - Tell students to listen for the answers to the questions.
> - 🎧 Play the audio.
> - Ask students for the answers. Write them on the board. Underline *managed to, couldn't, can*.

Exercise ❶

- Have students look at the examples and study the boldfaced words.
- Ask students which sentences are about permanent abilities (left column).
- Point out that modals for permanent ability can be used both in the present and past, while modals for one-time ability are used in the past only.

Exercise ❷

- Have students look at the examples again.
- Explain the task: Students complete the rules using *can (not), could (not), (not) be able to,* or *(not) manage to*.
- Go over the answers with the class.
- Refer students to Grammar Reference page 145, as needed.

> **Answer key**
>
> can
> could; was able to
> was/were able to; managed to
> couldn't; wasn't/weren't able to; didn't manage to

> **CULTURE NOTE**
>
> Although *salsa music* is popular music of Latin American origin, clubs and classes featuring salsa music have become popular in many areas of the U.S.

Exercise ❸

- Explain the task: Students complete the sentences with the correct form of *can, could, be able to,* or *manage to*. Point out that they should use each form at least once, and that there may be more than one correct answer in some cases.
- Go over the example with the class. Explain that *managed to* or *was able to* are both possible because the sentence expresses something that was possible at one particular occasion. On the other hand, *could* is not possible because the sentence does not express a permanent ability.
- Set a time limit of 5 minutes. Students complete the sentences.
- Have students work with a partner to check their answers.
- Go over the answers with the class.

> **Answer key**
>
> 1. managed to / was able to
> 2. can
> 3. managed to / was able to
> 4. could
> 5. couldn't / wasn't able to / didn't manage to
> 6. managed to / was able to
> 7. can
> 8. managed to / was able to
> 9. didn't manage to / wasn't able to / couldn't
> 10. couldn't / wasn't able to

EXTENSION

- Pair students. Write *can, could, be able to,* and *managed to* on the board. Have students write four sentences that are true for them using each of the words on the board. Set a time limit of 8 to 10 minutes.
- Call on individual pairs and ask them to read a sentence containing the word you point to at the board. Make sure you cover all the modals.

Pronunciation

Exercise ④

- 🎧 Play the audio and have students listen. Ask them to notice the difference in the pronunciations of *can* and *can't* and of *could* and *couldn't*. Call attention to the different colors used to show the weak and strong pronunciations.
- Explain that in the middle of a sentence, *can* and *could* usually have weak pronunciations.
- Ask students to listen to the vowel sounds in the weak and strong pronunciations. Elicit, or point out, that the weak pronunciations have the short, unclear vowel sound /ə/ (schwa) and the strong pronunciations have clearer vowel sounds.

Exercise ⑤

- 🎧 Play the audio. Stop it after each sentence and ask students to repeat it chorally.
- Ask a few individual students to repeat the sentences and check their pronunciation.
- Focus on making the weak forms short. You can use the respellings "kn" and "kd" to illustrate the weak pronunciations of *can* and *could*.
- Students may have difficulty with the syllabic /n/ in *couldn't*. Encourage them to pronounce the *n* without adding a vowel sound before it. The tip of the tongue goes to the roof of the mouth to pronounce /d/ and stays there without moving to make the following /n/ sound.

Exercise ⑥

- Tell students they are going to listen to the sentences in their books. Explain the task: Students listen for the word *can, can't, could,* or *couldn't* in each sentence and write the word they hear.
- 🎧 Play the audio. If necessary, stop the audio after each sentence and play it more than once.

> **Answer key**
> 1. can   4. couldn't
> 2. could   5. can't
> 3. can't   6. can

Speaking

Exercise ⑦

- Pair students. Explain the task: Students do ability tests like the ones Mike and Juliana did. Hold up your book and point to the chart. Read or have a student read aloud the four tests. To check understanding of *flip a coin*, demonstrate flipping and catching a coin.
- Tell students to take notes in the chart about their results. Remind students to be sure to use their left hand if they're right-handed, and vice versa.
- Set a time limit of 10 minutes for the students to complete the tests and take notes. Walk around the room, helping as needed.

Exercise ⑧

- Combine two pairs to form groups of 4. Go over the example in the book. Remind students to use *can, could, couldn't,* and so on.
- Have students in each pair take turns talking about their results. Tell students to find out how their partners did.

> **WRAP-UP**
>
> Call on a few students to report to the class how their partners did.

TRB For additional interactive grammar practice, have students do the reproducible activity for this unit in the *Teacher's Resource Book*.

Writing

Exercise ⑨

- Assign the writing task for class work or homework. Remind students to use the modals of ability and some of the vocabulary from the unit.
- **TRB** Optionally, give students a copy of the model (see the *Teacher's Resource Book,* Writing Models). Ask them to read the model and notice the modals of ability that are used.
- If students don't have the model, write the following on the board:

    I didn't do very well on the ability tests. I can't do much with my "other hand."

    Walk around the room to make sure students understand the task.
- If the assignment is done in class, have a few students read aloud as time permits.

For suggestions on how to give feedback on writing, see page xiv of this *Teacher's Edition*.

CONVERSATION TO GO

- As the students leave class, have them read the dialogue.
- Check understanding by asking students another way to say B's line. (*It was easy.*)

HOMEWORK

- 📖 For homework, assign *Workbook* page 44, Grammar Exercises 3 and 4, and page 45, Pronunciation Exercises 7 and 8.
- 💿 If students do not have the *WorldView Workbook*, assign listening homework from the Student CD. Write on the board:

    Track 24
    Who was able to use the scissors easily?
- 🎧 Tell students to listen to the audio and write their answer. Have them bring it to the next class. (*both Mike and Juliana were able to*)

Pronunciation

4 🎧 Listen. Notice the short, weak pronunciation of *can* and *could* and the stronger pronunciation of *can't* and *couldn't* in these sentences.

She **can** throw a ball with either hand.

He **could** play chess when he was four.

I **can't** draw with my left hand.

I **couldn't** cook until I got married.

5 🎧 Listen again and repeat.

6 🎧 Listen. Write the word you hear in each sentence: *can, can't, could,* or *couldn't*.

1. They __can__ dance very well.
2. She _____ ride a bike.
3. He _____ play the guitar.
4. My grandmother _____ speak English.
5. I _____ read without glasses.
6. He _____ write with his left hand.

Speaking

7 **BEFORE YOU SPEAK.** Do the ability tests in the chart. Use your "other" hand. Take notes in the chart.

8 **PAIRS.** Take turns. Tell each other how you did on the ability tests.

A: *I was able to write* have fun, *but no one could read it!*
B: *I couldn't write with my left hand. It was impossible!*

> throw a paper ball into a wastepaper basket
>
> write the words "have fun"
>
> flip and catch a coin
>
> draw a face

Writing

9 Write a brief report describing your results on the ability tests. Were you surprised by your results? Use *can, could, be able to,* and *manage to*.

CONVERSATION TO GO

A: Did you **manage to** fix the car?
B: Yes, it was **a piece of cake**!

UNIT 11

Trading spaces

Vocabulary Furniture
Grammar Present perfect for indefinite past
Speaking Talking about changes you can see

Lesson A

Getting started

1 **PAIRS.** Match the words with the furniture and other items in the photo.

armchair _m_	basket ____	bookcase ____	cabinet ____
carpet ____	drapes ____	fireplace ____	lamp ____
magazine rack ____	plants ____	picture ____	rug ____
sofa ____	stereo speakers ____	throw pillow ____	window ____

2 Match the sentences with the responses.

1. I don't like the sofa that color. _e_
2. That window needs some drapes. ____
3. The cabinet looks terrible there. ____
4. The floor in this room looks old. ____
5. That throw pillow on the arm chair is ugly. ____

a. You're right. Let's make some.
b. Why don't we refinish it?
c. Let's throw it out and get a new one.
d. Let's move it to the other side of the room.
e. Me, neither. Why don't we cover it?

3 **PAIRS.** Share your opinions about the room in the photo.

Trading spaces

UNIT 11

OBJECTIVES

Students will:

- activate vocabulary related to furniture and home redecoration
- use the present perfect for indefinite past
- practice listening for and saying different sounds represented by the letter *a*

BACKGROUND INFORMATION

"Trading Spaces" is a popular TV show in the U.S. In the show, couples trade places and re-decorate a room in each other's home. Each couple is given a budget and the help of professional designers. TV viewers like the show not only to see how the rooms are redecorated, but also to watch the reactions of the people as they see the changes. The word *space* can mean someone's home, so in this case the title of the show means trading homes.

WARM-UP: WHO WOULD YOU CHANGE SPACES WITH?

- Tell students this unit is about redecorating a home and describing the changes.
- Have students think about people they know (friends, a family members, co-workers). Ask them to choose someone they would want to exchange houses with.
- Form groups of 3. Set a time limit of 4 minutes. Students take turns telling each other who they would want to trade houses with and why.
- Call on a few students. Ask them to tell the class about one person they want to exchange houses with and why.

Getting started

LANGUAGE NOTES

- *Curtains* and *drapes* are both large pieces of hanging cloth that cover a window. Drapes are heavy curtains, typically found in a living room, while curtains are usually lighter.
- Note that in unstressed syllables, the letter *a* often has the sound /ə/: *sofa, magazine*.

OPTION: VOCABULARY PREVIEW

- Ask students to think about the rooms in a house. Write on the board:

  cook breakfast   eat dinner
  watch TV   wash clothes
  brush teeth   park car
  sleep

- Have students say which rooms you do the activities in. Explain any words students don't understand.

Exercise 1

- Pair students. Have them look at the photo.
- Explain the task: Students match the words in the book with the furniture and other things in the photo. Go over the example.
- Set a time limit of 5 minutes. While students are working, walk around the room, helping as needed.
- Combine 2 pairs to compare their answers.
- Go over answers with the class.

Answer key

armchair **m**	magazine rack **n**
basket **b**	plants **f**
bookcase **k**	picture **g**
cabinet **e**	rug **p**
carpet **o**	sofa **a**
drapes **h**	stereo speakers **j**
fireplace **c**	throw pillow **l**
lamp **d**	window **i**

Exercise 2

- Explain the task: Students match the sentences with the responses. Tell students the sentences on the left are opinions about the room, and the sentences on the right are suggestions for changes. Go over the example.
- Set a time limit of 5 minutes. Walk around the room, helping as needed.
- Go over the answers with the class. Explain that *Why don't we* and *Let's* are phrases used to make suggestions.

Answer key

1. e   2. a   3. d   4. b   5. c

EXTENSION

Have students work with a partner to practice reading the conversations.

Exercise 3

- Pair students. Tell them to share their opinions about the room in the photo, using the sentences in Exercise 2 as their model. Instead of *Let's . . .* or *Why don't we . . .* students can also use the formula *I'd (I would)*.
- Have students talk about specific details, such as the carpet or the picture, and ask what they would change.
- Set a time limit of 5 minutes. Tell students to take notes on their opinions as they talk. Walk around the room, helping as needed.
- Call on a few pairs to report their opinions to the class.

T48

Pronunciation

Exercise 4

- Ask students to look at the example words at the top of the columns. Explain that all these words are spelled with the letter *a*, but that /a/ has a different sound in each.
- 🎧 Play the audio. Ask students to listen to the way /a/ is pronounced in each of the example words.
- You may want to stop the audio after each word and ask students to repeat it to check their awareness of the different pronunciations.

Exercise 5

- Explain the task: Students look at the words in the box and decide how the letter *a* (or the underlined *a*) is pronounced in each case.
- Do the first word as an example with the class. Write the word *armchair* on the board, underlining the first *a* (as in the *Student Book*). Ask students which column to write it in. Say the word, or ask students to say it, and ask students if they think the answer was correct.
- Pair students. Walk around the room, helping as needed.

Answer key

magazine:	table:	art:
rack	drapes	armchair
basket	bookcase	carpet
plants	fireplace	
cabinet		
lamp		

Exercise 6

- 🎧 Tell students to listen and check their answers. Play the audio.
- 🎧 Play the audio again and have students repeat each word chorally. (The words are grouped by sound.)
- Go over the answers with the class.

Reading

Exercise 7

- Hold up your book and read the title, *TV Choice*. Tell students this is a description of an episode of the TV program "Trading Spaces" that will be shown this week. Provide background information about the TV show to make it easier for students to follow the episode summary.
- Explain the task: Students read the show summary and answer the questions. Have students read the questions first. Set a time limit of 5 minutes.
- Walk around the room, helping as needed.
- Have students work with a partner to check answers.
- Go over answers with the class.

Answer key
They are neighbors.
They are redecorating a room in each other's house.
They have 2 days and one thousand dollars.

Listening

Exercise 8

- Tell the students that Pedro and Carla Macedo have returned home. They see their new living room for the first time. Have students listen to their reactions and decide who likes the room more.
- 🎧 Play the audio.
- 🎧 Go over the answer. Play the audio again as needed.

Answer key
Pedro likes it more.

Exercise 9

- Explain the task: Students listen again to find out the specific changes that were made. They match the columns to describe what was done. Tell students to read the questions first. Go over the example.
- 🎧 Play the audio.
- 🎧 Play the audio again so that students can confirm their answers.
- Have students work with a partner to check answers. Students can do this by reading the completed sentences aloud.
- Go over the answers with the class.

Answer key
1. e   4. a
2. c   5. b
3. d   6. f

🌐 Please go to www.longman.com/worldview for additional in-class model conversation practice.

HOMEWORK

- 📖 For homework, assign *Workbook* page 46, Vocabulary Exercises 1 and 2, and page 48, Listening Exercises 5 and 6.

Pronunciation

4 🎧 Listen. Notice the pronunciation of the letter *a* in each word.

m**a**gazine	t**a**ble	**a**rt

5 **PAIRS.** How is the letter *a* pronounced in the following words? Write each word in the correct sound group.

armchair   basket   bookcase   cabinet   carpet

drapes   fireplace   lamp   plants   rack

6 🎧 Listen and check your answers. Then listen and repeat.

Reading

7 Read about the program "Trading Spaces" in *TV Choice* and answer these questions.

1. What is the relationship between the Macedos and the Nelsons?
2. What are the two couples doing?
3. How much time and money do they have?

TV Choice

This week on "Trading Spaces," two pairs of neighbors, Pedro and Carla Macedo and John and Cassie Nelson, work with professional designers to completely redecorate a room in each other's home. They have two days and a budget of $1,000 each. When the Macedos and Nelsons return to their own homes, will they be pleased or angry? Watch "Trading Spaces" on Tuesday evening at 8:00 to find out.

Listening

8 🎧 Listen to Carla and Pedro's reactions to their new living room. Who likes the room more, Carla or Pedro?

9 🎧 Listen again. Match the columns to describe what the Nelsons have done to the Macedos' living room.

1. They've thrown away ____
2. They've painted ____
3. They've made ____
4. They've moved ____
5. They've bought ____
6. They've put ____

a. the sofa.
b. covers and throw pillows for the armchairs.
c. the walls red.
d. new drapes.
e. the bookcase.
f. the books in the cabinet.

Grammar focus

1 Study the examples of present perfect for the indefinite past.

What **have** they **done**?	They**'ve painted** the walls bright red.
What **has** he **made**?	He**'s made** new drapes.
Has she **bought** new armchairs?	No, she **hasn't**.

2 Look at the examples again. Underline the correct words to complete the explanations in the chart.

Present perfect for indefinite past

Use the present perfect to describe a **present / past** action.
The time of the action **is / is not** important.

Grammar Reference page 145

3 The Nelsons are looking at the kitchen that the Macedos have just remodeled. Use the present perfect form of the verbs in the box to complete the conversation. Sometimes more than one answer is correct.

change	hang	move	paint	put	replace	take

Before

After

Announcer: Hi, Cassie. Hi, John. Look at your new kitchen!

Cassie: Wow! Our neighbors Pedro and Carla
   (1) _have changed_ everything.

John: Yes, I see Pedro **(2)** _____ the stove over to
   this wall . . . and are those new kitchen cabinets?

Announcer: Yes, Pedro and Cassie **(3)** _____ them
   all, and they **(4)** _____ them all gray.

Cassie: I love the cabinets . . . , but what happened to the
   washing machine?

Announcer: Pedro **(5)** _____ it to the basement.

John: And over on that wall? What's all that?

Announcer: That was Carla's idea. She **(6)** _____ all the pots and pans up there.
   I think that's really handy.

Cassie: And the floor. There's something different about the floor.

John: Yes, they **(7)** _____ the floor, too. It now has beautiful red tiles. It feels
   like we have a whole new kitchen!

Grammar focus

LANGUAGE NOTES

- Remind students that the present perfect = *have* + past participle. Point out that the contraction of *he/she has* is *he's/she's* (*He's arrived, She's called*). In conversation, this sounds the same as the contraction for *he is/she is* (*He's tall, She's from Spain*). It's necessary to use context to know which is being used.

- To help students understand when to use the present perfect, instead of the simple past, one guideline is to use it to talk about an action in the past that has an impact or relevance in the present. For example, with *I wrote a letter*, the action was completed some time in the past; that's all we know.

- Contrast this with *I have written a letter*. Here, the action was in the past, but it is still relevant. I may either write another letter, or the impact of my writing the letter is somehow important now (e.g., *I've written a letter to the authorities complaining about noise on the street, so we should wait a few days before calling to complain again*). In Exercise 3 (and in the Reading and Listening sections), the use of the present perfect focuses on recent actions in the past (redecorating) whose impact is seen now (there are many changes to see).

WARM-UP

Note: Skip this warm-up if you're doing this lesson (Lesson B) during the same class period as Lesson A.

- Books closed. Tell students they are going to listen again to the conversation between Pedro and Carla.
- Tell students to think about if the actions they mention are in the present, the past, or the future and what verb phrases express this.
- 🎧 Play the audio for Lesson A, Exercises 8 and 9.
- Ask students about the actions (*the past*) and what verbs they remember (*they've redecorated/refinished/moved/done*).

Exercise ❶

- Have students look at the examples and study the boldfaced words.
- Ask students to focus on the first two examples. Elicit from students that they are questions and answers.
- Ask students to study the entire set of examples, then ask these questions:

    What do you notice about the verbs? (*Most of them have two parts.*)

    Which is the main verb in each sentence? (*do, paint, make, make, buy*).

    Which is the auxiliary (not main) verb in each sentence? (*have*)

    What do you notice about word order in questions? (*The verb comes before the subject.*)

Exercise ❷

- Have students study the examples again.
- Tell students to underline the correct word to complete each explanation.
- Have students work with a partner to read the examples aloud, and then check their answers.
- Go over the explanations with the class.
- Refer students to Grammar Reference page 145, as needed.

Answer key

past   is not

Exercise ❸

- Explain the task: Students complete the conversation with the present perfect forms of the verbs in the box. Point out that sometimes more than one answer is correct. Go over the example.
- Set a time limit of 5 minutes. Walk around the room, helping as needed.
- Have students work with a partner to check their answers.
- Go over the answers with the class.

Answer key

1. have changed
2. has moved/has taken
3. have hung/have replaced
4. have painted
5. has taken/has moved
6. has put/has hung/has moved
7. have replaced/have changed

EXTENSION

Have students work in groups of 3 to practice reading the conversation. If you want, you can also call on various trios to present their conversations to the class.

Teacher's Notes — Lesson B

Speaking

Exercise 4

- Pair students. Hold up your book and point to the before and after pictures of the apartment. Tell students a team of designers has just redecorated this room and made six changes.
- Explain the task: Students find the six changes in the pictures.
- Go over the example. Tell students to take notes as they discuss the pictures.
- If needed, do a quick vocabulary review for the names of the items that were not covered in the Getting started section (*wall, drapes, armoire, TV set*). Optionally, encourage students to use a dictionary.
- Set a time limit of 5 minutes. Walk around the room, helping as needed.
- Do not go over the answers with the class until they have completed Exercise 5.

Exercise 5

- Combine two pairs to form groups of 4.
- Have students in each pair compare their notes and decide if they found the same six changes.
- Go over the changes with the class. Have students give their answers using complete sentences.
- Optionally, write the answers on the board and have students check their verb forms and spelling.

> **Answer key**
> They have painted the walls green.
> They have changed the drapes.
> They have moved the armoire.
> They have hung a picture over the television.
> They have changed the color of the armchairs.
> They have cleaned the floor.

Exercise 6

- Have students stay in the same groups. Tell them to discuss the changes the designers made, and other changes they would make. Remind students of the expressions from Exercise 1 (*Why don't we, Let's*) they can use to share their ideas.
- Set a time limit of 5 minutes. Walk around the room, helping as needed.
- Call on one student from each group to summarize their ideas for the class.

TRB For additional interactive grammar practice, have students do the reproducible activity for this unit in the *Teacher's Resource Book*.

Writing

Exercise 7

- Assign the writing task for class work or homework. Remind students that they can write about changes that aren't true. A recent change in their life might include a new job, a new hobby, or a new apartment.
- **TRB** Optionally, give students a copy of the model (see the *Teacher's Resource Book*, Writing Models). Remind students to use present perfect and some of the vocabulary from the unit.
- If students don't have the model, write the following on the board:

    Dear Steven:
    Do you remember that in my last letter I told you I was planning to move to a more modern apartment? Well, I didn't move. Instead, I've totally redecorated my . . .

    Walk around the room to make sure students understand the task.
- If the assignment is done in class, have students read their work aloud in small groups as time permits.

For suggestions on how to give feedback on writing, see page xiv of this *Teacher's Edition*.

CONVERSATION TO GO

- As the students leave class, have them read the dialogue.
- Optionally, call on a few students to tell you other changes they have made in their homes.

HOMEWORK

- For homework, assign *Workbook* page 47, Grammar Exercises 3 and 4, and page 48, Pronunciation Exercises 7, 8, and 9.
- If students do not have the *WorldView Workbook*, assign listening homework from the Student CD. Write on the board:

    Track 28
    Where is the sofa now?

- Tell students to listen to the audio and write their answer. Have them bring it to the next class. (*It's under the window.*)

Speaking

4 **PAIRS.** A team of designers has just redecorated this room. Look at the *before* and *after* photos and find the six changes the design team has made. You have five minutes. Take notes.

A: *They've painted the walls green.*
B: *Right. And they've changed the drapes.*

Before

After

5 **GROUPS OF 4.** Compare your notes. Have you found the same six changes?

6 Do you like the changes? Are there any different changes you would make?

Writing

7 Write a letter to a friend. Describe recent changes you have made either in your home or in your life. You can use your imagination. Use the present perfect for indefinite past.

CONVERSATION TO GO

A: **Have you decorated** the house?
B: We**'ve painted** the walls, but we **haven't done** anything else.

Lesson B

51

UNIT 12

A soccer fan's website

Vocabulary Time expressions with *in*, *on*, *at*, or no preposition
Grammar Modals: *may*, *might*, *could* for possibility
Speaking Talking about possible future arrangements

Lesson A

Getting started

1 **PAIRS.** Write the time expressions in the correct columns.

~~last Friday afternoon~~	the evening	Thursday
next Monday evening	the morning	yesterday morning
noon	this Thursday	6:45 P.M.

in	on	at	no preposition
			last Friday afternoon

2 🎧 Listen and check your answers.

3 **PAIRS.** Complete the sentences with a preposition where necessary.

1. I met Josephine for lunch __at__ noon.
2. Where were you _____ last night?
3. Pedro came home _____ 4 A.M.
4. I might go to a soccer game _____ Saturday afternoon.
5. Su-ki may phone you _____ the evening.
6. Did you see Yori _____ yesterday evening?
7. Her plane left _____ midnight.
8. I have to go to soccer practice _____ Monday.

Pronunciation

4 🎧 Listen. Notice the weak pronunciation of the prepositions *at*, *in*, and *on*.

We're leaving *at* ten.
We can walk around *in* the morning.
I think I'll go shopping *on* Tuesday.

We arrive *at* four *in* the afternoon.
There's a tour *at* noon *on* Sunday.
Let's meet *at* our hotel *in* the evening.

5 🎧 Listen again and repeat.

6 **PAIRS.** Take turns reading the sentences in Exercise 3.

A soccer fan's website

UNIT 12

OBJECTIVES

Students will:
- activate vocabulary related to schedules and plans
- use modals for possibility: *may, might, could*
- practice weak pronunciations of *in, at, on* in prepositional phrases

WARM-UP: I'M BUSY ON . . .

- Tell students this unit is about schedules and future plans. Ask students to think about their own plans.
- Form pairs. Set a time limit of 3 minutes. Have students tell each other about their weekly schedule. Give an example. *On Mondays, I go to the gym.*
- Call on some students to tell you about any changes in their schedule for next week. Give an example. *I usually go to the gym on Mondays, but next week I'm going on Tuesday.*

Getting started

Teaching Tip! Prepositions

Preposition combinations for time are difficult to master. Be sure that students understand:

- *In* is used with periods of time: *in the morning/ the afternoon/evening.*
- *At* is used with a specific time: *at noon, at 6:00 P.M.*
- *On* is used with days of the week: *on Tuesday.*

(**Note:** *At night* is the exception to these rules.)

OPTION: VOCABULARY PREVIEW

- Write the following on the board: *English class, washed your car, drink coffee.* Call on students and ask questions using the prompts, e.g, *When do you have English class? (On . . . and . . .), What time is the class? (At . . .), When is the last time you washed your car? (Last . . .), When do you drink coffee? (In . . .).*
- As the students answer, write the prepositions in columns on the board.

Exercise 1

- Pair students. Have students look at the time expressions above the chart.
- Explain the task: Students write the expressions in the correct column in the chart. Go over the example. Write on the board, *I went to the bank last Friday afternoon.* Point out there is no preposition before *last*.
- Set a time limit of 5 minutes. While students are working, walk around the room, helping as needed.

Exercise 2

- 🎧 Tell students to listen and check their answers. Play the audio.

- 🎧 Play the audio again, as needed, for students to confirm their answers.
- Go over the answers with the class.

Answer key

in: the evening, the morning
on: Thursday
at: noon, 6:45 P.M.
no preposition: last Friday afternoon, yesterday morning, next Monday evening, this Thursday

Exercise 3

- Divide students into new pairs. Explain the task: Students complete the sentences. Go over the example.
- Set a time limit of 3 minutes. As students work, walk around the room and provide help as needed.
- Go over the completed sentences with the class.

Answer key

1. at
2. no preposition
3. at
4. no preposition
5. in
6. no preposition
7. at
8. on

Pronunciation

Exercise 4

- Explain that prepositions are usually unstressed and have weak pronunciations.
- 🎧 Play the audio and have students listen. Ask them to notice the weak sound of the prepositions.
- You can contrast the strong and weak pronunciations of *at* /ət/ and *in* /ən/ by saying the words first by themselves and then in a sentence: *at* /ət/, *We're leaving at* /ət/ *ten; in* /ən/, *We arrive in* /ən/ *the afternoon.*
- Remind students that weak pronunciations often have the short, unclear sound /ə/.

Exercise 5

- 🎧 Play the audio. Stop the audio after each line and have students repeat it chorally.
- Encourage students to read each prepositional phrase as a whole and to stress the noun; for example: *at our **hotel** in the **evening**.*
- Ask a few individual students to repeat the sentences to check their pronunciation.

Exercise 6

- Explain the task: Students work with a partner to read the completed sentences in Exercise 3 aloud.
- Pair students. Walk around the room, helping as needed.

T52

Teacher's Notes — Lesson A

Teacher's Notes — Lesson A

Reading

BACKGROUND INFORMATION

Manchester United is a famous soccer team from Manchester, England. They have fans worldwide.

Heathrow Airport is one of two main airports that serve London for international travel.

Raffles Hotel is a popular hotel and tourist spot in Singapore with several well-known restaurants.

Exercise 7

- Have students look at the web page. Elicit what students know about Manchester United. Students who are soccer fans will have heard of the team, and may also know its current players. Provide information as needed.
- Pair students. Have them read the sentences in the book and fill in the blanks.
- Go over the answers with the class.

Answer key   soccer, football

Teaching Tip! Reading dates

In a schedule, *the* is said before the date: *Sunday the twenty-first*. Contrast: *I was born June twenty-first / I was born the twenty-first of June / We're leaving on Sunday the twenty-first*. Remind students that dates in American English follow the month/day/year format: 6/21/04 (*June 21, 2004*).

Exercise 8

- Hold up your book, point to the web page and read the heading, "Peter Gibson's Manchester United web page." Ask, *What is he organizing?* Elicit the answer (*a trip for Manchester United's Southeast Asia tour*). To familiarize students with the web page, ask a few questions and have students scan for the answers. This will help students practice reading for specific information. Example questions: *Where are they leaving from? What day is the bus tour? When do they arrive at Heathrow?*
- Explain the task: Students read the web page to answer the questions. Have students read the questions first.
- Set a time limit of 1 minute. Walk around the room, helping as needed.
- Go over answers with the class.

Answer key

1. Kuala Lumpur, Singapore, Bangkok   3. 10 days
2. three

EXTENSION

Have students read the itinerary in more depth. Ask more detailed questions, such as *How long will they stay in Kuala Lumpur? Where are they having dinner in Singapore? When does their return flight leave?*

WRAP-UP

Have students say whether or not they would like to join this trip, and give reasons. Divide students into pairs to share their ideas. Set a time limit of 5 minutes.

Listening

Exercise 9

- Tell students they are going to listen to a phone conversation between Peter and another fan who is going on the trip. Peter calls to explain that there may be some changes to the schedule.
- Explain the task: Students listen and circle the information on the website that might change.
- 🎧 Play the audio.
- 🎧 Play the audio one more time so that students can confirm their answers.
- Go over the answers with the class.

Answer key

(Friday) 12:00 noon   (Monday) at Raffles
(Saturday) 6:00 A.M.   (Tuesday) sightseeing tour
(Sunday) bus tour

Exercise 10

- Have students look at the questions or read them aloud with a class.
- 🎧 Play the audio again. Have students listen for the answers and make brief notes. If needed, play the audio again.
- Have students work in pairs to check their answers.
- Go over the answers with the class.

Answer key

1. He's calling to tell him about a few possible changes to the trip schedule.
2. The restaurant is full that night.
3. Yes, because he might have to buy some things for his girlfriend.

EXTENSION

🎧 Play the audio again. Give students other details to listen for, such as *Why are they considering a walking tour on Sunday instead? What might happen if someone cancels the reservation at Raffles? Does the other fan seem upset about the changes?* (*No*)

💻 Please go to www.longman.com/worldview for additional in-class model conversation practice.

HOMEWORK

- 📖 For homework, assign *Workbook* page 49, Vocabulary Exercises 1 and 2, and page 51, Listening Exercises 5 and 6.

Reading

7 *PAIRS.* Manchester United is a well-known sports team. The sport is called _____ in the U.S. and _____ in most other English-speaking countries.

8 Peter is a big fan of Manchester United. Read his web page and answer the questions.

1. Which three cities is Peter planning to visit?
2. How many games is he going to?
3. How long is the trip?

Peter Gibson's Manchester United WEBPAGE

I'm organizing a trip for MANCHESTER UNITED'S tour of SOUTHEAST ASIA.

Travel plans as of the 10th

Date	Time	Activity
Friday 20th	12:00 noon	Leave London Heathrow Airport
Saturday 21st	6:00 A.M.	Arrive in Kuala Lumpur
	7:00 P.M.	Group dinner at hotel
Sunday 22nd	10:00 A.M.	Bus tour
	9:00 P.M.	Manchester United vs. Malaysian Allstars at Bukit Jalil Stadium
Monday 23rd	9:00 A.M.	Fly to Singapore
	7:00 P.M.	Group dinner at Raffles
Tuesday 24th	10:00 A.M.	Sightseeing tour
	8:00 P.M.	Manchester United vs. Singapore League XI – National Stadium
Wednesday 25th	10:00 A.M.	Fly to Bangkok
Thurs. 26th – Sat. 28th		Sightseeing, group meals, etc.
Sunday 29th	6:30 P.M.	Manchester United vs. Thailand National Team
Monday 30th	5:00 A.M.	Return flight to U.K.
	11:00 A.M.	Arrive at London Heathrow Airport

Interested in joining us? Click here.

Listening

9 🎧 Listen to Peter's phone conversation with another fan. Circle the information on the web page that might change.

10 🎧 Listen again and answer the questions.

1. Why is Peter calling Charles?
2. What is the problem with the dinner at Raffles?
3. Does Charles think that a shopping trip is a good idea? Why?

Lesson B

12

Grammar focus

1 Study the examples of modals of possibility.

> It **could** be difficult to get a taxi.
> I **couldn't** ask for any more time off.
> You **may** need to get up earlier.
>
> Some people **may not** go sightseeing.
> We **might** leave at ten o'clock.
> We **might not** take a bus.

2 Look at the examples again. Fill in the blanks in the chart with *may, may not, might, might not, could,* and *couldn't.*

> **Modals: *may, might, could* for possibility**
>
> Use _____ , _____ , or _____ when it is possible that something will happen.
> Use _____ or _____ when it is possible that something won't happen.
> Use _____ when it is impossible that something will happen.

Grammar Reference page 146

3 Complete the conversation with the appropriate form of the words. More than one answer is possible in some cases.

> could (not)   may (not)   might (not)

Rob: I'm not sure yet, but I **(1)** _may not_ be able to go to the game on Saturday.

Ben: Why? I've got the tickets already!

Rob: I know, but they **(2)** _____ need me at work. They'll let me know tonight for sure.

Ben: Why do you have to work on the weekend?

Rob: We have this production deadline, and there **(3)**_____ be some last-minute changes.

Ben: Why don't you ask Chuck to work for you?

Rob: No, my boss **(4)** _____ get upset. I **(5)** _____ do that.

Ben: You never know. He **(6)** _____ mind, as long as someone's there!

Rob: Besides, Chuck **(7)** _____ have things to do on Saturday.

Ben: Or he **(8)** _____. You never know. He **(9)** _____ be free.

Rob: OK, let me call him. Chuck? Hi! It's me, Rob. I have a huge favor to ask. There's this game on Saturday, but I **(10)** _____ be able to go because I **(11)** _____ have to go to the office, and . . . OK, thank you.

Ben: What did he say?

Rob: He said yes, but he also said he **(12)** _____ ask me to work for him next weekend. I guess it's only fair!

54

Grammar focus

> **LANGUAGE NOTES**
> - *May, might,* and *could* in this section refer to the future. Point out that *could* is both the past tense of *can* (*I couldn't call you last night*) and also a modal to express future possibility (*I could be late for the meeting*).
> - *May, might,* and *could* have one form only, and there is no *–s* in the third person singular (*She might, he may*).
> - Questions are not formed with *may, might,* and *could*. Questions are formed with other phrases, such as in <u>When</u> *are you planning to go?* or <u>Are you going to</u> *a movie?* or <u>Do you think</u> *you'll go?* The answers often contain *may, might,* and *could: We* <u>may</u> *go next week, we* <u>might</u> *go, We* <u>could</u>.
>
> **Note:** It is not necessary to answer with a complete sentence if the meaning is clear: *Will you get home late tonight? / I might.*

WARM-UP

Note: Skip this warm-up if you're doing this lesson (Lesson B) during the same class period as Lesson A.

- Books closed. Tell students they are going to listen again to the conversation between Peter and Charles that they heard in the Listening section.
- Tell students to think about how they know the changes are not definite yet.
- 🎧 Play the audio for Lesson A, Exercise 9.
- Ask students what verb forms they remember that told them the changes are not definite yet. (*might, could, may*)
- Optionally, ask students if they remember any phrases they heard (*might leave, may arrive, could take*) and write them on the board.

Exercise ❶

- Have students look at the examples and study the boldfaced words.
- Ask students what they notice about the *could/may/might* + verb combinations. (*The main verb is always in the base form, without* to.)
- Elicit from students that *couldn't* is the contracted form of *could not*.
- Ask students whether the sentences refer to the past, present, or future (future possibility).

Exercise ❷

- Have students study the examples again.
- Tell students to complete the explanations using *may, may not, might, might not, could, couldn't*.
- Have students work with a partner to check their answers.
- Go over the answers with the class.
- Refer students to Grammar Reference page 146, as needed.

> **Answer key**
>
> *may, might,* or *could*
> *may not* or *might not*
> *couldn't* (*could not*)

Exercise ❸

- Explain the task: Students complete the conversation with the words in the box. Point out that more than one answer is possible in some cases.
- Have students look at the example. Ask students why *may not* is correct and which words helped them understand this. (*the first part,* <u>I'm not sure yet</u>.) Point out that *might not* is also correct here.
- Have students complete the exercise individually. Set a time limit of 5 minutes.
- Have students work with a partner to check their answers.
- Go over the answers with the class.

> **Answer key**
>
> 1. may not / might not
> 2. may / might / could
> 3. could / may / might
> 4. could / may / might
> 5. couldn't (could not)
> 6. may not / might not
> 7. may / might / could
> 8. may not / might not
> 9. may / might / could
> 10. may not / might not
> 11. may / might
> 12. may / might

WRAP-UP

Have students work in pairs to practice reading the conversations.

Speaking

Exercise 4

- Hold up your book and present the calendar page. Explain the task: Students fill in the calendar with four activities for Saturday. Remind students to include at least two definite and two possible activities, and tell them to leave at least three hours open in the afternoon or evening.
- Set a time limit of 3 minutes. Walk around the room, helping as needed.

(**Note:** If you find students have difficulty thinking of activities, review some activities with the class. Then give students another minute to complete their planners before continuing with Exercise 5.)

Exercise 5

- Pair students. Tell them to discuss their schedules and find a time on Saturday to go to a movie. Remind them the movie is two hours long, and they need to arrive at the theater 30 minutes early.
- Go over the example. Set a time limit of 5 minutes.
- Call on various pairs to say when they plan to meet. If they couldn't find a time to meet, ask them to explain why.

TRB For additional interactive grammar practice, have students do the reproducible activity for this unit in the *Teacher's Resource Book*.

Writing

Exercise 6

- Assign the writing task for class work or homework.
- **TRB** Optionally, give students a copy of the model (see the *Teacher's Resource Book*, Writing Models). Ask them to read the model and notice what modals are used.
- If students don't have the model, write the following on the board:

  Hi, Marcos –
  Just a quick note to let you know I might not be able to go skiing with you next month. I'm not sure yet, but I may have to go to a family reunion . . .

  Walk around the room to make sure students understand the task.

- Have a student read aloud the first few sentences or write them on the board.
- If the assignment is done in class, ask a few students to read their emails aloud.

For suggestions on how to give feedback on writing, see page xiv of this *Teacher's Edition*.

CONVERSATION TO GO

- As the students leave class, have them read the dialogue.
- Optionally, ask students to read the dialogue in pairs, switching parts.

HOMEWORK

- For homework, assign *Workbook* page 50, Grammar Exercises 3 and 4, and page 51, Pronunciation Exercises 7 and 8. Assign *Workbook* Self-quiz Units 9–12.
- If students do not have the *WorldView Workbook*, assign listening homework from the Student CD. Write on the board:

  Track 30
  How will the tour group get to the hotel in Kuala Lumpur?

- Tell students to listen to the audio and write their answer. Have them bring it to the next class. (*by taxi or bus*)

BEFORE NEXT CLASS

Have students review the material they have studied in these four units:

Unit no.	Review Grammar	Listen to Student CD	Study Grammar Reference
9	verb tenses	Track 22	Page 145
10	modals for ability: *can/could, be able to, manage to*	Track 24	Page 145
11	present perfect for indefinite past	Track 28	Page 145
12	modals for possibility: *may, might, could*	Track 30	Page 146

FOR NEXT CLASS

TRB Make copies of Quiz 3 in the *Teacher's Resource Book*.

Speaking

4 **BEFORE YOU SPEAK.** Complete the calendar page with four of the activities on the list, or add your own ideas. Include two activities that you might do, and two activities that you plan to do. Be sure to leave at least three hours open during the afternoon or evening.

- go to the gym
- visit my (relative)
- go shopping
- clean the house
- have coffee with (name)
- get a haircut

DAILY PLANNER	
Saturday	
11:00 A.M.	6:00 P.M.
12:00 P.M.	7:00 P.M.
1:00 P.M.	8:00 P.M.
2:00 P.M.	9:00 P.M.
3:00 P.M.	10:00 P.M.
4:00 P.M.	11:00 P.M.
5:00 P.M.	

5 **PAIRS.** Find a time to meet on Saturday to go to a movie together. You need to get to the theater at least half an hour before the show.

A: *Are you free on Saturday afternoon? I thought we could go to a movie.*
B: *Sure, what time?*
A: *What about two?*
B: *Well, I might have coffee with my friend Sarah at 1:30…*

PLAZA 3
555-6101
Show times:
12:00 P.M., 2:30 P.M., 4:40 P.M.,
7:10 P.M., 10:00 P.M.

Writing

6 Write a short email to a friend describing all the things you may/might/could do in the next few weeks or months. Use the modals for possibility.

CONVERSATION TO GO

A: I heard you **might not** go to the soccer game tomorrow.
B: If I get this work done tonight, I **may** go after all.

Review 3: Units 9–12

Unit 9 The river

1. 🎧 Listen to the model conversation.

2. **BEFORE YOU SPEAK.** Look at the brochure for the Chicago Trolley Tour. Pick three places that you'd like to visit and circle them.

3. **GROUPS OF 3.** Work together to plan your group's visit to Chicago. You probably won't be able to visit all the places that the Chicago Trolley Tour goes to. Agree on the places you'd like to visit and how long you'll stay at each place.

TOUR SCHEDULE:

Daily – 9 A.M. to 4:30 P.M. The first trolley heads out at 9 A.M. sharp. You can get on and off the trolley at any stop. Tour guides can show you around at many locations. The tour takes about three hours, but you can skip some stops and stay longer at others.

Boarding Locations/Stops:

* Sears Tower: Chicago's tallest building
* Marshall Field's: a grand old department store
* Chicago River South: take a walk along the beautiful Chicago River
* Art Institute: see our world-famous art museum
* Museum Campus: (includes the Field Museum of Natural History, the Shedd Aquarium, and the Adler Planetarium)
* Navy Pier: for great food, shopping, and entertainment
* Water Tower: the historic stone building that survived the Chicago Fire
* Rainforest Cafe: take a break and have a great lunch
* House of Blues: listen to great Chicago blues

Chicago's Old Town Trolley Tour

Unit 10 On the other hand

4. 🎧 Listen to the model conversation and look at the chart.

5. **PAIRS.** Take turns. Do the ability tests and take notes in the chart.

Test	You	Your partner
wink To wink is to close and open one eye as a signal to someone. Can you?		
wiggle your ears It takes great muscle control to move only your ears. Can you?		
touch your toes without bending your knees Some people are able to touch their toes without bending their knees. Can you?		
whistle a famous song Can you whistle a well-known song? Which one?		

6. **GROUPS OF 4.** Report your results to another pair.

Review 3: Units 9–12

📼 You may wish to use the video for Units 9–12 at this point. For video activity worksheets, go to www.longman.com/worldview.

Unit 9: The river

OBJECTIVE

Grammar: focus on using verb tenses for schedules and plans

Exercise 1

- Explain the task: Students listen to the model conversation.
- 🎧 Play the audio.
- Write on the board, a few phrases Speaker A uses to make suggestions: *I want to go . . . so I thought I'd . . .* and *Then I thought it would be (fun) to . . .* Also write down phrases Speakers B and C use to show agreement: *That sounds good, That's a good idea, That sounds perfect.*
- 🎧 Tell students to listen for these phrases. Then, play the audio again.

Exercise 2

- Students work alone. Explain the task: Students are going to take the Chicago Trolley Tour. They each look at the schedule, and decide three places they want to visit.
- Set a time limit of 3 minutes. While students are working, walk around the room, helping as needed.

Exercise 3

- Form groups of 3. Explain the task: Students work in their groups to plan their trolley tour. They discuss the differences in their plans and agree on some changes, as well as how long they will stay at each place. Encourage students to use the phrases on the board in their discussions.
- Set a time limit of 5 minutes. Walk around the room, helping as needed.

WRAP-UP

- Ask several students what they have planned for the tour. Depending on the level of the class, you may also have students explain what they each had planned to do as well as what they finally agreed to.
- To prompt students, write on the board: *I wanted to go to . . . , but (Maria) wanted to . . . , We decided to . . .* Time limit: 3 minutes.

Unit 10: On the other hand

OBJECTIVE

Grammar: focus on using modals for ability: *can/could, be able to, manage to*

Exercise 4

- Explain the task: Students listen to the model conversation.
- 🎧 Play the audio. Then write on the board the phrases: *I could only manage to . . .* and *I managed to . . . ; Can you . . . ? I can/couldn't.*
- 🎧 Play the audio again, and have the students listen to the conversation.

Exercise 5

- Form pairs. Explain the task: Students do the ability tests and take notes in the chart about how they did.
- Set a time limit of 10 minutes for students to do the tests, and take notes. Walk around the room, helping as needed.
- Have pairs discuss how they did on the tests. Remind them to use the phrases on the board.

Exercise 6

- Have pairs form groups of 4. Explain the task: Students compare how they did on the test with another pair.
- Call on pairs of students to report on how the other pair in their groups did.

WRAP-UP

- Work with the whole class. Take a poll and find out who could do each of the actions; ask: *Who can wink? Show the class.*
- Continue with the next two tests. For the last test, call on individual students to whistle, as time permits.

T56

Unit 11: Trading spaces

OBJECTIVE

Grammar: focus on using the present perfect for indefinite past

Exercise 7

- Explain the task: Students listen to the model conversation.
- 🎧 Play the audio. Then, ask students, *What did the mother change?* If students cannot answer, write on the board: *the stove, the cabinets*.
- 🎧 Play the audio again, and then ask the question again. (*She's moved the stove. She's redone the cabinets. She's painted them.*)

Exercise 8

- Form pairs. Explain the task: Students look at the photos and take turns saying what has been done to remodel the kitchen. Tell students to talk about the things listed. Before students begin, check vocabulary, and answer any questions they have.
- Set a time limit of 8 minutes. Have pairs talk about what the mother has done. Walk around the room, helping as needed.

Exercise 9

- Students continue in pairs.
- Explain the task: Students discuss the remodeling changes. They say if they are happy with the changes, and give reasons. Encourage students to talk about specific details as they give their reasons. Suggest that they take brief notes, as needed. Set a time limit of 5 minutes.

> **WRAP-UP**
>
> - Take a poll and find out which changes the students think are good and which changes they don't like.
> - For the changes they don't like, ask them to suggest alternative changes. Examples: *You don't like the color of the cabinets. What color would be better? You don't like where the stove is? Where would you like it?*

Unit 12: A soccer fan's website

OBJECTIVE

Grammar: focus on using modals for possibility: *may, might, could*

Exercise 10

- Explain the task: Students listen to the model conversation. Tell them two people are talking about what they are going to do this weekend.
- 🎧 Play the audio. Ask: *How do you know he hasn't decided yet?* (*He uses <u>might</u>, <u>could</u>, <u>may</u>.*)
- 🎧 Play the audio again, and have the students listen for what he might do.
- Conclude by asking them what he might do on Saturday morning (*meet with friends*), Saturday afternoon (*go to a movie*), and after the movie (*go to a party*).

Exercise 11

- Form groups of 3.
- Explain the task: Students take turns talking about their weekend plans. Each student names at least two things he or she might do and might not do each day. Tell students to take brief notes on each other's plans.
- Set a time limit of 5 minutes. Walk around the room, helping as needed.

> **WRAP-UP**
>
> Call on students to report to the class what someone in their group is doing. Example, *(Tanya) might go to the beach. She might not go to visit her family.*

Before   After

Unit 11 Trading spaces

7 🎧 Listen to the model conversation and look at the pictures.

8 **PAIRS.** While you were away at school, your mother has completely remodeled the kitchen. Look at the photos and take turns saying what she's done. Talk about these kitchen items.

| cabinets | counter top | dishwasher | pots and pans |
| sink | spice rack | stove | |

9 Are you happy with the changes? Why or why not?

Unit 12 A soccer fan's website

10 🎧 Listen to the model conversation.

11 **GROUPS OF 3.** Take turns talking about your weekend plans. Name at least two things you might do each day and two things you might not do.

World of Music 2

My Way
Frank Sinatra

Vocabulary

1 **PAIRS.** Match the expressions with their meanings.

1. He faced the final curtain. _e_
2. He followed a charted course. ___
3. I bit off more than I could chew. ___
4. I saw it through. ___
5. They stood tall. ___
6. He had his fill. ___
7. I took the blows. ___

a. I finished it completely.
b. I took on more than I could handle.
c. I accepted the consequences.
d. He had enough.
e. He met the end without fear.
f. He had a plan for his actions.
g. They were proud and determined.

Listening

2 🎧 Listen to the song. What kind of person does the song portray?

1. regretful and depressed
2. proud and independent
3. adventurous and irresponsible

3 🎧 Listen to the song again and complete the lyrics on page 59.

4 **PAIRS.** Compare your answers.

> From the 1940s through the 1980s, **Frank Sinatra** was probably the most famous entertainer in the U.S. Sinatra lived his life without caring what people thought, and the song, "My Way," became his signature song.

World of Music 2

OBJECTIVES

- introduce Frank Sinatra's song, "My Way"
- vocabulary: symbolic language
- express personal interpretation of a song

> **WARM-UP**
> - Books closed. Ask: What does independence mean to you? (Possible answers: *working alone, not asking for help, doing what is right, acting the way I want to*)
> - Ask students what, in their opinions, makes a person independent. Write the answers on the board as students say them.
> - Tell students they will be listening to a song about independence. Tell them to keep in mind their ideas about independence as they listen to the song.

Reading

- Tell students to read the information about Frank Sinatra. Tell them they are going to listen to one of Frank Sinatra's most popular songs, "My Way." Ask them if they know the song or if they have heard of it. Encourage the class to hum or sing parts of the song that they know.
- Ask: *Why is "My Way" known as Frank Sinatra's signature song? (Because it expressed his personality very well.)* Encourage students to explain their answers. (*He was very independent, because he didn't care what people thought about him.*)

Vocabulary

Exercise ❶

- Pair students.
- Explain the task: Students match the expressions with their meanings.
- Go over the example. (**Note:** "The final curtain" may refer to the last performance of a performer, but it also symbolizes death. This can be mentioned later after the students work with the song.)
- Set a time limit of 5 minutes. While students are working, walk around the room, helping as needed.
- Go over the answers with the class. Explain that these are expressions that many people are familiar with.

> **Answer key**
> 1. e   5. g
> 2. f   6. d
> 3. b   7. c
> 4. a

Listening

Exercise ❷

- Explain the task: Students listen to the song and then decide what kind of person the song portrays. Encourage students to consider the melody and tone of the song as well as the lyrics.
- Ask students to read the adjective pairs listed. Check if students have any questions about the vocabulary.
- 🎧 Play the song as students listen. Then have students mark their answer choice.
- 🎧 Tell students to listen again and confirm their answer. Then play the song again.
- Go over the answer. Encourage students to give reasons.

> **Answer key**
> Answer may vary, but 2 is the most likely choice.

T58

Exercise ❸

- Explain the task: Students listen to the song again and complete the blanks on page 59.
- 🎧 Play the song. Play the song again for the students to confirm their answers.
- Do not go over answers with the class until they have completed Exercise 4.

Exercise ❹

- Form pairs. Have pairs check their answers.
- Go over the answers with the class. One way to do this is to call on individual students to read a section of the lyrics aloud for the class.

> **Answer key**
>
> *My Way*
> Frank Sinatra
> Writer(s): Revaux/François/Anka
> Notes: First performed by Claude François ("Comme d'habitude")
> Translated and arranged by Paul Anka for Frank Sinatra.
>
> And now, the end is near;
> And so I face the final <u>curtain</u>.
> My friend, I'll say it clear,
> I'll state my case, of which I'm certain.
>
> I've <u>lived</u> a life that's full.
> I've <u>traveled</u> each and ev'ry highway;
> And more, much more than this,
> I <u>did</u> <u>it</u> my way.
>
> Regrets, I've <u>had</u> a few;
> But then again, too few to mention.
> I did what I <u>had</u> to do
> And <u>saw</u> it through without exemption.
>
> I <u>planned</u> each charted course;
> Each careful step along the byway,
> And more, much more than this,
> I <u>did</u> <u>it</u> my way.
>
> Yes, there were times, I'm sure <u>you</u> <u>knew</u>
> When I <u>bit</u> <u>off</u> more than I <u>could</u> chew.
> But through it all, when <u>there</u> <u>was</u> doubt,
> I ate it up and spit it out.
> I <u>faced</u> it all and I <u>stood</u> tall;
> <u>And</u> <u>did</u> <u>it</u> my way.

> I've <u>loved</u>, I've laughed and <u>cried</u>.
> I've <u>had</u> my fill; my share of losing.
> And now, as tears subside,
> I find it all so amusing.
>
> To think I did all that;
> And may I say—"Not in a shy way,"
> "Oh, oh no, not me,
> I <u>did</u> <u>it</u> my way."
>
> For what is a man, what has he got?
> If not himself, then he has not
> to say the things he truly feels;
> And not the words of one who kneels.
> The record shows I <u>took</u> the blows—
> <u>And</u> <u>did</u> <u>it</u> my way!

Speaking

Exercise ❺

- Form groups of 3. Explain the task: Students discuss the questions. Have students read the questions, or read them aloud for the class.
- Set a time limit of 10 minutes. Remind students to explain their opinions and to find lines and phrases in the song that support their point of view. Walk around the room, helping as needed.
- Conclude by calling on groups to share their ideas with the class. Ask: *After listening to this song, what do you think was important to Frank Sinatra?* Help students make a list of words and expressions to describe him. (Possible answers: *proud, strong, independent, true to himself, he didn't regret what he did in the past*)

> **OPTION**
>
> 🎧 Play the song and have the students sing along after they go over the answers. Play again as time permits. Ask students what kind of mood or feeling they have after listening to the song.

My Way

And now, the end is near;
And so I face the final ____.
My friend, I'll say it clear,
I'll state my case, of which I'm certain.

____ ____ a life that's full.
____ ____ each and ev'ry highway;
And more, much more than this,
I ____ ____ my way.

Regrets, ____ ____ a few;
But then again, too few to mention.
I did what I ____ to do
And ____ it through without exemption.

I ____ each charted course;
Each careful step along the byway,
And more, much more than this,
I ____ ____ my way.

Yes, there were times, I'm sure ____ ____
When I ____ ____ more than I ____ chew.
But through it all, when ____ ____ doubt,
I ate it up and spit it out.
____ ____ it all and I ____ tall;
____ ____ ____ my way.

____ ____, ____ laughed and ____.
____ ____ my fill, my share of losing.
And now, as tears subside,
I find it all so amusing.

To think I did all that;
And may I say – "Not in a shy way,"
Oh no, oh no, not me,
I ____ ____ my way.

For what is a man, what has he got?
If not himself, then he has not
to say the things he truly feels,
And not the words of one who kneels.
The record shows I ____ the blows –
____ ____ ____ my way!

Speaking

5 **GROUPS OF 3.** Discuss these questions.

What lines from the song best explain the character's personality?
Sinatra announced his retirement two years after recording "My Way."
Do you think the singer is expressing a personal feeling in this song?
Why or why not?

UNIT 13

Green card

Vocabulary Immigration
Grammar Review: present perfect with *for* and *since*
Speaking Talking about how long you have done something

Getting started

1 **PAIRS.** Complete the text with the words in the box.

| green card | ID (identification) card | immigration | nationalities |
| passport | permanent resident | ~~tourist visa~~ | work permit |

GOING TO THE UNITED STATES

Before you visit the United States, check to see if you need a (1) *tourist visa*. Some (2) _____ need to have one, but others don't. If you have a valid visa but want to stay longer than 90 days, you can apply to the (3) _____ department for an extension. If you want to work in the U.S., you need a (4) _____. If you want to live and work in the U.S. permanently, you need to go through a long process to get a (5) _____. When you get it, you are considered a (6) _____ of the United States. No matter what your status, it is a good idea to carry an (7) _____ or your (8) _____ with you so that you can prove who you are.

2 🎧 Listen and check your answers.

3 **PAIRS.** Talk about a trip you'd like to take to another country. Use as many words from Exercise 1 as you can.

I'd like to go to Spain. First I need to get a passport. I don't need a tourist visa because . . .

Green card

UNIT 13

Teacher's Notes — Lesson A

OBJECTIVES

Students will:

- activate vocabulary related to foreign travel and immigration
- review the present perfect with *for* and *since*
- practice listening for and saying strong, weak, and contracted forms of *have/has*

WARM-UP: IMMIGRATION

- Tell students this unit is about immigration and foreign travel, and that *immigration* is the process of entering another country in order to live there. Explain that a *green card* is a kind of identification card for people who move to the United States and become permanent residents.
- Pair students. Explain the task: Students make a list of the reasons someone might immigrate to another country. Give an example, *to get a better job*.
- Set a time limit of 2 minutes. While students are working, walk around the room, helping as needed.
- Call on a few students to read their ideas. Compile a list on the board.

Getting started

LANGUAGE NOTES

- *Green card* (See *Warm-Up*, above.)
- The short form *ID* (*card*) is typically used instead of the full word *identification* (*card*). In addition, the verb form is *to ID*: *The teacher needs to ID all students before the trip.*

OPTION: VOCABULARY PREVIEW

- Form groups of 3. Set a time limit of 3 minutes. Have students study the words in the box in Exercise 1.
- Ask students to group the words in the following categories: documents (*green card, passport, ID card, tourist visa, work permit*), word/s about someone's status (*permanent resident*), words about people coming to a country (*immigration, nationalities*).
- Go over the answers with the class. Explain any words students don't understand.

Exercise ❶

- Pair students. Hold up your book and present the text *Going to the United States*. Tell students this is a page from a travel guide. It has tips on visas and other information.
- Go over the list and ask the class which documents from the box they would need to visit a foreign country (*ID card, passport, tourist visa*).
- Elicit from students the meaning of *resident* (*person who lives in a country*) as opposed to *tourist* (*person visiting a country*). Then ask students which documents from the box they would need if they moved to another country (*work permit; green card, if the country is the United States*).
- Explain the task: Students use the words in the box to complete the text. Remind them to use the context to help them understand new words and phrases.
- Set a time limit of 5 minutes. Walk around the room, helping as needed.
- Have pairs form groups of 4 to compare their answers.
- Do not go over the answers with the class until they have completed Exercise 2.

Exercise ❷

- 🎧 Play the audio. Students check their answers.
- 🎧 Play the audio again as needed.
- Go over the answers with the class.

Answer key

1. tourist visa
2. nationalities
3. immigration
4. work permit
5. green card
6. permanent resident
7. ID (identification) card
8. passport

WRAP-UP

Have students work in pairs to practice reading the completed text.

Exercise ❸

- Form new pairs. Explain the task: Students talk about a trip they'd like to take to another country. Go over the example or provide a personal example.
- Tell students to use as many of the words from Exercise 1 as they can. Remind students to use *I'd like to . . .* Point out that if they are not sure what is required for a particular country, they can talk about what they *might* need to do. (*I might need a tourist visa. I have to find out.*)
- Set a time limit of 3 minutes. Walk around the room, helping as needed.
- Call on a few students to present to the class.

EXTENSION

Have students work in pairs to quiz each other on the words in Exercise 1. Student A says *I need this when I go on vacation to some (countries)*, and Student B says *tourist visa*. Students take turns giving the clue and identifying the vocabulary word.

Teacher's Notes — Lesson A

Reading

BACKGROUND INFORMATION

There are a few ways a foreign national can legally stay indefinitely in the U.S.: one way is to get a green card; another is to marry a U.S. citizen. The immigration service sometimes checks to find out if a couple is married "in name only" (a U.S. citizen has married someone only to help that person stay in the U.S. and gain permanent residency). An immigration officer will ask questions to find out if they live together and share a life together. This situation was depicted in the film *Green Card* (1990). In it, a Frenchman marries an American woman because he wants to be able to stay in the U.S.

Exercise 4

- Present the situation in the book. Elicit ideas of why the immigration officer is interviewing Kate and Rod Bolton. Provide some information as needed.
- Ask students to write down why they think the immigration officer is interviewing them.

Exercise 5

- Hold up your book and point to the interview form and illustrations of Rod and Kate. Ask students to identify what the case number is. (*247*)
- Explain the task: Students read the notes to find out the reason for the interview. Tell students to read quickly to find the answer.
- Set a time limit of 1 minute.
- Go over the answer with the class.

Answer key

The immigration officer is interviewing them to see if they have a real marriage.

Exercise 6

- Tell students to read the officer's notes again. Have students pay attention to the questions in the chart.
- Tell students that for now they will not write anything in Kate's column. They will return to the chart in Exercise 7.
- Have students complete the chart with the information Rod gave. Walk around the room, helping as needed.
- Pair students and have them check their answers.
- Go over the answers with the class.

Answer key

1. 8 months ago
2. San Francisco
3. 6 months ago
4. at a party in New York
5. 3 months ago
6. dance teacher
7. yes

Teaching Tip! Listening for content

Having students listen first without writing their answers will allow them to focus on understanding the content of the interview.

Exercise 7

- Tell students the officer is also going to interview Kate. Elicit ideas about why he is asking her the same questions. (*He wants to compare their answers.*)
- Explain the task: Students listen to the interview with Kate and complete the chart with Kate's information.
- 🎧 Play the audio as students listen, without writing.
- 🎧 Play the audio again for students to write their answers.
- Pair students and have them check their answers.
- Go over the answers with the class.

Answer key

1. 8 months ago
2. Los Angeles
3. 4 months ago
4. at a party
5. 3 months ago
6. dance teacher
7. no

Exercise 8

- Tell students to look at the information in their chart and see what is different. Go over the example.
- Pair students, and set a time limit of 5 minutes. Walk around the room, helping as needed.
- Have pairs work with another pair to compare their answers. Then have them decide whether Kate and Ron have a real marriage (or if it is only so that she can stay in the U.S.).
- Go over the answers with the class.

Answer key

Rod and Kate gave different information about:
where Kate lived before she went to New York. (He said San Francisco, she said Los Angeles.)
how long ago they met. (He said 6 months, she said 4 months.)
whether they like doing the same things. (He said they do, she said they don't.)

🌐 Please go to www.longman.com/worldview for additional in-class model conversation practice.

HOMEWORK

- 📖 For homework, assign *Workbook* page 54, Vocabulary Exercises 1 and 2, and page 56, Listening Exercises 5 and 6.

Reading

4 Kate and Rod Bolton recently got married. They are from different countries. Why do you think an immigration officer is interviewing them?

5 Read the officer's notes and check your answer.

Case number: 247 – Kate Bolton (English) Rod Bolton (American)

Reason for interview: Kate Bolton – application for green card. Check that the marriage is a real marriage.

Summary of what Rod Bolton said during his interview:

- Kate came to the U.S. eight months ago, but she lived in San Francisco when she first got here.
- He (Rod Bolton) met Kate at a party in New York six months ago, and they fell in love immediately.
- They were married three months ago.
- Kate is a dance teacher.
- They usually do everything together. They like the same things.

6 Read the officer's notes again and complete the first column of the chart with the information Rod gave him.

	Rod's answers	Kate's answers
1. When did Kate come to the U.S.?	8 months ago	
2. Where did she live before she came to New York?		
3. When did Kate and Rod meet?		
4. Where did they meet?		
5. When did they get married?		
6. What is Kate's job?		
7. Do they like doing the same things?		

7 🎧 Listen to the immigration officer's interview with Kate. Complete the chart in Exercise 6 with Kate's information.

8 **PAIRS.** Look at the information in Exercise 6. What information is different?

Kate said she met Rod four months ago, but Rod said it was six months ago.

Lesson B

13

Grammar focus

1 Study the examples of present perfect with *for* and *since*.

> (+) I've known him **for** four months.
> (−) She hasn't been to the U.K. **since** last year.
> (?) Has she lived in New York **for** a long time?
>   Yes, she has. / No, she hasn't.

2 Look at the examples again. Underline *for* or *since* to complete the rules in the chart.

Present perfect with *for* and *since*
Use **for** / **since** to talk about a period of time.
Use **for** / **since** to talk about a specific point in time.

Grammar Reference page 146

3 Write the expressions from the box in the correct columns.

> ~~a couple of days~~   ages   an hour   ~~Friday~~   4:00 A.M.   I was a child
> last summer   May   nine months   two years   2001

for	since
a couple of days	Friday

4 Use the correct form of the verb in parentheses or *for* or *since* to complete the conversation between Rod (R) and the immigration officer (I).

I: Nice cat. **(1)** _Have you had_ (you/have) him **(2)** ___for___ a long time?

R: Yes, I **(3)** _____ (have) him **(4)** _____ ten years.

I: And how long **(5)** _____ (you/live) in this apartment, Mr. Bolton?

R: **(6)** _____ April 15.

I: And your wife? How long **(7)** _____ (she/be) in the United States?

R: **(8)** _____ last September.

I: And how long **(9)** _____ (you/know) your wife?

R: **(10)** _____ six months.

I: And you **(11)** _____ (be) married **(12)** _____ February?

R: Yes, we **(13)** _____ .

I: And your wife **(14)** _____ (not be) to England **(15)** _____ last September?

R: No, she **(16)** _____ .

Grammar focus

> **LANGUAGE NOTE**
> The present perfect is used in this context to talk about something that started in the past and continues up to now. It is used with *since* to talk about a specific point in time in the past when something began: *He has been studying English since 2002.* It is used with *for* to talk about a period of time that started in the past: *He has studied English for two years.* Since it is common for students to confuse *for* and *since*, review this with them.

> **WARM-UP**
>
> **Note:** Skip this warm-up if you're doing this lesson (Lesson B) during the same class period as Lesson A.
> - Books closed. Tell students they are going to listen again to the immigration officer's interview with Kate.
> - Tell students to listen for phrases about time. Give a few examples: *for two months, since January.* Tell them to write the phrases with the verb forms.
> - 🎧 Play the audio.
> - Write on the board: *For how long?*
> - Ask individual students what phrases about time they heard (*I've been in the U.S. for eight months, I've only been in New York for five months, I've known Rod since December, I've known him for four months, you've been married for three months*).

Exercise ❶
- Have students look at the examples and focus on the boldfaced words and the verb form.
- Explain to students that (+) means affirmative sentence, (–) means negative sentence, and (?) means a question.
- Elicit the verb tense (present perfect).
- Point out the short form of the answer to the question; it is not necessary to repeat all of the information (the main verb is not needed; only the subject and the appropriate form of *have*).
- Optionally, review the formation of the present perfect (*have* + past participle of the verb). Explain that *have* functions as an auxiliary verb in these sentences and that *has* is the third person singular of *have*.

Exercise ❷
- Have students study the examples again.
- Elicit what words follow *for* and *since* (*for* is followed by *four months, several months,* and *a long time; since* is followed by *December* and *last year*).
- Students underline *for* or *since* to complete each rule.
- Pair students and have them check their answers.
- Go over the answers with the class.
- Refer students to Grammar Reference page 146, as needed.

> **Answer key** for   since

Exercise ❸
- Explain the task: Students write the expressions in the correct columns. Remind them to use *for* with a period of time, and *since* with a point in time.
- Set a time limit of 5 minutes. Have students complete the exercise individually.
- Have students check their answers in pairs.
- Go over the answers with the class.

> **Answer key**
>
> **For:** a couple of days, two years, nine months, an hour, ages
>
> **Since:** Friday, 4:00 A.M., last summer, 2001, I was a child, May

> **EXTENSION**
>
> Draw a horizontal arrow on the board with a starting point marked with a vertical slash (|➔). Elicit points of time from students (*7:00, January, 2001*). Write a few of them above the starting point. Then elicit a few periods of time (*20 minutes, 3 months, 2 years*) and write them along the horizontal line.
>
> Call on individual students and ask, *How long have you studied English?* (*Since 2002/For . . . years*). If time allows, ask other questions that allow students to use *for/since* in their answers, for example, *How long have we been in class today?* (*We've been here since . . . o'clock/We've been here for . . . minutes*).

Exercise ❹
- Tell students this is a conversation between Rod and the immigration officer. Explain the task: Students write the correct form of the verb in parentheses or *for* or *since* to complete the conversation.
- Set a time limit of 5 minutes. Have students complete the exercise individually.
- Have students check their answers in pairs.
- Go over the answers with the class.

> **Answer key**
>
> 1. Have you had
> 2. for
> 3. have had
> 4. for
> 5. have you lived
> 6. Since
> 7. has she been
> 8. Since
> 9. have you known
> 10. For
> 11. have been
> 12. since
> 13. have
> 14. hasn't been
> 15. since
> 16. hasn't

> **WRAP-UP**
>
> Have students work with a partner to practice reading the conversation.

Pronunciation

Exercise 5

- 🎧 Play the audio. Have students listen to the different pronunciations of *have* and *has* and their contractions.
- Stop the audio after each expression in order to highlight the different weak and strong pronunciations.
- Point out the disappearing /h/ sounds in *How long have you been married?* and *How long has she been in the U.S.?*
- Ask students to notice where the different weak and strong pronunciations are used: *Have* and *has* have weak pronunciations before another word and strong pronunciations at the end of a sentence. *Haven't* and *hasn't* always have strong pronunciations.

Exercise 6

- 🎧 Play the audio. Stop the audio after each line and have students repeat it chorally.
- Ask a few individual students to repeat the sentences to check their pronunciation.
- Encourage students to use the weak and contracted forms of *have/has*.

Exercise 7

- Explain the task: Students work with a partner and practice reading the conversation in Exercise 4.
- Check that students are aware of the weak pronunciation of *for* in connected speech: *for* /fər/ *six months*.
- Pair students. Walk around the room, helping as needed.

Speaking

Exercise 8

- Combine pairs to form groups of 4 and assign roles: Students A, B, C, and D. Tell them they will do an immigration interview. Students A and B are a couple. Students C and D are immigration officers. The immigration officers will interview them both, but separately, in order to decide if they are really married.
- Tell Students A and B to turn to page 138, and Students C and D to turn to page 140. They should not look at each other's books.
- Give students 5 minutes to prepare. Students A and B work together to decide on the personal information they will both say. Students C and D prepare a list of questions that they will ask. Remind students that because the interviews will be done separately, they both need to write down the information or the questions. Walk around the room, helping as needed.

Exercise 9

- Students stay in the same groups. Explain the task: Student C interviews Student A and Student D interviews Student B. Help students arrange their seating so that they can't hear each other's answers.
- Tell Students C and D to take notes about the interviews.

- Go over the example in the book.
- Set a time limit of 10 minutes. Walk around the room, helping as needed.

Exercise 10

- Students stay in the same groups. Tell Students A and B to compare their interviews and find out if they answered the questions the same way. Have Students C and D compare their notes, then decide if A and B are really married.
- Have Students C and D tell Students A and B their conclusion, and their reasons for it. Encourage Students A and B to challenge C and D's conclusion and give their own reasons.

TRB For additional interactive grammar practice, have students do the reproducible activity for this unit in the *Teacher's Resource Book*.

Writing

Exercise 11

- Assign the writing task for class work or homework.
- **TRB** Optionally, give students a copy of the model (see the *Teacher's Resource Book,* Writing Models). Ask them to read the model and notice where the present perfect is used with *for* and *since*. Remind students to use some of the vocabulary from this unit.
- If students don't have the model, write on the board:

  I interviewed Kate and Rod Bolton on November 28th. My conclusion is that their marriage is not real because . . .

  Walk around the room to make sure students understand the task.
- If the assignment is done in class, have students exchange their papers with a partner, as time permits.

For suggestions on how to give feedback on writing, see page xiv of this *Teacher's Edition*.

CONVERSATION TO GO

- As the students leave class, have them read the dialogue.
- Optionally, elicit from students the note of humor in the dialogue (the character in the chair is a ghost).

HOMEWORK

- 📖 Assign *Workbook* page 55, Grammar Exercises 3 and 4, and page 56, Pronunciation Exercises 7 and 8.
- 💿 If students do not have the *WorldView Workbook,* assign listening homework from the Student CD. Write on the board:

  Track 31
  What does the interviewer ask to use?
- 🎧 Tell students to listen to the audio and write their answer. Have them bring it to the next class. (*the bathroom*)

Pronunciation

5 🎧 Listen. Notice the weak and strong pronunciations of *have* and *has*. Notice that the contracted form of *has* is the same as the contracted form of *is*.

How long **have** you been married?	We**'ve** been married for three months.
How long **has** she been in the U.S.?	She**'s** been here since September.
Has she been to England since then?	No, she **hasn't**. / Yes, she **has**.
Have you known each other for a long time?	No, we **haven't**. / Yes, we **have**.
Your neighbor **hasn't** seen you together.	We **haven't** lived here very long.

6 🎧 Listen again and repeat.

7 *PAIRS.* Practice the conversation in Exercise 4.

Speaking

8 *2 PAIRS.* Students A and B, you are a married couple. Prepare for an immigration interview. Look at page 138. Students C and D, you are immigration officers. Prepare your questions for the interview. Look at page 140.

9 *2 PAIRS.* Conduct the interviews. Student C, interview Student A. Student D, interview Student B. Interview them on opposite sides of the room so they can't hear each other's answers! Take notes.

C: *How long have you known each other?*
A: *We've known each other for about 10 months, since last September.*

10 *GROUPS OF 4.* Students A and B, compare your interviews. Did you give the same answers? Students C and D, compare your notes. Do Students A and B have a real marriage? Tell them your conclusion and your reasons for it.

Writing

11 Imagine you are the immigration officer who interviewed Kate and Rod. Write a brief report on your findings. Use the present perfect with *for* or *since* and some of the vocabulary from this unit.

CONVERSATION TO GO

A: How long **have** you **lived** here?
B: Oh, I**'ve** only **lived** here **for** a few days.
A: Really? I**'ve been** here **since** 1780.

UNIT 14

What's that noise?

Vocabulary Sounds people make
Grammar Modals: *must be, might be, can't be* for deduction
Speaking Making deductions

Lesson A

Getting started

1 Label the photos with the verbs in the box.

| cheer | clap | cry | laugh | scream | shout | whistle | yawn |

2 🎧 Listen and match the sounds with the photos.

1. _C_   2. ___   3. ___   4. ___

5. ___   6. ___   7. ___   8. ___

3 **PAIRS.** Take turns making the noises in Exercise 1 and saying what your partner is doing.

A: *(yawns)*
B: You're yawning.

64

What's that noise?

UNIT 14

OBJECTIVES

Students will:

- activate vocabulary related to human sounds and job-related sounds
- use modals for deduction: *must be, might be, can't be*
- practice listening for and saying reduced /t/ in *must/might/can't be*

WARM-UP: CAN YOU REPEAT THAT?

- Tell students this unit is about sounds people make and hear daily. Ask students to think about the sounds they hear every day. Tell students they are going to experiment with making sounds.
- Ask students to close their eyes, listen to some sounds, and say how they were made. Create a few sounds using classroom objects. (Close a book with force, drag a chair across the floor, crumple some paper.)
- Form groups of 4. Set a time limit of 2–3 minutes. Tell students to take turns making a sound for the group. The group members who are listening should close their eyes and then say how the sound was made or even try to imitate making the sound.
- Call on some students to say which sound was the softest and which sound was the most annoying.

Getting started

OPTION: VOCABULARY PREVIEW

- Tell students to study the words in the box in Exercise 1.
- Ask students to name the sounds that you are going to make. One by one, make all of the sounds listed.

Exercise 1

- Have students look at the photos of people making noises. Tell students to label the photos with the verbs in the box.
- Set a time limit of 3 minutes. While students are working, walk around the room, helping as needed.
- Have students work with a partner to compare their answers. Encourage students to use dictionaries as needed.
- Go over the answers with the class.

Answer key

A yawn	C cheer	E laugh	G cry
B whistle	D scream	F shout	H clap

Exercise 2

- 🎧 Tell students to listen and match the sounds with the photos. Play the audio.
- 🎧 Play the audio again, as needed, for students to confirm their answers.
- Go over the answers with the class.

Answer key

1. C	3. B	5. D	7. H
2. E	4. G	6. F	8. A

Exercise 3

- Pair students. Explain the task: Students take turns making the noises in Exercise 1 and saying what their partner is doing. Go over the example.
- Set a time limit of 3 minutes. As students work, walk around the room, helping as needed.

EXTENSION

Ask the class about common situations in which each of the sounds are heard (e.g., *cheer–sports events; clap–a speech or a concert; cry–a sad movie; laugh–a comedy; scream–a rollercoaster; shout–calling a taxi; whistle–a concert, calling a taxi; yawn–a boring lecture*).

Teacher's Notes — Lesson A

T64

Listening

Exercise 4

- Tell students they are going to listen to a radio phone-in contest. Explain that this is a contest in which the people call in to a radio show and answer questions.
- Explain the task: Students listen, then put a check (✓) next to the name of the person who wins the contest.
- 🎧 Play the audio.
- 🎧 Play the audio one more time as needed.
- Go over the answer with the class.

> **Answer key**
> Maria

Exercise 5

- Have students look at the questions or read them aloud with the class.
- 🎧 Play the audio. Encourage students to listen for the answers, and to make brief notes as they hear the answers to the questions. If needed, play the audio again.
- Have students check their answers in pairs.
- Go over the answers with the class.

> **Answer key**
> 1. train station, airport, car, bus, taxi driver, bus driver
> 2. bus driver
> 3. actor, musician, golfer, basketball player
> 4. volleyball player
> 5. tennis player

Exercise 6

- Pair students. Tell them to make a list of sounds that Maria and Steve heard. Challenge them to see how many they can remember.
- Go over the example. Set a time limit of 3 minutes. Walk around the room, helping as needed.
- 🎧 Play the audio again for students to confirm their answers and add to their lists. Tell students to listen carefully to the sounds they hear.

> **Answer key**
> Answers may include: people talking, walking, shouting; traffic, a whistle, coins dropping, doors shutting; crowd noises: cheering and clapping; tennis ball hitting racket

> **WRAP-UP**
> Ask students to name sounds they heard. Make a list on the board.

Exercise 7

- Tell students to listen to the audio again and decide if each statement is true or false. If it is false, they write the correct information. Have students look at the statements.
- 🎧 Play the audio again. Students listen for the answers, and take brief notes.
- Students write *T* or *F* and rewrite the false statements.
- Have students check their answers in pairs.
- Go over the answers with the class.

> **Answer key**
> 1. T
> 2. F The prize is two tickets.
> 3. F He hears a tennis player. He loses.

🌐 Please go to www.longman.com/worldview for additional in-class model conversation practice and supplementary reading practice.

HOMEWORK

- 📖 For homework, assign *Workbook* page 57, Vocabulary Exercises 1 and 2, and page 59, Listening Exercises 5 and 6.

Listening

4 🎧 Listen to this radio phone-in contest. Who won the contest? Put a check (✓) next to the name(s).

Maria
Steve

5 🎧 Listen again and answer the questions.
1. Which possible places and jobs does Maria mention?
2. What is Maria's final answer?
3. Which four possible jobs does Steve mention?
4. What is Steve's final answer?
5. What is the correct answer?

6 **PAIRS.** Make a list of the sounds that Maria and Steve heard. How many can you remember?

A: People talking.
B: Yes, we also heard traffic.

7 🎧 Listen to the radio phone-in contest again. Write *T* (true) or *F* (false) after each statement. If the statement is false, write the correct information.

1. Callers have to listen and guess what the people's jobs are.
2. The prize is four tickets to the radio show.
3. Steve hears a volleyball player. Steve wins.

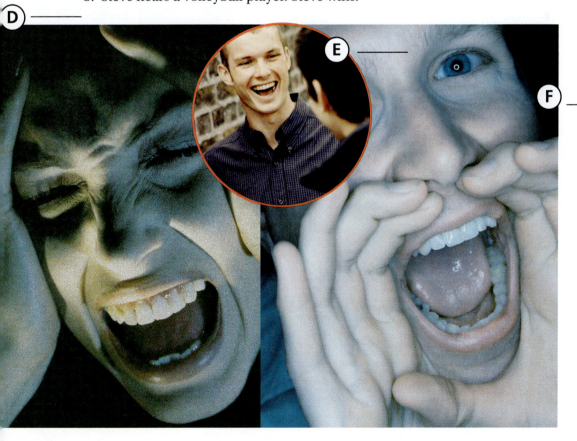

D ____
E ____
F ____

14

Grammar focus

1 Study the examples of modals of deduction.

> He **might be** a bus driver, but I'm not sure.
> He **must be** a bus driver. Look at his uniform.
> He **can't be** a bus driver. He's too young.

2 Look at the examples again. Write *must be*, *might be*, or *can't be* next to the correct description in the chart.

Modals: *must be, might be, can't be* for deduction
How sure are you?
Almost 100% sure something is true. _____
About 50% sure something is true. _____
Almost 100% sure something is NOT true. _____

Grammar Reference page 146

3 Complete the conversations with *must be*, *might be*, or *can't be*.

1. A: How long was your flight from Singapore?
   B: Twenty-six hours.
   A: Wow! You __must be__ really tired.

2. A: Who's that woman talking to Won-jin?
   B: Well, she looks a lot like her, so it _____ her sister.

3. A: I can't find my glasses.
   B: They _____ in the bathroom. You leave them there sometimes.

4. A: What's that noise upstairs?
   B: I don't know, but it _____ the cat. She's outside.

5. A: Sam never studies, but he always passes his exams.
   B: Well, they _____ very difficult exams then.

6. A: Listen to his accent. He _____ American.
   B: Not necessarily. He _____ from Canada.

7. A: Linda and Jeff are going to Bermuda again. It's their fourth vacation there this year!
   B: They _____ very wealthy.

8. A: I can't find the scissors.
   B: You just had them a minute ago, so they _____ very far away.

Grammar focus

LANGUAGE NOTES
- Remind students that modals of deduction are used when the speaker is commenting on something based on logic and the information or facts available. Which modal the speaker uses depends on the degree of certainty. *She might be a teacher* has less certainty than *She must be a teacher*. *Can't* is used when the speaker feels it is impossible to conclude differently: *She can't be a teacher* (I saw her working at the department store).
- Remind students that *might, must,* and *can* have the same form in all persons (*I might call you/She might call you*).

WARM-UP

Note: Skip this warm-up if you're doing this lesson (Lesson B) during the same class period as Lesson A.

- Books closed. Tell students they are going to listen again to the radio phone-in contest that they heard in the Listening section.
- Remind students that Maria and Steve are trying to guess what the people's jobs are. Ask them to think about what verb phrases tell them Maria and Steve are guessing.
- 🎧 Play the audio for Lesson A, Exercise 4.
- Ask students what verb phrases they heard Maria and Steve use when they were guessing: (*might be, must be, can't be*).
- Ask students which is the "stronger" guess: *might be* or *must be* (*must be*).

Exercise ❶
- Have students look at the examples and study the boldfaced words.
- Tell students to use *might be, must be,* or *can't be* to talk about a deduction. Explain that a deduction is the process of making a judgment or decision about something based on the information available. Which phrase the students decide to use depends on how sure they are. This is often based on how much information they have.

Exercise ❷
- Have students look at the examples again.
- Tell students to complete the blanks in the chart.
- Have students check their answers in pairs.
- Go over the descriptions with the class.
- Refer students to Grammar Reference page 146, as needed.

Answer key

| must be | might be | can't be |

EXTENSION
Use the context of the classroom or the place you live to practice deductions. For example, if a student is absent, comment that he or she might be sick/must be late, and so on. Ask students questions (*Where do you think [Ana] is today?*) and elicit answers with *might be, must be,* or *can't be*. Also ask students about any sounds that can be heard outside the classroom. Ask, *What can that be?* (*It must be a car/a truck . . .*).

Exercise ❸
- Explain the task: Students complete the conversation with *might be, must be,* or *can't be*. Remind students to read carefully for words that will help them decide how sure the speaker is.
- Ask students to look at the example. Ask students why *must be* is correct and which words helped them understand this (*The flight was twenty-six hours long!*).
- Have students complete the exercise individually. Set a time limit of 5 minutes.
- Have students check their answers in pairs.
- Go over the answers with the class.

Answer key

1. must be
2. must be/might be
3. might be
4. can't be
5. can't be
6. must be/might be
7. must be
8. can't be

WRAP-UP
Have students work in pairs to practice reading the conversations.

Pronunciation

Exercise 4

- Explain that when we link words together in a phrase, the sounds in the words are sometimes pronounced differently.
- 🎧 Play the audio and have students listen. Ask them to notice the pronunciation of the /t/ in *might be, can't be,* and *must be.*
- Point out that the /t/ is often not pronounced in *must be.*
- Tell students that the /t/ in *might be* and *can't be* is often pronounced as a glottal stop. Explain that this is the sound at the beginning and in the middle of *uh-oh.*

Exercise 5

- 🎧 Play the audio. Stop the audio after each line and have students repeat it chorally.
- Ask a few individual students to repeat the sentences to check their pronunciation.
- Encourage students to link words together smoothly. Although it is not necessary for students to pronounce /t/ as a glottal stop in *might be* and *can't be* or to omit /t/ in *must be,* check to see that they do not pronounce the /t/ in these phrases too strongly or add an extra sound after the /t/.

Exercise 6

- Explain the task: Students work in pairs and practice saying the conversations they completed in Exercise 3.
- Pair students. Walk around the room, helping as needed.

Speaking

Exercise 7

- Pair students. Explain the task: Students participate in a contest similar to the one in Exercise 4 on page 65. Explain that on the audio there are clues. They will listen and write their answers in the chart under Game 1.
- Give students 1 minute to read the directions and look over the chart.
- Check that students understand what to do at each step.

    Step 1: listen and write down all the possible jobs.
    Step 2: listen, then decide which of the jobs listed in Step 1 aren't possible.
    Step 3: listen and decide which job it must be.
    Step 4: listen to all the clues and confirm their answers.

- 🎧 Play the audio one clue at a time. Pause for students to fill in the chart and talk to their partners.
- **Note:** Students should use *might be* for the first clue, *might be/can't be* for the second clue, and *must be* for the third clue.
- To conclude, play the complete sequence, then ask students if they were correct.

> **Answer key**
> A teacher

Exercise 8

- Pair students with different partners. Tell them they are going to play the game again. They will listen to another mystery job and write their answers under Game 2.
- 🎧 Play the audio and follow the procedure for Exercise 7.

> **Answer key** A flight attendant

EXTENSION

- Form groups of 3 or 4. Explain the task: Students write the clues for other mystery jobs.
- Tell each group to decide on a mystery job, and then write at least three clues about it. Ask one group at a time to present their clues to the class.
- Have the rest of the class guess the mystery job. If students have difficulty guessing, encourage them to ask the group some questions.

TRB For additional interactive grammar practice, have students do the reproducible activity for this unit in the *Teacher's Resource Book.*

Writing

Exercise 9

- Assign the writing task for class work or homework.
- **TRB** Optionally, give students a copy of the model (see the *Teacher's Resource Book,* Writing Models). Ask them to notice which modals of deduction are used.
- Explain to students they need to provide enough information so that someone else can make a deduction, but that they shouldn't make the job too obvious at the beginning. Write on the board:

    My friend does not work outdoors. She works on the third floor in a large building. She works from nine to five.

    Walk around the room to make sure students understand the task.

- If the assignment is done in class, ask students to take turns reading their clues in small groups, as time permits.

For suggestions on how to give feedback on writing, see page xiv of this *Teacher's Edition.*

CONVERSATION TO GO

- As the students leave class, have them read the dialogue.
- Ask students why B is sure it isn't John? (*He's in Brazil.*)

HOMEWORK

- 📖 Assign *Workbook* page 58, Grammar Exercises 3 and 4, and page 59, Pronunciation Exercises 7, 8, and 9.
- 💿 If students do not have the *WorldView Workbook,* assign listening homework from the Student CD. Write on the board:

    Track 33
    What's the name of the radio contest?

- 🎧 Tell students to listen to the audio and write their answer. Have them bring it to the next class. (*What's that job?*)

Pronunciation

4 🎧 Listen. Notice the weak or disappearing sound of the *t* in *might be*, *can't be*, and *must be*.

He might be at an airport.   He can't be a taxi driver.   He must be a bus driver.

She might be British.   No, she can't be.   Then she must be Australian.

5 🎧 Listen again and repeat.

6 *PAIRS.* Practice the conversations in Exercise 3.

Speaking

7 🎧 *PAIRS.* You're going to be in a phone-in contest. Write your answers in the chart under *Game 1*.

1. Listen to the first clue. What are all the possible jobs? Tell your partner.
2. Listen to the next clue. Are all the jobs possible? Tell your partner why or why not.
3. Listen to the last clue. You should only have one job left.
4. Listen to the complete sequence. What is the job? Were you correct?

	Game 1	Game 2
1st clue: all possible jobs		
2nd clue: likely jobs / unlikely jobs		
3rd clue: final guess		
correct answer		

8 🎧 *PAIRS.* Play again. Listen to another mystery job. Follow the steps from Exercise 7. Record your answers in the chart under *Game 2*.

Writing

9 Write about a mystery job of a relative or a friend. Describe what the person does at his or her job, but do not make it obvious.

CONVERSATION TO GO

A: That **might be** John at the door.
B: No, it **can't be**. He's on vacation—in Brazil.
A: Then it **must be** Peter.

UNIT 15

Mumbai Soap

Vocabulary Topics for TV soap operas
Grammar will/won't for future
Speaking Predicting the future

Lesson A

Getting started

1. Do you watch soap operas on TV? Which is your favorite one?

2. Which five topics do you most often see in soap operas? Check (✓) the topics in the box.

crime	death	family life	greed	illness
marriage	misfortune	money	power	romance

3. **PAIRS.** Compare your answers.

Reading

4. Look at the photos of scenes from a television soap opera from India. Which topics in Exercise 2 do you think the soap opera is about?

5. Read Part One of the soap opera and check your answers to Exercise 4.

PART ONE

"NINA, you can't leave me," cries Sanjay, and Nina thinks her heart will break. She thinks about the soccer match in Mumbai where she met Sanjay. She knows her parents will never accept this man with no money or family connections. And she loves and respects her parents. They've told her, "Go to London and stay with our family there. You'll soon forget Sanjay."

6. How do you think Nina will solve her problem? Choose a, b, or c and say why.

   a. She'll run away and marry Sanjay.
   b. She'll stay in India, but she'll stop seeing Sanjay.
   c. She'll go to London.

Mumbai Soap

UNIT 15

Teacher's Notes — Lesson A

OBJECTIVES

Students will

- activate vocabulary related to schedules and plans
- use *will/won't* future
- practice listening for and saying contractions with *will*

WARM-UP: SOAPS

- Write the word *soap* on the board. Ask students to give you the definition. (Students will probably say: *something to clean your hands, body, things in your house with.*) Elicit from students what a *soap opera* is.
- Form groups of three. Set a time limit of 3 minutes. Have students discuss the following questions: *Who watches soap operas? Why are they popular?*
- Call on a few students to give their answers.

Getting started

OPTION: VOCABULARY PREVIEW

- Write the following on the board: *soap operas = life.* Tell students that soap operas dramatize real-life events, concerns, problems, etc.
- Form groups of 3. Set a time limit of 4 minutes. Explain the task: Students make a list of events, concerns, and problems.
- Ask students to give examples from their group's list. Write them on the board. Make sure to include: *crime, death, family life, greed, illness, marriage, misfortune, money, power, romance.*
- Go over any words that students don't know.

Exercise ❶

- Form groups of 3. Have students discuss the questions.
- Call on a few students to share their group's answers.

Exercise ❷

- Have students look at the topics. Verify that students understand the following words: *crime = activity that's against the law; misfortune = bad luck; greed = desire to have more money than you need; power = control over something or someone; family life = daily life in a family.* Ask for a couple of examples of each (*someone loses a job, gets sick*).
- Tell students to decide which five topics are most common.
- Set a time limit of 2 minutes. While students are working, walk around the room, helping as needed.
- Do not go over answers with the class until they have completed Exercise 3.

Exercise ❸

- Have students work in pairs to compare their answers from Exercise 2.
- Go over the answers with the class.

Answer key   Answers may vary.

Reading

BACKGROUND INFORMATION

Soap operas became popular in the U.S. in the early 20th century. They were called soap operas because the advertisers for the programs were soap companies.

Teaching Tip!   Making predictions

In Exercises 4–9, students practice making and checking predictions as they read three episodes of "Mumbai Soap." It is important that students do not read ahead or out of sequence. One way to promote this is to have the students cover the episodes (parts) with a piece of paper.

Exercise ❹

- Tell students they are going to read about a soap opera called "Mumbai Soap." Ask students to look at the first photo and describe what they see. Ask questions, such as *Who do you see? What is the man doing?*
- Have each student write down or circle the topics from Exercise 2 that they think the soap opera is about.
- Ask a few students to say which topics they chose. Ask them to give reasons.

Answer key   Answers may vary.

Exercise ❺

- Explain the task: Students read Part One of the soap opera. Tell them to check if the topics they predicted in Exercise 4 are correct.
- Set a time limit of 2 minutes. Walk around the room, helping as needed.
- Ask students if the topics they chose are correct.
- Check that students understand the problem by asking them to summarize it. (*Sanjay and Nina love each other, but her parents don't accept him. They've told her to go to London and forget about him.*)

Answer key   Answers may vary.

Exercise ❻

- Explain the task: Students decide how Nina will solve her problem.
- Give students time to choose *a, b,* or *c,* and take notes on their reasons.
- Pair students. Have them compare their choices.
- Walk around the room, helping as needed.

T68

Teacher's Notes — Lesson A

Exercise 7

- Tell students to read Part Two of the soap opera and check their predictions about what Nina will do.
- Set a time limit of 2 minutes. Walk around the room, helping as needed. Ask students what Nina decides to do (*go to London*). Elicit from students the information they used to make their choice (*Her emails tell Sanjay all about her life in London . . .*). Take a poll to find out how many students chose *c* in Exercise 6.
- Help students summarize Part Two. (*Nina is in London and emails Sanjay often. Ravi, a family friend also lives in London. He wants Nina to marry him. Nina is offered a role in a soap opera and Sanjay tells her to do it and forget about him.*)
- Ask students which topics from Exercise 1 are important here (*romance, marriage*).

Answer key
c

Exercise 8

- Tell students to predict what will happen next.
- Give students time to choose *a, b,* or *c,* and take notes.
- Pair students. Have them compare their choices.
- Walk around the room, helping as needed.

Exercise 9

- Tell students to read Part Three of the soap opera and check their predictions.
- Set a time limit of 2 minutes. Walk around the room, helping as needed.
- Pair students. Ask them to summarize Part Three and compare their predictions.
- Ask students what happens next. (*c. Nina accepts the job and stays in London.*) Elicit from students the information they used to make their choice. (*Sanjay turns on the TV in his Liverpool hotel room, He knows Nina is in London, He turns in surprise and sees her on the TV screen.*) Ask how many students chose c in Exercise 8.
- Help students summarize Part Three. (*Sanjay is visiting England. He is thinking about Nina. He turns on the TV and hears her voice.*)

Answer key
c

EXTENSION

Divide students into small groups. Assign roles: narrator, Nina, Sanjay, Ravi, and so on. Students may need to have more than one role depending on class size. Students read aloud Parts One through Three.

Please go to www.longman.com/worldview for additional in-class model conversation practice.

HOMEWORK

- For homework, assign *Workbook* page 60, Vocabulary Exercises 1 and 2, and page 62, Listening Exercises 5 and 6.

7. Read Part Two of the story and check your predictions.

PART TWO

"WILL we see each other again?" asks Sanjay. "Of course," promises Nina. "And I'll email every day." Her emails tell Sanjay all about her life in London and her acting classes. But they don't mention Ravi, a family friend also living in London. "Marry me, Nina," Ravi says. Nina asks for time to think. The next day she gets a call offering her an important role in a popular British soap opera. When Sanjay finds out about this, he writes, "I know you're happy in London. Please forget me." "No!" cries Nina.

8. What do you think will happen next? Choose *a*, *b*, or *c* and say why.

   a. Nina will go back to India and marry Sanjay.
   b. She'll accept the job and tell Sanjay about Ravi.
   c. She'll accept the job and stay in London.

9. Read Part Three of the story and check your predictions.

PART THREE

FIVE years later, Sanjay turns on the TV in his Liverpool hotel room. Tomorrow he will play soccer for India. He knows Nina is in London, but he doesn't think he'll see her. He still remembers her last email: "I won't marry anyone else, but I must stay in London. It's not just the job . . . it's also my family. I'll always love you." Sanjay can hear her voice. He turns in surprise and sees her on the TV screen. "She's as beautiful as ever. Is it too late?" he asks himself.

Grammar focus

1 Study the examples with *will* and *won't*.

Will for future	*Will* for predictions
(+) I'**ll** (**will**) always **love** you.	She **thinks** her heart **will break**.
(−) I **won't** (**will not**) **marry** anyone else.	He **doesn't think** he'**ll see** her again.
(?) **Will** you **remember** me?	**Do** you **think** it **will be** too late?

2 Look at the examples again. Underline the correct words to complete the explanations in the chart.

will/won't for predictions
Use *will* or *won't* to talk about something that you **think / know** is going to happen.
Use *don't think* + subject + *will* to talk about something you think **is / isn't** going happen.

Grammar Reference page 146

3 Complete the text with *will* or *won't* and a verb from the box. Use contractions when possible.

call   get   go   happen   marry   meet   recognize   speak

What do you think **(1)** __will happen__ in the final episode of "Mumbai Soap"?

I think Sanjay **(2)** _____ Nina's phone number from a mutual friend. He

(3) _____ her, but he'll hear a man's voice and he **(4)** _____ (**not**).

But Nina and Sanjay **(5)** _____ again. I think Nina **(6)** _____ to

Liverpool to watch the soccer game with friends. I don't think she **(7)** _____

Sanjay at first. But he'll be the hero of the game. Do you think Nina **(8)** _____

Sanjay at last?

Pronunciation

4 🎧 Listen. Notice the pronunciation of the contracted and weak forms of *will*.

I'**ll** always	I'**ll** always love you.
you'**ll** forget	You'**ll** forget me.
it'**ll** be	Do you think it'**ll** be too late?
her heart w**ill** break	She thinks her heart w**ill** break.

5 🎧 Listen again and repeat.

Grammar focus

> **LANGUAGE NOTE**
>
> The modal *will/will not* and the contracted form *won't* are used to make predictions. *I think* + *will* can be used to make predictions based on personal opinions (e.g., *I think she'll marry him. Do you think she'll marry him?*). For negatives, it is common to use the structure *I don't think he'll marry her.*

> **WARM-UP**
>
> Note: Skip this warm-up if you're doing this lesson (Lesson B) during the same class period as Lesson A.
>
> - Books closed. Tell students they are going to listen to Parts One through Three from the soap opera that they read in the Reading section.
> - Ask students to listen for phrases that tell them what time period Nina and Sanjay are worried about: the past or the future.
> - 🎧 Play the audio of the Reading section.
> - Write on the board a few phrases from the reading selection with *will* (examples: *her heart will break; Will we see each other again?; I'll email every day; I'll always love you*). Underline *will* and point out the contraction *'ll*. Explain that Nina and Sanjay are worried about the future.

Exercise ❶

- Have students look at the examples and study the boldfaced words.
- Remind students that (+) means *affirmative*, (–) means *negative*, and (?) means *question*.
- Elicit from students that *will* is used in affirmative sentences and that *won't* is the contraction of *will not*. Elicit from students that *will* and *won't* are the same for all persons.
- Elicit from students which form of the main verb always follows *will/won't* (the base form, or infinitive without *to*).
- Elicit or point out word order in questions (the subject comes between *will* and the main verb).

Exercise ❷

- Have students look at the examples again.
- Tell students to complete the rules by underlining the correct choice.
- Have students check their answers in pairs.
- Go over the explanations with the class.
- Refer students to Grammar Reference page 146, as needed.

> **Answer key**
>
> think   isn't going to

> **LANGUAGE NOTES**
>
> - Remind students that a *TV episode* is a TV program that is one of a series of programs that together tell a story.
> - A *mutual friend* here is someone who is a friend of both Sanjay and Nina.

Exercise ❸

- Explain the task: Students complete the text with *will* and *won't* and a verb from the box. Tell students to use a contraction when possible.
- Ask students to look at the example. Check that students understand what a *TV episode* is.
- Students complete the exercise individually. Set a time limit of 5 minutes.
- Have students check their answers in pairs.
- Go over the answers with the class.

> **EXTENSION**
>
> Have students work in pairs to take turns reading the text like a TV announcer. Encourage students to read with expression.

> **Answer key**
>
> 1. will happen   5. will meet
> 2. will get   6. 'll go
> 3. 'll call   7. 'll recognize
> 4. won't speak   8. will marry

Pronunciation

Exercise ❹

- Tell students that English speakers generally use contractions rather than full forms when they speak.
- 🎧 Play the audio and have students listen. The contracted and weak forms are said in short phrases first to highlight their pronunciation.
- Ask students to notice the way the pronouns are pronounced in the first four lines.
- Demonstrate the difference in the sound of the pronouns when they are said by themselves and in the contractions.

Exercise ❺

- 🎧 Play the audio. Stop the audio after each item to allow students to repeat chorally first the phrase and then the sentence.
- If necessary, write the last phrase on the board with a contraction to show the pronunciation: *her heart'll break*.
- Ask a few individual students to repeat the sentences to check their pronunciation.

Speaking

Exercise 6

- Hold up the book and point to the chart. Ask students to think about what will happen in the final episode of "Mumbai Soap," and tell them to write their notes in the chart. Encourage them to review their notes and answers from earlier exercises as needed. Prompt them by asking, *What predictions can you make?*
- Have students work alone. Set a time limit of 5 minutes. Walk around the room, helping as needed.

Exercise 7

- Form groups of 4. Explain the task: Students take turns telling each other how they predict "Mumbai Soap" will end.
- Go over the example. Point out the phrases *I think* and *I don't think*. Remind students these are used to express predictions or opinions. In addition, emphasize that they are all just making "good guesses" based on what they know; they can't determine who is right or wrong at this point.
- Set a time limit of 10 minutes. Walk around the room, helping as needed.
- Write on the board, *I think . . . because . . . .* Conclude by asking a few students to share their predictions and their reasons.

Exercise 8

- Tell students to listen to the last episode of "Mumbai Soap" and check their predictions. Encourage students to take brief notes as they listen so that they can compare what happens with what they predicted.
- 🎧 Play the audio.
- 🎧 Play the audio again for students to check their notes.
- Conclude by asking a few students to summarize the final episode.

> **WRAP-UP**
>
> Have students return to their groups to discuss the final episode and their predictions. Call on a few students to say if their predictions were correct.

TRB For additional interactive grammar practice, have students do the reproducible activity for this unit in the *Teacher's Resource Book*.

Writing

Exercise 9

- Assign the writing task for class work or homework. Make sure students understand they only need to make predictions about one of the things listed.
- **TRB** Optionally, give students a copy of the model (see the *Teacher's Resource Book*, Writing Models). Ask them to read the model and notice where *will* and *won't* are used for future predictions.
- If students don't have the model, explain that this is a simple, informal note to a friend. They can start it with *Dear (name of friend),* and end it with just their name. Write on the board:

    Hi, Sue—
    I think I know what will happen in the next episode of "Power and Love"! Julia won't marry Bruce. She'll tell him she's in love with Matthew just a few hours before the wedding. Then she'll run away because her parents will get angry at her.

    Walk around the room to make sure students understand the task.

- If the assignment is done in class, ask students to exchange their writing with a partner to compare predictions, as time permits.

For suggestions on how to give feedback on writing, see page xiv of this *Teacher's Edition*.

CONVERSATION TO GO

- As the students leave class, have them read the dialogue.
- Optionally, ask students to predict why B says this. What do they think might have happened?

HOMEWORK

- 📖 Assign *Workbook* page 61, Grammar Exercises 3 and 4, and page 62, Pronunciation Exercises 7 and 8.
- 💿 If students do not have the *WorldView Workbook*, assign listening homework from the Student CD. Write on the board:

    Track 35
    Did Nina know Sanjay was in England?

- 🎧 Tell students to listen to the audio and write their answer. Have them bring it to the next class. (*No, she didn't.*)

Speaking

6 **BEFORE YOU SPEAK.** What do you think will happen in the final episode of "Mumbai Soap"? Write your notes in the chart.

	I think . . .	I don't think . . .
Nina		
Sanjay		
Ravi		
Nina's Parents		

7 **GROUPS OF 4.** Take turns telling each other how you predict the soap opera will end.

Family life is very important to Nina, so I think she'll tell her parents about Sanjay. I don't think they'll be happy . . .

8 Listen to the summary of the last episode and check your predictions.

Writing

9 Write a note to a friend. Make predictions about one of these things. Use *will* or *won't*.
- What will happen in the next episode of your favorite TV program?
- What will be the result of the next big sports event in your area?
- What will be the main story in tomorrow's newspapers?

CONVERSATION TO GO

A: **Will** you **ever** see her again?
B: No, I **don't think** I **will**.

UNIT 16

The message behind the ad

Vocabulary Adjectives used in advertisements
Grammar Future factual conditional (*If* + simple present + *will*)
Speaking Talking about future possibilities

Lesson A

Getting started

1 Underline the best adjectives to complete the sentences about the products.

1. Medallion is a **delicious** / **shiny** new coffee. Try it—you'll love it.
2. You'll have **shiny / fresh** hair every time you use Gloss shampoo. So, for **reliable / healthy-looking** hair, use Gloss today.
3. Sunease sunscreen will keep your skin **fast / safe** from sunburn all through the day. And it keeps your skin **delicious / soft**, too!
4. Drink **safe / fresh** Sundew orange juice for breakfast—the **clean / healthy** way to start your day.
5. Now Lux-Clean laundry soap is even better. Your clothes will always be **clean / delicious** and very **reliable / soft**.
6. If you dream of working with a **soft / fast** and totally **healthy / reliable** computer, try the new VMC laptop today.

2 **PAIRS.** Compare your answers.

The message behind the ad

UNIT 16

OBJECTIVES

Students will:

- activate vocabulary related to advertisements and describing products
- use future real conditional (If + simple present + will)
- practice intonation in future real conditional sentences

WARM-UP: MY FAVORITE AD

- Write the following on the board: *an ad* and *a commercial*. Ask students to think about what these words have in common (information that encourages people to buy something) and how they are different. (We usually say *ad* to talk about advertisements on billboards or in print material such as magazines and newspapers, and we say *commercial* to talk about ads on TV or on the radio.)
- Pair students. Set a time limit of 2 minutes. Have students think about ads they have recently heard or seen. Explain the task: Students choose one ad per pair and answer the following questions: *What is the ad for? Do you like the ad? Why/why not? Would you buy the product?*
- Call on a few students to answer the questions and tell the class about the ad their group chose.

Getting started

OPTION: VOCABULARY PREVIEW

- Make mind maps on the board with the following words in the circles: *a cup of coffee, your hair, a glass of juice, sunscreen/sun cream, your skin, clothes, a computer*. Set a time limit of 1 minute. Ask students to brainstorm words that can describe what is in each circle. Have students make lists.
- Ask students to compare their answers with a partner. Students should add words to their list that their partner has.
- Call out one of the mind map words and ask students to say the words they thought of. Write them on the mind map. If students haven't suggested the following words, make sure to add them: *delicious, shiny, fresh, reliable, healthy-looking/healthy, fast, safe, soft, clean*.
- Explain any words that students don't know.

LANGUAGE NOTE

Although the following terms are not needed to complete Exercise 1, you might want to do a quick review if students seem to need them in their discussion: *glass of (juice), cup of (coffee), can of (coffee), box of (soap), container of (soap), bottle of (sunscreen)*.

Exercise ❶

- Ask students to look at the photos of the products and identify what each product is. Ask students to consider how each product might be described. For example, *What would you say about coffee if you wanted people to buy it?*
- Explain the task: Students read the sentences, and then underline the best adjectives to describe the products.
- Set a time limit of 5 minutes. While students are working, walk around the room, helping as needed.
- Do not go over answers with the class until they have completed Exercise 2.

Exercise ❷

- Pair students. Ask them to compare answers. Students can take turns reading their completed sentences aloud.
- Go over the answers with the class.

Answer key
1. delicious
2. shiny, healthy-looking
3. safe, soft
4. fresh, healthy
5. clean, soft
6. fast, reliable

EXTENSION

- Pair students. Student A is a radio announcer and Student B is the "voice" of a radio ad. Have students perform a skit by acting out the situations and sentences in Exercise 2.
- Student A—the announcer—can "finish" a program and then announce the ad for a product: *coffee, shampoo, sunscreen, orange juice, laundry soap, a computer*.
- Student B—the voice of the ad—can use the corresponding sentence in Exercise 2 to advertise the product. If possible he/she should add more information using the vocabulary in Exercise 1.
- Choose a student and role-play the following model for the class:

    A: . . .and that's the international news for today. Now a word about _____. (*coffee, shampoo*, etc.)

    B: Medallion, a delicious new coffee. Make it fresh in the morning and start your day right. Try it—you'll love it.

- Walk around the room, helping as needed.

WRAP-UP

Ask a few pairs to perform one of their skits for the class.

Teacher's Notes — Lesson A

T72

Teacher's Notes — Lesson A

Reading

Exercise 3

- Have students look at the magazine article. Read the title, "Talking Back to Ads," and elicit ideas on what the article is about. Prompt students by explaining that to "talk back" means to respond or give an opinion.
- Explain the task: Students read the article and decide if the viewers' reactions are positive or negative. Ask students to predict the answer from the title. Remind students that they will read the article twice, and this time they only need to read quickly to get a general idea of the viewers' reactions.
- Have students read the first paragraph only. Then check that students understand what viewers were asked about (*how people in the ads are portrayed*), and why (*advertisers wanted to know viewers' opinions of the ads*).
- Set a time limit of 2 minutes for students to complete the article. Walk around the room, helping as needed.
- Take a poll to find out how many students thought the reactions were positive/negative.
- Ask if students have any questions about new vocabulary. Check understanding of the verbs *target* (to try to make something affect a limited group), *offend* (to make someone angry or upset), and *portray* (to show in a particular way).

> **Answer key**
> negative

Exercise 4

- Tell students to read the article again and pay attention to the details.
- Have students read the questions first so that they can focus on the information they need to complete the task.
- Set a time limit of 5 minutes for students to read and answer the questions.
- Have students check their answers in pairs.
- Go over the answers with the class.

> **Answer key**
> 1. call or write to companies that use offensive ads
> 2. normal people in ads, not just supermodels
> 3. children might think that physical appearance is the most important thing

Listening

Exercise 5

- Form groups of 3. Explain the task: Students describe an advertisement they've seen recently, and say what the message of the ad was. Remind students to consider how the message comes from more than just the words; it comes from the music, the pictures, people's facial expressions, and so on.
- Go over the example. Tell students to listen carefully because they may have to report to the class about their partner's ad.
- Set a time limit of 3 minutes. Students take turns telling about their ad. Walk around the room, helping as needed.
- Call on a few students to report on one of their group's ads.

Exercise 6

- Explain the task: Tell students they are going to listen to an interview with an advertising executive. Students listen and check (✓) the pictures of the products in Exercise 1 that they talk about.
- 🎧 Play the audio. Walk around the room, helping as needed.
- 🎧 Play the audio again. Have students check their answers.
- Go over the answers with the class.

> **Answer key**
> sunscreen, shampoo, orange juice

Exercise 7

- Have students look at the questions or read them aloud with the class.
- 🎧 Play the audio again. Encourage students to listen for the answers, and to make brief notes as they hear the answers to the questions. If needed, play the audio again.
- Pair students and have them check their answers.
- 🎧 Go over the answers with the class. Then ask the students what the message is of each ad. Play the audio again, as needed, for students to answer.

> **Answer key**
> 1. young, good-looking, who have a lot of money
> 2. sunscreen
> 3. because people remember funny ads

⊙ Please go to www.longman.com/worldview for additional in-class model conversation practice.

HOMEWORK

- 📖 For homework, assign *Workbook* page 63, Vocabulary Exercises 1 and 2, and page 65, Listening Exercises 5 and 6.

Reading

3 Read the article about viewers' reactions to television ads. Are their reactions positive or negative?

Talking Back to Ads

ADS ON TV ARE A ONE-WAY STREET – they talk and we listen. But, does it have to be that way? Last week, we encouraged television viewers to talk back to advertisers about how people in the ads are portrayed. If you believe you can make a difference, read what some people had to say about most TV ads.

Yoko, a college student, said, "Advertisers seem to think that if they show thin, attractive people, everyone will want to buy what they're selling, whether it's a car, a soft drink, or perfume. I like to see ads that have real people in them, not just good-looking models."

Roger, a computer analyst, is especially worried about ads that target young children. "I have an eleven-year-old son, and I don't want him to think that physical appearance is the most important thing in life. A lot of TV ads tell kids that if they don't wear certain clothes, they won't be popular with other kids."

If you call or write to the advertiser and the TV network every time you see an ad that offends you, you will be able to change the way advertisers portray people. Let advertisers know what you think!

4 Read the article again and answer the questions.

1. What does the article encourage people to do? Why?
2. What kind of people would Yoko like to see on TV?
3. Why is Roger especially worried about ads that target young children?

Listening

5 **GROUPS OF 3.** Describe an advertisement you've seen recently. What was the message of the ad?

The new ad for Super-Fresh shampoo shows beautiful women having a great time dancing. The message is, "Use this shampoo and you'll be beautiful and happy."

6 🎧 Listen to the interview with an advertising executive. Check (✓) the photos of the products in Exercise 1 that they talk about.

7 🎧 Listen again and answer the questions.

1. What kind of people do they use in car advertisements?
2. Which products often use families in their advertisements?
3. Why is humor a good thing to use in ads?

Grammar focus

1 Study the examples of the future real conditional.

> (+) If you **buy** this car, you**'ll meet** a beautiful woman.
> People **will remember** the ad **if** it**'s** funny.
> (−) If you **use** this sunscreen, your kids **won't get** sunburned.
> You **won't** regret it **if** you **try** our product.
> (?) What **will happen if** I **buy** this car?

2 Look at the examples again. Underline the correct word or phrase to complete the rules in the chart.

Future real conditional
Use the future real conditional to talk about things that may or may not happen.
The verb in the *if* clause is in the **simple present / future**.
When the *if* clause comes first, it **is / isn't** usually followed by a comma (,).

Grammar Reference page 146

3 Complete the sentences with the correct form of the verbs in parentheses.

1. You *'ll lose* (**lose**) weight quickly if you *don't eat* (**not eat**) sweet things.
2. If you _____ (**try**) this lemonade, you _____ (**not want**) to drink anything else.
3. If you _____ (**use**) Gloss shampoo, your hair _____ (**look**) really shiny.
4. You _____ (**have**) more energy if you _____ (**eat**) lots of fresh fruit.
5. If the machine _____ (**break**), we _____ (**repair**) it free of charge.
6. If you _____ (**drink**) Vita-mint, you _____ (**have**) lots of energy all day long.
7. You _____ (**not feel**) so tired if you _____ (**exercise**) at our gym every day.
8. Your skin _____ (**be**) softer if you _____ (**wash**) with Callon soap every day.

Pronunciation

4 🎧 Listen. Notice the intonation in these conditional sentences.

If you buy this car, you'll meet a beautiful woman.

If the ad is funny, people will remember it.

If you use this sunscreen, your kids won't get sunburned.

If you try our product, you won't regret it.

5 🎧 Listen again and repeat.

Grammar focus

> **LANGUAGE NOTE**
> The future real conditional, also known as first conditional, *If* + simple present + *will* + base form (infinitive without *to*), is used to talk about things that are likely to happen as a result of another action or event. This is typically used to talk about real situations, such as *If you study hard, you will learn a lot.*

> **WARM-UP**
> **Note: Skip this warm-up if you're doing this lesson (Lesson B) during the same class period as Lesson A.**
> - Books closed. Tell students they are going to listen again to the interview with the advertising executive that they heard in the Listening section.
> - Tell students to listen for what she says the message of each ad is. Remind students that the message usually starts with *if*.
> - 🎧 Play the audio for Lesson A, Exercises 6 and 7.
> - Ask students what messages they remember. Write the following on the board: *If you buy this car, you'll meet a beautiful woman. If you try our product, you won't regret it. Your kids won't get sunburned if you use this sunscreen. If you don't drink orange juice, the sun won't come up.* Underline *if* + the simple present verbs (*buy, try, use*) + *will* in each of the messages.

Exercise 1
- Have students look at the examples and study the boldfaced type.
- Remind students that (+) means affirmative, (–) means negative, and (?) means question.
- Elicit from students that the sentences express a condition: something needs to happen before something else happens.
- Elicit from students that *you'll* is the contracted form of *you will* and that *won't* is the contracted form of *will not*.

Exercise 2
- Have students look at the examples again.
- Tell students to complete each rule.
- Pair students and have them check their answers.
- Go over the explanations with the class. Also point out that when the *if* clause comes second, a comma is not used.
- Check that students understand the sentence *If you buy this car, you'll meet a beautiful woman* is the kind of language used in ads. The ad wants people to believe that buying the car and meeting a beautiful woman are somehow connected.
- Check comprehension by asking *Will you regret it if you don't try our product?* (*Yes, I will.*)
- Refer students to Grammar Reference page 146, as needed.

> **Answer key**   simple present   is

Exercise 3
- Explain the task: Students complete the sentences with the correct form of the verbs in parentheses.
- Ask students to look at the example. Ask students why *'ll lose* and *don't* are correct (*'ll lose* is the verb in the resulting clause; *don't eat* is the verb in the *if* clause).
- If needed, do the second example with the class. Elicit from students that *try* must be in the present tense (*try*) and *not want* must be in the future with *will* (*won't want/will not want*).
- Have students complete the exercise individually. Set a time limit of 5 minutes.
- Have students check their answers in pairs.
- Go over the answers with the class. Then have students work in pairs to practice reading the sentences aloud.

> **Answer key**
> 1. will lose / don't eat
> 2. try / won't want
> 3. use / will look
> 4. will have / eat
> 5. breaks / will repair
> 6. drink / will have
> 7. won't feel / exercise
> 8. will be / wash

Pronunciation

Exercise 4
- 🎧 Play the audio. Ask students to notice the different intonation in the two clauses of each sentence.
- Explain that the word in red is the most important word in each clause.
- As you play the audio, you can move your hand up and down to show how the intonation rises slightly at the end of the first clause and falls to a low note at the end of the sentence.
- Draw attention to the general principle of rising intonation in the middle of the sentence, indicating that it is unfinished, and falling to a low note at the end.
- 🎧 You may want to play the audio again, this time stopping the recording after the first clause (*If you buy this car*) in the first sentence. Ask students if the sentence sounded finished. Repeat this process with the second clause (*you'll meet a beautiful woman*) and then with one or more of the other sentences.

Exercise 5
- 🎧 Play the audio. Stop the audio after each sentence and have students repeat it chorally.
- If necessary, remind students to make the words in red long. The words in red are stressed and also have a change in pitch.
- Encourage students to use different intonation in the two clauses of each sentence. You may want to have students repeat each clause separately and then the entire sentence.
- Ask a few individual students to repeat the sentences and check their pronunciation.

Teacher's Notes — Lesson B

Speaking

Exercise 6

- Hold up your book and present the photos. Ask students to describe the situations and people they see. Ask questions to focus students on the details in the photos, such as *Where is the girl? How is she feeling? How do you know? What is she wearing?*
- Wait to discuss what products are being sold until students have completed Exercise 7.
- Pair students. Tell them to identify what products are being sold, and who the advertisers are targeting (who they are selling to). You can either read or have the students read aloud the list of possible targets.
- Set a time limit of 5 minutes. Walk around the room, helping as needed.
- Ask a few pairs who they think the advertisers are targeting. Encourage them to give reasons and explain their choices. Point out that there are no absolute right or wrong answers to the questions, and that any answer is acceptable as long as they can give reasons.

Exercise 7

- Students stay in the same pairs. Hold up your book and point to each ad. Ask students to read aloud the slogan for each ad (*cool guy, cool beer,* etc.). Tell students to decide what the message is for each ad, and then write a new slogan.
- Set a time limit of 10 minutes. Walk around the room, helping as needed.

Exercise 8

- Ask each pair to say their slogans or write them on the board.
- Have the class vote on the best slogan for each ad.

> **EXTENSION**
>
> Bring to class several interesting pictures that students can use to write advertisements. The ads do not need to be for an obvious product. Point out to students that it is fairly common to have little relationship between the picture and the product being sold. Encourage students to use their imaginations to come up with a product to sell, and a slogan to use.

TRB For additional interactive grammar practice, have students do the reproducible activity for this unit in the *Teacher's Resource Book*.

Writing

Exercise 9

- Assign the writing task for class work or homework.
- **TRB** Optionally, give students a copy of the model (see the *Teacher's Resource Book*, Writing Models). Ask them to read the model and notice the vocabulary and grammar from the unit.
- If students don't have the model, write on the board:

    In an ad for the new dishwashing liquid Soft Hands, the messages we want to send are:
    - "If you wash the dishes with Soft Hands, your hands will be soft."
    - "If you use Soft Hands . . . "

    Walk around the room to make sure students understand the task.
- If the assignment is done in class, ask students to exchange their writing in small groups.

For suggestions on how to give feedback on writing, see page xiv of this *Teacher's Edition*.

CONVERSATION TO GO

- As the students leave class, have them read the dialogue.
- Optionally, ask students who the car dealer thinks will give her a lot of attention.

HOMEWORK

- For homework, assign *Workbook* page 64, Grammar Exercises 3 and 4, and page 65, Pronunciation Exercises 7 and 8. Assign *Workbook* Self-quiz Units 13–16.
- If students do not have the *WorldView Workbook*, assign listening homework from the Student CD. Write on the board:

    Track 37
    What kind of people are in ads for expensive cars?

- Tell students to listen to the audio and write their answer. Have them bring it to the next class. (*young, good-looking men or women*)

BEFORE NEXT CLASS

- Tell students that the next class will be a review class covering units 13–16.
- Have students review the material in the units to prepare for the activities in Review 4.

Unit no.	Review Grammar	Listen to Student CD	Study Grammar Reference
13	present perfect with *for* and *since*	Track 31	Page 146
14	modals for deduction: *must be, might be, can't be*	Track 33	Page 146
15	*will / won't* future	Track 35	Page 146
16	future real conditional	Track 37	Page 146

FOR NEXT CLASS

TRB Make copies of Quiz 4 in the *Teacher's Resource Book*.

Speaking

6 *BEFORE YOU SPEAK.* Look at the advertisements above. Who are the advertisers "targeting" (trying to sell the products to)? Make notes.

- young, middle-aged, or older people?
- men, women, or both?
- single or married people?
- people with children?

7 *PAIRS.* Discuss each ad. Who are the advertisers targeting? What is the message behind each ad?

I think they're targeting . . .
To me, the message is, "If you use this . . ."

8 Report on the messages. Do your classmates agree?

Writing

9 You work for an advertising agency. Write a paragraph with ideas for an ad to sell a product you use and like. Use the future real conditional.

CONVERSATION TO GO

A: If you **buy** this car, you**'ll get** a lot of attention.
B: Especially from my mechanic!

Review 4: Units 13–16

Unit 13 Green card

1. 🎧 Listen to the model conversation.

2. *2 PAIRS.* Break into pairs. Students A and B, look at page 139. Students C and D, look at page 140.

3. Students A and C, interview each other. Students B and D, interview each other. Take notes.

4. *GROUPS OF 4.* Students A and B, compare your notes. Students C and D, compare your notes. Are Students A and B really roommates? Are Students C and D? How do you know?

Unit 14 What's that noise?

5. 🎧 Listen to the model conversation.

6. *PAIRS.* Write down the name of four places and a few of the sounds you hear in each, for example, *concert: people clapping, people singing.*

7. *2 PAIRS.* Take turns telling the other pair the sounds you wrote down in Exercise 6. Do not say the name of the place. The other pair can have only three guesses. Each guess is one point. Keep score. The pair with the lowest number of points wins the game.

Review 4: Units 13-16

📼 You may wish to use the video for Units 13–16 at this point. For video activity worksheets, go to www.longman.com/worldview.

Unit 13: Green card

OBJECTIVE

Grammar: reviewing the present perfect with *for* and *since*

Exercise 1
- Explain the task: Students listen to the model conversation.
- 🎧 Play the audio. Point out the question starter: *How long have you . . . ?* and the phrases: *for about five years; since last April; for over a year.*
- 🎧 Play the audio again, and then have students repeat.

Exercise 2
- Form two pairs and assign roles: Student A and B; C and D. Tell them they will do an interview with their landlord. They will take turns pretending to be roommates and landlords. The landlords will interview the roommates separately in order to decide if they are really roommates.
- Tell Students A and B to turn to page 139, and Students C and D to turn to page 140. Tell them to read the directions and prepare for the interviews. Each pair works together to decide on the answers they will both give.
- Give students 5 minutes to prepare. While students are working, walk around the room, helping as needed.

Exercise 3
- Explain the task: Students A and C interview each other, and Students B and D interview each other. Remind students to take notes.
- Set a time limit of 5 minutes for students to conduct their interviews.

Exercise 4
- Explain the task: Students A and B compare their notes. Students C and D compare their notes. Students A and B decide if Students C and D are really roommates; Students C and D decide if Students A and B are really roommates.
- Set a time limit of 5 minutes. Remind students to give reasons for their decisions.
- Conclude by asking a few students to say what they decided and why.

Unit 14: What's that noise?

OBJECTIVE

Grammar: focus on using modals for deduction: *must be, might be, can't be*

Exercise 5
- Explain the task: Students listen to the model conversation.
- 🎧 Play the audio. Then write on the board the phrases: *it might be . . .* and *then it must be . . .*
- 🎧 Play the audio again, and then have students repeat.

Exercise 6
- Form pairs. Explain the task: Students work together to make a list of four places, and the sounds you can hear in them. Students should think of at least two sounds for each of the places they list.
- Set a time limit of 4 minutes. Walk around the room, helping as needed.

Exercise 7
- Combine two pairs to form groups of 4. Explain the task: Pairs take turns telling the sounds that can be heard in the places on their list, without giving the name of the place. The other pair has only three chances to guess what the place is. Point out that pairs should try to get the correct answer in as few guesses as possible.
- Students should keep score. Each guess is worth one point; the pair with the lowest number of points wins.
- While students are playing, walk around the room, helping as needed.

Unit 15: Mumbai Soap

OBJECTIVE

Grammar: focus on using *will/won't* future

Exercise 8

- Explain the task: Students listen to the model conversation and look at the photos.
- 🎧 Play the audio. Point out that the speakers are talking about what they think *will/won't* happen on a soap opera. Write on the board, *What do you think will happen?* and *I think that they'll . . .*
- 🎧 Tell students to listen for sentences with these phrases. Play the audio again.

Exercise 9

- Explain the task: Tell the students to read the TV guide and predict what will happen on Wednesday and on Friday.
- Set a time limit of 5 minutes. Remind students to write down their predictions.
- Walk around the room, helping as needed.

Exercise 10

- Pair students and have them share their predictions.
- Call on a few pairs to tell the class their predictions.

> **WRAP-UP**
>
> Have students write a short paragraph about what happens in the final episode of "Love Me or Leave Me." They can use their own prediction or that of a classmate.

Unit 16: The message behind the ad

OBJECTIVE

Grammar: focus on using future real conditional *(if +* simple present *+ will)*

Exercise 11

- Explain the task: Students listen to the model conversations. Each speaker is saying a short advertising slogan for a product.
- 🎧 Play the audio. Ask students what products the ads are for (*shampoo, a car, a vitamin drink*). Write on the board, *If you . . . , you will . . .* and *You will . . . if you . . .*
- 🎧 Tell students to listen again for conditional sentences. Play the audio again.

Exercise 12

- Tell students to each choose a product and write an advertising slogan using an *if* clause (the future real conditional).
- Students work alone. Walk around the room, helping as needed.

Exercise 13

- Form groups of 3. Tell students to take turns presenting their ad slogans, and then decide who came up with the best/funniest/most creative slogan.
- Set a time limit of 10 minutes for students to present and discuss their slogans. Walk around the room, helping as needed.

> **WRAP-UP**
>
> Ask each group to report which of their slogans they thought was the best/funniest/most creative.

Unit 15 Mumbai Soap

8 **BEFORE YOU SPEAK.** Read the TV guide. What do you think will happen on Wednesday? What do you think will happen on Friday?

TV GUIDE - WEEK IN REVIEW

Final week of
Love Me or Leave Me

MONDAY
Five days before their wedding, Linda and Evan have a huge fight and break up.

TUESDAY
Linda visits an old boyfriend in San Francisco, and Evan goes fishing.

WEDNESDAY
Evan a... make... are ... th...

THURSDAY
Linda and Evan go to the wedding rehearsal. The radio station BRMB is there to broadcast the wedding and interview them live before and after their wedding.

FRIDAY
Tune in for the grand finale – the final episode of "Love Me or Leave Me."

9 🎧 Listen to the model conversation and look at the photos.

10 **PAIRS.** Share your predictions.

Unit 16   The message behind the ad

11 🎧 Listen to the model conversation.

12 **BEFORE YOU SPEAK.** Choose a product and write an advertising slogan using an *if* clause.

13 **GROUPS OF 3.** Share your slogan with two classmates. Who came up with the best slogan? The funniest slogan? The most creative slogan?

UNIT 17 Willpower

Vocabulary Phrasal verbs
Grammar Verbs + gerund; verbs + infinitive
Speaking Talking about changing habits

Lesson A

Getting started

1 *Willpower* is the ability to control your mind and body in order to achieve something. Match the phrasal verbs about willpower with the correct definitions. You will use one definition twice.

Phrasal verbs	Definitions
1. I heard that you **took up** yoga recently. _d_ 2. I can't believe she **threw away** all the chocolates! ___ 3. I finally **gave up** drinking coffee in the afternoon. ___ 4. You'll have to **cut down on** desserts if you want to lose weight. ___ 5. I **keep on** going to the gym every day, even though I hate it. ___ 6. Every day she has a new excuse to **get out of** exercising. ___ 7. Many people **cut back on** carbohydrates to lose weight. ___ 8. I **turned down** their dinner invitation because I'm on a diet. ___	a. stopped doing something that you did regularly before b. did not accept an offer or opportunity c. continue to do something d. started doing a particular activity e. avoid doing something that you should do f. put something in the trash g. reduce the amount, number, or size of something

2 **PAIRS.** Take turns telling each other about something you've begun doing or cut back on recently. Use some of the phrasal verbs in Exercise 1.

Last summer, I took up tennis. I tried to cut down on sweets, but I just couldn't give up ice cream.

3 **PAIRS.** Discuss these questions.
Which of these things take a lot of willpower?
Which don't take much willpower?

- exercising
- giving up drinking coffee
- getting organized
- giving up watching television
- learning to speak a new language
- learning to play a musical instrument

78

Willpower

UNIT 17

Teacher's Notes — Lesson A

OBJECTIVES

Students will:

- activate vocabulary of phrasal verbs related to changing personal habits
- use verbs + *gerunds* and verbs + *infinitives*
- practice listening for and pronouncing the weak form of *to* in infinitives and the blended form "wanna" for *want to*

WARM-UP: I'VE GOT THE POWER

- Tell students this unit is about willpower. Explain that willpower is the ability to control your mind and/or body so that you can do something difficult.
- Form groups of 4. Set a time limit of 2 minutes. Write *start* and *stop* on the board. Ask students to make a list of things they want to start or stop doing.
- Call on different groups to say some of the things in each category.
- Optionally, take a poll of the class to see which items are the most important in someone's life.

Getting started

FYI

In this unit, the focus is on phrasal verbs as vocabulary items in context. The meanings should therefore be clear, and there is no need to go into the grammatical rules behind them at this stage. (The grammar will be treated in *WorldView 4*, Units 23 and 27.)

OPTION: VOCABULARY PREVIEW

- Write the following on the board in two columns:

take up _____ (noun)	do something more
throw away _____ (noun)	say *no*
give up _____ ing	complete something
cut down on _____ (noun)	start
keep on _____ ing	increase
get out of _____ ing	quit
cut back on _____ (noun)	stop
turn down _____ (noun)	keep

- Ask students to match the phrasal verb on the left with the word that has the opposite meaning on the right.
- If you think your students will need help, you may want to write a phrase with the phrasal verb to help make it clear: *take up yoga/dance classes; throw away all sweets in my house; give up smoking;* etc.
- Go over answers with the class. Go over any words students don't know.

Answer key

take up _____ (noun)	quit
throw away _____ (noun)	keep
give up _____ ing	start
cut down on _____ (noun)	do something more
keep on _____ ing	stop
get out of _____ ing	complete something
cut back on _____ (noun)	increase
turn down _____ (noun)	say *no*

Exercise ❶

- Ask students to look at the sentences. Remind them that the verbs in bold are phrasal verbs, and that they are made up of two parts, the verb and the particle. Point out that all of these phrasal verbs except for *turned down* are inseparable.
- Explain the task: Students match the phrasal verbs with the correct definitions. Go over the example. Remind students they will use one definition twice.
- Set a time limit of 5 minutes. While students are working, walk around the room, helping as needed.
- Go over answers with the class.

Answer key

1. d   2. f   3. a   4. g   5. c   6. e   7. g   8. b

Exercise ❷

- Pair students. Explain the task: Students take turns using phrasal verbs to tell each other about something they have begun doing or cut back on recently.
- Go over the example.
- Set a time limit of 3 minutes. Walk around the room, helping as needed.
- After 3 minutes, call on a few students to say what they have done recently, using the phrasal verbs.

Exercise ❸

- Pairs continue working together or form new pairs. Explain the task: Students decide which activities require willpower and which don't.
- Ask students to read the definition of willpower, and then think of something that takes willpower. Give an example (e.g., *You need willpower to stop smoking*).
- Have students look at the photo and the list of activities.
- Set a time limit of 5 minutes. Walk around the room, helping as needed.
- Have pairs work with another pair to compare their ideas.
- Take a poll for each activity to find out how much willpower the students think is required.

Answer key   Answers will vary.

T78

Reading

Exercise 4

- Have students look at the magazine quiz. Read the title, "Do you have willpower?" Read or have the students read the introduction to the quiz. Explain the task: Students read each situation and circle *a, b,* or *c.* Ask students if they have ever done a magazine quiz like this before.
- Set a time limit of 5 minutes for students to complete the quiz. Walk around the room, helping as needed.
- Ask if students have any questions about new vocabulary. Check understanding of *lose your temper* (get angry) and *anger management class* (a class where people learn to control their anger). Review *be out of shape / get in shape.*

Exercise 5

- Tell students to count the *a*'s, *b*'s, and *c*'s that they circled, then turn to page 137 to find out how much willpower they have. Encourage students to read the other answers as well.
- Walk around the room, helping as needed.

Teaching Tip! Discussing results

Some students may be uncomfortable discussing their quiz results. For this reason, it might be better to steer the discussion towards general ways to improve willpower, then conclude with a general *Yes/No* question about the results *(Were you surprised by the results, yes or no?).*

Exercise 6

- Pair students. Explain the task: Students tell each other the results of the quiz and say whether they agree or disagree. Then they discuss what they can do to have more willpower. Tell students to listen carefully because they may have to report to the class about their partner's ideas on how to increase willpower.
- Set a time limit of 5 minutes. After 5 minutes, call on a few students to report about their partners.

> **WRAP-UP**
>
> Ask students if they were surprised by their results on the quiz. Encourage them to give reasons.

Please go to www.longman.com/worldview for additional in-class model conversation practice.

HOMEWORK

- For homework, assign *Workbook* page 68, Vocabulary Exercises 1 and 2, and page 70, Listening Exercises 5 and 6.

Reading

4 Take the the quiz to find out how much willpower you have.

Do you have willpower?

Can you do things even if they're difficult? Can you finish what you start? Read each situation and circle *a*, *b*, or *c*.

1 You have stopped eating sweets, but today you're home alone and you're hungry. There's a box of chocolates in the kitchen. Do you decide to:
a. eat all the chocolates but not buy any more?
b. throw away the whole box and give up eating sweets forever?
c. eat one or two and then throw away the rest?

2 You love buying new things, but you already have too much charged on your credit card. You realize you need to cut down on spending. Will you:
a. try to shop only when there are sales?
b. quit shopping until all your bills are paid?
c. only shop when you really need to buy something?

3 You have a bad temper and your family dislikes going places with you. Do you decide to:
a. not worry about how your family feels?
b. take an anger management course and learn to control your temper?
c. practice not losing your temper, but if you do, be sure to apologize?

4 You don't enjoy exercising, but you want to get in shape. You take up jogging. One day as you start jogging, you meet a good friend who invites you for coffee. Will you:
a. stop to have a cup of coffee with your friend?
b. give an excuse to get out of having coffee and keep on jogging?
c. promise to meet him or her in five minutes and only jog around the park once?

5 Count the number of *a*'s, *b*'s, and *c*'s you circled. Then turn to page 137 to find out how much willpower you have.

6 **PAIRS.** Tell your partner your results on the willpower quiz. Do you agree or disagree with the results? Why? What can you do to have more willpower?

17

Grammar focus

1 Study the examples of verbs followed by gerunds and infinitives.

Verbs + gerund	Verbs + infinitive
(+) He **kept on** running.	I **want to eat** something.
(−) I don't **enjoy doing** exercise.	You **don't need to have** a cup of coffee.
(?) Did you **give up drinking** soda?	Did he **learn to control** his temper?

2 Look at the verbs in the box. Find these verbs in the quiz in Exercise 4. Put them into the correct column in the chart.

decide	give up	cut down on	need	quit
dislike	practice	learn	enjoy	get out of
want	take up	keep on	stop	promise

Verbs followed by gerund	Verbs followed by infinitive
give up	decide

Grammar Reference page 147

3 Complete the paragraph with the correct form of the verbs in parentheses.

Before I went to Mexico on vacation, I decided _____ Spanish classes.
                                                    1. (take)

I needed _____ work early to get to class. The class was hard, so I quit
          2. (leave)

_____ it and got some Spanish cassettes. I didn't enjoy _____ to
3. (take)   4. (listen)

the cassettes, but I didn't want _____ _____ Spanish. I kept on
                                 5. (give up) 6. (learn)

_____ to study, but I didn't have enough time. So I finally stopped
7. (try)

_____ . When I got to Mexico, I found that many people there speak
8. (try)

some English, and they were happy to practice _____ English with me!
                                              9. (speak)

80

Grammar focus

LANGUAGE NOTES

- An infinitive is *to* + base form *(to run)*. A gerund is the *–ing* form of a verb that can have different functions in a sentence. It can be used as the subject *(Running is good exercise)*, the direct object *(He kept on running)*, or as a modifier *(Those running shoes are expensive!)*. Here, it is used as the direct object.
- With some verbs, both the gerund and infinitive form can be used as the direct object *(He likes running / He likes to run)*. It is necessary to memorize which verbs take which forms. In addition, some verbs can be followed by a gerund or an infinitive without a change in meaning; for example, *start (He started running/He started to run)*.
- Interrogatives are formed according to the same rules: *Do you like to run? = Do you like running?*

WARM-UP

Note: Skip this warm-up if you're doing this lesson (Lesson B) during the same class period as Lesson A.

- Books closed. Tell students they are going to listen to a audio of the "Do you have willpower?" quiz that they read in the Reading section.
- Write the following phrases on the board. Tell students to listen for the words that come right after: *give up . . . , You love . . . , cut down on . . . , you take up . . .*
- Write an example on the board, *You have stopped,* then *eating sweets. (You have stopped eating sweets.)*
- 🎧 Play the audio for Lesson A, Exercise 4.
- Ask students for the phrases they heard. Write them on the board: *give up eating sweets, You love buying new things, cut down on spending, You take up jogging.*
- Ask students what they notice about the phrases (they have a word ending in *–ing* / a gerund).

Exercise ❶

- Have students look at the examples and study the boldfaced words.
- Remind students that (+) means *affirmative*, (–) means *negative*, and (?) means *question*.
- Elicit from students that gerunds are the *–ing* forms of the verbs *(running)* and that here they are used as the direct object. Also review that the infinitive is *to* + base form *(to eat)*.

Exercise ❷

- Have students look at the examples again.
- Explain the task: Students read the verbs in the box. They then look for these verbs in the Reading on page 79 and put them in the correct column.
- Set a time limit of 10 minutes. Walk around the room, helping as needed.
- Have students check their answers in pairs.
- Go over the answers with the class. Draw the chart on the board and ask a few students to fill it in.
- Refer students to Grammar Reference page 147, as needed.

Answer key

Verbs followed by gerund	Verbs followed by infinitive
cut down on	decide
dislike	learn
enjoy	need
get out of	promise
give up	want
keep on	
practice	
quit	
stop	
take up	

Exercise ❸

- Explain the task: Students complete the paragraph with the correct form of the verbs in parentheses.
- Set a time limit of 5 minutes.
- Have students check their answers in pairs.
- Go over the answers with the class.

Answer key

1. to take
2. to leave
3. taking
4. listening
5. to give up
6. learning
7. trying
8. trying
9. speaking

Pronunciation

Exercise 4

- Tell students that *to* is usually unstressed and has a weak pronunciation. Remind them that weak pronunciations often have the short, unclear sound /ə/.
- 🎧 Play the recording and have students listen. Ask them to notice the weak pronunciation of *to* in all the sentences and the way the words are blended together in *want to*.
- Say the words in *want + to* separately and then in the blended form "wanna" to highlight the way they sound different. Explain that English speakers often use the blended pronunciation in conversation.

Exercise 5

- 🎧 Play the audio. Stop the audio after each sentence and have students repeat it chorally.
- Ask a few individual students to repeat the sentences to check their pronunciation.
- Encourage students to pronounce the words in *want to* together as if they were a single word. Use the respelling "wanna" to illustrate this.

Speaking

Exercise 6

- Hold up your book and present The Willpower Game. Tell students to use the game board in their books and follow the instructions.
- Form groups of 3. Check that all students have a coin. Demonstrate tossing a coin and choosing one side to mean *go forward one square* and the other side to mean *go forward two squares*.
- Explain that the goal of the game is to be the first to reach the end by making statements in correct English. When students land on a square, they talk about the topic, and tell the truth about themselves. **Note:** There are several sentences possible for any square. Remind the players to listen closely to make sure the sentence is correct. Optionally, ask group members to make corrections.
- Walk around the room, helping as needed. Tell students to raise their hands when they reach the end.

> **EXTENSION**
>
> Have students write down five sentences they said or heard that used gerunds or infinitives. Have them rewrite the sentences using the other verb form (*I enjoy watching TV. / I like to watch TV. / I like to play sports. / Playing sports is my hobby.*).

TRB For additional interactive grammar practice, have students do the reproducible activity for this unit in the *Teacher's Resource Book*.

Writing

Exercise 7

- Assign the writing task for class work or homework. Make sure students understand that they should use their imaginations in order to include things they have given up, cut back on, or taken up. Encourage students to use gerunds and infinitives and some of the phrasal verbs from this unit.
- **TRB** Optionally, give students a copy of the model (see the *Teacher's Resource Book*, Writing Models). Ask them to read the model and notice the vocabulary and grammar from the unit.
- If students don't have the model, write on the board:

    Dear Paul,
    I'm planning a vacation to St. John in the Caribbean, so I want to lose weight and get in shape. I've changed both my diet and my lifestyle! I've given up drinking coffee . . .

    Walk around the room to make sure they understand the task.
- If the assignment is done in class, ask students to exchange their writing with a partner as time permits.

For suggestions on how to give feedback on writing, see page xiv of this *Teacher's Edition*.

CONVERSATION TO GO

- As the students leave class, have them read the dialogue.
- Optionally, point out the humor in the dialogue.

HOMEWORK

- 📖 Assign *Workbook* page 69, Grammar Exercises 3 and 4, and page 70, Pronunciation Exercises 7 and 8.
- 💿 If students do not have the *WorldView Workbook*, assign listening homework from the Student CD. Write on the board:

    Track 39
    If a person loses his or her temper, what's the first thing he or she could do?

- 🎧 Tell students to listen to the audio and write their answer. Have them bring it to the next class. (*He or she could apologize.*)

Pronunciation

4 🎧 **Listen. Notice the weak pronunciation of *to* in the verbs followed by infinitives and the disappearing /t/ sound in *want to* ("wanna").**

I want to lose weight.

I need to get more exercise.

I learned to play tennis.

But then I wanted to eat more.

I want to eat less.

I decided to stop eating chocolate.

I decided to go jogging every day.

And I needed to lose more weight.

5 🎧 **Listen again and repeat.**

Speaking

6 **GROUPS OF 3.** Take turns. Toss a coin (one side of the coin = move one space, the other side of the coin = move two spaces). When you land on a space, use the cues to make a sentence. If your sentence is correct, stay on the space. If it is incorrect, move back to where you started your turn. The first person to reach FINISH wins.

Writing

7 Write a letter to a friend. Describe recent changes you have made either in your work life or personal life, including things you have given up, cut back on, or taken up. You can use your imagination. Use verbs + gerund, verbs + infinitive, and some of the phrasal verbs from this unit.

CONVERSATION TO GO

A: Could I have a piece of your chocolate?
B: Sure. But didn't you **quit eating** chocolate?
A: No. I only **gave up buying** chocolate.

UNIT 18 Wave of the future

Vocabulary Words related to new trends
Grammar *Used to* and *would*
Speaking Comparing past and present trends

Lesson A

Getting started

1 Think about some trends in the world today. Complete the sentences with the words or phrases in the box.

| alternative medicine | genetic engineering | hybrid cars | instant messaging |
| renewable resources | telecommuting | vegetarianism | |

1. People are looking for ways to use <u>renewable resources</u>, like solar energy or windmills, for their energy needs.
2. _____ is quickly replacing the telephone as an easy way to communicate, especially among teenagers.
3. Many restaurants have responded to the trend toward _____ and serve meals using vegetables and grains, but no meat.
4. Instead of traveling to an office, many people are turning to _____. They use phones, faxes, mail, and the Internet to do their jobs without leaving home.
5. _____ use both gasoline and electricity. They are considered friendly to the environment.
6. Acupuncture, herbal remedies, and other traditional Chinese practices have become popular forms of _____ in the U.S.
7. Scientists use _____ to alter agricultural products like corn.

2 **PAIRS.** Compare your answers. Are these trends also happening in your country?

3 Look at the photos. Which of the trends in Exercise 1 does each one show?

4 **GROUPS OF 3.** Discuss these questions.

What's one advantage and one disadvantage of each trend in Exercise 1?
Which trends do you think will most likely become widespread?
Which trends will die out?

A: *Telecommuting has the advantage that you don't have to waste time getting to and from work.*
B: *I agree, but a disadvantage is that you have no personal contact with your coworkers.*

A

Wave of the future

UNIT 18

OBJECTIVES

Students will:

- activate vocabulary related to new trends and technology
- use *used to* and *would*
- practice listening for and saying the blended pronunciation "useta" for *used to/use to*

> **WARM-UP: POPULAR NOW**
>
> - Tell students this unit is about new trends. Explain that a trend is something that is starting to become popular. Give examples of trends, *One trend is more people are concerned about their health and being in shape.*
> - Work together with the class to list on the board at least five things or activities that are popular right now. Possible topics include: *extreme sports, recycling, using wireless devices, eating international foods.*

Getting started

OPTION: VOCABULARY PREVIEW

Tell students to look at the photos. Ask students to describe the people and things they see in the photos. Ask questions such as *What do the people look like? What are they doing? Where are they? What objects do you see in the pictures?*

Exercise ❶

- Have students look at the photos again. Ask them to briefly describe what they see. Focus students on details, such as who or what is in each photo, but not on what trend is being shown.
- Explain the task: Students complete the sentences using the words from the box. Remind students to use context clues to help them figure out new words.
- Go over the example, and then set a time limit of 10 minutes. While students are working, walk around the room, helping as needed.
- Do not go over answers with the class until they have completed Excercise 2.

Teaching Tip! Using context clues

Students are often uncomfortable using context clues to guess the meaning of new words, rather than looking them up in the dictionary. After students have completed a vocabulary exercise, it's helpful to ask them to share which context clues they used to decide what a word means.

Exercise ❷

- Form pairs. Students compare their answers.
- Go over the answers with the class. For 7, check that students know *alter* means "change."

> **Answer key**
>
> 1. renewable resources
> 2. instant messaging
> 3. vegetarianism
> 4. telecommuting
> 5. hybrid cars
> 6. alternative medicine
> 7. genetic engineering

Exercise ❸

- Explain the task: Students look at the photos and identify which of the trends in Exercise 1 each photo shows.
- Go over the answers with the class. Ask, for example, *What does the (first) photo show?*

> **Answer key**
>
> A. hybrid car   B. telecommuting   C. vegetarianism

Exercise ❹

- Form groups of 3. Explain the task: Students discuss the questions.
- Have students read the questions, or read them aloud for the class. Check that students understand that *widespread* means *more popular* or *more common* and that *die out* means *to stop being popular.* If there is a trend familiar to the class that has either become more widespread or has died out, use this as an example.
- Go over the example. Remind students of some expressions they can use to show agreement (*I agree/That's true*) and disagreement (*That may be true, but . . . / I don't think so / I disagree*). Tell students to take turns saying their opinions.
- Set a time limit of 10 minutes.
- Conclude by calling on groups to share one of their ideas.

EXTENSION

Write on the board the following words from the box: *alternative medicine, renewable resources, hybrid cars.* Ask students to work in small groups to list examples of each that they know of. Then call on groups to share their examples, and compile lists on the board.

Teacher's Notes — Lesson A

T82

Listening

Exercise 5

- Explain the task: Tell students they are going to listen to a conversation between Beth and Han-su. Ask them to listen to answer the question, *What's Beth's job?*
- 🎧 Play the audio for the first part of the conversation.
- Go over the answer with the class.

> **Answer key**
> Beth is a trend spotter. She predicts trends.

Exercise 6

- Tell students to listen to the second part of the conversation and decide if the sentences are true or false.
- Have students look at the questions, or read them aloud with the class.
- 🎧 Play the audio. Encourage students to make brief notes as they hear the answers to the questions.
- 🎧 Have students mark their answers, and then play the audio again for students to confirm their answers.

> **Answer key**
> 1. T   4. F
> 2. F   5. T
> 3. T   6. F

Exercise 7

- Pair students. Have them compare their answers and correct the false statements.
- Go over the answers with the class.

> **EXTENSION**
>
> In the conversation, Beth says that electronic books didn't become a trend. Ask students why they think this happened. Ask them to explain which they prefer, traditional books or electronic books, and give their reasons. Give an example, *I like to hold a book and read it when I'm riding the bus.*

Please go to www.longman.com/worldview for additional in-class model conversation practice and supplementary reading practice.

HOMEWORK

- For homework, assign *Workbook* page 71, Vocabulary Exercises 1 and 2, and page 73, Listening Exercises 5 and 6.

Listening

5 🎧 Listen to the first part of the conversation between Beth and Han-su. What's Beth's job?

6 🎧 Listen to the second part of the conversation. Write *T* (true) or *F* (false) after each statement.

According to Beth . . .
1. people used to think that regular books and magazines would disappear. T
2. telecommuting is not very common.
3. people know we need to use renewable resources.
4. people don't worry about wasting energy.
5. solar panels will soon be on every home and business.
6. SUVs are a wave of the future.

7 **PAIRS.** Compare your answers.

Grammar focus

1 Look at the examples. Which of these express a past action? Which of these express a past state? Write *PA* or *PS* next to each one.

> **(+)** People **used to** think that regular books would disappear.
> We **would** get up, get dressed, and go to our work places.
> My sister **used to** drive a small car. Now she drives an SUV.
>
> **(–)** People **didn't use to** worry about wasting energy.
> A few years ago, people **wouldn't** stop talking about e-books.
>
> **(?) Did** she **use to** drive a large car?

2 Look at the examples again. Fill in the blanks with *used to* or *would* to complete the rules in the chart.

Used to and *would*
Use both _____ and _____ for repeated past actions.
Use _____ only to talk about a past state (with *be, have, like, hate* . . .).
NOTE: *Would* usually needs a time reference *(every day, when I was a child)*. *Used to* is more common at the beginning of a narrative. Use *would* in later sentences, especially to avoid repetition.

Grammar Reference page 147

3 Make sentences with a similar meaning, using the correct form of *used to*.

1. When my brother was younger, he worked twelve hours every day.
   When my brother was younger, he used to work twelve hours every day.
2. I hated sports when I was in school, but now I'm a big soccer fan.
3. In the past, my boss drove her car to work every day, but now she uses public transportation.
4. Telecommuting was not very popular years ago, but now many people work from home.
5. Tania is a vegetarian now. She ate meat at least once a day when she was younger.
6. Beto drives a hybrid car now. He had a regular car before.
7. When she was younger, Kim went to the beach every weekend.

4 In which sentences from Exercise 3 could you also use *would*?

Grammar focus

LANGUAGE NOTES

- *Used to* + base form is used to show an habitual state, an event, or an action that was true in the past but is no longer true. *Would* + base form is used to show an event or action that occurred regularly in the past.
- Students need to be aware that both can be used to express past actions, but only *used to* can be used to show a past state, possession, or location. *(He used to like pizza/own a car/live in Paris.)*
- They should also be aware that *used to* is used to contrast the past with the present: *He used to like pizza* implies he no longer likes it.

WARM-UP

Note: Skip this warm-up if you're doing this lesson (Lesson B) during the same class period as Lesson A.

- Books closed. Tell students they are going to listen again to the conversation between Beth and Han-su that they heard in the Listening section.
- Write *used to* on the board. Tell students to listen and write down the verb phrases with *used to*.
- 🎧 Play the audio for Lesson A, Exercises 5 and 6. Play it again, as needed, for students to confirm their answers.
- Ask students what phrases they heard. Write each answer on the board (*used to think, used to say, used to think, used to drive*).
- Ask students if *used to* is used to talk about the past, present, or future (*the past*).

Teaching Tip! Stative verbs

Before students do Exercise 1, review with the students that a verb that expresses a state is a verb such as *think, believe, realize, understand, remember, seem, know, feel, like, love, have*. These verbs don't express any action.

Exercise ❶

- Have students look at the examples. Explain the task: Students decide if each sentence expresses a past action or a past state. For a past action, they write *PA*, and for a past state, they write *PS*. Remind students that if they aren't sure of the answer, they can ask themselves: *Is there an action, like drive or talk?*
- Go over the answers. One way to do this is to call on a student to read each sentence, and have the class say if it is a past action or a past state.

Answer key

(+) PS   (–) PS   (?) PA
PA   PA
PA

Exercise ❷

- Have students look at the examples again and underline the correct word to complete the sentences.
- Draw the chart on the board, and fill in the answers.
- Point out that *would* needs a time reference *(every day)*, and that *used to* is more common at the beginning of a narrative or conversation.
- Refer students to Grammar Reference page 149, as needed.

Answer key

used to, would   used to

Exercise ❸

- Explain the task: Students make sentences with a similar meaning using the appropriate form of *used to*.
- Ask students to look at the example. Point out that *used to* is used here because it was a repeated action in the past.
- Have students complete the exercise individually. Set a time limit of 7 minutes.
- Have students check their answers in pairs.
- Go over the answers with the class.

Answer key

1. used to work   5. used to eat
2. used to hate   6. used to have
3. used to drive   7. used to go
4. didn't use to be

Exercise ❹

- Tell students to decide in which sentences from Exercise 3 they could also use *would* and to rewrite them using *would*. Remind them that *would* is usually used with a time reference (such as *when he was younger*).
- Have students complete the exercise individually. Walk around the room, helping as needed.
- Pair students and have them check their answers.
- Go over the answers with the class.

Answer key

Sentences 1, 3, 5, 7
1. would work   5. would eat
3. would drive   7. would go

EXTENSION

- Ask students to think of a teacher they had when they were younger and to recall things the teacher did. Have them write at least three sentences about the teacher.
- Prompt the students with some sentence starters on the board: *She used to . . . Every day, he would . . .* Ask students to share their sentences in small groups.

T84

Pronunciation

Exercise 5

- Explain that the word *used* on its own is pronounced /yuzd/, but in the expression *used to* for a past habit, the two words are blended together and pronounced as "useta."
- 🎧 Play the audio and have students listen. Ask them to notice the way the words are blended together in *used to* and *use to*.
- Say the words *used* and *to* separately and then in the blended form "useta" to highlight the way they sound different. Point out that the /z/ sound in *used* changes to /s/ in "useta" and that *to* has its weak pronunciation /tə/.

Exercise 6

- 🎧 Play the audio. Stop the audio after each item to allow students to repeat chorally.
- Ask a few individual students to repeat and check their pronunciation.
- Encourage students to link the words together in *used to* and to stress the first syllable. Putting stress on the first syllable will help them produce the weak form of *to*.

EXTENSION

- Pair students. Have them take turns saying the sentences with *used to* that they wrote for Exercise 3.
- Walk around the room, helping as needed.

Speaking

Teaching Tip! Follow-up questions

Remind students that it is important to ask follow-up questions to keep a conversation going. The questions are usually related to the topic. If someone wants to change the topic, some expressions that can be used are *Speaking of* (chocolate) or *Not to change the topic, but . . .*

Exercise 7

- Explain the task: Students complete the sentences to make true statements about their past and current habits. Tell them they can also create some information if they cannot think of anything true.
- Set a time limit of 8 minutes. Walk around the room, helping as needed.

Exercise 8

- Pair students. Ask them to take turns telling each other about their past and present habits. Tell them to ask follow-up questions to keep the conversation going.
- Go over the example, and then set a time limit of 8 minutes.
- Walk around the room, helping as needed.

Exercise 9

- Ask students to report to the class. Have them tell the class about one of their partner's habits, *(Ana) used to play tennis, but she took up golf instead this year.*

TRB For additional interactive grammar practice, have students do the reproducible activity for this unit in the *Teacher's Resource Book*.

Writing

Exercise 10

- Assign the writing task for class work or homework. To help students get started, work with the class to compile a list on the board of topics related to lifestyle, such as *work, place to live, food, leisure activities, modern conveniences*. Remind students to include what is different and what things are better or worse.
- **TRB** Optionally, give students a copy of the model (see the *Teacher's Resource Book*, Writing Models). Ask them to read the model and notice *used to* and *would*.
- If students do not have the model, write on the board:

    My parents' lifestyle used to be quieter and less hecic. They would go to work and then come home and relax. Sometimes they would . . .

    Walk around the room to make sure students understand the task.

- If the assignment is done in class, ask students to exchange their writing in pairs and compare their parents' lifestyles.

For suggestions on how to give feedback on writing, see page xiv of this *Teacher's Edition*.

CONVERSATION TO GO

- As the students leave class, have them read the dialogue.
- Point out that *I'd* is the contraction of *I would*.

HOMEWORK

- 📖 Assign *Workbook* page 72, Grammar Exercises 3 and 4, and page 73, Pronunciation Exercises 7 and 8.
- 💿 If students do not have the *WorldView Workbook*, assign listening homework from the Student CD. Write on the board:

    Track 57
    What are two renewable resources?

- 🎧 Tell students to listen to the audio and write their answer. Have them bring it to the next class. (*wind power and solar power*)

Pronunciation

5 🎧 **Listen.** Notice that *used to* and *use to* are pronounced the same way: "useta."

used to	She used to drive a small car.
use to	Did you use to work in an office?
didn't use to	I didn't use to like vegetables.

6 🎧 Listen again and repeat.

Speaking

7 **BEFORE YOU SPEAK.** Think about your past and current habits. Complete the sentences.

8 **PAIRS.** Take turns telling each other about your past and present habits. Ask follow-up questions.

A: I used to eat a lot of chocolate.
B: Really? Would you have chocolate every day?
A: Yes, I would.

9 Tell the class about one of your partner's habits.

Writing

10 Compare your lifestyle with that of your parents when they were your age. What is different? What things were better or worse? Use *used to* and *would*.

1. Eating habits
   I used to eat a lot of _____.
   I would buy _____.
   Now I _____ all the time.

2. Commuting _____.
   I used to go to school/ work by _____ (form of transportation).
   I would spend _____ (amount of time) getting ready and traveling.
   Now I _____

3. Other _____.
   I used to _____
   I would _____.
   Now _____.

CONVERSATION TO GO

A: I **used to** live in the city, but last year we moved to the countryside.
B: I did the opposite. I **used to** have a house in the suburbs, and **I'd** drive two hours to work every day.

Lesson B

UNIT 19

Made in the U.S.A.

Vocabulary Materials; possessions
Grammar Passive (simple present)
Speaking Describing where things come from

Lesson A

Getting started

1. Look at the pictures of items you can buy at Fisherman's Wharf in San Francisco. Match each item with the material.

   1. cotton __G__   2. glass _____   3. gold _____   4. leather _____
   5. pewter _____   6. lycra _____   7. silver _____   8. wood _____

2. 🎧 Listen and check your answers. Then listen again and repeat.

3. **PAIRS.** Take turns asking and answering the questions.

   What things do you typically buy that are made of wood or glass?

   Do you prefer silver or gold jewelry? Why?

   Do you prefer cotton or polyester clothing? Why?

   What kinds of leather clothes or accessories do you like?

   What is your most treasured possession? What material is it made of?

Visit Fisherman's Wharf
with its spectacular view of the bay and handicrafts from all over the world

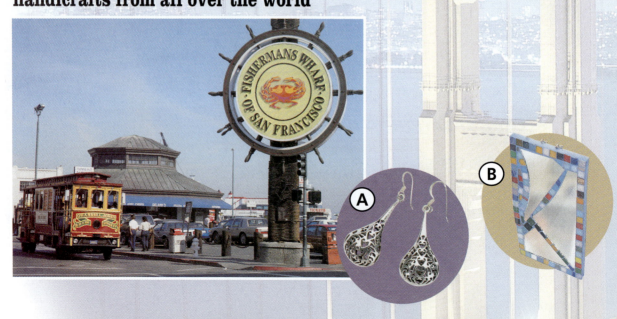

Made in the U.S.A.

UNIT 19

Teacher's Notes — Lesson A

OBJECTIVES

Students will:
- activate vocabulary related to materials and possessions
- use the passive (simple present)
- listen for and pronounce words in which /n/ and /l/ form a syllable with no vowel sound

BACKGROUND INFORMATION

The Golden Gate Bridge is a suspension bridge that links San Francisco, California, with Marin County to the north. It was opened in 1937, and is a famous landmark of the city.

Fisherman's Wharf is another popular internationally-known tourist destination. It was named for the many fishing boats that used to dock there, but is now a long mall of over a hundred stores and restaurants.

WARM-UP: WHAT'S IT MADE OF?

- Tell students this unit is about personal possessions and the materials used to make them. "Made in the U.S.A." means that an item was manufactured or produced in the United States.
- As a class brainstorm a list of products that are made in the student's country. Write them on the board.
- If you have time, you may want to make a list of other products that students use or see constantly and where they are from. If students are not sure, they can go online after class to find the information.

Getting started

LANGUAGE NOTES

- All of the materials presented in this unit, with the exception of *wood*, can be used as both nouns and adjectives; for example, *silver: a silver necklace*. The adjective form of *wood* is *wooden: a wooden bowl*.
- *Pewter* is a gray, nonshiny metal, made by mixing lead and tin. It is used to make candlesticks, vases, and other decorative items.
- You might want to point out that *treasured possession* doesn't need to be worth a lot of money, only that it is special to the person who owns it.

OPTION: VOCABULARY PREVIEW

- Ask students to look around the room and identify three items, such as a table, a book, a light, and so on. Tell them to write down the name of the item and what they think it is made from.
- Form groups of 4. Set a time limit of 2 minutes. Write the following on the board: *It's a _____. It's made of _____.* Ask students to talk about their lists.

- Call on each group to tell the class about two items. Make a list on the board.
- Make sure the following materials are on the list: *cotton, glass, gold, leather, pewter, lycra, wood*. If not, point out an item made from the material or give an example. Answer any questions students may have about the vocabulary.

Exercise 1

- Tell students to look at the pictures of the items you can buy at Fisherman's Wharf. Ask them if they are familiar with Fisherman's Wharf. If anyone has been there, invite the student to briefly tell the class about it.
- Explain the task: Students match each item with the material it is made of. Have students look at the materials. Verify that they are familiar with them.
- Go over the example, and then set a time limit of 5 minutes. While students are working, walk around the room, helping as needed.
- Do not go over answers with the class until they have completed Exercise 2.

Exercise 2

- 🎧 Play the audio and have students check answers.
- Go over the answers with the class.

Answer key
1. cotton G   4. leather F   7. silver A
2. glass B   5. pewter D   8. wood H
3. gold C   6. lycra E

Exercise 3

- Pair students. Explain the task: Students take turns asking and answering the questions. Have the students read the questions, or read them aloud with the class.
- Set a time limit of 10 minutes. Walk around the room, helping as needed.
- For each question, call on a pair of students to ask and answer it. Encourage students to give reasons.

Answer key
answers will vary

EXTENSION

- Form groups of 3. Have students discuss their most treasured possessions. Encourage them to ask and answer questions such as *How long have you had it? Where did you get it? Why is it special to you?*
- Call on volunteers from various groups to report.

T86

Listening

Exercise 4

- Explain the task: Students listen to two tourists, Marcela and Peter, who are shopping at Fisherman's Wharf. Students then complete the chart for the items that Marcela and Peter talk about. Check that students understand *country of origin* means the country where something is made; hold up an object and say *This was made in (China). Its country of origin is (China).*
- 🎧 Play the recording. Walk around the room, helping as needed.
- 🎧 Play the recording one more time so that students can confirm their answers.
- Go over the answers with the class.

Answer key

	Item	Material	Country of origin	Price
1	mirror	glass	Holland	$100
2	box	wood	Morocco	$50
3	earrings	silver	Mexico	$25

Exercise 5

- Explain the task: Students listen, and then circle the picture of the item that Peter buys.
- 🎧 Play the recording.
- Go over the answer with the class.
- Optionally, do a quick review of comparatives and superlatives. Say, *Of the things Marcela and Peter looked at, which is more expensive, the mirror or the earrings? The box or the earrings? Which is the most/least expensive?*

Answer key

earrings

Exercise 6

- Pair students. Have them read and answer the question.
- Go over the answer with the class. **Note:** You may want to point out that *cheap* can mean *inexpensive* or it can mean *poor quality*. Here, it means *inexpensive*.

Answer key

because they are cheap

🌐 Please go to www.longman.com/worldview for supplementary reading practice.

> **EXTENSION**
>
> Pair students. One takes Marcela's part, and the other takes Peter's. Have them use the information in the listening to role-play the conversation. Emphasize that they should create their own lines, using the ideas they have heard, not memorize lines from the conversation.

Pronunciation

Exercise 7

- Explain that most syllables have a vowel sound, but that sometimes an /n/ or /l/ can make a syllable by itself, without any vowel.
- 🎧 Play the recording and have students listen. The words with syllabic consonants are said in isolation first to highlight their pronunciation.
- Point out that even though there is usually a vowel in the spelling, the vowel is not pronounced.

Exercise 8

- 🎧 Play the recording of the individual words. Stop the recording after each word and have students repeat chorally. Then ask a few individual students to repeat and check their pronunciation.
- Encourage students to pronounce the syllabic /n/ or /l/ without adding a vowel sound before it. Have them start to say a word like *cotton, wooden,* or *metal,* but stop after the /t/ or /d/ sound. Then tell them to try to say /n/ or /l/ without moving the tongue away from the roof of the mouth.
- Check to make sure students put stress on the syllables shown in bold type and not on the syllables with syllabic /n/ or /l/.
- 🎧 Then play the recording of the sentences. Stop the recording after each sentence and have students repeat first chorally and then individually.

🌐 Please go to www.longman.com/worldview for additional in-class model conversation practice.

HOMEWORK

- 📖 For homework, assign *Workbook* page 74, Vocabulary Exercises 1 and 2, and page 76, Listening Exercises 5 and 6.

Listening

4 🎧 Listen to Marcela and Peter, tourists at Fisherman's Wharf in San Francisco. Complete the chart with information on the items they talk about.

Item	Material	Country of origin	Price
mirror			

5 🎧 Listen again. Circle the picture of the item Peter buys.

6 **PAIRS.** Why does Peter buy it?

Pronunciation

7 🎧 Listen. Notice that the sound /n/ or /l/ can form a syllable without a vowel sound.

cott*o*n   wood*e*n   di*d*n't

met*a*l   sand*a*ls   cand*le*sticks

8 🎧 Listen. Notice how the words with these sounds are pronounced in the sentences.

They didn't buy the cotton shirt.   They didn't buy the wooden boxes.

They didn't buy the sandals.   They didn't buy the metal candlesticks.

9 🎧 Listen again and repeat.

Grammar focus

1 Study the examples of the active and passive voice.

Active voice	Passive voice
They make the mirrors in Holland by hand.	The mirrors **are handmade** in Holland.
Artists hand-paint the mirrors.	The mirrors are hand-painted by artists.
The big stores sell it for at least $75.	It's sold in the big stores for at least $75.
Where do they make it?	Where **is** it **made**?

2 Look at the examples again. Circle *a* or *b* to answer the questions.

Simple present passive

In the passive sentences, which is more important?

a. the people who make, sell, or buy things   b. the things that they make, sell, or buy

How do you form the simple present passive?

a. *have* + the past participle   b. *be* + the past participle

Grammar Reference page 147

3 Rewrite the sentences in the passive. Do not mention the agent (the person or thing that does the action) unless it is necessary to understand the sentence.

1. We call rugs from Turkey, Iran, and Pakistan Oriental rugs.

    Rugs from Turkey, Iran, and Pakistan are called Oriental rugs.

2. Cosmetics companies use fish scales to make lipstick.
3. The U.S. imports most of its electronics from Japan.
4. Both the medical industry and the photography industry use silver.
5. Swiss companies manufacture most of the gold watches in the world.
6. Factories in Canada produce most of the foreign cars sold in the U.S.
7. Food companies add preservatives to food to make it last longer.
8. The supply of materials affects the price of the product.

Grammar focus

> **LANGUAGE NOTES**
> - In general, the passive is used when an action, or the result of an action, is more important to communicate than who did the action. It's also commonly used when the speaker doesn't know who performed an action.
> - In this unit, the passive is used because the focus is on the materials, the origin, and other characteristics of possessions. *Who* painted the item, or *who* made it (unless it was hand-made) is less important.

> **WARM-UP**
>
> Note: Skip this warm-up if you're doing this lesson (Lesson B) during the same class period as Lesson A.
> - Books closed. Tell students they are going to listen again to the conversation between Marcela and Peter that they heard in the Listening section.
> - Tell students to listen for what Marcela asks about the boxes and what the shopkeeper tells her. Also ask them to listen for what the shopkeeper says about the jewelry.
> - 🎧 Play the recording for Lesson A, Exercises 4 and 5.
> - Ask students what Marcela asks (*Where are they made?*), and what the shopkeeper tells her. (*They're made in Morocco. They're hand-painted.*) Then ask what the shopkeeper says about the jewelry. (*All of my silver jewelry is bought in Mexico.*) Write each answer on the board.

Exercise ❶

- Have students look at the examples and study the bold-faced words.
- Ask students to focus on the passive voice column.
- Elicit that present tense passive is formed with *am/is/are* + past participle.

Exercise ❷

- Have students look at the examples and circle *a* or *b* to answer the questions.
- Go over the answers. Provide more information as needed to make sure students understand why the passive is being used here (*to focus on the objects*).
- Refer students to Grammar Reference page 147, as needed.

> **Answer key**
> 1. b   2. b

Exercise ❸

- Explain the task: Students rewrite the sentences in the passive. Remind students not to include who did the action unless it is necessary for the meaning to be clear.
- Ask students to look at the example. Point out that the passive is used here because the focus is on how much paper is used; it's understood that people use it.
- Have students complete the exercise individually. Set a time limit of 10 minutes.
- Have students check their answers in pairs.
- Go over the answers with the class. Point out that the "doer" is mentioned in sentences 4, 5, and 8 because otherwise the meaning wouldn't be clear.

> **Answer key**
> 1. Rugs from Turkey, Iran, and Pakistan are called Oriental rugs.
> 2. Fish scales are used to make lipstick.
> 3. Most of the electronics in the U.S. are imported from Japan.
> 4. Silver is used by both the medical industry and the photography industry.
> 5. Most of the gold watches in the world are manufactured by Swiss companies.
> 6. Most of the foreign cars sold in the U.S. are produced in Canada.
> 7. Preservatives are added to food to make it last longer.
> 8. The price of the product is affected by the supply of materials.

Speaking

> **LANGUAGE NOTE**
>
> Some students confuse *made of* versus *made from*. Generally, *made of* is used to talk about the material; for example, *the shoes are made of leather, the shirt is made of cotton*. *Made from* is used when the material is processed in some way so that its form is different; for example, *Tortillas are made from corn, ice cream is made from cream and sugar, tofu is made from soybeans, wine is made from grapes or other fruit.*

Exercise 4

- Explain the task: Students talk to each other and try to find someone who has something or who is wearing something made of the materials listed in the chart. They should also find out if the item is handmade and where it was made.
- Form students into small groups, or tell students to stand up and walk around the room to talk to classmates. Remind students to fill in their charts as they gather their information. Go over the example.
- Set a time limit of 10 minutes. Walk around the room, helping as needed.
- After 10 minutes, ask students to return to their seats. If students haven't completed their surveys, extend the time another few minutes.

Exercise 5

- Pair students. Ask them to take turns telling each other about their survey results.
- Go over the example, and then set a time limit of 5 minutes.
- Walk around the room, helping as needed.

Exercise 6

- Draw a five-column chart on the board with the headings: *cotton, gold, leather, silver, wood*. Ask students what things people have that are made of each of these materials. Fill in their answers, or have a student come to the board and fill in the answers.
- Conclude by asking students to count up the items in each column and decide which material is the most common.

> **EXTENSION**
>
> Bring a variety of objects to class. Do not show them to the whole class. Instead, form small groups of students, and give each group an object. Each group writes down the features of the item as they did for Exercise 4, but not what the object is. Groups then exchange papers and try to guess what the object is. Encourage students to ask each other for more details until they can guess correctly.

TRB For additional interactive grammar practice, have students do the reproducible activity for this unit in the *Teacher's Resource Book*.

Writing

Exercise 7

- Assign the writing task for class work or homework.
- **TRB** Optionally, give students a copy of the model (see the *Teacher's Resource Book,* Writing Models). Ask them to read the model and notice the vocabulary and grammar from the unit.
- If students don't have the model, write on the board:

    One of my most treasued possessions is a brown purse that my sister gave me. The purse is made of beautiful dark brown leather . . .

    Walk around the room to make sure they understand the task.

- If the assignment is done in class, ask students to exchange their writing in small groups.

For suggestions on how to give feedback on writing, see page xiv of this *Teacher's Edition*.

CONVERSATION TO GO

- As the students leave class, have them read the dialogue.
- Optionally, tell students to look around the room, and then ask, *Is anyone in the room wearing anything made of silver?*

HOMEWORK

- Assign *Workbook* page 75, Grammar Exercises 3 and 4, and page 76, Pronunciation Exercises 7, 8, and 9.
- If students do not have the *WorldView Workbook*, assign listening homework from the Student CD. Write on the board:

    Track 43
    How much money does Peter ask Marcela for?

- Tell students to listen to the audio and write their answer. Have them bring it to the next class. (*$10*)

Speaking

4 Find someone in the class who has something with him or her today, or who is wearing something, made of the materials listed below. Complete the chart with the answers. Find out other details.

A: Are you wearing anything made of cotton?
B: Yes, my jacket is made of cotton.
A: Is it handmade?
B: No.
A: Is it imported?

Person	Material	Object	Handmade?	Imported?
	cotton			
	gold			
	leather			
	silver			
	wood			

5 **PAIRS.** Take turns telling each other about the results of your survey.

Min-ja's jacket is made of cotton. It's not handmade. It's made in Korea.

6 Take a poll of the class. Find out what things people have that are made of cotton, gold, leather, silver, and wood.

Writing

7 Write a paragraph about something special that you bought on a trip or that someone gave you. Say what it is made of, who made it, and where it was made. Use the passive voice.

CONVERSATION TO GO

A: Did you make that ring?
B: Yes, I did.
A: What's it **made of**?
B: Silver.

UNIT 20

At the movies

Vocabulary Types of movies
Grammar *so, too, neither, (not) either*
Speaking Talking about favorite movies

Lesson A

Getting started

1 Match the comments about movies with the words in the box.

a) an action movie   b) an animated film   c) a comedy
d) a drama   e) a horror movie   f) a martial arts film   g) a musical
h) a science fiction movie   i) ~~a thriller~~   j) a western

1. It was very intense. The ending was totally surprising. __i__
2. I laughed all the time. _____
3. I loved the music and the dancing. _____
4. It was really scary. I had to close my eyes every five minutes. _____
5. There were lots of fights between cowboys. _____
6. It's set in the future, when computers run the world. _____
7. The hero fought off a whole army with his bare hands. _____
8. It's full of exciting scenes, with lots of explosions and car chases. _____
9. It's a very emotional story about a man who lived alone on an island. _____
10. It's a computer-animated comedy about friendly monsters. _____

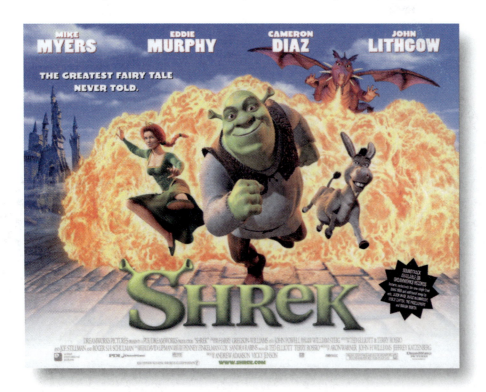

90

At the movies

UNIT 20

OBJECTIVES

Students will:
- activate vocabulary related to types of movies
- use *so, too, neither, (not) either*
- practice listening for and pronouncing syllables and word-stress patterns

WARM-UP: MOVIE TIME

- Tell students this unit is about movies.
- Ask students: *What makes a good movie? Is it the actors, the music, the story, the special effects?* Tell students to discuss the factors that they think make a movie good.
- Form groups of 3. Set a time limit of 3 minutes. Students take turns saying their opinions.
- After 3 minutes, take a poll to find out what factors the students think are most important. Ask: *Is it the actors? Is it the special effects?* and so on.

BACKGROUND INFORMATION

Movies in the posters:

Lord of the Rings, a movie trilogy (2001, 2002, 2003) directed by Peter Jackson, is an epic tale of good versus evil. In it, a Hobbit, Frodo, has the ancient Ring and must journey through Middle Earth to destroy it, which he does in the final movie.

Shrek (2001) is an animated fairytale about a sweet ogre named Shrek and a talking donkey who go on a journey to save a princess from a mean lord. They are successful and everyone lives happily ever after.

Crouching Tiger, Hidden Dragon (Wu hu cang long) (2000), directed by Ang Lee, takes place in feudal China. It is the story of two warriors seeking a stolen sword and a fugitive. It is based on themes of pain, revenge, and duty.

Getting started

OPTION: VOCABULARY PREVIEW

- Form groups of 3. Set a time limit of 2 minutes. Ask students to make a group list of five movies. They can include favorite movies, famous movies, classics, movies they have heard about, etc.
- Have students work through their list and (1) think about what type of movie it is and write words that describe the movie, and (2) write words that describe the different atmospheres in the movie and the feelings they had while watching the movie. You may want to write some examples on the board: *James Bond's Goldfinger: suspense, crime, action / surprise, romantic, good over evil. Notting Hill: romantic comedy / funny, romantic, sad, a happy ending.*

- While students are working, walk around the room, helping as needed.
- Ask each group to say one of their movies and the words they wrote about it. Write the words from each group on the board. You may want to group them in categories: type of film (make sure all of the words in Exercise 1 are on the board); feelings (*funny, sad, exciting,* etc.); themes (*good over evil, happy endings,* etc.).

Teaching Tip! Key words

To do Exercise 1, students need to read each sentence carefully and look for the word or words that give them the "key" information they need to decide what kind of movie it refers to. After students complete the exercise, you may want to quickly review each sentence and ask students to identify the "key" words they used. This can benefit the whole class, particularly those students who missed the context clues and therefore made errors.

Exercise 1

- Ask students to look at the movie posters. Check if students are familiar with these movies. Point out that these were all popular movies in the early 2000s. Provide other background information as needed.
- Explain the task: Students match the words in the box with the comments about movies. Explain that the words in the box are all types of movies. Go over the example. Ask students what words in the sentence told them it was a thriller (*very intense* and *ending/totally surprising*). Emphasize that they need to read each sentence carefully and look for the "key" words.
- Set a time limit of 7 minutes. While students are working, walk around the room, helping as needed.
- Go over the answers with the class. You can write on the board *It was a* to use as a prompt as students answer the questions. (*It was a thriller.*)

Answer key

1. a thriller
2. a comedy
3. a musical
4. a horror movie
5. a western
6. a science fiction movie
7. a martial arts film
8. an action movie
9. a drama
10. an animated film

Teacher's Notes — Lesson A

Pronunciation

Exercise 2

- Check that students understand what the circles mean.
- Remind them that the circles represent the number of syllables. The big circle represents main stress.
- Ask students to count the number of syllables and write each word in the correct stress group.
- Do the first word as an example. Write *drama* on the board and count out the syllables on your fingers. Say the word with stress on different syllables to elicit the correct stress (**dra**ma). Mark the correct stress.
- 🎧 Play the audio and have students listen. Stop the audio after each item to give students time to write.
- Do not go over answers with the class until they have completed Exercise 3.

Exercise 3

- 🎧 Play the audio. Have students listen and check their answers to Exercise 2.
- 🎧 Then play the audio again, and ask students to repeat the items chorally.
- Encourage students to make the vowel in the stressed syllable long.
- Ask a few individual students to repeat the words to check their pronunciation.

Answer key

●●	●●●	●●●●	●●●●
drama	musical	science fiction	action movie
western	comedy	martial arts film	horror movie
thriller			animated

Exercise 4

- Pair students. Ask them to look at the posters again. Explain the task: Students tell each other about the movies in the posters. They decide which words from the box describe each movie.
- Set a time limit of 5 minutes. Have the students read the questions, or read them aloud for the class.
- Encourage students to use the vocabulary from Exercise 1. Walk around the room, helping as needed.
- Ask several pairs to share their answers with the class. Check that they use the correct stress in the words.

Answer key

Lord of the Rings: drama, action movie
Shrek: animated film, comedy
Crouching Tiger, Hidden Dragon: martial arts film, drama

Listening

> **BACKGROUND INFORMATION**
>
> The listening selection refers to the original *Star Wars*, directed in 1911 by George Lucas. The complete *Star Wars* series is six films long.
>
> *E.T.* (1982), directed by Steven Spielberg, is the story of a group of Earth children who become friends with an alien named E.T. who has come to Earth.
>
> *Titanic* (1997), directed by James Cameron, is a drama/romance based on the true story of the *Titanic* disaster. The movie won eleven Academy Awards (Oscars).

Exercise 5

- Pair students. Tell students to read the questions and the names of the movies. Ask students if they are familiar with these movies. Provide information as needed.
- Have students work together to guess the answers.

Exercise 6

- Explain the task: Students listen to an interview and check their answers. Check that students know a *fan* is someone who likes something or someone very much.
- 🎧 Play the audio.
- 🎧 Play the audio one more time so that students can confirm their answers.
- Go over the answers with the class.

Answer key 1. (c) *Titanic*   2. (c) *Titanic*

Exercise 7

- Have students look at the statements, or read them aloud with the class.
- 🎧 Play the audio again. Encourage students to make brief notes as they hear the answers to the statements.
- 🎧 Have students mark their answers, and then play the audio again for students to confirm their answers.
- Go over the answers with the class. Ask students to correct the false statements.

Answer key

1. F/The interviewer and the guest both think *Star Wars* is one of the best action movies ever made.
2. T
3. F/There are no perfect movies.
4. F/The most frequent mistake involves the actors and extras wearing watches.

🌐 Please go to www.longman.com/worldview for additional in-class model conversation practice and supplementary reading practice.

HOMEWORK

- 📖 For homework, assign *Workbook* page 77, Vocabulary Exercises 1 and 2, and page 79, Listening Exercises 4 and 5.

Pronunciation

2 🎧 Listen to the words from the box in Exercise 1. Notice the number of syllables and the stress. Write each word in the correct group.

●●	●●●	●●●●	●●●●
drama			

3 🎧 Listen and check your answers. Then listen again and repeat.

4 **PAIRS.** Use the words from Exercise 1 to say at least two things about each of the movies in the posters.

Listening

5 **PAIRS.** Guess the answer to each question.

1. Which of these movies made the most money at the box office?
   a. *Star Wars*
   b. *E.T.*
   c. *Titanic*

2. Which of these movies was the most expensive to make?
   a. *Lord of the Rings*
   b. *Star Wars*
   c. *Titanic*

6 🎧 Listen to the interview and check your guesses.

7 🎧 Listen again. Write *T* (true) or *F* (false) after each statement. If the statement is false, write the correct information.

1. The interviewer and the guest both think *Star Wars* is one of the best animated films ever made.

2. Both the interviewer and the guest were surprised at *Titanic*'s success.

3. Not many movies have mistakes in them.

4. The most frequent mistake in movies involves the clothes the actors and extras wear.

20

Lesson B

Grammar focus

1 Study the examples of additions with *so, too, neither,* and *not either.*

> The editors are upset, and **so** are the directors.
> The editors are upset, and the directors are, **too**.
> I didn't know that, and **neither** did the fans.
> I didn't know that, and the fans did**n't either**.

2 Look at the examples again. Underline the correct information to complete the rules in the chart.

Additions: *so, too, neither, (not) either*
Additions always use a form of *be*, an auxiliary verb (such as *have* or *do*), or a modal (such as *can, should,* or *will*). The verb tense in the addition must match the verb tense in the first sentence.
Use *so* or *too* if the addition follows **an affirmative / a negative** statement.
Use *neither* or *not either* if the addition follows **an affirmative / a negative** statement.
In additions with *so* and *neither*, the subject comes **after / before** the verb.

Grammar Reference page 147

3 Rewrite the sentences using *so, too, either,* or *neither*. Remember to use commas correctly.

1. Both Silvia and Pedro are movie experts.
   Silvia is a movie expert, and so is Pedro.
2. Bruce and David can't go to the movies tonight.
3. Frank and Lois were disappointed in the musical they saw.
4. Russell Crowe and Cameron Diaz are famous actors.
5. Two comedies, *All Day Long* and *Mother*, are playing tonight.
6. Yi-Lian and her friend don't like horror movies.
7. Pat and Omar thought the acting was terrible.
8. Alice and Vera didn't like the ending to the thriller.

4 **PAIRS.** Compare your answers from Exercise 3. If your answers are the same, what other way could you say the same thing?

Silvia is a movie expert, and Pedro is, too.

Grammar focus

> **LANGUAGE NOTES**
> - One way to help students understand that there are alternative ways of expressing the same information is to set up equations:
>
>   *Dan is a jazz musician and so is Jerry = Dan is a jazz musician and Jerry is, too.*
>   *Dan doesn't like rock music and neither does Jerry = Dan doesn't like rock music and Jerry doesn't either.*
>
> - Remind students to pay attention to the word order: *I didn't know that* (the subject "I" comes before "did") and *neither did Thomas* (the subject follows "did").

> **WARM-UP**
>
> **Note:** Skip this warm-up if you're doing this lesson (Lesson B) during the same class period as Lesson A.
>
> - Books closed. Tell students they are going to listen again to the interview that they heard in the Listening section.
> - Tell students to listen to answer the following questions: 1. *What does the interviewer say about the car in the field in* Lord of the Rings? 2. *Who is upset when they see actors wearing watches?*
> - 🎧 Play the audio for Lesson A, Exercises 6 and 7.
> - Ask students for the answers. Write them on the board:
>   1. *I didn't know that and <u>neither</u> did a lot of fans.*
>   2. *The editors must be upset <u>and so</u> are the directors.*
>   Underline *neither* and *and so*.
> - Underneath 1 write *I didn't know that and a lot of fans <u>didn't either</u>*. Underneath 2 write *The editors must be upset and the directors are, <u>too</u>*.
> - Have students read each pair of sentences. Explain that the sentences in each pair have the same meaning.

Exercise ❶

- Have students look at the examples and study the boldfaced words.
- Ask students to focus on the first two examples.
- Elicit from students that the sentences have the same meaning.
- Ask students to focus on the second two examples.
- Elicit from students that the sentences have the same meanings.

Exercise ❷

- Have students look at the examples again and underline the correct information to complete the rules in the box.
- Have students check their answers in pairs.
- Go over the rules with the class.
- Refer students to Grammar Reference page 147, as needed.

> **Answer key**
>
> an affirmative   a negative   after

EXTENSION

- To make sure students understand the rules, have them work in pairs to write eight simple descriptive sentences of people and objects in the classroom. For example, *Tina is tall, and Ana is tall, too. / Robert is tall and so is José. / Leo isn't wearing a jacket, and Marco isn't either. / Hiro doesn't have a backpack, and neither does Hideki.*
- Have pairs work with another pair to exchange papers and check each other's sentences. For an added challenge, ask one pair at a time to read a sentence for the class. Have the class listen, then restate the information in a different way. For example, pair one says *Tina is tall, and Ana is tall, too*. Another student listens, and responds *Tina is tall and so is Ana*.

Exercise ❸

- Explain the task: Students rewrite the sentences using *so, too, either,* or *neither*.
- Ask students to look at the example. Point out that "both" in the first sentence means *Silvia is an expert and Pedro is an expert*. Explain that using "and so" is a simpler way of saying it.
- Set a time limit of 10 minutes, and have students complete the exercise individually. Walk around the room, helping as needed.
- Go over the answers with the class.

Exercise ❹

- Pair students. Explain the task: Students compare their answers from Exercise 3. If their answers are the same, have them say the sentence a different way.
- Go over the example.
- Set a time limit of 5 minutes. Walk around the room, helping as needed.
- Call on a few students to say their sentences.

> **Answer key**
>
> **Note:** For each sentence there are two possible rewrites.
> 1. Silvia is a movie expert, and so is Pedro. (Pedro is, too)
> 2. Bruce can't go to the movies tonight, and neither can David. (David can't either)
> 3. Frank was disappointed in the musical they saw, and so was Lois. (Lois was, too)
> 4. Russell Crowe is a famous actor, and so is Cameron Diaz. (Cameron Diaz is, too)
> 5. *All Day Long* is playing tonight, and so is *Mother*. (*Mother* is, too)
> 6. Yi-Lian doesn't like horror movies, and neither does her friend. (her friend doesn't either)
> 7. Pat thought the acting was terrible, and Omar did, too. (so did Omar)
> 8. Alice didn't like the ending to the thriller, and neither did Vera. (Vera didn't either)

Teacher's Notes — Lesson B

Speaking

Exercise 5

- Continue in the same groups or form new groups of 3. Explain the task: Students take turns asking each other about their favorite movies, and take notes in the survey form in their books. Encourage students to ask follow-up questions to find out what the person especially likes about each movie.
- Go over the example with the class.
- Set a time limit of 15 minutes. Walk around the room, helping as needed.

Exercise 6

- Explain the task: Students report to the class what they found out about their classmates' tastes in movies. Go over the example.
- Call on individual students to report to the class as time permits.

> **EXTENSION**
>
> Have students write short reviews of movies, based on their discussions in Exercise 5. Remind students to use vocabulary from the unit. They can present to the class or in small groups as time permits.

TRB For additional interactive grammar practice, have students do the reproducible activity for this unit in the *Teacher's Resource Book*.

Writing

Exercise 7

- Assign the writing task for class work or homework.
- **TRB** Optionally, give students a copy of the model (see the *Teacher's Resource Book*, Writing Models). Ask them to read the model and notice the vocabulary and grammar from the unit.
- If students don't have the model, write on the board:

    Florencia and I often go to the movies together because we like the same kinds of movies. Florencia loves good comedies, and so do I . . .

    Walk around the room to make sure they understand the task.
- If the assignment is done in class, ask students to exchange their writing in small groups as time permits.

For suggestions on how to give feedback on writing, see page xiv of this *Teacher's Edition*.

CONVERSATION TO GO

- As the students leave class, have them read the dialogue.
- Optionally, ask students how they could say the same thing a different way. (A: *Terry loves action films and Alex does, too.* B: *Well, I don't like them at all, and Dana doesn't either.*)

HOMEWORK

- Assign *Workbook* page 78, Grammar Exercise 3, and page 79, Pronunciation Exercises 6 and 7. Assign *Workbook* Self-quiz Units 17–20.
- If students do not have the *WorldView Workbook*, assign listening homework from the Student CD. Write on the board:

    Track 47
    Which movie has a car where it shouldn't?

- Tell students to listen to the audio and write their answer. Have them bring it to the next class. (*Lord of the Rings*)

BEFORE NEXT CLASS

- Tell students that the next class will be a review class covering Units 17–20.
- Have students review the material in the units to prepare for the activities in Review 5.

Unit no.	Review Grammar	Listen to Student CD	Study Grammar Reference
17	verb + gerunds; verbs + infinitives	Track 39	Page 147
18	*for . . ./to . . .* after adjective/noun to express opinions	Track 41	Page 147
19	passive (simple present)	Track 43	Page 147
20	*so, too, neither, (not) either*	Track 47	Page 147

FOR NEXT CLASS

TRB Make copies of Quiz 5 in the *Teacher's Resource Book*.

Speaking

5 **GROUPS OF 3.** Take turns asking each other about the kinds of movies you like. What are your favorite movies? Take notes on the survey form.

A: *Do you like action movies?*
B: *Yes. My favorite action movie is* The Matrix Reloaded.

Movie Madness

	Student 1		Student 2	
	like?	favorite	like?	favorite
action movie				
animated film				
comedy				
drama				
horror movie				
martial arts film				
musical				
science fiction				
thriller				
western				

6 Report to the class. Tell what you found out about your classmates' taste in movies.

Senna doesn't like romantic comedies, and neither does Flavia.

Writing

7 Choose two similar movies (for example, two action movies or two comedies). Write a review comparing the two movies. Give some examples from the movies. Use the additions *so*, *too*, *either*, or *neither*.

CONVERSATION TO GO

A: Terry loves action films, and **so does** Alex.
B: Well, I don't like them at all, and **neither does** Dana.

Review 5: Units 17–20

Unit 17 Willpower

1 🎧 Listen to the model conversation.

2 **GROUPS OF 3.** With your group, make up a fictional story. Use at least six verbs from the box plus gerunds or infinitives. Each member of the group contributes at least three sentences to the story.

decide	dislike	enjoy	give up	keep on	learn
need	practice	quit	stop	take up	want

3 Take turns sharing your story with the other groups.

Unit 18 Wave of the future

4 Check (✓) the things your parents used to do in the past. Add two more habits to the list.

Did your parents use to . . .	Name
buy records?	
write long letters to friends and relatives?	
drive a very big car?	
waste electricity?	

5 🎧 Listen to the model conversation.

6 Talk to your classmates. Ask questions until you get "yes" answers to all your questions. Write your classmates' names in the column on the right. Ask follow-up questions.

94

Review 5: Units 17–20

You may wish to use the video for Units 17–20 at this point. For video activity worksheets, go to www.longman.com/worldview.

Unit 17: Willpower

OBJECTIVE

Grammar: focus on using verbs + *gerunds* and verbs + *infinitives*

Exercise 1

- Explain the task: Students listen to the model conversation. Write the following questions on the board: *What does Matthew enjoy doing? What does he need to find? What does he also want to take up?* Ask students to listen for the answers.
- 🎧 Play the audio. Ask students the answers. (*Matthew enjoys playing soccer. He needs to find a team. He also wants to take up running.*)
- 🎧 Play the audio again as students listen.

Exercise 2

- Form groups of 3. Ask students to read the words in the box. Explain the task: Students write a story using at least six of the verbs in the box with gerunds or infinitives. Tell each member of the group to contribute at least three sentences.
- Brainstorm a list of topics to write about with the class. Compile a list on the board. Examples: *take up a new hobby or sport, quit a bad habit, learn a new skill.*
- Set a time limit of 10 minutes. While students are working, walk around the room, helping as needed.

Exercise 3

- Have two groups of 3 form a group.
- Tell the groups to take turns sharing their stories.
- Conclude by asking one or two groups to share their stories with the class.

Unit 18: Wave of the future

OBJECTIVE

Grammar: focus on using *used to* and *would*

Exercise 4

- Have students look at the chart. Ask them to check (✓) the things they used to do in the past. Hold up your book and demonstrate making a check in the first column after the question.
- Tell students to add two more habits to the list. These can be their habits or other activities.
- Set a time limit of 3 minutes for students to complete the chart.

Exercise 5

- Explain the task: Students listen to the model conversation.
- 🎧 Play the audio. Write on the board, *Did you use to . . . ?* and *I used to . . .* Underline *use to* and *used to*.
- 🎧 Play the audio again, and have the students listen.

Exercise 6

- Explain the task: Students walk around the room and ask their classmates the questions in the chart in Exercise 1. Tell them to try to find an affirmative answer for each of the questions. When they find someone, they fill in the name in the chart.
- Remind students to ask follow-up questions. Give an example, *What kind of car did you use to drive?*
- Set a time limit of 10 minutes. While students are working, walk around the room, helping as needed.

Unit 19: Made in the U.S.A.

OBJECTIVE

Grammar: focus on reviewing the simple present in statements and questions

Exercise 7

- Form pairs. Have students look at the chart.
- Explain the task: Students complete the chart. In the first column they write three items they own that they might sell, then what the items are made of, and where they were made.
- Go over the example: *The earrings are silver and gold. They were made in Brazil.*
- Give students 2 minutes to complete the chart.

Exercise 8

- Explain to the students that they will hear a conversation between a customer and someone selling something. Ask them to listen for what questions the customer asks.
- 🎧 Play the audio as students listen to the model conversation.
- Elicit the questions and write them on the board: *What are you selling today? What are they made of? Where are they made? But what else do you have?*
- 🎧 Explain that Maine is a state in the northeast part of the United States. Play the audio again, and have the students repeat.

Exercise 9

- Form two pairs.
- Explain the task: Students go shopping in pairs. They take turns asking the other pair what they sell, what the items are made of, and where they are from. Then they decide which item(s) to buy.
- Students switch roles with the other pair.
- Set a time limit of 8 minutes. Walk around the room, helping as needed.

> **WRAP-UP**
> Call on several pairs to tell the class which things they decided to buy. Remind them to include what the items are made of, and where they are from.

Unit 20: At the movies

OBJECTIVE

Grammar: focus on using *so, too, neither, (not) either*

Exercise 10

- Tell the students that they will hear a conversation about two movies. The speakers give opinions about the movies. Ask the students if the speakers agree or disagree and how they know.
- 🎧 Play the audio as students listen to the model conversation.
- Write on the board: *So do I* and *I don't either.* Elicit that the speakers both like comedies and neither likes movies with car chases.
- 🎧 Play the audio again.

Exercise 11

- Form groups of 4. Explain the task: Students take a survey within their group. Each student writes down three movies or TV shows to talk about, and then surveys the other group members. Remind students to ask follow-up questions and take notes in the chart.
- Give students time to write down the names of three movies or TV shows.
- Set a time limit of 10 minutes for students to complete their surveys. Remind students to fill in their charts as they talk. Walk around the room, helping as needed.

Exercise 12

- Explain the task: Students tell what they found out about their classmates.
- Go over the example.
- Call on students to report to the class about their groups.

Unit 19 Made in the U.S.A.

7 **PAIRS.** What are some things you have now that you can try to "sell"? What are they made of? Where are they made? Complete the chart.

Item	Material	Origin
Earrings	Silver and gold	Brazil

8 🎧 Listen to the model conversation.

9 *2 PAIRS.* You and your partner are shopping. Take turns asking the other pair what they are selling, what materials the items are made of, and what countries they come from. Which things would you buy? Switch roles with the other pair.

Unit 20 At the movies

10 🎧 Listen to the model conversation.

11 **GROUPS OF 4.** Write the names of three movies (or TV programs) to talk about. Survey your group members about their opinions. Ask follow-up questions to find out what each person especially likes or dislikes about each movie. Take notes in the chart.

12 Tell the class the results of your survey.

Ron didn't like Endless Night, *and neither did John.*

What did you think of . . .?

What do you think of . . .	Name	Name	Name	Name

World of Music 3

You've Got a Friend
Carole King

Vocabulary

1 **GROUPS OF 3.** What do you think these phrases or sentences mean? Choose the best answer.

1. You're down and troubled and need some love and care.
    a. You fell and need help to get up again.
    b. You're sad and in need of a friend.
    c. You don't feel well and need medicine.

2. If the sky above you grows dark
    a. It will get dark soon
    b. If the day gets dark
    c. If things don't go right for you

3. Keep your head together.
    a. Get close to me.
    b. Stay calm.
    c. Avoid an accident.

4. They'll desert you.
    a. They'll stay with you.
    b. They'll trick you.
    c. They'll forget about you.

*Songwriter **Carole King** says that "You've Got a Friend" is one of only two songs that she created through sheer inspiration. The song is a signature tune for singer James Taylor, a long-time friend of King's.*

Listening

2 🎧 Listen to "You've Got a Friend," by Carole King. What is the main idea of the song?

a. The singer is offering her friendship to somebody.
b. The singer is promising to visit someone.
c. The singer is sad and needs a friend to help her.

3 🎧 Listen again and complete the lyrics on page 97.

World of Music 3

- introduce Carol King's song "You've Got a Friend"
- vocabulary: figures of speech
- express personal interpretation of a song

WARM-UP
- Books closed. Ask: *When you feel sad or you need to talk to someone, who do you run to? Why?*
- Ask students what, in their opinions, are the qualities of a friend. Write the answers on the board.
- Tell students they will be listening to a song about friendship. Tell them to keep in mind their ideas about the qualities of a friend as they listen to the song.

Reading

- Tell students to read the information about Carole King. Tell them they are going to listen to one of Carole King's most popular songs, "You've Got a Friend." Ask them if they know the song or if they have heard of it. Encourage the class to hum or sing parts of the song that they know.
- Ask: *What kind of a relationship did Carole King and James Taylor have?* (*The two were good friends.*)
- Ask them what they know about Carole King and James Taylor. (*Carole King is known for her songwriting skill. Among her more famous compositions are "You've Got a Friend," and "You Make me Feel Like a Natural Woman." James Taylor is known for such songs as "Sweet Baby James" and "Fire and Rain." King and Taylor were good friends.*)
- Sing, or encourage students to sing, a line or two from the songs mentioned above to refresh their memory of these popular '70s songs.

Vocabulary

Exercise 1

- Divide the class into groups of 3. Explain that they will work together to guess the meanings of the four sentences.
- Have students read the sentences. Remind them that the four sentences are used in the song "You've Got a Friend." Ask them what sentences 2 and 3 are. (*They are figures of speech.*) Ask: *What is a figure of speech?* (*It is a word or an expression that is used to create a mental picture. For example, "I died laughing" is a figure of speech.*)

- Set a time limit of 2 minutes.
- Call on individual students to give the answers.

Answer key
1. b   2. c   3. b   4. c

Listening

Exercise 2

- Have students read the three sentences quickly and underline any unfamiliar vocabulary. Elicit, or explain, the meanings of unfamiliar words if any.
- Tell students they will listen to the song. Explain that they will listen for the main idea and circle the letter of the sentence that expresses the main idea.
- 🎧 Play the song.
- Have students circle the correct answer.

Answer key
a. The singer is offering her friendship to somebody.

Exercise 3

- Explain the task: Students listen to the song again while they read the lyrics. They fill in the missing words.
- Have students read through the lyrics once and underline any unfamiliar words and phrases. Elicit, or clarify, the meanings of these words and phrases.
- 🎧 Play the song.
- Set a time limit of 6 minutes. Walk around the room, helping as needed. You may need to play the song again to give students more time to complete the exercise.
- Have students compare their answers with a partner. Encourage them to change any incorrect answers.

Answer key

Line 3: nothing, nothing	Line 20: door
Line 4: eyes	Line 24: again
Line 6: darkest	Line 30: people
Line 9: again	Line 31: hurt
Line 11: have to	Line 32: take
Line 15: clouds	Line 37: again
Line 16: wind	Line 38: Winter, summer
Line 17: call	Line 39: call

Speaking

Exercise ❹

- Divide the class into groups of 3. Have each group discuss the answers to the questions. Encourage them to use the lines from the song.
- 🎧 If needed, play the song again.
- Have volunteers share their answers to the questions.

> **Answer key**
> Answers will vary, possible answers include:
> When you're down and troubled and need
> a helping hand
> And nothing is going right
> If the sky above you should grow dark and full of clouds

EXTENSION

Encourage students to interpret or explain specific lines of the song, for example, "I will be there to brighten up even your darkest nights."

OPTION

🎧 Play the song again and have students sing along.

You've Got a Friend

When you're down and troubled
and you need some love and care
and _____, _____ is going right.
Close your _____ and think of me
and soon I will be there
to brighten up even your _____ night.

You just call out my name,
and you know wherever I am
I'll come running to see you _____.
Winter, spring, summer, or fall,
all you _____ ____ do is call
and I'll be there.
You've got a friend.

If the sky above you
grows dark and full of _____
and that old north ____ begins to blow
Keep your head together and _____
my name out loud
Soon you'll hear me knocking at
your _____.

You just call out my name,
and you know wherever I am
I'll come running, running, yeah, yeah
to see you _____.
Winter, spring, summer, or fall
all you have to do is call
and I'll be there, yes, I will.

Now, ain't it good to know that you've
got a friend
when ____ can be so cold?
They'll _____ you, yes and desert you.
And _____ your soul if you let them.
Ah, but don't you let them.

You just call out my name,
and you know wherever I am
I'll come running, running, yeah, yeah
to see you _____.
_____, spring, _____, or fall,
all you have to do is _____.
And, I'll be there, yes, I will.
You've got a friend.
You've got a friend. Yeah, baby.
You've got a friend.
Ain't it good to know you've got
a friend?
Ain't it good to know you've got
a friend?
Oh, yeah now.
You've got a friend.
Oh yeah.
You've got a friend.

Speaking

 GROUPS OF 3. Discuss these questions. Use lines from the song to explain your answer.

1. When does the singer think a friend is especially useful?
2. How strong are the singer's feelings towards her friend?

UNIT 21 How polite are you?

Vocabulary Phrasal verbs with *turn, switch, go*
Grammar Modals: *Could you, Would you, Would you mind* for polite requests
Speaking Making or responding to requests

Lesson A

Getting started

1 Complete the sentences with the word or words in the box. You will use some words more than once.

| down | ~~off~~ | on | up | over to |

1. I hate it when my alarm goes ___off___ in the morning.
2. That music is too loud. Could you turn it _____, please?
3. Can you turn _____ the lights? I can't see what I'm reading.
4. Please turn _____ all cell phones in the aircraft now.
5. I love that song. Can you turn _____ the volume, please?
6. Would you mind switching _____ Channel 13? I want to watch that Japanese movie.

2 **PAIRS.** Compare your answers.

3 **PAIRS.** Talk about the things you usually turn on when you get home at night. Think about your TV, computer, lights, etc. What do you turn on first, second, and so on?

When I get home, the first thing I turn on is the lights. Then I always . . .

98

How polite are you?

UNIT 21

OBJECTIVES

Students will:

- activate vocabulary: phrasal verbs with *turn, switch, go*
- use modals: *Could you, Would you, Would you mind . . . ?* for polite requests
- practice the informal blended pronunciations of *would you* and *could you*

WARM-UP

- Tell students this unit is about making polite requests. Explain that one place people make polite requests is in a public situation, such as on a bus or in a store, where the people don't know each other. Give an example: On a bus someone might say, *Would you please close the window?*
- Ask students to think of other public situations where they would make a polite request.
- Form groups of 4. Set a time limit of 2 minutes. Students work together to list other public places where they would make a polite request.
- After 2 minutes, call on students to read from their lists. Compile a list of places on the board. (Other possible answers: *an airport, a subway, a train, a train platform.*)

Getting started

Teaching Tip! Phrasal verbs

- Review with students that some phrasal verbs are separable, and some are inseparable. With a separable verb, the verb and the particle can be separated by a direct object. With an inseparable verb, the particle cannot be separated from the verb.
- In this unit, the phrasal verbs that are separable include: *turn off, turn on, switch on, switch off.* The phrasal verbs that are inseparable include: *go off, switch over to.*
- If you want to preteach the vocabulary, demonstrate the phrasal verbs by doing actions in the class. For example, say *I need to turn on the light,* and then turn the light on. Continue with the other phrasal verbs, where possible.

OPTION: VOCABULARY PREVIEW

- Write the following on the board in columns:

    turn on
    turn off   make something _____
    turn up   (stop, louder, start, quieter)
    turn down

- Pair students. Set a time limit of 2 minutes. Ask students to fill in the blank for each phrasal verb. You may want to show an example on the board: *turn on = make something start.* Answer any questions about the phrasal verbs and their meanings.

Exercise 1

- Explain the task: Students complete the sentences with the word or words in the box. Ask students to look at the words. Explain that the verbs in the sentences are phrasal verbs, and that they are made up of two parts, the verb and the particle. The words in the box are particles. Review that the particle looks like a preposition but that it is part of the verb phrase and that it changes the meaning of the verb.
- Go over the example.
- Set a time limit of 5 minutes. While students are working, walk around the room, helping as needed.
- Do not go over the answers until the class has done Exercise 2.

Exercise 2

- Pair students. Ask them to compare answers.
- Go over answers with the class. For 6, two answers are possible. *Switch on* means the TV is not turned on yet. *Switch over to* means the TV is on, and the speaker wants to watch a different channel.

Answer key

1. off   3. on   5. up
2. down   4. off   6. on/over to

Exercise 3

- Pairs continue working together or form new pairs. Explain the task: Students talk about things that they usually turn on when they get home at night.
- Go over the example. You may want to review with the students the words they can use to say what they did first, second, and so on (*first, then, next, and then, next, finally*).
- Set a time limit of 5 minutes. Walk around the room, helping as needed.
- Take a poll with the class: *Who turns on the lights? Who turns on the TV?*

EXTENSION

- Form groups of 3. Set a time limit of 3 minutes. Write the following on the board: *turn down, turn off, turn up, turn over to.* Ask students to make a list of things in their daily lives, their jobs, school, a restaurant, and other situations that they *turn _____.* For example: *turn off the lights, turn up the music, turn down the radio.*
- Call on various groups to pick a phrasal verb and say the items on their list. You may want to write the lists on the board. Ask other groups for words that are not yet on the board. Go over any vocabulary words that students don't know.

Teacher's Notes — Lesson A

T98

Reading

Exercise 4

- 🎧 Tell students they will hear people making different noises. Ask them to listen to the noises. Play the recording and have the students listen only.
- 🎧 Then, play the recording again, and pause for the students to identify each sound.
- Ask students which sounds they find annoying, and which sounds they don't mind (are OK).

> **Answer key**
>
> cell phone
> person whistling
> music from a person's headphones
> person banging on a piano
> person drumming his or her fingers on something
> person jangling coins in his or her pocket

Exercise 5

- Pair students. Ask students to discuss the questions.
- Have the students read the questions, or read them aloud for the class.
- Set a time limit of 5 minutes. After 5 minutes, call on a few students to say if they are noisy, and if so, when.

Exercise 6

- Students work individually. Explain the task: Students read the situations and the responses. They have to decide which response they would use in each situation. Students circle their answers.
- Set a time limit of 5 minutes. Walk around the room, helping as needed.
- Do not go over answers with the class until they have completed Exercise 7.

Exercise 7

- Pair students. Ask them to discuss their answers, and decide which answers are most polite and which are rude. Verify that they understand *rude* and *polite* are opposites.
- Go over answers with the class. Remind students that answers may vary.

> **Answer key**
>
> Answers may vary, but generally, response **A** is the most polite for all situations, and **C** ruder. Response **B** is also rude, but shifts the conflict to another person (the conductor, the waiter, and so on).

🌐 Please go to www.longman.com/worldview for additional in-class model conversation practice.

HOMEWORK

- 📖 For homework, assign *Workbook* page 82, Vocabulary Exercises 1 and 2, and page 84, Listening Exercises 5 and 6.

Reading

4 🎧 Listen to some noises and say what they are. How do you feel about them?

5 *PAIRS.* Discuss these questions. Are you a noisy person? If so, when? Do you feel comfortable asking people to stop making noise?

6 Read the situations in "Excuse me . . ." Circle your answers to the questions.

7 *PAIRS.* Discuss your answers. Which answers are most polite? Which are rude?

"Excuse me . . ."

1 **You're on a bus. The person next to you is playing loud music. What do you say?**
- A "Would you mind turning your music down, please?"
- B "Driver! Can you tell this guy that it's illegal to play music on the bus?"
- C "You're being very rude."

2 **You're on a train. The passenger behind you is kicking your seat. What do you say?**
- A "Could you stop doing that, please? I can't concentrate."
- B "Conductor! He's kicking my chair!"
- C "Stop that now!"

3 **It's the middle of the night. Your neighbor's dog is barking. You can't sleep. You . . .**
- A call your neighbor and say, "Could you make Mitzy stop barking, please?"
- B call the police and say, "Would you come quickly, there's a dangerous animal next door!"
- C open the window and shout, "Be quiet!"

4 **You're having a romantic dinner in a restaurant. A man near you is speaking loudly on his cell phone. What do you say?**
- A "Would you mind lowering your voice, please?"
- B "Waiter! Please tell this man to go outside."
- C "We're trying to have a nice, quiet dinner, and you're disturbing us."

Grammar focus

1 Study the examples of polite requests and responses.

Would you please **turn** the music down?	Of course.
Could I **turn** on the TV?	Sure.
Would you **mind lowering** your voice?	No, of course not.
	Not at all.

2 Look at the examples again. Underline the correct words to complete the rules in the chart.

Could you / Would you / Would you mind for polite requests

Use *would you* or *could you* + **the gerund / the base form of the verb** to make polite requests.

Use *Would you mind* + **the gerund / the base form of the verb** to make polite requests.

If you answer *No* to a *would you mind* question, you are saying that you **will / won't** do what the person requests.

Grammar Reference page 148

3 Look at the pictures. Write polite requests and responses for each situation.

1. A: Would you mind making less noise, please?
   B: No, of course not.

2. _____

3. _____

4. _____

5. _____

Grammar focus

LANGUAGE NOTES

- The answer *No* to a *would you mind* question may be confusing for some students; they may interpret it as a refusal. Explain that in conversation, often, a speaker will add to a simple *No* response and say *No, I don't mind* or *No, no problem.*
- Students should also be aware that sometimes a speaker will say *Sure, go ahead* or *Sure, no problem* or *Sure, certainly,* all of which have the same basic meaning as *No, I don't mind.*

WARM-UP

Note: Skip this warm-up if you're doing this lesson (Lesson B) during the same class period as Lesson A.

- Books closed. Tell students they are going to listen to a recording of the situations and responses that they read in the Reading section.
- Tell students to pay attention to the **A** responses, and to listen for the verb phrases used to make polite requests. Ask students to write down the verb phrase they hear in each **A** response. Write an example on the board: *Could you.*
- 🎧 Play the recording for Lesson A, Exercise 6. Play again, as needed.
- Ask students what verb phrases they heard. Write them on the board:

    Would you mind (*turning your music down*), *Could you* (*stop*), *Could you* (*make*), *Would you mind* (*lowering your voice*).

- Ask students what they notice about *Would you mind* (the *-ing* form is used after it).

Exercise ❶

- Have students look at the examples and study the boldfaced words.
- Ask students to focus on the first three examples.
- Elicit from students that the sentences use the base form of the verb.
- Ask students to look at the last example. Elicit that it uses the gerund (base form of the verb + *–ing*).

Exercise ❷

- Have students look at the examples again, and then underline the correct words to complete the rules in the box. You may want to quickly review that gerunds are the *-ing* forms of verbs that are used here as part of the direct object. Also review that the base form (*turn*) looks like the infinitive without the "to."
- Go over the rules with the class. Ask students to point out the gerunds and base forms in the examples (*turn, lowering*).
- Refer students to Grammar Reference page 148, as needed.

Answer key

the base form of the verb   the gerund   will

Exercise ❸

- Explain the task: Students look at the pictures and make polite requests and responses for each situation.
- Go over the example. Point out that the response, *No, of course not* means *No, of course I don't mind.*
- Set a time limit of 5 minutes. Have students complete the exercise individually.
- Pair students and have them check their answers. They can do this by reading their written conversations aloud.
- Go over the answers with the class. One way to do this is to call on different student pairs to read for the class.

Answer key

Answers will vary, but may include:
1. Would you mind being more quiet, please? We're trying to sleep.
   No problem.
2. It's hot in here. Could I open the window?
   Sure.
3. This is a library! Would you mind talking somewhere else?
   No, of course not.
4. Excuse me, but I'm trying to sleep. Could you turn down your TV?
   Sure. No problem. I'm sorry about that.
5. Could I borrow your dictionary for a minute?
   Of course you can.

EXPANSION

- Form groups of 4. Have students take turns making polite requests about classroom objects. Give an example, *Would you mind lending me your dictionary, Tara?* Tell each student to make at least two requests.
- Have the student in the group who answers then make the next request. You might want to demonstrate this with a group first.

    You ask: *Could you give me a piece of paper, Alex?*
    S2 (Alex): *Sure, here you are.*
    S2 (Alex): *Can I borrow your pen, Carlos?*
    S3 (Carlos): *No problem, I have two.*

Pronunciation

Exercise 4

- Explain that English speakers link words and sometimes blend them together.
- 🎧 Play the audio and have students listen. Ask them to notice the pronunciation of *would you* and *could you*.
- Say the words in *would + you* and *could + you* separately and then in the blended forms "wouldja" and "couldja" to highlight the way they sound different.
- Tell students that the blended pronunciations are common in informal conversation. Explain that students do not need to use these pronunciations when they speak, but they need to be able to recognize them.
- Point out that the spellings "wouldja" and "couldja" are used only to show the way the blended pronunciations sound. Students should not use these spellings in their writing.

Exercise 5

- 🎧 Play the audio. Stop the audio after each item and ask students to repeat it chorally.
- Ask a few individual students to repeat the sentences and check their pronunciation.
- Encourage students to practice the blended pronunciations, saying the words in *would you* and *could you* together as if they were each a single word. Tell students that practicing these pronunciations will help them recognize the forms when they hear them.
- Encourage students to use polite intonation for the requests, with a high voice pitch and rising intonation at the end. An intonation that is too flat can sound rude.

Exercise 6

- Pair students. Explain the task: Students practice the short conversations they wrote for Exercise 3. Set a time limit of 3 minutes.
- Walk around the room, helping as needed. Encourage students to use the blended pronunciations of *would you* and *could you*.

Speaking

Exercise 7

- Pair students. Assign roles: Student A and Student B for each pair.
- Explain the task: Students role-play the situations using polite requests and vocabulary from the unit.
- Have Student A look at this page, and Student B look at page 142.
- Set a time limit of 10 minutes for students to complete their role-plays. Tell students to switch parts and do the role-plays again if they finish early. Walk around the room, helping as needed.
- Conclude by calling on a few pairs to role-play a situation.

EXTENSION

Bring up the fact that sometimes a polite request is not met with a polite response. What can the students say in those cases? You might mention that they can repeat the request politely by saying something like *Well, I'd appreciate it if (you would turn down your radio)*.

TRB For additional interactive grammar practice, have students do the reproducible activity for this unit in the *Teacher's Resource Book*.

Writing

Exercise 8

- Assign the writing task for class work or homework. Some students might not have been in situations like those in Reading, Exercise 6. If this is the case, tell them to substitute a similar situation in which they needed to make a polite request. Encourage students to use some of the phrasal verbs and vocabulary from this unit.
- **TRB** Optionally, give students a copy of the model (see the *Teacher's Resource Book*, Writing Models). Ask them to read the model and notice the different parts of the letter and the punctuation used. Point out how quotation marks are used when writing a coversation.
- If students do not have the model, write on the board:

  My next-door neighbor, Mrs. Jones, must have about ten dogs. Last Sunday, they were all barking! I couldn't study, so I called Mrs. Jones, and said, "Hi. This is Jason, your next-door neighbor . . ."

  Walk around to make sure students understand the task, and answer any questions.
- If the assignment is done in class, ask students to share their writing with a partner as time permits.

For suggestions on how to give feedback on writing, see page xiv of this *Teacher's Edition*.

CONVERSATION TO GO

- As the students leave class, have them read the dialogue, or read aloud chorally.
- Optionally, ask students why the first speaker has to repeat the request. (*Because the music is really loud.*)

HOMEWORK

- 📖 Assign *Workbook* page 83, Grammar Exercises 3 and 4, and page 84, Pronunciation Exercises 7 and 8.
- 🔊 If students do not have the *WorldView Workbook*, assign listening homework from the Student CD. Write on the board:

  Track 48
  What is the neighbor's dog's name?
- 🎧 Tell students to listen to the audio and write their answer. Have them bring it to the next class. (*Mitzy*)

Pronunciation

4 🎧 Listen. Notice the way the words *would you* and *could you* are linked and blended together: "wouldja" and "couldja."

Would you	Would you please turn the music down?
	Would you mind lowering your voice?
Could you	Could you please stop doing that?
	Could you make your dog stop barking?

5 🎧 Listen again and repeat.

6 *PAIRS.* Practice the conversations you wrote in Exercise 3.

Speaking

7 *PAIRS.* Role-play situations using polite requests. Student A, look at this page. Student B, look at page 142.

Role-play #1
You left your wallet at home, and you need to borrow money for lunch from Student B, a close friend.

Role-play #2
Student B is your co-worker. Listen and reply.

Role-play #3
You need to stay at home to take care of your sick child. Ask your boss, Student B, for permission to work from home. You will turn on your cell phone so people can call you from work.

Role-play #4
Student B is your neighbor. Listen and reply.

Writing

8 Look at the quiz in Exercise 6 on page 99. Have you ever been in a situation like any of those? Describe what happened and include the conversation you had with the annoying person.

CONVERSATION TO GO

A: **Could you turn** your music **down**?
B: What did you say?
A: **Would you mind turning** it **down**?
B: **No, of course not.**

Lesson B

UNIT 22

The art of crime

Vocabulary Words related to crime
Grammar Passive (simple past)
Speaking Describing a crime

Lesson A

Getting started

1 Look at the words associated with crime. Complete the chart.

Crime	Criminal	Verb (+ someone or something)	Meaning
robbery	robber		take money or property illegally from a person or place
burglary		burglarize (a place)	enter a building illegally and take money or goods
mugging	mugger		attack and take something from a person
scam	con artist		use a dishonest plan to get money from somebody
shoplifting		shoplift (something)	take goods from a store without paying
theft		steal (something)	take something illegally

2 🎧 Listen and check your answers. Then listen again and repeat.

3 *PAIRS.* Rank the crimes in Exercise 1 in order of seriousness (1 = the most serious, 6 = the least serious).

4 *GROUPS OF 4.* Decide what punishment each type of criminal deserves.

Should the criminal:
- go to prison? (say for how long)
- pay a fine? (say how much)
- do community service? (say what kind of service)

A: A bank robber should go to prison for thirty years.
B: Thirty years is too much, especially if no one got hurt.

102

The art of crime

UNIT 22

OBJECTIVES

Students will:
- activate vocabulary related to crime
- use the passive (simple past)
- practice rhythm in passive sentences

WARM-UP

- Tell students this unit is about crime. Elicit from the students what a "crime" is. (*illegal activity*)
- Pair students. Set a time limit of 2 minutes. Ask the students to brainstorm different types of crimes. Put a few examples on the board: *stealing money from a bank, taking candy from a store without paying for it.*
- Ask various pairs for three or four items on their lists. Write a list of the student's ideas on the board.
- Ask students to vote on the most serious crime and the least serious crime. Ask a few students to give the reasons behind their votes.

Getting started

LANGUAGE NOTE

Make students understand *rob a person or place* and *steal something from someone*. In addition, the expression is *to commit a crime* and not *to do a crime*.

OPTION: VOCABULARY PREVIEW

- Write the following verbs on the board: *steal, rob, mug, scam, burglarize, shoplift.*
- Form groups of 3. Set a time limit of 5 minutes. Read the situations. Have students match the verb with the situation.
  1. Someone with a gun walks in a bank and demands money.
  2. Someone comes up from behind you and makes you give them your money.
  3. Someone sells you a sports car for $1,000. Later the police show up and take it because it is a stolen car.
  4. Someone you know takes a shirt from the local department store without paying.
  5. Someone takes your car from a parking lot.
  6. Someone enters your house in the night and takes your computer and TV.
- Go over the answers with the class. Answer any questions students have about the vocabulary.

Answer key

1. rob 3. scam 5. steal
2. mug 4. shoplift 6. burglarize

Exercise 1

- Explain the task: Students look at the words associated with crime and complete the chart. Remind students to use prior knowledge to make "good guesses." For example, write on the board *teach* and *teacher*. Remind students that *-er* means "person who does this." Tell students to think about this as they fill in the blanks.
- Go over the example, and then set a time limit of 5 minutes. While students are working, walk around the room, helping as needed.

Exercise 2

- 🎧 Play the audio so that students can confirm their answers. Play the audio again.
- Go over the answers with the class.
- Conclude by briefly discussing the picture of the Eiffel Tower being sold, and why this is a scam.

Answer key

robbery; robber; rob (a place)
burglary; burglar; burglarize (a place)
mugging; mugger; mug (someone)
scam; con artist; scam (someone)
shoplifting; shoplifter; shoplift (something)
theft; thief; steal (something)

Exercise 3

- Pair students. Explain the task: Students rank the crimes in Exercise 1 in order of seriousness. Encourage students to give reasons.
- Set a time limit of 5 minutes. Walk around the room, helping as needed.
- Call on several pairs of students to tell their ranking. Ask students to give reasons.

Answer key

Answers will vary.

Exercise 4

- Explain the task: Students decide what punishment each type of crime deserves.
- Go over the punishment choices. Make sure that students understand that *prison* and *jail* are the same; that *a fine* is money paid as a punishment, and that *community service* includes unpaid work done in the community such as picking up trash along the highway.
- Form groups of 4. Go over the example. Set a time limit of 5 minutes. Walk around the room, helping as needed.
- Ask a few students what they decided and why.

Teacher's Notes — Lesson A

T102

Listening

BACKGROUND INFORMATION

The Mona Lisa, painted from 1503–1506 by Leonardo Da Vinci, is not only world famous, but considered to have been his favorite. He took it everywhere with him. There are many theories about the smile on the woman's face, but no one knows for sure why he painted it this way. Art historians do know that he was interested in light and shadow, and this may explain the smile. The Mona Lisa is currently on display in the Louvre, in Paris.

Exercise 5

- Form pairs. Have students look at the painting. Tell them to read the questions, or read them aloud for the class.
- Walk around the room, helping as needed.
- Conclude by asking the students what they know about the Mona Lisa. Provide information as needed.

Exercise 6

- Tell students that in 1911 the Mona Lisa disappeared. Explain that they are going to listen to a story about it, and then match the questions with the answers.
- 🎧 Have students read the questions, or read them aloud for the class. Then, play the audio. Students match the questions with the answers.
- 🎧 Play the audio again for students to confirm their answers.
- Go over the answers with the class.

Answer key

1. a   2. c   3. b

Exercise 7

- Explain the task: Students listen to the audio again and decide if the statements are true or false.
- Have students look at the questions, or read them aloud with the class.
- 🎧 Play the audio again. Encourage students to make brief notes as they hear the answers to the questions.
- 🎧 Have students mark their answers, and then play the audio again for students to confirm their answers.
- Go over the answers with the class.

Answer key

1. F The Mona Lisa was painted by Leonardo Da Vinci.
2. F It was found in 1913.
3. F Perugia was arrested.
4. T

🌐 Please go to www.longman.com/worldview for additional in-class model conversation practice and supplementary reading practice.

HOMEWORK

- 📖 For homework, assign *Workbook* page 85, Vocabulary Exercises 1 and 2, and page 87, Listening Exercises 5 and 6.

Listening

5 **PAIRS.** Look at the painting and read the questions. How much do you know about this painting? Discuss your answers with your partner.

1. It's called the Mona Lisa in English. Do you know what it's called in your language?
2. Who painted it?
3. What happens if you look at the woman's eyes from different angles?

6 🎧 In 1911, the Mona Lisa disappeared. Listen to the story and match the questions with the answers.

1. Who had the idea for the theft? __
2. Who stole the painting? __
3. Who believed the copies were real? __

a. Eduardo de Valfierno
b. rich collectors
c. Vincenzo Perugia

7 🎧 Listen again. Write *T* (true) or *F* (false) after each statement. Correct the false statements.

1. The Mona Lisa was painted by Michelangelo. **F**
   The Mona Lisa was painted by Leonardo Da Vinci.
2. The painting was never found.
3. None of the thieves was ever arrested.
4. Six copies of the painting were made.

Grammar focus

1 Study the examples of active and passive sentences and questions.

Active sentences			Passive sentences		
Subject	**Verb**	**Object**	**Subject**	**Verb**	**Agent**
Da Vinci	painted	the Mona Lisa.	The Mona Lisa	**was painted by**	Da Vinci.
Someone	stole	the painting.	The painting	**was stolen**.	
The police	caught	the thieves.	The thieves	**were caught**.	

Passive questions			
Question word	**Auxiliary**	**Subject**	**Past participle (by)**
Who	**was**	the Mona Lisa	**painted by**?
When	**was**	the thieves	**stolen**?
How	**were**	the painting	**caught**?

2 Look at the examples again. Underline the correct information to complete the explanation in the chart.

> **Simple past passive**
>
> Use the **passive / active** when the action is more important than the person or thing that did the action.

Grammar Reference page 148

3 Rewrite the sentences in the passive. Do not mention the agent (the person or thing that did the action) unless it is important or necessary to understand the sentence.

1. They took over $150,000 from the bank.
   Over $150,000 was taken from the bank.
2. Somebody broke into our house last month.
3. Security personnel arrested many shoplifters during the holiday season.
4. They stole my car yesterday.
5. According to legend, con artists sold the Eiffel Tower dozens of times.
6. The police discovered thousands of pirated CDs.
7. People made copies of the movie months before it reached the video stores.
8. Eduardo de Valfierno sold the Mona Lisa six times.

Grammar focus

LANGUAGE NOTES

- In general, the passive is used when an action, or the result of an action, is more important to communicate than who or what performed the action.
- This unit demonstrates how questions can be formed with the passive to emphasize different pieces of information (i.e., *who* versus *when* versus *how*). Point out that students can choose to ask questions in several ways depending upon what they want to focus on.

WARM-UP

Note: Skip this warm-up if you're doing this lesson (Lesson B) during the same class period as Lesson A.

- Books closed. Tell students they are going to listen again to the information about the Mona Lisa that they heard in the Listening section.
- Ask students to listen for verb phrases with *was/were*. Tell them to each write down at least three phrases. Give an example, The Mona Lisa *was painted*.
- 🎧 Play the audio for Lesson A, Exercises 6 and 7.
- 🎧 Play it again for students to confirm their answers.
- Ask students what verb phrases with *was/were* they heard. Write their answers on the board. (Possible answers: *it was painted, the painting was stolen/was found, it was offered, Perugia was arrested, the painting was in Perugia's apartment, the theft was planned, copies were made, Valfierno was paid, the Mona Lisa was returned*.) **Note:** There are other phrases with *was/were* that are not in the passive that students might include.

Exercise ❶

- Have students look at the examples and study the boldfaced words.
- Ask students to focus on the passive sentences. Elicit that the past passive is formed with *was/were* + past participle.
- Ask students to focus on the passive questions. Elicit or point out that the past participle follows the subject in questions.

Exercise ❷

- Have students look at the examples again and underline the correct information to complete the explanation.
- Go over the sentences and the questions. Point out that the plural of *thief* is *thieves*. Provide more information as needed to make sure students understand that the passive is being used here to focus on the actions rather than who or what did the actions.
- Refer students to Grammar Reference page 148, as needed.

Answer key

the passive

Exercise ❸

- Explain the task: Students rewrite the sentences in the passive. Remind students not to include who did the action unless it is necessary for the meaning to be clear.
- Ask students to look at the example. Remind students that the passive is used here because the focus is on how much money was taken, and not who stole it.
- Have students complete the exercise individually. Set a time limit of 5 minutes.
- Pair students and have them check their answers.
- Go over the answers with the class. Point out that the subject needs to be included in sentences 6 and 8 because it's important to know who did the action.

Answer key

1. Over $150,000 was taken from the bank.
2. Our house was broken into last month.
3. Many shoplifters were arrested during the holiday season.
4. My car was stolen yesterday.
5. According to legend, the Eiffel Tower was sold dozens of times.
6. Thousands of pirated CDs were discovered by the police.
7. Copies of the movie were made months before it reached the video stores.
8. The Mona Lisa was sold six times by Eduardo de Valfierno.

EXTENSION

- Pair students. Explain the task: Students prepare a news report on how the Mona Lisa was lost and found, based on the information they heard in the Listening section. Tell them to prepare it like a broadcaster might do on the evening news. Remind them to use the passive.
- Call on a few students to present to the class.

Pronunciation

Exercise 4

- Remind students that in English, only the important words in a sentence are stressed. These words are longer and clearer than other words.
- 🎧 Play the audio and have students listen. Ask them to listen to the stress in the sentences here.
- Call attention to the passive forms, by writing one or more of them on the board. Ask students to notice which words are stressed in the passive.
- Ask students what they notice about the total number of syllables and the number of stressed syllables in the sentences here. (The sentences have different numbers of syllables, but the same number of stressed syllables.)

Exercise 5

- 🎧 Play the audio. Stop after each sentence and ask students to repeat it chorally.
- Ask a few individual students to repeat and check their pronunciation.
- Check that students stress only the important words (or syllables in these words). You can tap out the strong beats in the sentences to reinforce the rhythm.
- Encourage students to use the weak pronunciations of *was* and *were*. If necessary, remind students to make the vowels /ə/ and /ɚ/ short.

Speaking

Exercise 6

- 🎧 Pair students and assign parts, Student A and Student B. Explain the task: Students each have an article about the *Great Train Robbery* with some information missing. Students need to ask each other questions about the missing information.
- Have Student A turn to page 140, and Student B turn to page 142. Students read their part of the story.
- Set a time limit of 8 minutes. Walk around the room, helping as needed. If students have difficulty forming the questions, prompt them, or provide the questions listed below.
- After 8 minutes, check that the students have all of the information they need. If they don't, extend the time another 2 minutes.

   Student A's questions:
   1. What was stolen from the train?
   2. What was the crime named?
   3. Where was the train stopped?
   4. Where was the money taken?

   Student B's questions:
   1. Who was attacked?
   2. How many bags of bills were stolen?
   3. Who was arrested?
   4. What was recovered?

Exercise 7

- Students continue in same pairs. Have them take turns telling the story of the Great Train Robbery. Tell students to ask questions about parts that are wrong or unclear.
- Conclude by asking the class to tell the story together. Explain that you will call on one student at a time to say the next part of the story.
- Start by saying the first line of the story, or call on a student to do so. Then call on one student at a time to continue. Remind students to listen carefully, and to raise their hands if they hear something that isn't correct.

TRB For additional interactive grammar practice, have students do the reproducible activity for this unit in the *Teacher's Resource Book*.

Writing

Exercise 8

- Assign the writing task for class work or homework.
- Together make a list on the board of some real crimes that have happened recently. Point out the four pieces of information they need to include: what, where, to whom it happened, and if anyone was arrested.
- **TRB** Optionally, give students a copy of the model (see the *Teacher's Resource Book*, Writing Models). Ask them to read the model and notice the passive verbs used.
- If students do not have the model, write on the board:

   A suspected bank robber was caught yesterday. On September 12, over $150,000 was stolen from . . .

   Walk around the room to make sure students understand the task.

- If the assignment is done in class, ask a few students to read their writing aloud as time permits.

For suggestions on how to give feedback on writing, see page xiv of this *Teacher's Edition*.

EXTENSION

Have students use their written work as scripts to prepare a news broadcast of "people and places in the news." Students can practice in small groups, and then present as time permits.

CONVERSATION TO GO

- As the students leave class, have them read the dialogue.
- Optionally, ask students if the car was found.

HOMEWORK

- 📖 Assign *Workbook* page 86, Grammar Exercises 3 and 4, and page 87, Pronunciation Exercises 7 and 8.
- 💿 If students do not have the *WorldView Workbook*, assign listening homework from the Student CD. Write on the board:

   Track 50
   Where was the real Mona Lisa from 1911 to 1913?

- 🎧 Tell students to listen to the audio and write their answer. Have them bring it to the next class. (*in Perugia's apartment*)

Pronunciation

4 🎧 Listen to the rhythm in these sentences. Notice that the stressed syllable of each important word is long and clear and that unstressed syllables and unimportant words are short and weak.

How were the **thieves caught**?   **When** was the **paint**ing **sto**len?

Copies of the **paint**ing were **made**.   The **cop**ies were **sold** to coll**ect**ors.

The o**rig**inal was **off**ered to a **deal**er.   The **paint**ing was re**turned** to the museum.

5 🎧 Listen again and repeat.

Speaking

6 *PAIRS.* You're going to read parts of an article about a famous robbery. Student A, look at page 140. Student B, look at page 142. Read the article. Ask and answer questions about the missing information in your article.

7 Tell the story (without looking at pages 140 and 142) of the Great Train Robbery.

The Great Train Robbery

Writing

8 Write a short newspaper article about a real or imaginary crime that happened recently. Use the passive voice. Include:

- the type of crime
- where/when it happened
- who it happened to
- whether or not the criminal was arrested

> ### CONVERSATION TO GO
>
> A: When **was** your car **stolen**?
> B: Last year. The thieves **were** never **caught**.

UNIT 23 A balanced life

Vocabulary Expressions with *take*
Grammar Review verbs for likes/dislikes followed by gerund and/or infinitive
Speaking Discussing work and after-work activities

Lesson A

Getting started

1 Look at the pictures and read the conversations. Write the expressions with *take* next to the correct definitions in the chart.

Expression with *take*	Definition
1. take part in	participate in an activity
2.	agree to do something
3.	relax
4.	begin something new
5.	arrange to have time away from work
6.	stop and have a rest

A balanced life

UNIT 23

OBJECTIVES

Students will:

- activate vocabulary related to work and leisure; expressions with *take*
- use verbs for likes/dislikes + gerunds and/or infinitives
- practice pronouncing consonant sound groups

WARM-UP: TIME TO RELAX

- Tell students this unit is about work and leisure activities. Explain that the title of the unit is "A balanced life" and that this refers to finding a balance between work and play.
- Ask students to think about things they do to relax each week. Give several examples, *I try to get some exercise. Sometimes, I go to the park and walk around. I watch TV.*
- Form pairs. Tell students to say at least four things they do to relax in their leisure time. Set a time limit of 2 minutes.
- After 2 minutes, call on a few students to tell the class one or two activities they do.

Getting started

OPTION: VOCABULARY PREVIEW

- Read aloud or write on the board the expressions *take on, take it easy, take a break, take up, take part in, take the day off*.
- Ask the class if they know what any of the expressions mean. Have a few volunteers share what they know. Do not write the words on the board. Instead, tell students that they will check their understanding in Exercise 1.

Exercise ❶

- Tell the students they are going to practice using expressions with *take*. Have the students look at the pictures.
- Explain the task: Students read the conversations, and then write the expressions with *take* next to the correct definitions in the box. Remind students to use the context to help them figure out the meaning. For example, in the first picture, the man says *Peter didn't come in today*. This context clue helps the students to decide that *arrange to have time away from work* is the best choice for *take the day off*.
- Set a time limit of 5 minutes for students to fill in the chart. While students are working, walk around the room, helping as needed.
- Do not go over answers with the class until they have completed Exercise 2.

Teacher's Notes — Lesson A

T106

Teacher's Notes — Lesson A

Exercise 2

- Pair students. Have them compare their answers.
- Go over the answers with the class. Remind students to think of these expressions as units; for example, *take part in* is one unit. Also point out that *take a break* is often followed by *from* (e.g., *take a break from studying*).

Answer key

1. take part in
2. take on
3. take it easy
4. take up
5. take the day off
6. take a break

Exercise 3

- Pair students. Explain the task: Students take turns talking about three things they want to *take part in, take up,* or *take a break from*. Tell students to ask and answer follow-up questions.
- Go over the example. Then, set a time limit of 5 minutes. Walk around the room, helping as needed.
- Conclude by calling on pairs to ask and answer about what they want to do.

Answer key

Answers will vary.

EXTENSION

- Pair students. Set a time limit of 4 minutes. Explain the task: Students each discuss two things or situations in their lives that use expressions with *take*. You may want to write the expressions on the board: *take off, take on, take it easy.*
- You may want to give an example: *I need to take off a day from work, because I have a doctor's and a dentist's appointment. / I really don't want to take on any more projects. I'm too busy. / I'm going to take it easy this weekend and just relax and read my new book.*

Listening

Exercise 4

- Form pairs. Explain the task: Students look at the photo of Marta and Ian and discuss the questions.
- Have the students read the questions, or read them aloud for the class. This is a good opportunity to review the present continuous. *(He is sitting on the couch. He is reading the newspaper. She is smiling. She is standing there, holding her gym bag.)* Ask students to imagine what Marta and Ian are saying to each other.
- Give students time to discuss their answers to the questions.
- Call on students for their answers.

Answer key

Answers will vary.

Exercise 5

- Explain the task: Tell students they are going to listen to Marta and Ian. Ask students to predict what the conversation is about.
- 🎧 Have students read the questions. Tell them to take notes on their answers. Then play the audio.
- 🎧 Play the audio one more time so that students can confirm their answers.
- Go over the answers with the class.

Answer key

1. He's been taking on too much and needs to take the evening off.
2. She is upset and confused about why Ian has changed his mind.
3. He wants to watch basketball and eat pizza with his friend.

EXTENSION

- Ask students how Marta felt when she slammed the door. (Possible answers: *angry, irritated.*) Then ask them to imagine the conversation between Marta and Ian after she gets back home from the gym.
- Have students work in pairs to role-play the conversation. Then call on one or two pairs to perform for the class, as time permits.

Please go to www.longman.com/worldview for additional in-class model conversation practice and supplementary reading practice.

HOMEWORK

- For homework, assign *Workbook* page 88, Vocabulary Exercises 1 and 2, and page 90, Listening Exercises 5 and 6.

2 **PAIRS.** Compare your answers.

3 **PAIRS.** Talk about something you want to *take part in*, something you want to *take up*, or something you want to *take a break from*. Ask and answer follow-up questions.

A: *I want to take up karate.*
B: *Are you sure? It requires a lot of dedication.*

Listening

4 **PAIRS.** Look at the photo of Marta and Ian and discuss these questions.
What is happening in the photo?
What are they saying to each other?

5 🎧 Listen to the conversation and answer the questions.

1. What reason does Ian give for not going to the gym?
2. How does Marta react?
3. What is Ian's real reason for not going?

Lesson A

Grammar focus

1 Study the examples of verbs to express likes and dislikes.

> Marta **likes to go** to the gym, but Ian **likes watching** basketball on TV.
> Marta **hates watching** sports on TV, but she **loves to work out**.
> He **can't stand working out**, so he **doesn't mind staying** in tonight.
> I **love watching** basketball, but I **hate to watch** the games alone.
> Ian **doesn't enjoy exercising**. He **can't stand to go** to the gym.
> She**'s sick of running**. She**'s into doing** yoga now.

2 Look at the examples again. Complete the rules in the chart.

Verbs for likes/dislikes followed by gerunds and/or infinitives
Use the gerund or infinitive after the following verbs: _____, _____, _____, and _____.
Use only the gerund after the following verbs and phrasal verbs: _____, _____, _____, and _____.

Grammar Reference page 148

3 Write sentences using the prompts. Make any necessary changes. Sometimes more than one correct answer is possible.

1. I really / can't stand / exercise
   I really can't stand exercising.
2. I / sick of / be out of shape, / so I / decided to / take up jogging
3. Now that it's light out / at 6:00 A.M., / I / not mind / get up early
4. You / really into/ practice / yoga now?
5. I / enjoy / play tennis, / but after an hour / I / like / take / a break
6. Kate's boyfriend / not like / go / to the gym

Pronunciation

4 🎧 Listen. Notice the groups of consonant sounds.

I ca**n't st**and **pl**aying tennis, but I do**n't mi**nd **sw**imming.

She ha**tes** watching **sp**orts, but she lo**ves pract**icing yoga.

He li**kes ex**ercising, but sometimes he nee**ds** to take a **br**eak.

5 🎧 Listen again and repeat.

Grammar focus

> **LANGUAGE NOTE**
> Notice that a question formed with an infinitive can be answered using either a gerund or an infinitive. Examples: *What do Marta and Ian like to do? She likes to go to the gym. He likes watching TV.*

> **WARM-UP**
> Note: Skip this warm-up if you're doing this lesson (Lesson B) during the same class period as Lesson A.
> - Books closed. Tell students they are going to listen again to the conversation between Marta and Ian that they heard in the Listening section.
> - Write on the board: *You said you were really into . . . / I need to . . . / I don't mind . . . / you love . . .*
> - Tell students to listen and complete the phrases.
> - 🎧 Play the audio for Lesson A, Exercise 5. Play again for students to confirm the phrases.
> - Ask students about the phrases (*You said you were really into exercising and losing weight. / I need to take a break. I don't mind staying in and taking it easy. / . . . you love watching basketball!*)
> - Write each answer on the board. Underline the gerunds and infinitives.

Exercise 1
- Have students look at the examples and study the boldfaced words.
- Elicit that some verbs can be followed by gerunds or infinitives, but other verbs can only be followed by gerunds.

Exercise 2
- Have students look at the examples again and complete the rules in the box using the verbs from the example.
- Go over the examples and rules. Check that students know *can't stand* means *really don't like*; that *(he) doesn't mind* means *(it) doesn't bother him*, and that *sick of = tired of*.
- Refer students to Grammar Reference page 148, as needed.

> **Answer key**
> like, hate, love, can('t) stand
> mind, enjoy, be sick of, be into

> **OPTION**
> Present question formation in the Language Note. Have students work in pairs to practice asking and answering questions using gerunds and infinitives.

Exercise 3
- Explain the task: Students write sentences using the prompts. Remind students to make any necessary changes, and that sometimes more than one correct answer is possible.
- Ask students to look at the example. Point out that *exercise* was changed to *exercising* and that *to exercise* would also be correct here.
- Have students complete the exercise individually. Set a time limit of 7 minutes.
- Pair students and have them check answers by reading their sentences aloud.
- Go over the answers with the class. For 4, explain that *to be really into* something means to really enjoy it. Examples: *He is really into cooking. They are really into skiing.*

> **Answer key**
> 1. I really can't stand *exercising / to exercise*.
> 2. I was sick of *being* out of shape, so I decided to take up jogging.
> 3. Now that it's light out at 6:00 A.M., I don't mind *getting up* early.
> 4. Are you really into *practicing* yoga now?
> 5. I enjoy *playing* tennis, but after an hour, I like *taking / to take* a break.
> 6. Kate's boyfriend doesn't like *going / to go* to the gym.

Pronunciation

Exercise 4
- 🎧 Play the audio and have students listen. Ask them to notice the groups of consonant sounds, shown in bold-faced type.
- Point out that English often has long groups of consonant sounds where words come together.
- Students may need help distinguishing consonant sounds from consonant letters. Point out, or elicit, that the number of consonant sounds and the number of consonant letters is not always the same. For example, the single letter *x* in *exercising* represents the two sounds /ks/, while the three letters *tch* in *watching* represent the single sound /tʃ/.
- You may want to point out places where a vowel letter is not pronounced, as in *likes* or *loves*, resulting in a consonant cluster. This is very common when a word has an *–es* ending pronounced as /s/ or /z/.

Exercise 5
- 🎧 Play the audio. Stop the audio after each item to allow students to repeat chorally. The sentences are divided in half to make them more manageable to say.
- If students have difficulty, break the sentences down further, starting at the end and building the sentences up again. Students may need to practice individual words and shorter phrases before practicing the longer clauses and sentences here.
- Ask a few individual students to repeat and check their pronunciation.
- Encourage students to go smoothly from one word to the next, without inserting a vowel sound between words. If students tend to add a vowel before the /s/ in *sports, stand*, or *staying*, it can help to have them start these words by saying a long /sss/ sound.

Speaking

> **LANGUAGE NOTE**
> The expression *to be in shape* means to be physically fit = to be healthy and strong. The opposite is *to be out of shape*. Note that *unfit* is generally not used to mean out of shape. *Unfit* means unsuitable, and is used in sentences such as, *The food was unfit for humans to eat.*

Exercise 6

- Ask the students what they are willing to do to be physically fit. Verify that they understand *physically fit* means to be healthy and strong. Have them read the survey, and then add two more ideas of their own at the bottom. Check that they know what *grains* means by giving two examples: *rice* and *wheat*. Also remind them that the phrase *once a day (week)* = *once per day (week)*.
- Hold up your book and demonstrate making a check next to *take up a sport* in the "You" column.
- Set a time limit of 5 minutes, and have students work alone to take the survey. Walk around the room, helping as needed.

Exercise 7

- Form groups of 3. Ask students to take turns asking each other the survey questions. Tell them to take notes on their partners' answers.
- Go over the example, and then set a time limit of 10 minutes. Walk around the room, helping as needed.
- Conclude by asking individual students to report on their partners' answers. Give an example: *Jake is willing to take up a sport. He isn't willing to eat mainly vegetables and grains.*

TRB For additional interactive grammar practice, have students do the reproducible activity for this unit in the *Teacher's Resource Book.*

Writing

Exercise 8

- Assign the writing task for class work or homework.
- **TRB** Optionally, give students a copy of the model of an email (see the *Teacher's Resource Book,* Writing Models).
- If students don't have the model, write on the board:

    Hi!
    How are you? I'm great! I've been really successful at balancing work and play lately, and I'm proud of myself. Last year I took on too much work, and I was always too busy!

- Make sure students understand that the task is to describe how successful (or unsuccessful) they have been at balancing work and play. To do this, they need to include examples and details. Walk around the room to make sure students understand the task.
- If the assignment is done in class, ask students to exchange their writing in pairs and respond to the email, as time permits.

For suggestions on how to give feedback on writing, see page xiv of this *Teacher's Edition.*

CONVERSATION TO GO

- As the students leave class, have them read the dialogue.
- Optionally, point out *I love to work* and *I love getting more money.*

HOMEWORK

- Assign *Workbook* page 89, Grammar Exercises 3 and 4, and page 90, Pronunciation Exercises 7 and 8.
- If students do not have the *WorldView Workbook,* assign listening homework from the Student CD. Write on the board:

    Track 52
    What is Dave bringing?

- Tell students to listen to the audio and write their answer. Have them bring it to the next class. (*a pizza*)

Speaking

6 BEFORE YOU SPEAK. What are you willing to do to be physically fit? Check (✓) the things that you are willing to do. Add two more ideas of your own.

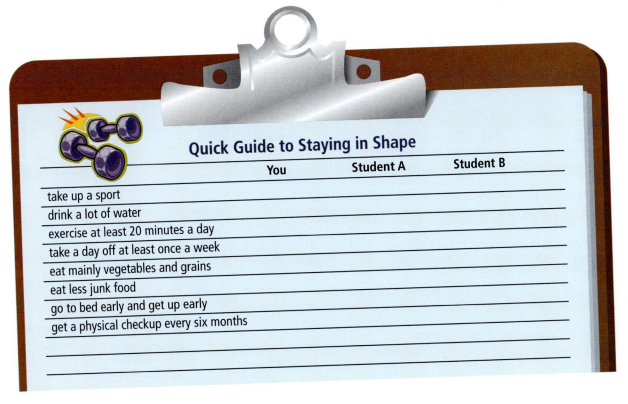

Quick Guide to Staying in Shape	You	Student A	Student B
take up a sport			
drink a lot of water			
exercise at least 20 minutes a day			
take a day off at least once a week			
eat mainly vegetables and grains			
eat less junk food			
go to bed early and get up early			
get a physical checkup every six months			

7 GROUPS OF 3. Take a survey. Take turns asking one another what you are willing to do. Take notes on the other students' answers.

A: Would you take up a sport?
B: Yes, why not? I like to play soccer, so I don't mind going to the park on weekends and kicking the ball for a while.
C: I really like sports, but I just don't have time right now.

Writing

8 Write an email to your friend describing how successful (or unsuccessful) you have been at balancing work and play. Use expressions with *take* and verbs for likes and dislikes.

CONVERSATION TO GO

A: I **don't mind working** late once in a while, but I **can't stand working** late every night.
B: Actually, I **like to work** overtime because I **love getting** more money!

UNIT 24

Digital age

Vocabulary Technical equipment
Grammar Relative clauses with *that, which, who, where*
Speaking Describing people, places, and things

Lesson A

Getting started

1 Look at the names of technical equipment and answer the questions below.

| cell phone | computer | digital camera | digital TV |
| laptop | DVD player | printer | scanner |

1. Which one lets you make and receive calls? <u>cell phone</u>
2. Which two have a screen and a keyboard? _____ _____
3. Which one can put pictures or text on paper? _____
4. Which two make pictures that you can look at on a computer? _____ _____
5. Which one has a screen and a remote control? _____
6. Which one connects to your TV to show movies? _____

SCREEN

2 **PAIRS.** Compare your answers.

REMOTE CONTROL

KEYBOARD

Pronunciation

3 🎧 Listen. Notice the stress. Some of the words in Exercise 1 have two strong syllables.

•keyboard   •digital •cam•era

4 **PAIRS.** Draw a circle over the strong syllable(s) in each word or phrase. The number (2), indicates that there are two strong syllables.

| cell phone | computer | digital TV (2) | DVD player |
| laptop | printer | remote control (2) | scanner |

5 🎧 Listen and check your answers. Then listen and repeat.

6 **GROUPS OF 3.** Discuss these questions.

Which of the technical equipment in Exercise 1 do you have?
Which would you like to have?
Which do you think is the most useful?

110

Digital age

UNIT 24

OBJECTIVES

Students will:

- activate vocabulary related to technical/digital equipment
- use relative clauses with *that, which, who, where*
- practice listening for and saying word stress in nouns and noun phrases

WARM-UP: WHAT DID YOU USE?

- Tell students this unit, "Digital age," is about technical equipment, especially digital equipment. Write the following in columns on the board:

    Me   My grandparents   Early civilization

- Ask students to suggest different tasks we do every day and write them in the "Me" column, for example: *wash clothes, buy milk, go to work, watch TV.*
- Ask students about how their grandparents did the same task and how people in early civilization performed those tasks.
- To conclude, you can take a poll to see what students think: *Who has the "easier" life?*

Getting started

LANGUAGE NOTE

In the U.S., people refer to wireless phones as *cell phones* or *cellular phones,* while in Great Britain and other countries, they are usually referred to as *mobile phones.*

OPTION: VOCABULARY PREVIEW

- Write the following words on the board: *cell phone, computer, digital camera, digital TV, laptop, DVD player, printer, scanner.*
- Ask several students what these items are used for.

Exercise ❶

- Ask students to look at the names of technical equipment written in the box, and use them to answer the questions.
- Go over the example. Set a time limit of 5 minutes.
- Walk around the room, helping as needed.
- Do not go over answers with the class until they have completed Exercise 2.

Exercise ❷

- Pair students. Ask them to compare answers.
- Go over answers with the class. One way to do this is to ask the individual students to answer the questions.

Answer key
1. cell phone
2. computer, laptop
3. printer
4. scanner, digital camera
5. digital TV
6. DVD player

Pronunciation

Exercise ❸

- 🎧 Play the audio. Students listen to the first example.
- Explain that *keyboard* is a compound noun—a noun made from two words that come together to make a noun with a new meaning. Tell students that compound nouns have one main stress, usually on the first word: **keyboard**.
- Play the second example. Explain that *digital camera* is made up of an adjective + a noun and is not a compound noun. It has stress on both words.
- You may want to have students repeat the two examples to reinforce the stress pattern. Note that *camera* is pronounced as two syllables, with the *e* silent.

Exercise ❹

- Pair students. Explain the task: Students work with a partner to identify the stressed syllable (or syllables) in each word. Words with the number 2 after them have two stressed syllables. Students draw a circle over the stressed syllables, as in the examples in Exercise 3.
- Encourage students to say the words aloud as they work.
- Set a time limit of 3 minutes. Walk around the room, helping as needed.
- Do not go over answers with the class until they have completed Exercise 5.

Exercise ❺

- 🎧 Play the audio. Have students listen and check their answers to Exercise 4.
- 🎧 Then play the audio again, and ask students to repeat the items chorally.
- Encourage students to make the stressed syllables long.
- Ask a few individual students to repeat the words to check their pronunciation.

Exercise ❻

- Form groups of 3. Tell students to discuss the questions. Have the students read the questions, or read them aloud for the class.
- Set a time limit of 5 minutes. Students take turns talking about which of the equipment in Exercise 1 they own, which they would like to have, and which they find the most useful. Tell students to listen carefully and take notes.
- Walk around the room, helping as needed.
- Call on students to tell the class what their partners said. Get groups to compare answers.

Teacher's Notes — Lesson A

T110

Reading

BACKGROUND INFORMATION

- In 1927, Philo Farnsworth of the United States received a patent for the first TV. As early as 1935, the BBC experimented with broadcasting in London several hours a day. However, it wasn't until the early 1950's that black-and-white TVs started to become popular in people's homes. Traditional TV used an analog signal that was broadcast. In the 1980's cable TV was introduced, and in the 1990's high definition TV was developed.
- The main difference between digital TV and traditional TV is that digital TV converts an analog signal to digital code, and the result is a clearer picture. It isn't necessary to explain the technical differences, but some students may know this. Many students will be familiar with digital devices and will understand the word digital to imply "better quality."

Exercise 7

- Form pairs. Explain the task: Students discuss how TVs today are different from the first TVs.
- Ask students to consider any features they can think of, such as *color* versus *black and white*, *size*, *flat screen* versus *large wooden cabinets*, *remote controls* versus *knobs*. **Note:** It isn't necessary to go into the technical differences in how the TV image is created (*digital* versus *analog*), but some students may be familiar with this and able to explain it.

Exercise 8

- Explain the task: Students read the article about digital television and decide if the questions are true or false.
- Have students look at the questions, or read them aloud with the class.
- Set a time limit of 10 minutes for students to read the article and mark the sentences *T* or *F*.
- Go over the answers with the class. Call on volunteers to correct the false statements.

OPTION

Have students work in pairs to correct the false statements.

Answer key
1. T
2. T
3. F (Traditional images cannot be compressed.)
4. F (The pictures of buildings are only sent once.)
5. F (You can only receive digital TV where the service is available.)

Exercise 9

- Pair students. Tell students to read the article again and answer the questions.
- Have students read the questions before they begin reading.
- Walk around the room, helping as needed.
- Go over the answers with the class.

Answer key
1. With digital TV we can order things from advertisers, answer quiz questions, or vote on our favorite programs.
2. Because the information is in digital form and it can be compressed.
3. You need either a special TV or a special box that works with your nondigital TV.

Please go to www.longman.com/worldview for additional in-class model conversation practice.

HOMEWORK

- For homework, assign *Workbook* page 91, Vocabulary Exercises 1 and 2, and page 93, Listening Exercises 5 and 6.

Reading

7 **PAIRS.** TVs today are different from the first TVs. Can you describe some differences?

8 Read the article about digital television. Write *T* (true) or *F* (false) after each statement.

1. We can communicate with digital TVs. T
2. Traditional TV pictures use more space than digital pictures.
3. Traditional television images can be compressed.
4. Digital pictures of buildings are sent many times.
5. You can receive digital TV anywhere you are.

9 **PAIRS.** Read the article again and answer the questions.

1. What is one thing that we can't do with traditional TV that we can do with digital TV?
2. Why can digital systems send and receive more information?
3. What equipment do you need to get digital TV?

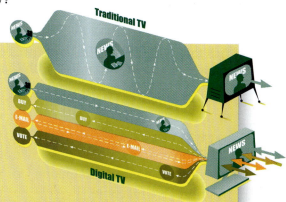

What is digital TV?

In the past, we usually just watched TV. But digital TV is interactive. With digital TV we can easily order things from advertisers, answer quiz questions, or vote on our favorite programs using the remote control. In places where digital TV is very advanced, viewers can get a service that lets them watch any program, whenever they want.

HOW DOES DIGITAL TV WORK?
As you know, a TV studio is a place where they produce TV programs. These programs are "the information" sent from the TV studio to our homes. Traditional TV needs a lot of space to send the information. With digital systems, the information is in digital form and it can be compressed, so the system can send and receive more information.
 Additionally, digital TV systems only send the parts of the picture that change. So they send a picture of a building once, because it doesn't move. But they send a lot of pictures of people who are walking or cars that are moving around that building.

DO I NEED A SPECIAL TV?
In areas where the service is available, you need either a special TV or a special box that can put the pictures together for your nondigital TV. Then you can watch your favorite program and even "talk" to the station.

24

Grammar focus

1 Study the examples of relative clauses.

> They send a lot of pictures of people **who** are walking.
> They send a lot of pictures of people **that** are walking.
> They only send the parts of the picture **that** change.
> They only send the parts of the picture **which** change.
> A television studio is a place **where** they make programs.

2 Look at the examples again. Complete the rules in the chart with *that, which, who,* or *where*.

Relative clauses with *that*, *which*, *who*, and *where*
To introduce relative clauses, use:
_____ for places.
_____ or _____ for things.
_____ or _____ for people.

Grammar Reference page 148

3 Match the beginnings of the sentences on the left with the endings on the right. Then make complete sentences with *that, which, who,* or *where*.

A pilot is someone who flies planes.

1. ~~A pilot is someone~~
2. A garage is a place
3. A laptop is something
4. A computer analyst is someone
5. A printer is a machine
6. A bank is a place
7. A scanner is something
8. A photographer is a person

a. writes computer programs.
b. takes pictures.
c. ~~flies planes.~~
d. puts words and pictures on paper.
e. transfers information into a computer.
f. you can carry around easily.
g. you park your car.
h. you can get money.

112

Grammar focus

LANGUAGE NOTES

- The restrictive clauses here are also called identifying adjective clauses because they identify which member of a group the sentence is about. Commas are not used because the information is necessary to identify who or what is being talked about. (*The man who lives next to me is very nice.*) A simple test students can do is to cover up the clause and try to read the sentence without it. If the sentence doesn't make sense without the clause, they know it is restrictive and they don't need commas.
- In contrast, nonrestrictive, or nonidentifying adjective clauses, use commas because the information is added information; it is not needed to identify who (or what) is being talked about. (*Evan, who is a teacher, lives next door.*)

WARM-UP

Note: Skip this warm-up if you're doing this lesson (Lesson B) during the same class period as Lesson A.

- Books closed. Tell students they are going to listen to an audio of the article about digital TV that they read in the Reading section.
- Write the following questions on the board. Tell students to write down the words they hear that answer the question: *What is a TV studio? What do TV digital systems send a lot of pictures of?*
- 🎧 Play the audio for Lesson A, Exercise 8. Play it again for students to confirm their answers.
- Ask students for the answers. Write them on the board: *A TV studio is a place where they produce TV programs. TV digital systems send a lot of pictures of people who are walking or cars that are moving around that building.*
- Underline the relative clause markers: *where, who,* and *that.* Say, *These tell us which place/people/cars.*

Exercise ❶

- Have students look at the examples and study the boldfaced words.
- Ask students to focus on the first pair of sentences. Elicit or explain that *who = that*; both sentences have the same meaning.
- Have students focus on the second pair of sentences. Elicit or explain that *which = that*; both sentences have the same meaning.
- Point out that only *where* is correct in the last sentence. It cannot be replaced with *that.*

Exercise ❷

- Have students look at the examples again and write the correct word to complete the explanations in the box.
- Go over the answers with the class. Emphasize which pronouns are used for people, which for things, and which for places, as it is fairly common for students to choose the wrong pronoun. Also point out that no commas are used here between the main clause and the relative clause, because the information in the clause is necessary.
- Refer students to Grammar Reference page 148, as needed.

Answer key
where   *that, which*   *that, who*

Exercise ❸

- Explain the task: Students match the beginnings of sentences on the left with the endings on the right and then write complete sentences using *who, which, that,* or *where.*
- Have students complete the exercise individually. Set a time limit of 10 minutes. Walk around the room, helping as needed.
- Pair students and have them check their answers. One way to do this is to have the students read their sentences aloud.
- Go over the answers with the class. Review that *who* is used with people and *where* and *that* with things.

Answer key
1. A pilot is someone who/that flies planes. (c)
2. A garage is a place where you park your car. (g)
3. A laptop is something which/that you can carry around easily. (f)
4. A computer analyst is someone who/that writes computer programs. (a)
5. A printer is a machine which/that puts words and pictures on paper. (d)
6. A bank is a place where you can get money. (h)
7. A scanner is something which/that transfers information into a computer. (e)
8. A photographer is a person who/that takes pictures. (b)

EXTENSION

Have students use classroom objects for additional practice. Ask students to look around the room and write about objects they see. Give an example: *A dictionary is a book that you can use to look up words.* Have students work in pairs to write four sentences. Set a time limit of 5 minutes. After 5 minutes, call on a few pairs to read their sentences for the class.

Speaking

Exercise 4

- Form groups of 3 and assign parts. Hold up your book and present the "Definitions Game." Tell Student A to turn to page 138, Student B to page 141, and Student C to page 142 and to follow the instructions given.
- Tell students to look at the example for their part and to raise their hands if they have any questions.
- Give students time to look at the cues for their parts and make unfinished sentences using *who, that/which, where*. Walk around the room, helping as needed.
- Have students play the game. Explain that they take turns reading their unfinished sentences. The person in the group who finishes the sentence first with the correct word gets one point.
- Walk around the room, helping as needed.

Answer key

Student A sentences
1. who/that (a pilot)
2. that (a microwave oven)
3. where (a bookshelf)
4. that (a horror movie)
5. who/that (a groom)
6. where (a hotel)

Student B sentences
1. who/that (a lefty)
2. that (a credit card)
3. where (a museum)
4. that (a comedy)
5. where (a lobby)
6. who/that (a bride)

Student C sentences
1. that (an action movie)
2. who/that (an interior designer)
3. where (a fitness center)
4. who/that (a con artist)
5. that (a soap opera)
6. where (a hospital)

TRB For additional interactive grammar practice, have students do the reproducible activity for this unit in the *Teacher's Resource Book*.

Writing

Exercise 5

- Assign the writing task for class work or homework. Make sure students understand that they can use their imaginations to come up with a piece of equipment. Encourage students to use relative clauses and some of the vocabulary from this unit.
- **TRB** Optionally, give students a copy of the model (see the *Teacher's Resource Book*, Writing Models). Ask them to read the model and notice the relative clauses used.
- If students do not have the model, write on the board:

  I'd like to have a videophone. A videophone is a telephone that has a screen and a camera, so the people who are speaking can see each other's faces...

  Walk around the room to make sure students understand the task.
- If the assignment is done in class, ask students to work with a partner to read each other's work, as time permits.

For suggestions on how to give feedback on writing, see page xiv of this *Teacher's Edition*.

CONVERSATION TO GO

- As the students leave class, have them read the dialogue, or read aloud chorally.
- Optionally, ask students if they know where to buy a good digital camera locally.

HOMEWORK

- Assign *Workbook* page 92, Grammar Exercises 3 and 4, and page 93, Pronunciation Exercises 7 and 8. Assign *Workbook* Self-quiz Units 21–24.
- If students do not have the *WorldView Workbook*, assign listening homework from the Student CD. Write on the board:

  Track 55
  What happens to programs sent to digital systems?
- Tell students to listen to the audio and write their answer. Have them bring it to the next class. (*They are compressed.*)

BEFORE NEXT CLASS

- Tell students that the next class will be a review class covering Units 21–24.
- Have students review the material in the units to prepare for the activities in Review 6.

Unit no.	Review Grammar	Listen to Student CD	Study Grammar Reference
21	modals from polite requests: *Could you, Would you, Would you mind?*	Track 48	Page 148
22	passive (simple past)	Track 50	Page 148
23	verbs for likes/dislikes + gerunds/infinitives	Track 52	Page 148
24	relative clauses with *that, which, who, where*	Track 55	Page 148

FOR NEXT CLASS

TRB Make copies of Quiz 5 in the *Teacher's Resource Book*.

Speaking

4 **GROUPS OF 3.** Play the Definitions Game. Take turns reading your definitions. Who can guess the word?

Student A, look at page 138. Student B, look at page 141. Student C, look at page 142.

A: *A person who flies planes is . . .*
B: *A pilot.*
A: *Correct. You get a point.*

Writing

5 Think about all the technical equipment for work or entertainment that you'd like to have. (It could be something that doesn't exist yet, and the cost is not important.) Write a paragraph describing each piece of equipment. Use relative clauses and some of the vocabulary from this unit.

CONVERSATION TO GO

A: I want a digital camera **that's** easy to use.
B: I know a place **where** you can buy a really good one.

Review 6 — Units 21–24

Unit 21 How polite are you?

1 🎧 Listen to the model conversation.

2 **PAIRS.** Role-play some situations with requests. Student A, use the information below. Student B, look at page 136.

Student A

Role-play #1
You are a teacher. Student B is your student. You are explaining a difficult math problem, but your student doesn't understand.

Role-play #2
You are riding on a bus. Student B gets on and asks you something.

Role-play #3
You are trying to enjoy a quiet evening in your apartment. Student B is your neighbor, and he or she has the music turned up very loud. Ask your neighbor to turn it down.

Unit 22 The art of crime

3 Read the crime story. Complete the sentences to make your own article. Use your imagination to make the article interesting.

Last night, **(1)** _____ was broken into, and

(2) _____ was stolen. **(3)** _____ and

(4) _____ were attacked by the thief and another

person. Police suspect that the stolen goods were placed

in a **(5)** _____ and taken to **(6)** _____.

Some observers think the crime was an inside job.

4 🎧 Listen to the model conversation.

5 **PAIRS.** Ask questions to find out what your partner's crime story is. Then answer his or her questions about your story.

Review 6: Units 21–24

📼 You may wish to use the video for Units 21–24 at this point.
For video activity worksheets, go to www.longman.com/worldview.

Unit 21: How polite are you?

OBJECTIVE

Grammar: focus on using modals *Could you, Would you, Would you mind . . . ?* for polite requests

Exercise 1

- Explain the task: Students listen to the model conversations.
- 🎧 Play the audio. Then write on the board: *Could you . . . ?* and *Would you mind . . . ?*
- 🎧 Play the audio again, and then have students repeat.

Exercise 2

- Explain the task: Students role-play requests and responses.
- Form pairs and assign parts. Tell Student A to use the information on the page, and Student B to turn to page 136.
- Give students time to read the situations and think about their lines.
- Set a time limit of 10 minutes for students to do the role-plays. While students are working, walk around the room, helping as needed.
- Conclude by calling on a few pairs to role-play for the class.

Unit 22: The art of crime

OBJECTIVE

Grammar: focus on using the passive (simple past)

Exercise 3

- Have students look at the picture. Explain the task: Students listen to the model conversation.
- 🎧 Play the audio. Then, write the questions from the audio on the board: *What was broken into? What was stolen? Who was attacked?* Point out that the questions are in the passive. Remind students that *broken into* means burglarized.
- 🎧 Play the audio again as the students listen.

Exercise 4

- Students work alone.
- Explain the task: Students fill in the blanks to make their own article about a crime. (Answers will vary.) Encourage them to use their imaginations to make their stories interesting.
- Set a time limit of 10 minutes for students to complete their articles. Walk around the room, helping as needed.

Exercise 5

- Form pairs. Have students take turns asking questions to find out what their partner's story is.
- Go over the example. Then set a time limit of 5 minutes for students to ask and answer questions.
- Call on a few students to share their partner's story.

> **WRAP-UP**
>
> - Have students use their stories as scripts to do a news broadcast. First have students work in pairs to practice reading their articles.
> - Call on students to present for the class. Encourage them to use gestures and props; for example, they can be on-the-scene reporters at the crime scene.

Unit 23: A balanced life

OBJECTIVE

Grammar: focus on verbs for likes/dislikes + gerunds and/or infinitives

Exercise 6

- Explain the task: Students listen to the model conversation.
- 🎧 Play the audio. Then write on the board the questions: *What is your job? What do you do on the weekends? Would you say you have a balanced life?*
- 🎧 Play the audio again as the students listen.

Exercise 7

- Form pairs. Tell the students to take turns asking each other about work and leisure activities. Remind students to take brief notes about their partners' answers.
- Set a time limit of 5 minutes. Walk around the room, helping as needed.

Exercise 8

- Have two pairs work together. Explain the task: Each student tells the other pair about his or her partner's life.
- Go over the example. Remind students that *to be really into* something means to like it a lot. Set a time limit of 5 minutes.
- Conclude by calling on a few students to tell the class about their partner.

> **WRAP-UP**
>
> Do a question-and-answer exchange with the class for further practice with gerunds and infinitives. Ask questions such as: *Who enjoys going to work? Who likes to go to movies? Who likes exercising on the weekends? Who thinks they have a balanced life?*

Unit 24: Digital age

OBJECTIVE

Grammar: focus on using relative clauses with *that, which, who, where*

Exercise 9

- Explain the task: Students each think of five items or occupations and write short definitions of them.
- Go over the example. Remind students that the word defined can also be an occupation, such as a reporter or a chef.
- Give students time to write their definitions. Walk around the room, helping as needed.

Exercise 10

- Explain the task: Students listen to the model conversation.
- 🎧 Play the audio. Then write on the board: *What do you call a . . . ?* and *Oh, I know. A . . .*
- 🎧 Play the audio again and have the students repeat.

Exercise 11

- Form groups of 3. Explain the task: Students take turns reading their definitions aloud and guessing the answers. The first person to guess each item or job wins a point.
- Set a time limit of 8 minutes. Walk around the room, helping as needed.

> **WRAP-UP**
>
> Have a representative from each group present two definitions to the class. The rest of the class then calls out the answer.

Unit 23 A balanced life

6 🎧 Listen to the model conversation.

7 **PAIRS.** Ask and answer questions about each other's work and leisure activities.

8 **GROUPS OF 4.** Tell the other pair about your partner's life.

Sylvie has a balanced life. She is really into her job and enjoys going to work every day. She doesn't mind her boss, except when he's in a bad mood . . .

Unit 24 Digital age

9 Think of five items or occupations and write short definitions for them.
Palm Pilot: thing where you can keep your schedule and all your addresses

10 🎧 Listen to the model conversation.

11 **GROUPS OF 3.** Take turns reading your definitions aloud and guessing the answers. The first person to guess each item gets 1 point.

UNIT 25

Arranged marriages

Vocabulary Wedding party; expressions with *get*
Grammar *It's* + adjective / noun + infinitive to express opinion
Speaking Talking about relationships

Lesson A

Getting started

1 Look at the photo of the wedding party. Identify the people.

bride _D_   best man ___   bridesmaids ___

groom ___   groomsmen ___   maid of honor ___

2 Complete the story with the expressions in the boxes.

| ~~got engaged~~ | get on each other's nerves | got to know |

1. Carla and Greg _got engaged_ three years ago. During that time, they _____ each other very well! Carla and Greg _____ at times, but most of the time they have a great time together.

| get along | got married | gotten over |

2. Carla and Greg _____ yesterday. The wedding ceremony was fine, but there was some tension during the reception. Phil, the best man, is Greg's best friend. Jenny, Carla's sister, was the maid of honor. Jenny and Phil went out together for a year. Jenny has never _____ Phil, and she doesn't _____ with Phil's new girlfriend.

| get back with | get divorced | got upset |

3. At some point during the reception, Jenny told Carla that she would like to _____ Phil. Phil's new girlfriend overheard the conversation and _____. Carla and Greg started arguing about Jenny. People thought they were going to _____ before their honeymoon. After a few minutes, everyone calmed down. Phil told Greg that he was very sorry about the situation.

3 **PAIRS.** Compare your answers.

4 **GROUPS OF 3.** Tell each other about a wedding you've been to recently.

116

Arranged marriages

UNIT 25

OBJECTIVES

Students will:

- activate vocabulary related to couples and weddings
- use *for . . . /to . . .* after adjective/noun to express opinions
- practice listening for and saying /t/ when it links to a following word

WARM-UP: WHAT'S IMPORTANT

- Tell students this unit is about couples and marriages. Explain that the title of the unit is "Arranged marriages," but that they will explore other marriages as well.
- Pair students. Ask students, *What are three important characteristics for a partner to have?* Give an example (*A husband or wife should be honest*).
- Set a time limit of 2 minutes. Write on the board: *A husband/wife should be . . .* Have students work together to list at least three characteristics.
- After 2 minutes, call on students to share their ideas. Write a list on the board.

OPTION: VOCABULARY PREVIEW

- Ask students to imagine the following situation: Two people are getting married and you are at the wedding ceremony. Who do you see?
- Form groups of 3. Set a time limit of 2 minutes. Ask students to brainstorm a list of words that identify the people who are in the wedding party.
- Call on pairs to say words from their lists. Make sure the following words are on the board: *bride, groom, best man, groomsmen, bridesmaid, maid of honor*. You may want to write all the words on the board. Go over any words that students don't understand.

CULTURE NOTE

In addition to the members of the wedding party in the photo, it is common to have a flower girl and a ring bearer. The flower girl is a young girl who carries flowers and enters the ceremony before the bride. The ring bearer is a young boy who carries a pillow on which the wedding rings are placed.

Exercise ❶

- Have students look at the photo. Explain that the people will all be part of a wedding. Ask students to identify the people. Go over the example, *The bride is D.*
- Set a time limit of 2 minutes. As students work, walk around the room, helping as needed.
- Go over the answers with the class.

EXTENSION

Have students work in pairs to describe the people in the wedding party. They can give physical as well as emotional characteristics. Give a few examples: *The groom is tall. The bride looks happy.* Vary the examples depending on the level of the class.

Answer key

bride D groom E
best man B groomsmen F
bridesmaids A maid of honor C

LANGUAGE NOTE

All of the vocabulary items in Exercise 2 start with the verb *get*. Before students begin, you might want to point this out, and review the tenses: *get/got/(have) gotten*. Students might be unfamiliar with some of the *get* phrases: *get on each other's nerves* = irritate each other; *to get over (someone)* = to no longer be in love with the person; *get back with* = start a relationship again; *get along (with)* = have a good relationship (with).

Exercise ❷

- Explain the task: Students complete the story with the expressions in the boxes. Point out that the story is in three parts, and that they complete one section at a time.
- Set a time limit of 5 minutes. Walk around the room, helping as needed. Encourage students to use the context to make "good guesses."

Answer key

1. got engaged / got to know / get on each other's nerves
2. got married / gotten over / get along
3. get back with / got upset / get divorced

Exercise ❸

- Pair students. Have student compare answers. They can do this by reading the story aloud. Have students take turns reading the paragraphs.
- Conclude by going over the answers with the class.

Exercise ❹

- Form groups of 3. Explain the task: Students tell each other about a wedding they went to. Encourage students to use vocabulary from Exercises 1 and 2.
- Set a time limit of 5 minutes. Walk around the room, helping as needed.
- Call on a few groups to share one of their stories.

Teacher's Notes — Lesson A

T116

Pronunciation

LANGUAGE NOTES
- The pronunciation of /t/ at the end of a word changes depending on what comes after it.
- When /t/ at the end of one word is followed by another /t/ at the beginning of the next word, the two sounds are linked together and pronounced as one long /t/: *thattime*.
- In North American English, when /t/ at the end of a word comes after a vowel or *r* and is followed by a vowel sound at the beginning of the next word, the /t/ is pronounced like a quick /d/ sound: *ge*t *upset*. To make this sound, the tip of the tongue lightly taps the roof of the mouth just behind the front teeth.
- Note that many English speakers do not pronounce the *t* at the end of *went* before a vowel: *wen*t *out*.

Exercise 5
- Remind students that when we link words together, the sounds that connect the word can change. Explain that /t/ has several different pronunciations in American English.
- 🎧 Play the recording and have students listen. Ask them to notice the pronunciation of the /t/ sounds.
- Call attention to the *t's* in the first two sentences. Tell students that when two /t/ sounds come together, they are pronounced as one long /t/.
- Call attention to the *t's* in the last three sentences. Point out that /t/ sounds like a very fast /d/ when it comes before a vowel.

Exercise 6
- 🎧 Play the recording. Stop the recording after each item and have students repeat it chorally. The sentences are broken down into smaller parts to highlight the pronunciation of /t/ and to make the sentences more manageable for students to say.
- Ask a few individual students to repeat the sentences to check their pronunciation.
- Encourage students to link words together smoothly.
- Although it is not necessary for students to use the voiced /t/ sound when they speak, practicing it will help with comprehension.

Listening

BACKGROUND INFORMATION
Monsoon Wedding is an Indian movie about the efforts of a family to marry their daughter to someone they have chosen for her, even though she doesn't know him. The movie portrays the tension between traditional and modern values, and the importance of family within Indian culture.

Exercise 7
- Pair students. Have students look at the questions. You might want to present the term "marry for love" and have students compare it to an arranged marriage.
- Set a time limit of 3 minutes. Walk around the room, helping as needed.

Exercise 8
- Explain the task: Students listen to Monica and Carlos talk about the movie *Monsoon Wedding* to find out what Carlos thinks of arranged marriages. Elicit if any students are familiar with the movie, and if so, what they remember about it.
- 🎧 Play the audio. Remind students to listen for Carlos's opinion of arranged marriages.
- Go over the answer with the class.

Answer key
Carlos thinks arranged marriages are a bad idea.

Exercise 9
- Have students look at the questions or read them aloud with the class.
- 🎧 Play the audio again. Encourage students to listen for the answers, and to make brief notes as they hear the answers to the questions. If needed, play the audio again.
- Have students check their answers in pairs.
- Go over the answers with the class
- 🎧 Tell students to listen again and decide if each statement is true or false.
- 🎧 Play the audio again. Students listen for the answers, and take brief notes.
- Have students check their answers in pairs.
- Go over the answers with the class.
- 🌐 Please go to www.longman.com/worldview for additional in-class model conversation practice and supplementary reading practice.

Answer key
1. T 2. F 3. T 4. T

HOMEWORK
- 📖 For homework, assign *Workbook* page 96, Vocabulary Exercises 1 and 2, and page 98, Listening Exercises 5 and 6.

Pronunciation

5 🎧 Listen. Notice the different pronunciations of *t* at the end of a word when it links to another *t* and when it links two vowel sounds.

went out together	They went out together for three years.
during that time	During that time, they got to know each other well.
get upset	At times, they get upset with each other.
get on each other's nerves	Sometimes they get on each other's nerves.
get along well	But most of the time, they get along well.

6 🎧 Listen again and repeat.

Listening

7 *PAIRS.* What is an arranged marriage? Are they now or were they once common in your country?

8 🎧 Listen to Monica and Carlos talk about the movie *Monsoon Wedding*. What does Carlos think of arranged marriages?

9 🎧 Listen again. Write *T* (true) or *F* (false) after each statement.

1. In the movie, Aditi's parents want her to marry a man who works in Texas.
2. It's not important for Aditi to marry someone her parents like.
3. Monica thinks that Carlos and his fiancée should see the movie.
4. Carlos will probably go to see *Monsoon Wedding* with his fiancée.

Grammar focus

1 Study the examples. Notice the ways to express an opinion.

> It's **important to know** the person you're marrying.
> It's **important for her to marry someone** her parents like.
> It's **a good idea to let** your parents arrange things.
> It's not **a good idea for her to marry** a stranger.

2 Look at the examples again. Underline the correct information to complete the rules in the chart.

It's + adjective/noun to express opinion
It's can be followed by an adjective or a noun **+ infinitive / gerund.**
Use *for* + **subject / object** before the infinitive when you want to specify *who*.

> Grammar Reference page 148

3 Use the words in columns 1 and 3 to write eight logical sentences. Begin each sentence with *It's*. Make some sentences with the words in column 2 to specify *who*.

It's a bad idea for someone to get married just to please his or her parents.

1	2	3
		get married just to please his or her parents
(not) important		be engaged for three years before getting married
(not) a good idea	someone	get married without getting engaged first
(not) a bad idea	couples	get to know each other well before getting married
(not) crazy	parents	choose children's marriage partners
(not) absurd	people	try to get along with each other's parents
(not) wonderful		marry someone with similar interests
		maintain some independence

4 **PAIRS.** Compare your sentences.

Grammar focus

LANGUAGE NOTES

- The students are already familiar with this structure in a simpler form. The structure used here is the same as in *It's beautiful today* or *It's raining*. *It* is used as the subject of the sentence, but the "true" subject (i.e., what is being talked about) comes after the verb in the predicate. The sentence *It's important to know the person you are marrying* can also be written with the "true" subject first: *To know the person you are marrying is important*. Explain to the students that the sentence beginning with "It's" puts the emphasis on the opinion.
- You may want to point out that there is a difference in meaning between *It's important for her to marry someone her parents like* and *It's important to her to marry someone her parents like*. The first sentence means that it is important to her parents that she marry someone they like. The second sentence means that it is important to her to marry someone they like.

WARM-UP

Note: Skip this warm-up if you're doing this lesson (Lesson B) during the same class period as Lesson A.

- Books closed. Tell students they are going to listen again to the conversation between Monica and Carlos that they heard in the Listening section.
- Write the following on the board: *It's important for her to . . . It's more important to . . .* and *It's a good idea to . . .* Ask students to listen to complete these sentences.
- 🎧 Play the audio for Lesson A, Exercise 8.
- Call on students to say the completed sentences. Write them on the board. (*It's important for her to marry someone her parents like. It's more important to love the person you're marrying. It's a good idea to let your parents arrange things.*)
- Ask students if they heard any other examples using these phrases. Write their examples on the board.

Exercise 1

- Have students look at the examples again and study the boldfaced words.
- Ask students if this structure looks like another one they know. (It's the same as *It's hot today*.)
- Elicit that this structure is used to emphasize an opinion.

Exercise 2

- Have students look at the examples and underline the correct information to complete the rules.
- Have students check their answers in pairs.
- Go over the rules with the class.
- Refer students to Grammar Reference page 148, as needed.

Answer key   infinitive   object

EXTENSION

Have students work in pairs to make four original statements starting with *It's (not) a good idea to . . .* or *It's (not) important to . . .* They can write about marriage or about another topic they are interested in, such as sports or learning how to do something.

Exercise 3

- Explain the task: Students use the words in columns 1 and 2 to write eight logical sentences. Tell students to begin with *It's*, and to make some sentences with the words in column 2 to specify *who*.
- Go over the example. As you go over it, point out the words in each of the columns so that students understand how to choose from each column. If necessary, do another example with the class. Tell students that the opinions they write don't have to be true. Emphasize that there are many possible sentences to make.
- Set a time limit of 10 minutes. Have students complete the exercise individually. Walk around the room, helping as needed.

Answer key

Answers will vary, but may include:
1. It's a bad idea for someone to get married just to please his or her parents.
2. It's (not) wonderful to be engaged for three years before getting married.
3. It's (not) a good idea for people to get married without getting engaged first.
4. It's (not) a bad idea to get to know each other well before getting married.
5. It's (not) crazy (for parents) to choose children's marriage partners.
6. It's (not) important to try to get along with each other's parents.
7. It's (not) wonderful to marry someone with similar interests.
8. It's (not) important (for couples) to maintain some independence.

Exercise 4

- Have students compare their sentences in pairs.
- Conclude by calling on individual students to read one of their sentences for the class.

Speaking

Teaching Tip! Disagreeing politely

One way to soften a disagreement or opinion in a conversation is to first say a phrase such as *I see what you're saying, but . . .* or *I understand what you are saying, but . . .* This lets the other speaker know that his/her opinion is respected, even if it isn't accepted.

Exercise 5

- Tell the students that this is a page from a self-help guide that couples can read on their own to get advice. Elicit ideas on the kind of advice this guide might include.
- Explain the task: Students read the advice in the guide and add two more statements of their own.
- Give students 5 minutes to read the advice and write their own sentences. Walk around the room, helping as needed.

Exercise 6

- Pair students. Tell them to exchange opinions about each statement. After students have finished the statements in the book, have them take turns reading and responding to the statements they wrote in Exercise 3.

Exercise 7

- Have students take a class poll to see which statements most students agreed with. Set a time limit of 5 minutes.
- Call on a few students to share their results.

EXTENSION

Ask students to work in pairs to rewrite the sentences from the guide using *It's a good idea (for)*. Do the first two with the class: *It's a good idea to let your parents help you choose your spouse. It's a good idea for couples to stay close to their families after they get married.* Have pairs work with another pair to compare their sentences. Call on pairs to read for the class.

TRB For additional interactive grammar practice, have students do the reproducible activity for this unit in the *Teacher's Resource Book*.

Writing

Exercise 8

- Ask students if they ever read advice columns in the newspaper. If so, ask them to explain the types of topics people frequently write about (*marriages, romance, work*).
- Have students read the email on page 119. Together, summarize what the main problems are. (*He and his wife aren't getting along. They like to do different things. He wants some independence. He loves his wife.*)

- **TRB** Assign the writing task for class work or homework. Optionally, give students a copy of the model (see the *Teacher's Resource Book*, Writing Models). Tell students that they need to talk about the main points of the man's email in their responses. Walk around to make sure they understand the task.
- If students do not have the model, write on the board:

  Dear Confused,
  Some people think that if couples don't enjoy doing all the same things, they will never get along. This is not true. Couples do not need to do everything together, but . . .

- If the assignment is done in class, ask students to take turns reading their letters in small groups.

For suggestions on how to give feedback on writing, see page xiv of this *Teacher's Edition*.

CONVERSATION TO GO

- As the students leave class, have them read the dialogue.
- Point out the humor in the dialogue.

HOMEWORK

- Assign *Workbook* page 97, Grammar Exercises 3 and 4, and page 98, Pronunciation Exercises 7 and 8.
- If students do not have the *WorldView Workbook*, assign listening homework from the Student CD. Write on the board:

  Track 41
  When is Carlos getting married?

- Tell students to listen to the audio and write their answer. Have them bring it to the next class. (*next June*)

Speaking

5 **BEFORE YOU SPEAK.** Read the advice in the guide and add two more statements.

The Complete Guide for Couples

♥ You should let your parents help you choose your spouse.

♥ Couples should stay close to their families after getting married.

♥ You should choose someone you have known for a long time.

♥ Both spouses should develop and maintain their own interests.

♥ You should share all your problems with your spouse. Don't keep anything to yourself.

♥ Couples should enjoy doing the same kinds of things.

♥ _____

♥ _____

6 **PAIRS.** Share your opinions about each statement.

A: I think it's crazy to let your parents help you choose your spouse.

B: Well, I think it's OK to listen to their opinion, but you have to make the final decision, that's for sure.

7 Take a class poll. Are there any statements most people agree with?

Writing

8 Imagine that you write an advice column for a local newspaper. Today you received this email from a reader. Write your answer. Use *It's* + adjective or noun + infinitive.

To: Vanessa@timesadvice.com
Subject: need help!

I've been married for three years. I would say that, for the most part, my wife and I have had a happy relationship. But now we don't get along very well. She gets upset when I go out with my friends. And on Sundays, I like to watch soccer games. She wants me to go shopping with her, or to visit relatives, but that's really boring. I really love my wife, but I also need some independence. What should I do?

Yours,
Confused

CONVERSATION TO GO

A: I think **it's fine for you** to disagree with me all the time.
B: Oh, you're so wrong. I hardly ever argue with you.

Lesson B

UNIT 26

Money matters

Vocabulary Money and banks
Grammar Verbs with two objects
Speaking Talking about money

Lesson A

Getting started

1 Complete the sentences with a pair of expressions in the box. Make the necessary changes.

be in the red / be in the black	borrow money / lend money
invest money / save money	bank statement / bank account
checking account / savings account	deposit money / withdraw money
receive interest / pay interest	

1. When you owe money, you _are in the red_, but once you pay it all back, you _are in the black_ again.

2. You _____ when you put it in the bank, and you _____ if you need it to buy something.

3. People usually keep money for paying bills in a _____ but put their savings in a _____, so that the bank pays them some interest.

4. Banks usually send their customers a _____ every month explaining the activity in their _____.

5. People _____ on the money they have in the bank, but they _____ on money they borrow from the bank.

6. You _____ when you buy something (or shares in a company) to make a profit, and you _____ when you keep it and don't spend it.

7. You _____ from a bank (or someone) when you need more than you have. The bank (or someone) _____ to you.

2 **PAIRS.** Compare your answers.

3 Look at the bank statement and answer the questions.

1. How much money did the customer deposit?
2. How much money did the customer pay in checks?
3. Did the customer pay or receive interest? How much?
4. Is the customer in the black or in the red?

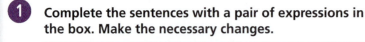

DirBanking

Statement of account   Checking account number: 81033917

Date		Credits	Debits	Balance
08/24	Balance brought forward			2,312.78
08/29	Check #1075		17.50	2,295.28
09/06	Check #1076		150.00	2,145.28
09/15	Electronic Deposit	500.00		2,645.28
09/21	Interest	14.52		2,659.80
09/22	Balance brought forward			2,659.80

4 **PAIRS.** Which of the things in Exercise 1 do you do the most?

120

Money matters

UNIT 26

OBJECTIVES

Students will:

- activate vocabulary related to money and banking
- use verbs with direct and indirect objects
- practice listening for and saying the weak pronunciation of object pronouns

WARM-UP: A TYPICAL DAY

- Tell students this unit is about money and banking. Explain that the unit title "Money matters" has two meanings: *matters* as a verb means money is important (*Money matters to him*); and *matters* as a noun means the subject of money (*He is worried about money matters*).
- Say, *Every day you probably spend a little money. Think about what you bought yesterday. Did you buy a newspaper? Did you buy a cup of coffee or some lunch? Did you pay for the bus or train? Do you know how much you spent?*
- Form groups of 3. Ask students to take turns saying what they spent money on. Tell them to listen carefully to their partners, and decide who spent the most in their group.
- Set a time limit of 2 minutes. After 2 minutes, call on a few students to report how much they spent, and who spent the most in their group.

Getting started

OPTION: VOCABULARY PREVIEW

- Write the phrases from Exercise 1 on the board or have students look at them in the book. Write the following in two columns on the board:

    money coming in   money going out

- Form groups of 3. Set a time limit of 3 minutes. Ask students to write the phrases from Exercise 1 in the correct group. Tell them that some phrases might be in both groups (*invest money, bank statement, bank account, deposit money*). While students are working, walk around the room, helping as needed.
- Ask different students to say one phrase and the group they put it in. Go over any words that students don't understand.

Exercise 1

- Tell the students that the sentences are about banking. Have students look at the expressions in the box. Point out that some of the pairs are opposites, such as *be in the red (owe money)/be in the black (not owe money); receive/pay interest; borrow/lend money; deposit/withdraw money*. For example, you *borrow* money from someone (or a bank), and they *lend* the money to you.

- Explain the task: Students complete each sentence with a pair of expressions from the box. Remind students to make any necessary changes in verb form. Also remind them to read the sentences carefully and to use context clues.
- Go over the example. Point out the phrase *owe money*. This context clue tells them to use the phrase *in the red*. Walk around the room, helping as needed.
- Do not go over the answers with the group until they have completed Exercise 2.

Exercise 2

- Pair students. Ask them to compare answers.
- Go over answers with the class.

Answer key

1. are in the red, are in the black
2. deposit money, withdraw money
3. checking account, savings account
4. bank statement, bank account
5. receive interest, pay interest
6. invest money, save money
7. borrow money, lends money

Exercise 3

- Have students look at the bank statement. Make sure students understand that *balance carried forward* means the amount of money in the account.
- Tell students to work individually to find the answers to the questions. Set a time limit of 2 minutes.
- Go over the answers with the class. Check that students understand *credit* means money deposited, and *debit* means money paid out.

Answer key

1. $500
2. $167.50
3. received interest; $14.52
4. in the black

Exercise 4

- Pair students. Ask them to discuss which of the activities in Exercise 1 they do the most.
- Conclude by polling the students. Ask, *How many of you (invest money)?*

Teacher's Notes — Lesson A

Reading

Exercise 5

- Have students look at the photos and elicit the three different ways of banking: *traditional banking* (going to the bank), *telephone banking* (using the phone to make transactions), and *e-banking* (all transactions done over the Internet).
- Pair students. Have them read the questions or read them aloud for the class.
- Set a time limit of 2 minutes for students to discuss the methods of banking and say which one they prefer and why.
- After 2 minutes, ask a few students their opinions and elicit some advantages and disadvantages of each type of banking.

Exercise 6

- Explain the task: Students read the website for DirBanking, and find three advantages of banking with this online service. Students can underline the advantages or take brief notes.
- Set a time limit of 5 minutes. Walk around the room, helping as needed.
- Call on individual students to report to the class. Tell the class to listen as each student speaks so that they don't say an advantage that was already mentioned. Continue calling on students until all advantages are reported.

> **Answer key**
>
> not waiting for a statement
> not waiting in line
> saving time and money
> banking 24 hours a day, 7 days a week
> banking by telephone or computer
> getting low interest rates
> getting advice on stocks

Exercise 7

- Explain the task: Students read the web page again and answer the questions. Remind students to read the questions before they begin.
- Set a time limit of 2 minutes. **Note:** Giving students only 2 minutes will help them target their reading and focus them on finding the specific information they need to answer the questions.
- After 2 minutes, go over the answers with the class.
- Conclude by asking students if they have any questions about new vocabulary. Check understanding of *financial security* (protection from dangerous money situations) and *peace of mind* (a feeling of being calm and not worried).

> **Answer key**
>
> 1. Customers save time because they don't have to wait in line—they can bank any time of the day or night.
> 2. The bank offers the best interest rates.
> 3. Accounts can be accessed by regular phone, cell phone, or computer.

EXTENSION

Have students work in pairs to use the information from the web page to make a radio advertisement for DirBanking. Have students practice saying the advantages and promoting the features of the bank. Students can then present their "ads" in small groups or to the whole class, as time permits.

Please go to www.longman.com/worldview for additional in-class model conversation practice.

HOMEWORK

- For homework, assign *Workbook* page 99, Vocabulary Exercises 1 and 2, and page 101, Listening Exercises 5 and 6.

Reading

5 **PAIRS.** Look at the photos showing different ways of banking. Discuss these questions.

What do you use banks for?

Which of the methods of banking in the pictures do you prefer? Why?

6 Read the web page for DirBanking. What are three advantages of banking with this online service?

7 Read the web page again and answer the questions.

1. How does DirBanking save you time?
2. Why would you want to borrow money from this bank?
3. How can you access your account?

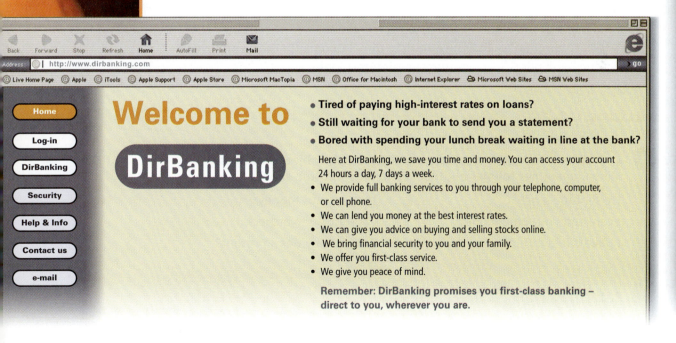

Welcome to **DirBanking**

- Tired of paying high-interest rates on loans?
- Still waiting for your bank to send you a statement?
- Bored with spending your lunch break waiting in line at the bank?

Here at DirBanking, we save you time and money. You can access your account 24 hours a day, 7 days a week.

- We provide full banking services to you through your telephone, computer, or cell phone.
- We can lend you money at the best interest rates.
- We can give you advice on buying and selling stocks online.
- We bring financial security to you and your family.
- We offer you first-class service.
- We give you peace of mind.

Remember: DirBanking promises you first-class banking – direct to you, wherever you are.

Grammar focus

1 Look at the examples with direct and indirect objects. Underline the direct object and circle the indirect object in each sentence.

> We can lend **you money**.
> We can lend **money to you**.
> We bring **your family financial security**.
> We bring **financial security to your family**.

2 Look at the examples again. Underline the correct words to complete the rules in the chart.

Verbs with two objects
When the indirect object comes **before** the direct object, **use / do not use** a preposition.
When the indirect object comes **after** the direct object, **use / do not use** a preposition (usually *to* or *for*).

Grammar Reference page 149

3 Rewrite each sentence by changing the order of the direct and indirect object.

1. I lent my sister ten dollars.
   I lent ten dollars to my sister.
2. I showed the bank statement to my accountant.
3. Can you send me the bill?
4. She teaches money management to high school students.
5. I can lend the money to you.
6. When will you send me the receipt?
7. Many companies give the option of direct deposit to their employees.
8. The bank offers its customers low-interest loans.

Pronunciation

4 🎧 Listen. Notice the weak pronunciation of the object pronouns. When *him* or *her* follows another word, the *h* is often silent.

He sent *me* a bill.   They owe *us* money.
I can lend *you* some money.   We sent *them* a check.
I gave *h̸im* a receipt.   Did you buy *h̸er* a present?

5 🎧 Listen again and repeat.

6 🎧 Complete the sentences with the word you hear: *her*, *him*, or *them*.

1. I showed _____ the statement.
2. We owe _____ money.
3. I gave _____ a check.
4. Did you give _____ a receipt?
5. I sent _____ a bill.
6. I lent _____ five dollars.

Grammar focus

> **LANGUAGE NOTE**
>
> Students should know that the indirect object often comes before the direct object. *(He gave me a book.)* If the typical word order is changed and the indirect object is placed *after* the direct object, this is indicated by the preposition *to*. *(He gave the book to me.)*

> **WARM-UP**
>
> Note: Skip this warm-up if you're doing this lesson (Lesson B) during the same class period as Lesson A.
>
> - Books closed. Tell students they are going to listen to an audio of the website for DirBanking that they read in the Reading section.
> - Write the following phrases on the board with blanks for students to fill in: *We provide full _____ to _____. We can lend _____. We can give _____ advice. We bring financial security to _____. We offer you first-class _____.*
> - Ask students to write down the phrases then listen to the audio and fill in the blanks.
> - 🎧 Play the audio for Lesson A, Exercise 6. Play the audio again for students to confirm their answers.
> - Call on students to come to the board and fill in the blanks. (*We provide full banking service to you. We can lend you money. We can give you advice. We bring financial security to you. We offer you first-class service.*)
> - Ask students what they notice about the sentences. (*They have two objects.*)

Exercise ❶

- Have students look at the examples and study the boldfaced words.
- Point out that the direct object usually tells who or what receives the action of the verb, and that the indirect object tells to or for whom or what the verb happens. (*She gave me a book = She gave a book to me.*) Remind students that the indirect object is only used with a direct object.
- Have students underline the direct object and circle the indirect object.

> **Answer key**
>
> direct objects = *money, financial security*
> indirect objects = *you, your family*

Exercise ❷

- Have students look at the examples again and underline the correct words to complete the rules.
- Go over the answers with the class. Refer students to Grammar Reference page 149, as needed.

> **Answer key**   do not use; use

Exercise ❸

- Explain the task: Students rewrite each sentence by changing the order of the direct and indirect object.
- Ask students to look at the example. Point out that *to* is added when the indirect object (*my sister*) is moved after the direct object (*ten dollars*).
- Have students complete the exercise individually. Set a time limit of 10 minutes.
- Pair students and have them check their answers.
- Go over the answers with the class.

> **Answer key**
>
> 1. I lent ten dollars to my sister.
> 2. I showed my accountant the bank statement.
> 3. Can you send the bill to me?
> 4. She teaches high school students money management.
> 5. I can lend you the money.
> 6. When will you send the receipt to me?
> 7. Many companies give their employees the option of direct deposit.
> 8. The bank offers low-interest loans to its customers.

Pronunciation

Exercise ❹

- Remind students that in English, words that give new or important information sound longer and stronger.
- 🎧 Play the audio and have students listen. Ask students to notice the weak pronunciation of the pronouns.
- Point out the disappearing /h/ sound in *him* and *her* and the way these words are linked to the words before them. Respellings like "gavim" and "buyer" can be useful.

Exercise ❺

- 🎧 Play the audio. Stop after each sentence and have students repeat it chorally.
- Ask a few individual students to repeat and check their pronunciation.
- Encourage students to put stress on the word before the pronoun to help them give it a weak pronunciation.

Exercise ❻

- Tell students they are going to listen to the sentences in their books. Ask them to write the word they hear in the blank: *her, him,* or *them*.
- Explain that the difference between these pronouns can be hard to hear when native speakers say them in conversation.
- 🎧 Play the audio. If necessary, stop the audio after each sentence to give students time to write.

> **Answer key**
>
> 1. him   3. her   5. them
> 2. them   4. her   6. him

Speaking

Exercise 7

- Explain the task: Students have won a $100,000 prize in a contest and they now have to decide how to spend it.
- Have students read the ideas listed or read them aloud for the class. Verify that students know a *charity* is an organization that gives money and help to people who need it. Tell students to be very specific as to how they will spend the $100,000.
- Set a time limit of 10 minutes. Walk around the room, helping as needed. Check that students' choices add up to $100,000.

Exercise 8

- Form groups of 3. Tell students to compare their decisions.
- Go over the example. Remind students to ask follow-up questions. Set a time limit of 10 minutes.
- Conclude by asking a few students what their partners would do with the money.

> **WRAP-UP**
>
> Ask the class to share different things people do when they suddenly get a lot of money.

TRB For additional interactive grammar practice, have students do the reproducible activity for this unit in the *Teacher's Resource Book*.

Writing

Exercise 9

- Assign the writing task for class work or homework. Make sure students understand that in their letter they need to explain how they would use one million dollars for social, community, and educational programs. Elicit ideas on the types of programs and activities that might be included, such as a summer sports program, or an after-school homework program.
- Encourage students to use verbs with two objects and some of the money and banking vocabulary from this unit. Remind them to be as specific as they can about how they would spend the money.
- **TRB** Optionally, give students a copy of the model of a letter (see the *Teacher's Resource Book*, Writing Models). Ask them to read the model and notice the vocabulary and grammar from the unit.

- If students don't have the model, write on the board:

  Dear Mr. Richmond:
  We need donations to provide a better quality of life to the people in our town and to support the different programs that we are working on at the moment. This is an example of how we would distribute a generous donation of $1,000,000 among the different social, community, and educational progams in our town . . .

  Walk around the room to make sure students understand the task.

- If the assignment is done in class, ask a few students to read their letters aloud as time permits.

For suggestions on how to give feedback on writing, see page xiv of this *Teacher's Edition*.

CONVERSATION TO GO

- As the students leave class, have them read the dialogue, or read aloud chorally.
- Optionally, ask students if it's a good idea to lend money to friends. Encourage them to give reasons why or why not.

HOMEWORK

- Assign *Workbook* page 100, Grammar Exercises 3 and 4, and page 101, Pronunciation Exercises 7 and 8.
- If students do not have the *WorldView Workbook*, assign listening homework from the Student CD. Write on the board:

  Track 58
  How can DirBanking customers access their accounts?

- Tell students to listen to the audio and write their answer. Have them bring it to the next class. (*through telephone, computer, or cell phone*)

Speaking

7 **BEFORE YOU SPEAK.**
Congratulations! You have won first prize in a contest—$100,000! Now you have to decide what to do with the prize money. Make a list. Be very specific. Use these ideas or other ideas of your own.

- buy presents for your friends (Who? What presents?)
- keep some for yourself (How much? Invest it?)
- lend some to a friend to start a business (How much? Receive interest?)
- give some to your family (How much?)
- give some to a charity (Which charity? How much?)

8 **GROUPS OF 3.** Compare your decisions. Ask and answer questions.

A: First, I'd buy my younger brother a sports car. That would cost about $40,000.
B: Wow! That's generous.
C: Why would you do that?

Writing

9 You are the head of an organization that gives money to important social, community, and educational programs in your city or town. Write a letter to a rich, local business owner, explaining how you would distribute one million dollars of his or her money. Use verbs with two objects. Be as specific as you can.

CONVERSATION TO GO

A: Can you lend **me ten dollars**?
B: Sorry, I never lend **money to friends**!

UNIT 27

Less is more

Vocabulary waste, use, spend, save + noun
Grammar Review and expansion: should/shouldn't, could, ought to for advice
Speaking Giving advice

Lesson A

Getting started

1 Look at the word web. It shows how the verb *waste* can go with these nouns.

2 **PAIRS.** Make word webs for the verbs *use*, *spend*, and *save*. Use the same nouns as in Exercise 1.

3 🎧 Listen and check your answers.

4 **PAIRS.** Look at the picture of the office. Make as many sentences as possible using the verb + noun combinations from Exercise 1.

A: They are wasting electricity because all the lights are on.
B: And I'm sure they also spend a lot of money on paper.

124

Less is more

UNIT 27

OBJECTIVES

Students will:

- activate vocabulary related to waste and natural resources and giving advice
- use modals: *should/shouldn't, could, ought to* for advice
- practice reductions of *should/could/ought to* in rapid speech

WARM-UP: RESOURCES

- Tell students this unit is about things people waste, like natural resources or electricity. Explain that the expression *less is more* means that it is sometimes better to have less of something, rather than more.
- Say that one natural resource is *wood*. Ask students to look around the room and find at least two items that are made from wood. Give examples: *a piece of paper, a pencil*. Tell them to write down the items they see.
- Form pairs. Set a time limit of 1 minute. After 1 minute, call on a few students to read their lists.

Getting started

OPTION: VOCABULARY PREVIEW

- Ask students to brainstorm a list of resources. Write their ideas on the board.
- Form groups of 3. Set a time limit of 4 minutes. Ask the groups to make a list (one per group) of four resources they use every day. Tell students to talk about how important each resource is to them.
- Set a new time limit of 4 minutes. Ask the groups to rank the list in order of importance and to make sure they have reasons for their decisions (1 = the most important and 4 = the least important on this list).
- Walk around the room, helping as needed.
- Ask a few groups for their lists and write them on the board. Ask students for some of the reasons behind their choices.

Exercise ❶

- Have students look at the word web. Explain that it shows how the verb *waste* can go with these nouns. Verify that they know *waste* means to not use something wisely, or to use more of something than you should.
- Go over the word combinations in the word web. Start by saying, *waste electricity*. Elicit a few ideas on how people waste electricity. (*They leave lights on.*) Continue around the word web with the other word combinations.

Exercise ❷

- Pair students. Explain the task: Students work together to make word webs for the verbs *use, spend,* and *save*. Tell them to use the same nouns as in Exercise 1.
- Point out that each verb cannot be used with all of the nouns, and they have to decide which combinations will work. For example, *use* doesn't go with *opportunities*.
- Set a time limit of 10 minutes. While students are working, walk around the room, helping as needed.

Exercise ❸

- Tell students to listen and check their answers.
- 🎧 Play the audio. Play it again, as needed.
- Go over the answers with the class.

Answer key

Use: paper; time; electricity/energy; money; space; resources
Spend: time; money
Save: paper; time; electricity/energy; money; space; resources
Verb + noun combinations that are not typical are: use opportunities, spend paper, spend electricity/energy, spend opportunities, spend space, spend resources, save opportunities.

Exercise ❹

- Pair students. Have them look at the picture of an office and observe how the office is being wasteful.
- Explain the task: Students make as many sentences as possible using the verb + noun combinations from Exercise 1. Go over the example. You might want to suggest that students first take a few notes.
- Set a time limit of 5 minutes. Walk around the room, helping as needed.
- Call on individual students to share their observations.

Answer key

Answers may vary, but might include:
The men are wasting time talking.
The women are wasting time drinking coffee.
They are wasting energy by letting all the heat go out the window.
The woman is spending a lot of money.
They should save electricity by turning some of the lights off.
They're wasting space by piling reports all over the table and floors instead of putting them on the shelves.
They might be wasting business opportunities by letting the phones ring.
They are wasting resources by throwing paper in the wastebasket instead of using the recycling bin.

Teacher's Notes — Lesson A

Teacher's Notes — Lesson A

Listening

Exercise 5

- Explain the task: Students look at the sentences and underline the words so that the sentences express their opinions. Emphasize that students should give their opinions; there are no correct answers.
- Give students time to underline the words. Walk around the room, helping as needed.

Exercise 6

- Pair students. Have them compare their answers to Exercise 5.
- Call on a few students to share their opinions with the class.

> **Answer key**
> Answers will vary.

Exercise 7

- Explain the task: Tell students they are going to listen to a radio interview with Laura Chang, author of a book called *Less Is More*. Elicit ideas on what the book is about.
- Tell students to listen for what Laura Chang thinks about the statements in Exercise 5. Encourage them to take brief notes as they listen.
- 🎧 Play the audio as students take notes on the author's opinions.
- 🎧 Play the audio one more time so that students can confirm their answers.
- Go over the answers with the class.

> **Answer key**
> 1. less   2. less   3. shorter   4. less

Exercise 8

- Pair students. Have students look at the questions, or read them aloud with the class.
- 🎧 Play the audio again. Encourage students to make brief notes as they hear the answers to the questions.
- 🎧 Play the audio again for students to confirm their answers.
- Have pairs ask and answer the questions.
- Go over the answers with the class.

> **Answer key**
> 1. People should work shorter hours so that they can have less stress and be more successful.
> 2. They will be tired and irritable and not very productive.
>   They will be wasting time and might become more tired.
> 3. Because a 10-minute nap gives you more energy than an extra hour of sleep at night.

EXTENSION

- Ask students to consider how they might apply the idea of "less is more" to their own lives. Ask them to each write three sentences about what they could do differently. Give examples: *If I buy fewer clothes, I won't have so many clothes to wash. If I study hard for a few hours, I will have more free time to do other things.*
- Have students share their sentences in small groups.

> **WRAP-UP**
> Ask students how their opinions compared to the author's.

🌐 Please go to www.longman.com/worldview for additional in-class model conversation practice and supplementary reading practice.

HOMEWORK

- 📖 For homework, assign *Workbook* page 102, Vocabulary Exercises 1 and 2, and page 104, Listening Exercises 5 and 6.

Listening

5 Underline the words so that the sentences express your opinion.

1. If you want to feel more energetic, then you should sleep **more / less.**
2. If you want to be more effective in business, you should use technology **more / less**.
3. To be more successful at work, work **longer / shorter** hours.
4. Eat **more / less** if you want to be healthier.

6 **PAIRS.** Compare your answers.

7 Listen to the radio interview with Laura Chang, author of the book *Less Is More*. What does she think about the statements in Exercise 5?

8 **PAIRS.** Listen again and answer the questions.

1. Why does the author think that people should work shorter hours?
2. What does the author say will happen if a person gets too little sleep? too much sleep?
3. Why does the author say people ought to try taking afternoon naps?

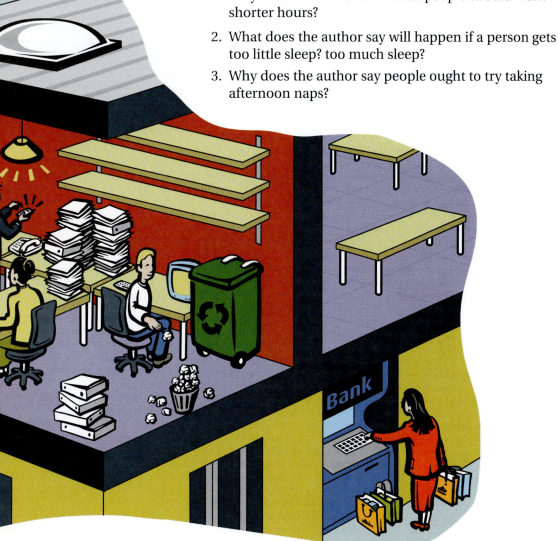

27

Lesson B

Grammar focus

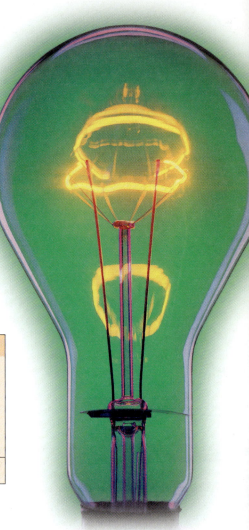

1 Study the examples with *should*, *could*, and *ought to*.

> **(+)** She's exhausted! She **should work** shorter hours.
> He's so unhealthy. He really **ought to eat** less.
> If they need to use less energy, they **could use** fluorescent bulbs, or they **could get** solar hot water panels.
>
> **(–)** We **shouldn't sleep** so much on the weekends. We never get anything done!
>
> **(?)** I can't finish all my work. What **should** I **do**?

2 Look at the examples again. Complete the rules in the chart with *could*, *should (not)*, or *ought to*.

Modals *could*, *should (not)*, *ought to* for advice and suggestions
Use _____ and *ought to* for advice.
Use _____ for suggestions.
Use only _____ in questions to ask for advice and suggestions.
Use only _____ in negative for advice.
NOTE: *Ought to* is never used in the negative form.

> Grammar Reference page 149

3 Rewrite the sentences using the appropriate form of *should*, *could*, or *ought to*. More than one answer is possible in some cases.

1. I want to have more energy. What is your advice?

   What should I do to have more energy?

2. One day the world will run out of oil, so it's important to invest in solar power now.

3. Don't use incandescent light bulbs. They waste a lot of resources.

4. To have more energy during the day, you have a couple of choices. Either sleep less at night, or take a nap in the afternoon.

5. If you want to save on your electric bill, here's my advice: use fluorescent bulbs as much as possible.

6. They need to get more done at work. What is your advice?

7. Don't leave the lights on if you're not in a room.

8. Here's a suggestion to do better at work: use less technology.

4 **PAIRS.** Compare your answers.

Grammar focus

> **LANGUAGE NOTES**
> - *Should* and *ought to* are both used to give advice. The speaker makes a suggestion about what he/she believes would be a good thing to do. *Should* is generally considered more formal: *You should get some rest. You ought to get some rest.*
> - *Could* is used to suggest something is a good idea when used with the first person: *I could try calling the airlines.* It sounds like advice when said to someone else: *You could try studying more.*
> - Only *should* is used to *ask for* advice. (*What should I do?*)
> - Remind students that modals have only one form: they don't have an *-s* in the third-person singular.

> **WARM-UP**
> Note: Skip this warm-up if you're doing this lesson (Lesson B) during the same class period as Lesson A.
> - Books closed. Tell students they are going to listen again to the interview with Laura Chang that they heard in the Listening section. Remind them that she talks about some things people should and shouldn't do.
> - Tell students to listen for phrases with *should*, and to write down at least three that they hear.
> - 🎧 Play the audio for Lesson A, Exercise 7.
> - Ask students for examples of phrases with *should*. (Possible answers: *we should work shorter hours; I think people shouldn't sleep so much; maybe I should; we should all spend less time at the computer; should we eat less, too?*)
> - Conclude by saying that these are all suggestions. She is giving advice about what she thinks people need to do.

Exercise ❶

- Have students look at the examples and study the boldfaced words.
- Remind students that (+) means *affirmative*, (–) means *negative*, and (?) means *question*.
- Ask students to look at the first three examples. Ask them what they notice about the verbs (the base form is used after *should, ought,* and *could*).
- Have students look at the next example. Point out that *should* is used with the negative but *ought* isn't.
- Ask students what they notice about the question (the modal *should* comes before the subject; and *should*, not *ought to*, is used).

Exercise ❷

- Have students look at the examples again and complete the rules in the box.
- Pair students and have them compare their answers.
- Go over the answers with the class.

- Ask a few questions to elicit the key points about the grammar. (*What do you use for suggestions? What do you use the base form after?*)
- Refer students to Grammar Reference page 149, as needed.

> **Answer key**
> should   could   should   shouldn't

Exercise ❸

- Explain the task: Students rewrite the sentences using the appropriate form of *should, could,* or *ought to*. Point out that more than one answer is possible in some cases.
- Ask students to look at the example. Point out that *could* is used here because it's a suggestion of a good idea, but *should* and *ought to* can also be used.
- Have students complete the exercise individually. Set a time limit of 10 minutes.
- Do not go over answers with the class until they have completed Exercise 4.

> **Answer key**
> Answers will vary, but should be similar to the sentences below.
> 1. What should I do to have more energy?
> 2. One day the world will run out of oil, so we should invest in solar power now.
> 3. You shouldn't use incandescent bulbs. They waste a lot of resources.
> 4. To have more energy during the day, you have a couple of choices. You could sleep less at night, or you could take a nap in the afternoon.
> 5. If you want to save on your electric bill, you should use flourescent bulbs as much as possible.
> 6. What should they do to get more done at night?
> 7. You shouldn't leave the lights if you're not in a room.
> 8. To do better at work, you should use less technology.

Exercise ❹

- Have students compare their answers in pairs.
- Go over the answers with the class.

> **EXTENSION**
> - Have students work in pairs to write questions with *should*, using the information in the sentences in Exercise 3. Tell them to read each sentence and write at least one question.
> - Point out that more than one question is possible for each sentence. Have pairs exchange questions with another pair and check each other's work. (Examples: *What should we invest in? Should we use incandescent light bulbs in the summer? Should we use fluorescent bulbs as much as possible? What should you get in the habit of doing? What should we try harder to do? Why should you set your thermostat higher in the summer?*)

Pronunciation

Exercise 5

- Remind students that modal auxiliaries usually have a weak pronunciation in the middle of a sentence.
- 🎧 Play the first two sentences on the audio. Ask students to listen to the weak pronunciation of *should*.
- 🎧 Play the next two sentences. Ask students to listen to the way the words are blended together in *ought to*.
- Say the words *ought + to* separately and then in the blended form "oughta" to highlight the way they sound different. You can use the respelling "oughta" to illustrate.
- 🎧 Play the last two sentences on the audio and ask students to listen to the weak pronunciation of *could*.

Exercise 6

- 🎧 Play the audio. Stop after each sentence and have students repeat it chorally.
- If necessary, break the longer sentences down into shorter phrases to make them easier to pronounce, starting at the end and building the sentences up again. For example: *at the computer—less time at the computer—spend less time at the computer—You could spend less time at the computer.*
- Ask a few individual students to repeat and check their pronunciation.
- Encourage students to make the weak pronunciation of *should* and *could* short and to use the blended pronunciation of *ought to*.

Speaking

Exercise 7

- Form groups of 3 and assign parts. Tell students they will take turns asking for and giving advice.
- Tell Student A to stay on this page; Student B to turn to page 137; Student C to turn to page 140.
- Give students time to look over their parts.
- Set a time limit of 10 minutes. Walk around the room, helping as needed.
- After 10 minutes, call on individual students to tell the class one of their problems and the advice they received.

TRB For additional interactive grammar practice, have students do the reproducible activity for this unit in the *Teacher's Resource Book*.

Writing

Exercise 8

- Assign the writing task for class work or homework. You may want to tell students they can write about a real or imaginary problem. In either case, they write a short letter to the person giving him or her advice.
- **TRB** Optionally, give students a copy of the model of a letter (see the *Teacher's Resource Book,* Writing Models). Ask them to read the model and notice the vocabulary and grammar from the unit.
- If students don't have the model, write on the board:

    Dear Lydia,
    You shouldn't worry so much. I think there's a solution to your problem! You are too worried about earning more and more money, and so you work longer hours each day. I don't think that you need to earn more money if you spend less money.

    Walk around the room to make sure students understand the task.
- If the assignment is done in class, ask students to exchange their writing with a partner as time permits.

For suggestions on how to give feedback on writing, see page xiv of this *Teacher's Edition*.

CONVERSATION TO GO

- As the students leave class, have them read the dialogue.
- Optionally, ask them if this is advice the woman can use. (*Probably not—she has two young children to take care of.*)

HOMEWORK

- 📖 Assign *Workbook* page 103, Grammar Exercises 3 and 4, and page 104, Pronunciation Exercises 7 and 8.
- 💿 If students do not have the *WorldView Workbook,* assign listening homework from the Student CD. Write on the board:

    Track 60
    What should you do in the afternoon?
- 🎧 Tell students to listen to the audio and write their answer. Have them bring it to the next class. (*Take a ten-minute nap.*)

Pronunciation

5 🎧 Listen. Notice the weak pronunciations of *should* and *could* and the linked pronunciation of *ought to* ("oughta").

What should I do?   You should work shorter hours.

You could take an afternoon nap.   You could spend less time at the computer.

You ought to relax more.   You ought to sleep less.

6 🎧 Listen again and repeat.

Speaking

7 **GROUPS OF 3.** Describe a situation. Ask for and give advice. Student A, look at this page. Student B, look at page 137. Student C, look at page 140.

Take turns sharing your problems and giving advice on what to do.

Student A

Problem #1
I can read and write English well, but when I try to have a conversation in English, I feel embarrassed. Do you have any suggestions?

Problem #4
It takes me too long to get to work and back home every day. I spend too much time commuting every day. Any ideas?

Problem #7
My colleagues at work always arrive late for meetings. I waste my time waiting for them. Help!

A: Maybe you should try . . .
B: Or, what about this? I think you should . . .

Writing

8 Think of a problem that a friend or relative has. Write the person a short letter giving him or her advice on that problem. Use the modals *should/shouldn't*, *could*, and *ought to* for giving advice.

CONVERSATION TO GO

A: What should I do?
B: You ought to relax more.

UNIT 28

Celebrate

Vocabulary Words related to parties
Grammar Present unreal conditional (*If* + simple past + *would* + verb)
Speaking Talking about imaginary situations

Lesson A

Getting started

1 Write the words and phrases from the box in the correct columns.

~~anniversary~~	barbecue	birthday	~~black tie~~
DJ	dinner	family reunion	graduation
live music	pianist	potluck dinner	wedding

Occasion	Type of party	Music
anniversary	black tie	

2 Complete the sentences with words from Exercise 1.

1. The company is having a _black tie_ party, so I guess I'll have to rent a tuxedo.
2. What are you taking to the _____ at Jack's house? I'm taking Thai chicken salad, my specialty!
3. _____ is always better than a DJ, don't you think?
4. I don't have _____ parties because I can't cook.
5. It's such a hot day. Let's have a _____ at the lake.
6. Jan's having a big _____ party in her backyard on Saturday. She's turning twenty-one on Friday.
7. My brother and I gave a party for my parents' twenty-fifth _____. All their friends and our family came.

3 **PAIRS.** Compare your answers.

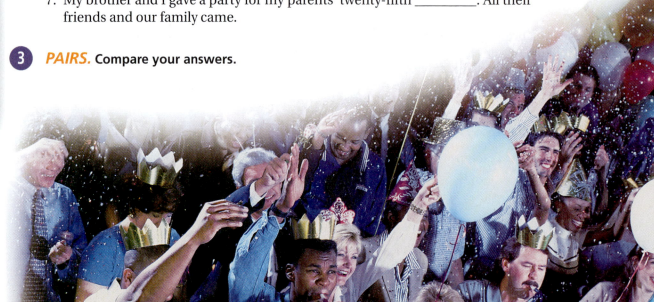

128

Celebrate

UNIT 28

OBJECTIVES

Students will:

- activate vocabulary related to parties and party-going
- use the present unreal conditional (*if* + simple past + *would* + verb)
- practice contracted and weak forms of *would*

> **WARM-UP: THE MOST IMPORTANT DAY . . .**
>
> - Pair students. Set a time limit of 3 minutes. Ask students to take turns telling each other about one of the most important days in their lives, and the event that occurred on it. Give examples: *wedding, graduation, birthday.* Encourage students to give as many details as possible.
> - Ask a few students to say when their most important day was and what happened on that day.

Getting started

> ***CULTURE NOTES***
>
> - A *potluck dinner* is a casual dinner to which everyone invited brings something to eat. It is called "potluck" because usually no one knows for sure what food people will bring.
> - A *barbecue* is a party at which food is cooked and eaten outdoors. Note that *barbecue* (noun) also means the outdoor stove used to cook on: *He cooked on a big barbecue.* It is also a verb: *He barbecued the chicken.*

> **OPTION: VOCABULARY PREVIEW**
>
> - Ask students to brainstorm different types of events and celebrations in their lives. Write their ideas on the board. Make sure to include: *anniversary, birthday, graduation, wedding, family reunion.*
> - Write the following words on the board: *black tie, a dinner, a barbeque, a potluck dinner, live music, a DJ.*
> - Ask students to think about the different ways we celebrate these events/celebrations. For example, is it a formal or informal celebration? Have students say which of the new words on the board would go with each event/celebration. Go through the list.
> - Answer any questions students have about vocabulary.

Exercise ❶

- Ask students to look at the picture of the New Year's party. Ask students to briefly describe what the people are doing. Help with vocabulary, as needed. (*They're cheering, blowing noisemakers, smiling.*)
- Have students look at the chart. Read the column heads: *Occasion, Type of party, Music.* Explain the task: Students put the words in the correct column. Go over the example. Check understanding of *DJ (disk jockey)* and have students write it in the *Music* column.
- Set a time limit of 7 minutes. Walk around the room, helping as needed.
- Have students compare their answers in pairs.
- Go over the answers with the class.

> **Answer key**
>
> | Occasion | Type of Party | Music |
> |---|---|---|
> | anniversary | barbecue | DJ |
> | birthday | black tie | live music |
> | family reunion | dinner | pianist |
> | graduation | potluck dinner | |
> | wedding | | |

Exercise ❷

- Explain the task: Students complete the sentences with words from the chart in Exercise 1. Point out that they will only need to use some of the words.
- Go over the example. Explain that a "black-tie" party or social event is one to which the guests have to wear formal clothes, such as tuxedos and floor-length dresses.
- Set a time limit of 5 minutes. Walk around the room, helping as needed.
- Do not go over answers with the class until they have completed Exercise 3.

Exercise ❸

- Form pairs. Have students compare answers.
- Go over the answers with the class.

> **Answer key**
>
> 1. black tie
> 2. potluck dinner
> 3. live music
> 4. dinner
> 5. barbecue
> 6. birthday
> 7. anniversary

> **EXTENSION**
>
> - Form pairs. Ask students to take turns describing a wedding or graduation party they have attended. Encourage them to give as many details as possible. Set a time limit of 5 minutes.
> - Call on a few students to tell the class about their partner's party.

> **WRAP-UP**
>
> Have pairs practice reading the completed sentences from Exercise 2 aloud.

Teacher's Notes — Lesson A

T128

Reading

Exercise 4

- Have students look at the magazine ad. Explain that a magazine is holding a competition. Tell students to read the advertisement and answer the questions. Remind students to read the questions before they begin.
- Set a time limit of 10 minutes. Walk around the room, helping as needed.
- Have students compare their answers in pairs.
- Go over the answers with the class. Have students reread sections, as needed.

> **Answer key**
>
> 1. to celebrate their 100th edition
> 2. describe your party plans
> 3. a free party of a lifetime for someone you love

EXTENSION

Ask students who can enter the competition (anyone over 16) and when the competition closes (December 31).

Exercise 5

- Pair students. Have them look at the pictures and briefly describe the two situations. (*Two people are imagining the kind of party they could have if they won the competition.*)
- Explain the task: Students read the sentences and match them with the pictures. They need to decide who said each statement, A or B.
- Go over the example. Point out how the men in tuxedos show it is a formal party (B).
- Set a time limit of 5 minutes.
- Go over the answers with the class. If students disagree, ask them to give reasons.

> **Answer key**
>
> 1. B   4. B
> 2. A   5. A
> 3. A   6. B

EXTENSION

- Have students continue with the same partner as Exercise 5, or form new pairs.
- Ask students to discuss which type of party they would rather go to, A or B, and the reasons why. Write on the board expressions they can use: *I'd rather go to A because . . . I'd prefer B because . . .*
- Walk around the room, helping as needed.
- Conclude by taking a poll to find out how many in the class would prefer A or B.

Please go to www.longman.com/worldview for additional in-class model conversation practice.

HOMEWORK

- For homework, assign *Workbook* page 105, Vocabulary Exercises 1 and 2, and page 107, Listening Exercises 5 and 6.

Reading

4 A magazine is holding a competition. Read the advertisement and answer the questions.

1. Why is the magazine having a competition?
2. What do you have to do to enter?
3. What's the prize?

5 *PAIRS.* Match the sentences with the pictures below.

1. If we had a formal dinner with the family, my parents would love it. __B__
2. If it were possible, I would have fireworks. _____
3. I'd have a party on a yacht if money were not a problem. _____
4. If the children couldn't come, it wouldn't be a real family reunion. _____
5. If we had live music, people would have a great time. _____
6. I would not serve the food myself if I had the money to hire a waitress. _____

It's party time

Help us celebrate our 100th edition

Win the party of a lifetime for someone you love. We'll pay for everything.

All you have to do is tell us your party plans. If you had the chance to have the party of a lifetime, who would it be for, when would you have the party, and what would you celebrate?

If money were no problem,
- what type of party would it be?
- where would you have the party?
- what food and drink would you choose?
- how many people would you invite?

To enter the competition you must be 18 or over. The competition closes on December 31.

Grammar focus

1 Study the examples of the present unreal conditional.

> (+) **If** I **were** a millionaire, I**'d have** a party on a yacht.
> (–) It **wouldn't be** a family reunion **if** the children **couldn't come**.
> (?) **If** you **invited** all your friends to a party, where **would** it **be**?

2 Look at the examples again. Underline the correct information to complete the rules in the chart.

Present unreal conditional
Use the present unreal conditional to talk about **real / imaginary** situations.
The verb in the *if* clause is in the **base form / past tense**.
Use **would / should** in the result clause.
Use a comma when the *if* clause comes **first / last**.
NOTE: Use *were* for all forms of *be*.

Grammar Reference page 149

3 Rewrite the sentences using the present unreal conditional.

1. I live in a small apartment, so I don't have large parties.
   If I didn't have a small apartment, I'd have large parties.
2. I don't have enough money, so I can't take a long vacation.
3. Etsu doesn't like to cook. That's why she invited us to a restaurant.
4. I don't have a barbecue every weekend only because I don't have a backyard.
5. Imad never invites his friends to his house because he lives too far out of town.
6. Magali is not a good dancer. That's why she doesn't go to clubs with her friends.
7. My neighbors complain about the noise, so I can't have a lot of parties.
8. A beach party is a great way to celebrate a birthday, but mine is in the winter.

Pronunciation

4 🎧 Listen. Notice the pronunciation of the weak and contracted forms of *would*.

Where **would** it be?   If you could have a party, where **would** it be?

I**'d** have the party at a restaurant.   I **wouldn't** cook.

We**'d** have live music.   They**'d** play salsa.

We**'d** dance all night.   Everyone **would** have a great time.

5 🎧 Listen again and repeat.

Grammar focus

> **LANGUAGE NOTES**
> - The present unreal conditional, also referred to as the second conditional, is about imaginary situations: *If I had a lot of money, I would buy a bigger house.* (I don't have a lot of money, so I can't buy a bigger house.)
> - Students can test the unreal conditional, by asking a question: *Do I have a lot of money? No, so I can't buy a bigger house.*
> - The use of the past simple in the *if* clause can be confusing for students. It's important to make it clear that the past isn't being talked about, but the imaginary present, for example, *If I had a lot of money . . .* (now) or an imaginary future, for example, *If I won the lottery . . . (next Saturday).*

> **WARM-UP**
>
> Note: Skip this warm-up if you're doing this lesson (Lesson B) during the same class period as Lesson A.
>
> - Books closed. Tell students they are going to listen to a recording of the advertisement that they read in the Reading section.
> - Ask students to pay attention to sentences with *if*. Ask them to listen for what verb tense is used with *if* sentences.
> - 🎧 Play the audio for Lesson A, Exercise 4.
> - Ask students what verb tense is used (*past*). Write on the board: *If you had the chance to have this party, who would it be for? / If money were no problem, what type of party would it be?* Underline *had* and *were*.
> - Tell students that even though the past tense form is used, the past isn't being talked about; it's the imaginary present. *(What would happen if . . . ?)*

Exercise 1

- Have students look at the examples and study the boldfaced words.
- Remind students that (+) means *affirmative*, (–) means *negative*, and (?) means *question*.
- Ask students to study the examples. Ask students what they notice about the verb in the *if* clause. (*They are in the past tense even though the sentences are about the present or the future.*)
- Ask students what they notice about the question. (*The verb in the* if *clause is in the past, but the question is about the future.*)

Exercise 2

- Have students look at the examples again and circle the correct information to complete the rules in the box.
- Have students compare their answers with a partner.
- Go over the explanations with the class. Point out that they need to use *were* for all forms of *be*.
- Refer students to Grammar Reference page 149, as needed.

> **Answer key**
> imaginary   past tense   would   first

Exercise 3

- Explain the task: Students rewrite the sentences using the present unreal conditional.
- Ask students to look at the example. Point out the verb forms that are used (*had, would take*).
- Have students complete the exercise individually. Set a time limit of 10 minutes.
- Have students check their answers in pairs.
- Go over the answers with the class. Remind students that the clause order can be reversed; the *if* clause can come second.

> **Answer key**
> Answers may vary slightly, and clauses may be reversed.
> 1. If I didn't live in a small apartment, I would have large parties. (If I lived in a big apartment . . .)
> 2. If I had enough money, I could take a long vacation.
> 3. If Etsu liked to cook, she would invite us to her house for dinner.
> 4. I would have a barbecue every weekend if I had a backyard.
> 5. Imad would invite his friends to his house if he didn't live so far out of town.
> 6. Magali would go to clubs with her friends if she were a good dancer.
> 7. If my neighbors didn't complain about the noise, I could have a lot of parties.
> 8. If my birthday were not in the winter, I would celebrate it with a beach party.

Pronunciation

Exercise 4

- 🎧 Play the audio and have students listen. Ask them to notice the pronunciations of *would*.
- Elicit, or point out, that *would* has a weak pronunciation in the middle of a sentence.
- Remind students that English speakers generally use contractions rather than full forms after pronouns. Point out that '*d* in the contractions here (*I'd, we'd, they'd*) is pronounced as the single sound /d/.

Exercise 5

- 🎧 Play the audio. Stop the audio after each sentence to allow students to repeat chorally.
- Ask a few individual students to repeat and check their pronunciation.
- Make sure that students pronounce the /d/ in *I'd, we'd,* and *they'd* and do not just say *I, we,* and *they*.

T130

Speaking

Exercise 6

- Hold up your book and point to the entry form for the competition. Ask, *What is your idea of a perfect party? Enter the competition.*
- Read aloud, or ask a student to read aloud the questions on the entry form. Tell students to take notes, and include any other ideas they have.
- Set a time limit of 10 minutes. Have students write down their ideas.
- Walk around the room, helping as needed.

Exercise 7

- Form groups of 3. Tell students to take turns asking and answering questions about the parties they planned. Encourage them to ask each other for details.
- Go over the example. Tell students to vote for the winning entry in their group after they have discussed all three parties.
- Set a time limit of 10 minutes. Walk around the room, helping as needed.

Exercise 8

- Call on several students to tell the class about their party.
- Conclude by asking groups which party they voted for and why. If time permits, take a class vote on which party they would most like to attend.

TRB For additional interactive grammar practice, have students do the reproducible activity for this unit in the *Teacher's Resource Book*.

Writing

Exercise 9

- Assign the writing task for class work or homework. Encourage students to be creative and add art work if possible. Remind them to include the information on the list.
- **TRB** Optionally, give students a copy of the model of an invitation (see the *Teacher's Resource Book*, Writing Models). Ask them to read the model and notice the vocabulary and grammar from the unit.
- If students don't have the model, write on the board:

  Dear J.K.,
  I'm having a surprise birthday party for my sister Camila on Saturday November 9th at 10:00 P.M. It's a costume party, so please wear a costume party, so please wear a costume! There will be . . .

  Walk around the room to make sure that students understand the task.

- If the assignment is done in class, have students share their work in small groups as time permits.

For suggestions on how to give feedback on writing, see page xiv of this *Teacher's Edition*.

CONVERSATION TO GO

- As the students leave class, have them read the dialogue, or read aloud chorally.
- Point out that *to throw a party* means to give a party.

HOMEWORK

- Assign *Workbook* page 106, Grammar Exercises 3 and 4, and page 107, Pronunciation Exercises 7 and 8. Assign *Workbook* Self-quiz 7.
- If students do not have the *WorldView Workbook*, assign listening homework from the Student CD. Write on the board:

  Track 62
  How many editions has the magazine published?

- Tell students to listen to the audio and write their answer. Have them bring it to the next class. (*100*)

BEFORE NEXT CLASS

- Tell students that the next class will be a review class covering Units 25–28.
- Have students review the material in the units to prepare for the activities in Review 7.

Unit no.	Review Grammar	Listen to Student CD	Study Grammar Reference
25	*used to* and *would*	Track 57	Page 148
26	verbs with direct and indirect objects	Track 58	Page 149
27	models for advice: *should/shouldn't, could, ought to*	Track 60	Page 149
28	present unreal conditional	Track 62	Page 149

FOR NEXT CLASS

TRB Make copies of Quiz 7 in the *Teacher's Resource Book*.

Speaking

6 ***BEFORE YOU SPEAK.*** What is your idea of a perfect party? Enter the competition. Take notes.

100th Edition "Party of a Lifetime"
Official Competition Entry Form

Place _____
Time/Occasion _____
Type of party _____
Food and drink _____
Music _____
Number of people _____
(Other ideas) _____
_____
_____

7 ***GROUPS OF 3.*** Tell each other about your party and answer questions about it. Then vote for the winning entry.

My party would be a surprise party for my boyfriend. It would be . . .

8 Tell the class about your party.

Writing

9 Write an invitation to the party you have arranged. Be creative and include information about the points on the list.

- occasion (reason for the party)
- type of party
- when and where the party is
- how to get there
- dress code (casual, elegant, . . .)

CONVERSATION TO GO

A: What **would** you **do if** you **won** a competition?
B: **If** I **won** a lot of money, **I'd throw** myself a big going-away party at work!

Lesson B

Review 7: Units 25–28

Unit 25 Arranged marriages

1 🎧 Listen to the model conversation.

2 **PAIRS.** What do you think makes a successful marriage? Use the phrases in the chart and your own ideas to make five statements expressing your opinion.

I think it's . . .	a good idea . . .	(for . . .) to . . .
	a bad idea . . .	get married
	crazy / absurd / wonderful . . .	get to know each other
	very / somewhat / not very important . . .	get engaged
		get upset
		get along
		get over something

Unit 26 Money matters

3 🎧 Listen to the model conversation.

4 **GROUPS OF 4.** Student A, you have just won a million dollars and you're trying to keep it a secret. Students B, C, and D, you've heard about Student A's winnings and are visiting him or her. Read your situation and then have a conversation. Keep talking until you reach an agreement.

Student A's situation: You're planning to have a family someday. You need this money to provide you and your family with financial security.

Student B's situation: You loaned Student A some money back in high school but he or she never paid you back. Now you want him or her to pay back what he or she owes—with interest!

Student C's situation: You have a great idea for a new business, but the bank won't give you a loan. You want Student A to invest some money in the business. He or she would be your partner.

Student D's situation: You were best friends with Student A when you were children. Now you are the president of a charity that helps feed hungry people all over the world. You want Student A to donate some of his or her money to this charity.

Review 7

Units 25–28

📼 You may wish to use the video for Units 25–28 at this point.
For video activity worksheets, go to www.longman.com/worldview.

Unit 25: Arranged marriages

OBJECTIVE

Grammar: focus on using *for . . . / to . . .* after adjective/noun to express opinions

Exercise ❶

- Explain the task: Students listen to the model conversations about arranged marriages. Ask students to listen for the phrases people use to express their opinions.
- 🎧 Play the audio. Then write on the board: *I think it's a good idea to . . . I think it's very important for . . .*
- 🎧 Play the audio again, and have the students listen.

Exercise ❷

- Form pairs. Ask the students what they think makes a marriage successful. Tell them to use the phrases in the chart with their own ideas to each make five statements expressing their opinions.
- Model an example: *I think it's a bad idea for people to get married too young.*
- Set a time limit of 8 minutes. Walk around the room, helping as needed.
- Call on several students to share their partner's opinions with the class.

Unit 26: Money matters

OBJECTIVE

Grammar: focus on using comparative adjectives and *as . . . as*

Exercise ❸

- Explain the task: Students listen to the model conversation. Tell students to listen for the numbers that are used.
- 🎧 Play the audio. Ask students what numbers they remember (*twenty years; a thousand dollars; thirty-six thousand dollars*).
- 🎧 Play the audio again, and have the students listen to check their answers.

Exercise ❹

- Form groups of 4. Assign roles: Student A, B, C, D.
- Explain the task: Student A has won a million dollars and is trying to keep it a secret. Students B, C, and D have heard about it and are visiting Student A. They each want some money from Student A, and present their points of view. Students continue their conversation until they reach an agreement.
- Give students 2 minutes to read their parts, and organize their ideas. Encourage students to take brief notes to use in their conversation.
- Set a time limit of 10 minutes for students to reach an agreement. Tell them to have one person in the group write down their final agreement so that they can explain it to the class. Walk around the room, helping as needed.

> **WRAP-UP**
>
> - Ask each group to explain their agreement. Tell the class to listen carefully to each group and take brief notes.
> - After all groups have presented, have the students compare the agreements either in their groups or as a whole-class discussion, and decide which agreement is the fairest.

Unit 27: Less is more

OBJECTIVE

Grammar: focus on modals: *should/shouldn't, could, ought to* for advice

Exercise 5

- Explain the task: Students listen to the model conversation.
- 🎧 Play the audio. Then write on the board the modals: *should, shouldn't, could, ought to*. Remind students these are used to give advice.
- 🎧 Tell the students to listen for these modals. Play the audio again as students listen.

Exercise 6

- Form pairs. Have the students look at the list of problems.
- Explain the task: Tell the students they have some of the problems. They take turns asking for and giving advice. They can choose any of the problems.
- Give an example, *I spend too much time working. What should I do?* Elicit advice from several students.
- Set a time limit of 10 minutes.
- Walk around the room, helping as needed.

> **WRAP-UP**
>
> - Do a question-and-advice chain with the class. Student 1 asks for advice *(I don't get enough exercise. What should I do?)* and then says a classmate's name *(Taro)*. Taro then gives some advice *(You should join a health club)*. Taro then asks a different classmate for advice about another problem.
> - Students continue asking and answering at random around the room. Saying the classmate's name *after* the question promotes active listening as all students must be ready to answer if their name is called.

Unit 28: Celebrate

OBJECTIVE

Grammar: focus on using the present unreal conditional (*if* + simple past + *would* + verb)

Exercise 7

- Explain the task: Students listen to the model conversation and look at the pictures.
- Have students look at the pictures and briefly describe what they see in each. Encourage them to use adjectives and describe details.
- 🎧 Play the audio. Write on the board: *If I had . . . , I would . . .* Underline the verbs. Review with students that this is the unreal conditional (*I don't have . . . , so I won't . . .*).
- 🎧 Tell the students to listen for the verb tenses used in the *if* sentences. Play the audio again as students listen.

Exercise 8

- Form groups of 3. Explain the task: Students take turns asking *what if . . .* questions about the situations listed. All of the students in the group should answer each question.
- Give an example, *If you could do anything you wanted on your birthday, what would you do?* Write the example on the board, and underline the verbs to remind students of the tenses they need to use.
- Set a time limit of 12 minutes for students to share their ideas. Walk around the room, helping as needed.
- Conclude by asking each group who had the most original idea for one of the situations.

Unit 27 Less is more

5 🎧 Listen to the model conversation.

6 **PAIRS.** Role-play. You have one of the problems below. Use your imagination to add details. Take turns asking for and giving advice.

You . . .
  spend too much time working/sleeping/shopping . . .
  don't spend enough time with your family/at your work/with your friends . . .
  don't have enough space to work/exercise/cook . . .
  spend too much money on clothes/food/jewelry . . .
  waste too much time on the Internet/playing cards/watching TV . . .

Unit 28 Celebrate

7 🎧 Listen to the model conversation and look at the pictures.

8 **GROUPS OF 3.** Take turns asking and answering *what if* . . . questions about the situations below. Give reasons for your answers. Who has the most original idea?

- win a contest
- don't have to go to school or work every day
- don't need to worry about money
- can live anywhere in the world
- have all the free time you want
- have dinner with a famous person

133

World of Music 4

If I Could Turn Back Time
Cher

Vocabulary

1 **GROUPS OF 3.** What do you think these sentences mean? Choose the best answer.

1. I'd take back those words that hurt you.
   a. I'd return that book to the store if you don't like it.
   b. I wish I hadn't said those hurtful things to you.
   c. I wish I hadn't done those terrible things to you.
2. Pride's like a knife; it can cut deep inside.
   a. Sharp knives are dangerous.
   b. Pride is similar to a knife because they can both cut you.
   c. Pride is similar to a knife because they can both hurt people.
3. Words are like weapons; they wound sometimes.
   a. Words can hurt someone as badly as a weapon.
   b. People can injure others easily if they aren't careful.
   c. People need to be careful with weapons because they might wound someone.

Listening

2 🎧 Listen to the song. Which word best describes the feelings of the speaker?

a. regretful   b. worried   c. joyful

3 🎧 Listen to the song and put each line of the chorus in order.

4 **PAIRS.** Compare your answers.

*Known for her outrageous costumes and wigs, **Cher** has faded from popularity many times over her long career but has always managed to emerge again into the limelight. "If I Could Turn Back Time" is one of Cher's many "comeback" songs.*

Speaking

5 **GROUPS OF 3.** Discuss the questions. Explain your opinions and ask and answer follow-up questions.

1. What do you think the story behind this song might be?
2. What might have happened to make the singer feel the way she does?

World of Music 4

OBJECTIVES

- introduce Cher's song, "If I Could Turn Back Time"
- vocabulary: imagery
- express personal interpretation of a song

WARM-UP

- Books closed. Say, *"Sticks and stones may break my bones, but words can never hurt me." Do you agree?* Encourage students to give reasons.
- Ask, *Has anyone ever hurt your feelings by saying something unkind? Were you able to forgive them?*
- Tell the class they are going to listen to a song about being sorry for saying something unkind. Tell them to think about their ideas as they listen to the song.

Reading

- Tell students to read the information about Cher. Tell them they are going to listen to one of Cher's best-known songs, "If I Could Turn Back Time." Ask them if they know the song, or if they have heard of it. Encourage the class to hum or sing parts of the song that they know.
- Ask them what they know about Cher.

Exercise 1

- Form groups of 3.
- Tell the students the sentences are lyrics from Cher's song, "If I Could Turn Back Time." Explain the task: They read the sentences, decide what they mean, and choose the best answer. Before they begin, have them read all of the sentences and answer choices.
- Set a time limit of 5 minutes. While students are working, walk around the room, helping as needed.
- Go over the answers with the class. For 1, explain that *take back* means to admit that what was said was wrong. Write on the board, *hurt* and *wound*. Check that students understand that in this context *hurt* means to make someone feel upset or unhappy, and *wound* means to hurt someone emotionally. You might want to point out that the expression "I'm sorry I hurt your feelings" is commonly used to apologize for saying something that upset someone, and that "I take back what I said" can be used in the same way. "To heal wounds" means to rebuild a relationship after someone has been hurt.

Answer key 1. b 2. c 3. a

Listening

Exercise 2

- Explain the task: Students listen to "If I Could Turn Back Time," and decide which word best describes the feelings of the speaker.
- Ask students to read the answer choices. Before playing the song, check that students know the meaning of *regretful* (feeling sadness about something because you wish it hadn't happened), *worried* (upset), and *joyful* (happy).
- 🎧 Play the song as students listen.
- Check the answer with the class. If students don't agree, ask them to give reasons.

Answer key a

Exercise 3

- Explain the task: Students listen to the song again and put each line of the chorus in order.
- 🎧 Play the song, and then pause for students to write.
- 🎧 Play the song again. Students to confirm their answers.
- Do not go over the answers with the class until they have completed Exercise 4.

Exercise 4

- Have students compare their answers with a partner.
- Go over the answers with the class.

Answer key (See complete lyrics on page T135.)

Speaking

Exercise 5

- Form groups of 3. Explain the task: Students discuss the questions. Encourage them to explain their opinions, and ask and answer follow-up questions.
- Set a time limit of 10 minutes. Walk around the room, helping as needed.
- Conclude by calling on a few students to present their ideas to the class.

OPTION

Play the song and have the students sing along. Play the song again as time permits.

T134

If I Could Turn Back Time

If I could turn back time
If I could find a way
I'd take back those words that have hurt you and you'd stay
I don't know why I did the things I did
I don't know why I said the things I said
Pride's like a knife it can cut deep inside
Words are like weapons, they wound sometimes
I didn't really mean to hurt you
I didn't wanna see you go
I know I made you cry, but baby

CHORUS:
If I could turn back time
If I could find a way,
I'd take back those words that hurt you
and you'd stay
If I could reach the stars
I'd give them all to you
then you'd love me, love me, like you used to do
if I could turn back time

My world was shattered I was torn apart
Like someone took a knife and drove it
deep in my heart
You walked out that door I swore that I didn't care
but I lost everything darling then and there
Too strong to tell you I was sorry

CHORUS

If I Could Turn Back Time

If I could turn back time

If I could find a way

I'd take back those words that have hurt you and you'd stay

I don't know why I did the things I did

I don't know why I said the things I said

Pride's like a knife it can cut deep inside

Words are like weapons, they wound sometimes

I didn't really mean to hurt you

I didn't wanna see you go

I know I made you cry, but baby

CHORUS

back / time / if / could / turn / I _____

way / if / could / I / find / a _____

take / I'd / back / words / those / you / hurt / that _____

you'd / and / stay _____

I / the / reach / if / could / stars _____

you / to / give / all / I'd / them _____

then you'd love me, love me,

used / do / to / you / like _____

I / time / back / if / could / turn _____

My world was shattered I was torn apart

Like someone took a knife and drove it

deep in my heart

You walked out that door I swore that I didn't care

but I lost everything darling then and there

Too strong to tell you I was sorry

CHORUS

Information for pair and group work

Unit 1, Exercise 6
Student A

Student A, this is your situation. Complete each sentence with information that is true for you. Use your imagination and add at least two more details!

- You went to high school (secondary school) with Student B, but you haven't seen each other in a few years.
- You used to be an actor, but now you're working at _____.
- You're taking _____ classes.
- You're living in _____.
- _____
- _____
- Ask about Student B's job and what he or she is doing these days.
- End your conversation.

Unit 7, Exercise 4
Student B

Student B, your impressions of the restaurant include:

- atmosphere not formal enough—hard to have a conversation
- waiters couldn't answer questions, not knowledgeable enough about the menu items
- pizzas were too bland and fatty—not enough spices and too much cheese
- good salad, but dressing too sweet
- only offered soft drinks—no iced tea or hot beverages
- much too expensive

With your partner, decide if you would go back to that restaurant again.

A: *I thought the salad was really fresh.*
B: *Yes, but I didn't like the dressing. I thought it was too sweet.*
A: *Really? I didn't think it was sweet enough. It seemed sour to me.*

Unit 3, Exercise 4
Student B

Read the brochure. Then take turns asking and answering questions about the facilities and services at your partner's hotel. Both hotels cost $115 per night. Together, choose one of the hotels.

A: *How many rooms does the Delta Hotel have?*
B: *It has 32 rooms. Does the Marina offer free airport transportation?*

The Delta Hotel

A cozy, charming hotel located in the heart of downtown offering:

- free airport transportation
- 32 guest rooms, each decorated with antique furniture and paintings
- television and telephone in all rooms, with high-speed Internet access
- exercise room and sauna
- 24-hour coffee shop and café

Our concierge will be happy to assist you with theater or opera tickets and can recommend fine restaurants within walking distance of the hotel.

Review 6, Exercise 2
Student B

Role-play #1

Student A is your teacher. He or she is explaining a math problem, but you don't understand. Ask the teacher to explain it again.

Role-play #2

You get on a bus with your elderly grandmother. Student A is sitting in the seat near the door. You ask him or her to let your grandmother sit there.

Role-play #3

You are having a party with some friends. Student A is your neighbor. He or she comes to your door to ask you something.

Unit 4, Exercise 7
Student A

You're a patient. Don't give the doctor your information all at once. Try to make the doctor ask you questions to find out what your problem might be. Choose one of the following situations:

- **Situation 1:** You have the following symptoms: red eyes, itchy throat, runny nose, headache. You arrive at the doctor's office very tired and depressed.

- **Situation 2:** You have the following symptoms: You have a very bad rash on your hands and face. It's red and itchy and painful. You have had it for almost a week. You never drink coffee or tea or milk. You only eat chocolate on special occasions. You don't have any pets, but you did go horseback riding last weekend. You went to the zoo two weeks ago.

- **Situation 3:** Your choice. You choose the symptoms.

Unit 27, Exercise 7
Student B

Take turns sharing your problems and giving advice on what to do.

A: Maybe you should try . . .
B: Or, what about this? I think you should . . .

Problem #2

I have a computer at home, but I can't use it much because every time I try to download something, it tells me it's out of memory. What can I do?

Problem #5

I have no problem learning new English words in class, but after a day or two, I always forget the new words or what they mean. What would you suggest?

Problem #8

I feel that I'm not saving enough money. I want to spend less and save more, but how?

Unit 9, Exercise 6
Student A

You and Student B are taking a weekend trip to Washington, D.C., together. Ask Student B questions and fill in the missing itinerary information about your trip. Remember to use the simple present to ask for information about schedules, timetables, and events. Answer Student B's questions.

A: What airline are we on?
B: We're on . . .

WorldView Travel
Here is your itinerary. Have a great trip!

FLIGHT INFORMATION

Airline: <u>Jet Airways</u>   Ticket/class: _____

to Washington, D.C.

Day/date: Friday, April 19
Time departs: _____
Time arrives: _____

from Washington, D.C.

Day/date: Sunday, April 21
Time departs: _____
Time arrives: _____

HOTEL INFORMATION

The Wellington Hotel
(Located 5 blocks from the White House)

Arrival date: Friday, April 19
Departure date: Sunday, April 21
Free airport transfers

Check-in time: 1:00 P.M.
Check-out time: 11:00 A.M.

Unit 17, Exercise 5

3–4 *a* answers: You have very little willpower and find it difficult to control your mind and body. Try harder!

3–4 *b* answers: It is easy for you to achieve things by controlling your mind and body. You have a lot of willpower. Congratulations!

3–4 *c* answers: You are like most people . . . you have some willpower, but not enough. Don't give up!

Information for pair and group work

Unit 1, Exercise 6
Student B

Student B, this is your situation. Complete each sentence with information that is true for you. Use your imagination and add at least two more details!

- You went to high school (secondary school) with Student A, but you haven't seen each other in a few years.
- You're a/an (your occupation). You're working at _____ .
- You're also taking _____ classes.
- _____
- _____
- Ask Student A where he or she is living now.
- Ask Student A if he or she is still acting.
- End your conversation.

Review 1, Exercise 8
Student B

Student B, use this information to answer Student A's questions.

Super Seven Hotel

- a budget motel with all the comforts of home
- just minutes from the airport
- 78 rooms ($59/night), all with television and telephone
- 24-hour coffee shop and café
- exercise room and sauna
- a conference room
- computer hookups and fax service available
- free baby-sitting service 24 hours a day

Unit 24, Exercise 4
Student A

Look at the cues and follow the model to make unfinished sentences using *who*, *that/which*, and *where*. Do not say the answer (in parentheses). Take turns saying your unfinished sentences to your group. The person who finishes it first with the correct answer gets 1 point.

A: A person who flies planes is . . .
B: A pilot.
A: Correct. You get a point.

1. person / flies planes
   (a pilot)
   A person who flies planes is . . .
2. machine / cooks food very fast
   (a microwave oven)
3. place / people store their books
   (a bookshelf)
4. movie / very scary
   (a horror movie)
5. man / getting married
   (a groom)
6. place / you can rent a room for a night
   (a hotel)

Unit 13, Exercise 8
Students A and B

You are a married couple in the U.S. Student A is from the U.S. Student B is from another country. Immigration officers are going to interview you both, but separately. You have five minutes to prepare for the interview. Work together to make sure you give the same information about:

- how long Student B has been in the U.S.
- how long you have known each other/been married
- where you met
- what your favorite thing about the other person is
- your wedding
- your jobs
- what you do in your free time

When the teacher calls "Time," go to page 63, Exercise 9.

Unit 8, Exercise 6
Student A

You are a very neat and responsible person. You enjoy cooking, you study a lot, and you always get to bed before 10:00 P.M. You wake up at 6:00 A.M. You love classical music.

These are some of the things you want your roommate to agree to. He or she has to:
- keep the house neat and clean
- take out the trash every day
- do his or her own laundry at least once a week
- take turns doing the housework
- pay 50% of all the bills

He or she can't:
- play loud music after 10:00 P.M.
- be late in paying the bills

Work out an agreement with your partner. Take notes on page 37.

You don't have to go to bed early, but you have to be quiet if you're up after ten, so you can't play loud music then.

Review 4, Exercise 2
Students A and B

1. Students A and B, you are roommates. Prepare for a meeting with your new landlord.

   Decide how long you've:
   lived in the U.S. _____
   known each other _____
   shared an apartment _____
   taken English classes together _____

2. Ask these questions to find out whether or not Students C and D are really roommates.

   How long have you:
   lived in the U.S.? _____
   known each other? _____
   shared an apartment? _____
   taken English classes together? _____
   had your dog? _____

Unit 9, Exercise 6
Student B

You and Student A are taking a weekend trip to Washington, D.C., together. Ask Student A questions and fill in the missing itinerary information about your trip. Remember to use the simple present to ask for information about schedules, timetables, and events. Answer Student A's questions.

A: *What airline are we on?*
B: *We're on . . .*

WorldView Travel

Here is your itinerary. Have a great trip!

FLIGHT INFORMATION

Airline: Jet Airways

to Washington, D.C.

Ticket/class: business class

from Washington, D.C.

Day/date: _____
Time departs: 7:00 A.M.
Time arrives: 12:00 noon

Day/date: _____
Time departs: 4:00 P.M.
Time arrives: 9:00 P.M.

HOTEL INFORMATION

The Wellington Hotel
(Located _____)
Arrival date: _____
Departure date: _____
Check-in time: _____
Check-out time: _____
Free airport transfers

Information for pair and group work

Unit 13, Exercise 8
Students C and D

You are immigration officers in the U.S. Students A and B are married. Student A is from the U.S. Student B is from another country. You think they may not have a real marriage. You have five minutes to work together to prepare questions to ask the couple. You will ask Students A and B the same questions separately and then compare their answers. Write your questions on a piece of paper. Ask questions about:

- how long Student B has been in the country
- how long they have known each other/been married
- where they met
- what their favorite thing about the other person is
- their wedding (When? Where? How many people attended? How long it lasted?)
- their jobs
- what they do in their free time

When the Teacher calls "Time," go to page 63, Exercise 9.

Review 4, Exercise 2
Students C and D

1. Ask these questions to find out whether or not Students A and B are really roommates.

   How long have you:
   lived in the U.S.? _____
   known each other? _____
   shared an apartment? _____
   taken English classes together? _____
   worked at the same place? _____

2. Students C and D, you are roommates. Prepare for a meeting with your new landlord.

   Decide how long you've:
   lived in the U.S. _____
   known each other _____
   shared an apartment _____
   taken English classes together _____

Unit 22, Exercise 6
Student A

1. Read the text and ask Student B questions to find out the missing information.

A: *What was stolen from a train?*

In England in 1963, (1) _____ was stolen from a train. The crime was called (2) _____. The train was stopped near (3) _____. The driver was attacked, and the train was then driven one kilometer down the track. One hundred and twenty bags of bills were stolen. The money was taken (4) _____, where the robbers even used some of it to play Monopoly. But very soon, the thirteen main thieves were arrested, and most of the money was recovered.

2. Now answer Student B's questions.

Unit 27, Exercise 7
Student C

Take turns sharing your problems and giving advice on what to do.

A: *Maybe you should try . . .*
B: *Or, what about this? I think you should . . .*

Problem #3

I'm out of shape and need to do more exercise. But running seems a waste of energy. Any ideas?

Problem #6

I never remember my friends' birthdays. OK, it saves money on cards and presents. But what's the answer?

Problem #9

I like everyone in class, but I feel more comfortable working alone than with others. Do you have any suggestions?

Unit 24, Exercise 4
Student B

Look at the cues and follow the model to make unfinished sentences using *who*, *that/which*, and *where*. Do not say the answer (in parentheses). Take turns saying your unfinished sentences to your group. The person who finishes it first with the correct answer gets 1 point.

B: *A person who writes with his or her left hand is . . .*
C: *A lefty.*
B: *Correct.*

1. person / writes with his or her left hand
   (a lefty)
2. plastic thing / you use instead of money
   (a credit card)
3. place / you can see famous paintings
   (a museum)
4. movie / makes you laugh
   (a comedy)
5. place in a hotel / you check in
   (a lobby)
6. woman / getting married
   (a bride)

Review 1, Exercise 8
Student A

Student A, use this information to answer Student B's questions.

The Drake Hotel
- a classic hotel in the heart of the city
- 5 minutes from fabulous stores, restaurants, and museums
- free transportation to and from the airport
- 153 modern rooms ($219/night) and 25 guest suites ($359/night)
- satellite TV, computer and fax hook-ups in all rooms
- a large ballroom
- 2 conference rooms
- 24-hour business service and translation service
- a fitness center
- an award-winning restaurant and café

Unit 8, Exercise 6
Student B

You are not a very neat person. You have no idea how to cook. You always go out to restaurants, and you like to have fun. Often you don't come home until after midnight. You love rock and roll music and like to play it loud on your stereo.

These are some of the things you want your roommate to agree to. He or she has to:
- do the housework
- not make a fuss if your room is messy
- let you invite friends over for parties
- keep his or her CDs and tapes separate from yours
- let you play rock and roll anytime
- not worry if the bills don't get paid on time

He or she can't:
- make noise before noon
- expect you to be home for dinner

Work out an agreement with your partner. Take notes on page 37.

I'm usually out late, so you can't make noise before noon. You don't have to leave the house, you just have to be quiet.

Information for pair and group work

Unit 22, Exercise 6
Student B

1. Read the text and answer Student A's questions.

In England, in 1963, almost four million dollars was stolen from a train. The crime was called the Great Train Robbery. The train was stopped near London. **(1)** _____ was attacked, and the train was then driven one kilometer down the track. **(2)** _____ bags of bills were stolen. The money was taken to a farm, where the robbers even used some of it to play Monopoly. But very soon, **(3)** _____ were arrested, and **(4)** _____ was recovered.

2. Now ask Student A questions to find out the missing information in your text.

Unit 24, Exercise 4
Student C

Look at the cues and follow the model to make unfinished sentences using *who, that/which,* and *where*. Do not say the answer (in parentheses). Take turns saying your unfinished sentence to your group. The person who finishes it first with the correct answer gets 1 point.

C: *A movie that has lots of fights and explosions is . . .*
B: *A thriller.*
C: *No.*
A: *An action movie.*
C: *Correct. You get a point.*

1. movie / has lots of fights and explosions
   (an action movie)
2. person / decorate homes or offices
   (an interior designer)
3. place / you go to work out
   (a fitness center)
4. person / tricks people into giving him or her money
   (a con artist)
5. TV program / usually involves love
   (a soap opera)
6. place / doctors and nurses work
   (a hospital)

Unit 21, Exercise 7
Student B

Role-play #1

Student A is your close friend. Listen and reply.

Role-play #2

You're in a new office and don't know where the light switches are. Ask a co-worker, Student A, to turn on the lights.

Role-play #3

Student A is your employee. Listen and reply.

Role-play #4

Your friends are visiting and want to listen to music. Ask your neighbor, Student A, if you can turn the volume up.

Grammar reference

Unit 1

Present continuous for the extended present

- Use the present continuous to talk about temporary events that are happening at this moment but that will be completed at some future time.
  *Halley's **taking** courses at the local college.*
  *She **isn't dating** anyone right now.*
  ***Are** you **walking** to the deli?*

Unit 2

Comparative adjectives, *as . . . as*

- Use the comparative form of adjectives with **than** to compare two things or people.

Adjective	Comparative form
one syllable	add *–er*
two syllable, ends with *–y*	change *y* to *i* and add *–er*
two syllables or more	use **more** + adjective
irregular (**good, bad**)	**better** than, **worse** than

*Boys are **louder than** girls.*
*Boys are **messier than** girls.*
*Girls are **more talkative** than boys.*
*Girls are **better than** boys at school.*

- Use *as* + adjective + *as* to say there is no difference between two people or things.
  *Boys are **as smart as** girls.* (They have the same intelligence.)
  *Girls are **as polite as** boys.* (They have the same manners.)

- Use **not as** + adjective + **as** to say there is a difference between two people or things.
  *Masako is **not as fast as** Robert.* (Robert is faster.)
  *Elysse is not **as hardworking as** her brother.* (Her brother is more hardworking.)

Unit 3

Review: Simple present statements and questions

Affirmative		
I/You/We/They	like	to order room service.
He/She	like**s**	
Negative		
I/You/We/They	don't	have a room with an ocean view.
He/She/It	doesn't	
Yes/No **question**		
Do	I/you/we/they	prefer a room with a balcony?
Does	he/she/it	
Short answer		
Yes,	I/you/we/they	do.
	he/she/it	does.
No,	I/you/we/they	don't.
	he/she/it	doesn't.
Wh– **question**			
What	do	I/you	base form of the verb ?
When			
Where	does	he/she/it	
Why			
How	do	we/they	

*Where **do** I **get** towels for the pool?*
*When **does** the restaurant **serve** breakfast?*
*Why **do** the premier suites **cost** more than the double deluxe rooms?*

Unit 4

Adjectives ending in *–ed* and *–ing*

- Use adjectives ending in *–ed* to describe the way a person feels.
  *Marissa is **annoyed**.* (She looks angry or upset.)
  *Luke was **shocked**.* (He looked very surprised.)
  *Jalil felt **embarrassed**.* (His face turned red.)

- Use adjectives ending in *–ing* to explain what or who makes a person feel a certain way.
  *Her allergies are **annoying**.* (They bother her.)
  *The news was **shocking** to Luke.* (He didn't expect it.)
  *The situation was **embarrassing**.* (Everyone stared at Jalil.)

143

Grammar reference

Unit 5
Subject and object questions

- The subject of a sentence does the action. The object of a sentence receives the action.

- When **who** is the subject of the question, put it before the verb. Don't use *do/does*.
  Who helps Ron? Mary does.
  Who sings the singing telegrams? Ron does.
  Who pays the agency? People who order telegrams do.
  (*Who* is the subject of these questions.)

- When **who** is the object of a question, use normal question word order and *do/does*.
  Who does Mary help? Mary helps Ron.
  Who does Ron sing to? He sings to people at parties.
  Who do people pay? They pay the agency.
  (*Who* is the object of these questions.)

Unit 6
Review: simple past vs. past continuous

- Use the simple past to talk about completed actions in the past, often with a time reference *(yesterday, last week, in 1999,* etc.).
  We **went** to Ireland on vacation **in 2003**.
  I **didn't go** on vacation **last year**.
  Did you **go** to the beach **in July**?

- Use the past continuous to talk about actions that continued for a period of time in the past.
  It **was raining** almost the whole time.
  People **weren't doing** much outside.
  Were you **considering** leaving early?

- Use the past continuous to set the scene in a story.
  The rain **was falling** and the wind **was blowing** through the trees in the dark forest . . .

- Use the simple past and past continuous together in one sentence if the first action was still going on when the second action happened.
  It **was raining** when suddenly the sun **came** through the clouds.
  We **weren't paying** attention when we **passed** the restaurant.
  What **were** you **doing** when you **heard** the news?

Unit 7
Too, enough

- Use **too** followed by an adjective to say "more than is needed or wanted."
  The restaurant was **too** noisy. (We couldn't hear because of the noise.)
  Is it **too** cold in here? (Is the temperature lower than you want?)

- Use an adjective followed by **enough** to say "as much as necessary or wanted."
  The desserts are sweet **enough**. (They don't need to be sweeter.)
  The food wasn't spicy **enough**. (It needed more spices.)
  Is the tea hot **enough**? (Does it need to be hotter?)

Notes:
- Do not put the adjective after **enough**.
  X *The water is enough cold.*
- Use **too** and **enough** with adverbs.
  He cooks **too plainly** for my taste.
  We didn't follow the recipe **carefully enough**.

Use **enough** followed by a noun to say "as much as necessary or wanted."
There is **enough** sauce on the pasta. (I don't want more.)
My coffee doesn't have **enough** sugar. (It needs more.)
Did you get **enough** salad? (Did you get all the salad that you wanted?)

Unit 8
Modals: *have to/don't have to, must, can't* for obligation and prohibition

- Use **must** to say that something is necessary.
  She **must** sign a prenuptial agreement before they get married. (He won't marry her if she doesn't.)
  He **must** give her $2,000 per month. (It's in the prenuptial agreement.)

- Also use **have / has to** to say that something is necessary.
  John **has to** pay $10,000. (That's what the contract says.)
  Do I **have to** wait for you? (Is it necessary to wait?)

- Use **don't have to** to say that something isn't necessary.
  They **don't have to** wash the dishes by hand. (They have a dishwasher.)
  He **doesn't have to** pay the bills. (His wife pays them.)

- Use **can't** to say that something is prohibited.
  He **can't** ask her for any money. (He's not allowed to ask for money.)
  You **can't** get married in any state if you are under 16 years old. (It is illegal.)

Unit 9

Simple present and present continuous for future

- Use the simple present to talk about schedules, timetables, and events in the future.
  The tour **starts** at 7:30 tomorrow.
  The movie **isn't** over until 8:00.
  Does the boat **leave** at 6:00?

- Use the present continuous to talk about personal plans in the future.
  I**'m seeing** the doctor at 4:00.
  We**'re not going** to the movies tonight, but we**'re going** tomorrow.
  Are you **leaving** in the morning or the afternoon?

Unit 10

Modal verbs for ability

- Use **can/can't** to talk about ability in the present.
  I **can** write with both hands.
  You **can't** draw with your left hand.
  Can Jane cut with her right hand?

- Use **could/couldn't** or **be able to** to talk about abilities that began at a specific moment or lasted for a period of time in the past.
  I **could** read when I was four.
  Sam **couldn't** write very well.
  Could you run fast when you were a child?
  She **was able to** write her name before going to school.
  Franklin **wasn't able to** ride a bike until he was ten.
  When **were** your children **able to** walk?

- Use **be able to** or **managed to** to talk about ability on a specific occasion in the past.
  It was difficult, but we **were able to** fix the car.
  I **managed to** escape out the window.
  Were they **able to** find the exit.
  Did they **manage to** find the exit?

- Use **not be able to**, **didn't manage to**, or **couldn't** to talk something that wasn't possible on a specific occasion in the past.
  We tried, but we **weren't able to** fix the car.
  I **didn't manage to** escape. I had to be rescued.
  They **couldn't find** the exit. They had to ask someone where it was.

Unit 11

Present perfect for indefinite past

- Use the present perfect to talk about actions that happened in the past when knowing the time of the action is not important.

| Affirmative | subject + **have/has** + past participle
We**'ve polished** the floorboards. |
|---|---|
| Negative | subject + **haven't/hasn't** + past participle
He **hasn't removed** the fireplace. |
| Question | **have/has** + subject + past participle
Have they **changed** the sofa covers? |
| Short answers | **Yes** + subject + **have/has**
Yes, they **have**. |
| | **No** + subject + **haven't/hasn't**
No, they **haven't**. |

Note: Add **–ed** to regular verbs to form the past participle. See page 150 for a list of irregular verbs.

Grammar reference

Unit 12

Modals: *may*, *might*, *could* for possibility

- Use *may*, *might*, or *could* to talk about something that is possible in the future.
  The group **may** stay in two different hotels. (It's possible that they won't all stay in the same hotel.)
  The guide **might** change the time of the tour. (It's possible that she'll change the time.)
  We **could** take a bus at 4:30, or we **could** wait until 6:00. (Two options are both possible: the 4:30 bus and the 6:00 bus.)

- Use *may not* and *might not* to talk about something that probably won't happen in the future.
  We **may not** have time to eat before we leave. (There is a possibility that we won't have time to eat.)
  The weather is going to be cloudy, but it **might not** rain. (There is a possibility that it won't rain.)

- Use *couldn't* to talk about something that is not possible in the future.
  I **couldn't** spend that much money on a trip. (I wouldn't have any money left.)
  She **couldn't** go on that trip. (They are going to fly, and she hates airplanes.)

Unit 13

Review: present perfect with *for* and *since*

- Use the present perfect with *for* or *since* to talk about actions that started in the past and continue into the present.
  I**'ve lived** in the United States **for** eight months. (I moved here eight months ago. I still live here now.)
  Peter **hasn't had** a pet **since** his dog died. (After his dog died, he didn't have a pet. He still doesn't have a pet now.)
  Has Sam **known** Claire **since** he was twenty? (Did he meet her when he was twenty? Does he still know her?)

- Use the present perfect with *for* to talk about a length of time.
  She**'s dated** him **for** two weeks.
  He **hasn't lived** in New York **for** a long time.
  Have they **worked** together **for** ten years?

- Use the present perfect with *since* to talk about a specific time that a continuing action started.
  They**'ve been** in there **since** 2:00.
  He **hasn't talked** to us **since** Tuesday.
  Have you **been** married **since** 2002?

Unit 14

Modals: *must be*, *might be*, *can't be* for deduction

- Use *must be* if you're very sure that something is true.
  You've traveled all night. You **must be** tired!
  He's eating two sandwiches. He **must be** hungry.

- Use *might be* if you are not sure if something is true.
  Your car keys **might be** on the kitchen table. (Sometimes you put them there.)
  They **might be** listening to music. (They are wearing headphones.)

- Use *can't be* if you are very sure that something isn't true.
  That woman looks like Carly, but it **can't be** her. (Carly is in Japan right now.)
  Edena **can't be** happy. (She just received bad news).

Unit 15

***Will/won't* for future and predictions**

- Use *will* and *won't* to talk about the future.
  Sanjay and Nina **will** get married.
  Nina's parents **won't** be happy.

- Use *think* and *don't think* followed by a subject + *will* to make predictions.
  I **think** Nina **will** convince her parents.
  I **don't think** they **will** cause any problems.
  Nina **thinks** they will have children someday.
  She **doesn't think** they'll live in London forever.

Unit 16

Future real conditional (*If* + simple present + *will*)

- Use two clauses to make future real conditional statements.

If clause	Result clause
if + simple present	***will/won't*** + base form of the verb

- Use the future real conditional to talk about things that may happen in the future and their results.
  If you **eat** this cereal, you**'ll** be strong and healthy.
  If you **don't hurry**, we**'ll** be late.
  If I **call** you tonight, **will you** be home?

- The *if* clause is often in the first position in a sentence, but it can also go second.
  He**'ll** fix the washing machine **if** it **breaks**.

146

Unit 17

Verbs + gerund and verbs + infinitive

- Use an infinitive after these verbs: **decide**, **learn**, **need**, **promise**, **want**.
  I **want to go** out tonight.
  José doesn't **need to buy** any new clothes.
  Have you **decided to start** a diet?

- Use a gerund after these verbs: **cut down on**, **dislike**, **enjoy**, **get out of**, **give up**, **keep on**, **practice**, **quit**, **stop**, **take up**.
  We **gave up eating** meat.
  I **don't enjoy cooking.**
  Is Karen **taking up swimming?**

Notes:
- Gerund = base form of the verb + *–ing*
- Infinitive = **to** + base form of the verb

Unit 18

Used to and would

- Use **used to/would** + base form of the verb to talk about repeated actions in the past that don't happen now.
  A lot of people **used to waste** energy (but now they don't).
  They **didn't use to recycle** most materials.
  Did you **use to buy** cars that used a lot of gas?
  I'**d use** things once and throw them away.
  We **wouldn't turn** down the heat at night.

- Use **used to** + base form of the verb to talk about states in the past that aren't that way now.
  Energy sources **used to seem** endless.
  People **didn't use to know** that they were hurting the environment.
  Did she **use to think** that recycling was important?

Unit 19

Passive (simple present)

- Use the passive when:
  - you're not interested in who or what does the action.
  - it's not important who or what does the action.
  - you don't know who or what does the action.

- The object of an active sentence becomes the subject of a passive sentence.
  People make **the boxes**.   (active)
  The boxes are made.   (passive)

Simple present passive
subject + *am/is/are* + past participle
The boxes **are made** in Morocco.
They **are sold** for $75.
The wood **is cut** by hand.
How **are** the boxes **made**? They **are made** by hand.

Unit 20

So, too, either, neither

- Use **so** and **too** to make additions to affirmative statements.
  He was surprised by the ending, and I was, **too**.
  He was surprised by the ending, and **so** was I.

- Use **not** + **either** and **neither** to make additions to negative statements.
  The acting wasn't great, and the story was**n't either**.
  The acting wasn't great, and **neither** was the story.

- Place the auxiliary, modal, or form of **be** or **do** before the subject in an addition with **so** or **neither**.

- Always use an auxiliary, a modal, or a form of **be** or **do** to make an addition. In the addition, use the appropriate form of the same auxiliary, modal, **be**, or **do** that appears in the statement.
  Renée Zellweger starred in the movie Chicago, and **so did** Catherine Zeta-Jones.
  She **is** a big fan of Keanu Reeves, and I **am**, **too**.
  Star Wars **didn't** make as much money as Titanic, and E.T. **didn't either**.
  Ben Affleck wasn't in The Lord of the Rings, and **neither was** Leonardo DiCaprio.

Grammar reference

Unit 21

Modals: *could you*, *would you*, *would you mind . . . ?* for polite requests

- Use **could you** and **would you** followed by the base form of the verb to make polite requests.

Could you	open the window?	Of course.
	please turn off the lights?	
	make less noise?	
Would you	turn up the volume?	Sure.
	stop doing that, please?	

- You can also use **would you mind** followed by a gerund to make polite requests.

Would you mind	closing the door?	No, of course not.
	please turn on the lights?	
	speaking louder?	
	turning down the volume?	
	continuing that, please?	Not at all.

Unit 22

Passive (simple past)

- Use the simple past passive when the action is more important than the person or thing that did the action.

Simple past passive
Subject + ***was/were*** + past participle
The cars **were stolen** on Tuesday.
A window **was broken**.

- The object of an active sentence becomes the subject of the passive sentence.
*Someone found **my wallet**.*
***My wallet** was found.*

- Use **by** + the person or thing to say who or what did the action.
*The manager **was hurt by** the robber.*
*The building **wasn't hit by** lightning.*
*What **was** the car **hit by**?*

Unit 23

Review: verbs for likes/dislikes followed by gerunds and/or infinitives

- Use a gerund or an infinitive after these verbs: **like**, **hate**, **love**, and **can('t) stand**.
*I **like to go** to the gym, but I **hate to lift** weights.*
*She **likes doing** aerobics, but she **hates running**.*
*We **love to eat** fatty foods, but we **can't stand to gain weight**!*
*They **love exercising** outside, but they **hate getting** a sunburn.*

- Use only a gerund after these verbs and phrasal verbs: **mind**, **enjoy**, **be sick of**, and **be into**.
*I don't **mind walking**; it's good exercise!*
*Do you **enjoy working** out?*
*He was **sick of taking** the same kinds of classes at the gym, and now he's **into doing** Pilates.*

Unit 24

Relative clauses with *that*, *which*, *who*, and *where*

- Use relative clauses with **that**, **which**, **who**, and **where** to define people, places, and things.
*A producer is someone **who** makes TV programs.*
*This is the computer **which** we saw at the first store.*
*A cell phone is something **that** makes communication convenient.*
*A garage is a place **where** you can park a car.*

- Use **who** or **that** for people, **which** or **that** for things, and **where** for places.

Unit 25

***It's* + adjective/noun + infinitive to express opinion**

- Use ***It's*** followed by an adjective or a noun phrase and an infinitive to express an opinion. You can add **for** + an object after the adjective or noun phrase, but it's not necessary.

It's	absurd	(***for*** + people) to get married.
	crazy	
	important	
	wonderful	
	a good idea	
	a bad idea	

*It's a good idea **to discuss** issues before marriage.*
*It's a good idea **for couples to discuss** issues before marriage.*
*It's important **to compromise** in a marriage.*
*It's important **for people to compromise** in a marriage.*

Unit 26

Verbs with two objects

- Some verbs can have a direct object. A direct object receives the action of the verb. A direct object answers the question *what* or *who*.
  *I received **my bank statement**.* (What did I receive? My bank statement.)
  *The accountant didn't return **her call**.* (What didn't he return? The call.)
  *When did you see **her**?* (Who did you see? Her.)

- Some verbs can also have an indirect object. An indirect object can come before the direct object. It answers the question *to whom* or *for whom*. The indirect object is usually a person.
  *We offer **customers** first-class service.* (Who do we offer service to? Customers.)
  *He doesn't owe **the accountant** money.* (Who doesn't he owe the money to? The accountant.)
  *Did the bank send **you** a letter?* (Who was the letter for? You.)

- Use *to* or *for* + the indirect object when it follows the direct object.
  *We offer first-class service **to customers**.*
  *He doesn't owe money **to the accountant**.*
  *Did the bank send a letter **to you**?*

Note: You can never have an indirect object without a direct object.
X *I gave my accountant.*

Unit 27

Review: Modals: *should/shouldn't, could, ought to* for advice

- Use **should, could,** or **ought to** tell someone you think something is a good idea.
  *You **should** get more sleep.*
  *We **could** try going to bed earlier.*
  *They **ought to** do more exercise during the day.*

- Use **should** to ask for advice.
  *What **should** I do?*
  *What time **should** we leave?*

- Use **shouldn't** to tell someone you think something is a bad idea.
  *You **shouldn't** work so hard.*
  *We **shouldn't** wait too long.*

Unit 28

Present unreal conditional (*If* + simple past + *would* + verb)

- Use two clauses to make present unreal conditional statements.

If clause	Result clause
if + simple past	*would/wouldn't* + base form of the verb

- Use the present unreal conditional to talk about unreal events or conditions in the present and their results.
  *If I **had** a million dollars, I'd throw a huge party.*
  *If her hip **didn't hurt**, Grandma **would** dance.*
  *If it **weren't** so far away, we'd all go to your house.*
  ***Would** you come to the party **if** you **had** time?*

- The *if* clause is often in the first position in a sentence, but it can also go second.
  *It **wouldn't** be difficult **if** everyone **helped** out.*

Note: Always use the **were** form of the verb **be** in the *if* clause with the present unreal conditional.
*If I **were** you . . .*
*If she **were** nicer . . .*
*If they **weren't** so tired . . .*

149

Irregular Verbs

Simple present	Simple past	Past Participle
be	was/were	been
become	became	become
begin	began	begun
break	broke	broken
build	built	built
buy	bought	bought
catch	caught	caught
choose	chose	chose
come	came	come
cost	cost	cost
do	did	done
draw	drew	drawn
drink	drank	drunk
drive	drove	driven
eat	ate	eaten
fall	fell	fallen
feel	felt	felt
fight	fought	fought
find	found	found
fly	flew	flown
forget	forgot	forgotten
get	got	gotten
give	gave	given
go	went	gone
grow	grew	grown
hang	hung	hung
have	had	had
hear	heard	heard
hurt	hurt	hurt
keep	kept	kept
know	knew	known
leave	left	left
lend	lent	lent

Simple present	Simple past	Past Participle
lose	lost	lost
make	made	made
mean	meant	meant
meet	met	met
pay	paid	paid
put	put	put
quit	quit	quit
read	read	read
ride	rode	ridden
run	ran	run
say	said	said
see	saw	seen
sell	sold	sold
send	sent	sent
shake	shook	shaken
show	showed	shown
sing	sang	sung
sit	sat	sat
sleep	slept	slept
speak	spoke	spoken
spend	spent	spent
stand	stood	stood
swim	swam	swum
take	took	taken
teach	taught	taught
tell	told	told
think	thought	thought
throw	threw	thrown
understand	understood	understood
wear	wore	worn
win	won	won
write	wrote	written

Vocabulary

Unit 1
complimenting
ending a conversation
greeting
introducing
making conversation
small talk

Unit 2
aggressive
cooperative
competitive
emotional
hardworking
messy
noisy
talkative

Unit 3
thirteen/thirty
fourteen/forty
fifteen/fifty
sixteen/sixty
seventeen/seventy
eighteen/eighty
nineteen/ninety

baby-sitting service
business center
ballroom
café
casino
conference room
fitness center
guest room
limousine service
lobby
restaurant
sauna
swimming pool
tennis court
video arcade

Unit 4
backache
cold
earache
headache
rash

sore throat
stomachache

Unit 5
deliver   a telegram
hire   a person
make   breakfast
pay   bills
send   a greeting card
spend   time
take   pictures
take out   the trash

Unit 6
awful
bad
big
boiling
cold
crowded
enormous
exhausted
fantastic
fascinating
freezing
good
hot
interesting
packed
tired

absolutely
really
very

Unit 7
casual
courteous
elegant
formal
indifferent
polite
romantic
rude

bland
greasy
healthful
hot
low-fat

nutritious
salty
sour
spicy
sweet

Unit 8
lose their temper
do the housework
make prenuptial agreements
have some kind of insurance
take care of financial obligations
sign a contract
react to problems
exchange wedding rings

Unit 9
break down
get off
go on
head out
put someone up
show someone around
start off

Unit 10
a piece of cake
challenging
complicated
doable
hard
impossible
manageable
no trouble
simple
straightforward
tough

Unit 11
armchair
basket
bookcase
cabinet
carpet
drapes
fireplace
lamp
magazine rack
picture
plants

Vocabulary

rug
sofa
stereo speakers
throw pillow
window

Unit 12
at + (a specific time)
at noon
in the evening
last night
last Sunday
next Sunday
on Sunday
on Sunday morning
this Sunday
yesterday afternoon

Unit 13
green card
ID (identification) card
immigration
nationalities
passport
permanent resident
tourist visa
work permit

Unit 14
cheer
clap
cry
laugh
scream
shout
whistle
yawn

Unit 15
crime
death
family life
greed
illness
marriage
misfortune
money
power
romance

Unit 16
clean
delicious
fast
fresh
healthy
reliable
safe
shiny
soft

Unit 17
cut back on
cut down on
get out of
give up
keep on
take up
throw away
turn down

Unit 18
alternative medicine
genetic engineering
hybrid cars
instant messaging
renewable resources
telecommuting
vegetarianism

Unit 19
cotton
glass
gold
leather
pewter
lycra
silver
wood

accessories
bathing suit
bicycling shorts
box
candlesticks
clothes/clothing
dress
earrings
gloves

jewelry
mirror
picture frame
ring
sandals
shirt
tray
vase
watch

Unit 20
action movie
animated film
comedy
drama
horror movie
martial arts film
musical
science fiction movie
thriller
western

Unit 21
go off
switch off
switch over to
turn down
turn off
turn on
turn up

Unit 22
robbery/robber/rob
burglary/burglar/burglarize
mugging/mugger/mug
scam/con artist/scam
shoplifting/shoplifter/shoplift
theft/thief/steal

get arrested
go to prison
pay a fine
do community service

Unit 23
take a break
take it easy
take off
take on
take part in
take up

Unit 24
cell phone
computer
digital camera
digital TV
DVD player
laptop
printer
scanner

Unit 25
best man
bride
bridesmaids
ceremony
groom
groomsmen
honeymoon
maid of honor
reception

get along
get back with
get divorced
get engaged
get married
get on each other's nerves
get over
get to know
get upset

Unit 26
bank account
bank statement
be in the black/red
borrow money
checking account
deposit money
invest money
lend money
pay interest
receive interest
save money
savings account
withdraw money

Unit 27
save energy
save money
save paper
save resources
save space
save time
spend money
spend time
use electricity
use money
use paper
use resources
use space
use time
waste electricity/energy
waste money
waste opportunities
waste paper
waste resources
waste space
waste time

Unit 28
anniversary
barbecue
birthday
black tie
DJ
dinner
family reunion
graduation
live music
pianist
potluck dinner
wedding

Student Book Audioscript

Unit 1 Nice to see you again

Getting started, Exercise 4, page 2

Conversation 1
A: I'd like you to meet my friend, Ana.
B: Hi. Nice to meet you.

Conversation 2
A: See you soon! Say hello to your family for me!
B: OK, thanks. Bye!

Conversation 3
A: Wonderful dinner! Everything was delicious.
B: Thanks! I'm glad you enjoyed it.

Conversation 4
A: Hi, how are you doing?
B: Great. How about you?

Conversation 5
A: It's a beautiful day, isn't it?
B: Yeah! I'm so glad it stopped raining.

Listening, Exercises 6 and 7, page 3

T= Tom   S= Sue   B= Bernardo

T: Sue? Hi! What a nice surprise.
S: Tom? I can't believe this. It's great to see you! What are you doing in San Diego?
T: I'm on vacation—visiting an old friend. Wow. You know, I haven't seen you since you left New York. How are you doing?
S: I'm doing really well. What about you? You look great!
T: Thanks! You look great, too.
S: Thanks! Oh, Tom, this is Bernardo, a good friend of mine. Bernardo, this is Tom. Tom and I used to work together in New York. At Green Advertising.
B: Nice to meet you, Tom.
T: Nice to meet you, too, Bernardo.
S: Tom is originally from Canada—from Toronto.
B: Really? Toronto is a great city . . . So how do you like California?
T: It's great. I love the weather here.
S: I know. The sun always seems to shine! So, are you still working at Green?
T: Yes, I'm still there. I'm a project manager now. So, what are you up to these days?
S: Well, I'm working at West Coast Advertising here in San Diego . . . with Bernardo. And I'm doing my master's.
T: Your master's degree? Really? In what?
S: Web design.
T: Cool! Good for you!
S: Uh oh, it's late! I'm sorry . . . but we have to get going. We have to meet my mother, and she always gets worried if I'm late.
T: Well, it was really good to see you again, Sue. And good to meet you, Bernardo.
B: Good to meet you, too. Enjoy the rest of your stay here.
S: Listen, Tom, why don't you give me a call later? Here's my number. We'll catch up. Maybe we can even try to have lunch while you're here.
T: That's a great idea. I'll call you.
S: OK then . . . See you!
T: OK, bye, Sue. Bye, Bernardo.

Pronunciation, Exercises 4 and 5, page 5

A: How are you doing?
B: Great! What about you?
A: So, how do you like California?
B: It's great. I love the weather here.
A: It was good to see you again.
B: Why don't you give me a call?

Unit 2 Why women iron

Getting started, Exercise 2, page 6

1. Ben is very hardworking. He studies every night.
2. My brother is very messy. He never cleans his room.
3. Marcelo never says anything, but his sister is the opposite. She's very talkative.
4. Could you please help? You're not being very cooperative.
5. Emilia is very competitive. She always wants to win.
6. Jack is always getting into fights. He's very aggressive.
7. I couldn't hear the movie. The people in front of me were too noisy.
8. I always cry at weddings. I'm very emotional.

Reading from page 7 for the optional Grammar Warm-up

Note: See the Reading on *Student Book* page 7 for the text of the audio.

Pronunciation, Exercises 4 and 5, page 8

Boys are stronger than girls.
Girls aren't as strong as boys.
Boys are more competitive than girls.
Girls aren't as competitive as boys.
Boys are as sensitive as girls.

Unit 3 Living in luxury

Getting started, Exercise 3, page 10

a baby-sitting service	a limousine service
ballrooms	a lobby
a business center	restaurants
cafés	a sauna
conference rooms	a swimming pool
a fitness center	tennis courts
guest rooms	

Listening, Exercise 5, page 11

58	1,217
218	13,000
560	14,850
715	140,000
850	16,000,000

Listening, Exercise 6, page 11

J = James   C = Caller

J: Four Seasons, reservations, this is James speaking. May I help you with a reservation today?

C: Yes, I'd like to ask about room availability on May 26th and 27th.

J: For which location, ma'am? There are 58 Four Seasons hotels and resorts worldwide, in over 27 countries.

C: Oh, I see, of course . . .

J: In fact, we have approximately 14,850 rooms and we employ 26,000 people . . .

C: Wow! That's very impressive . . .

J: So which Four Seasons can I check for you today, ma'am?

C: Miami . . .

J: OK, Miami. Yes, ma'am . . . and that is for, you say, the 26th and 27th . . .

C: Right. The 26th and 27th of May, yes, it's for our fifth wedding anniversary, and we'd like to reserve a suite . . .

J: Excellent choice, ma'am . . . there is an absolutely perfect suite overlooking Miami Beach. It's the Premier Suite.

C: Wow! An ocean view! And how much does the Premier Suite cost?

J: Let me check. OK. It goes for $1,300 a night . . .

C: . . . Well, maybe we don't need an 'absolutely perfect suite' . . . perhaps just a nice room . . .

J: Yes, certainly, ma'am, we have a deluxe double room, for just $550 a night . . . I'm sure you'd be very comfortable there. . . .

C: Does it have an ocean view?

J: No, I'm sorry, ma'am, it does not.

C: Well, yes, it *is* our anniversary, and I know Peter will be very happy . . .

Pronunciation, Exercise 7, page 11

eighty	fourteen
eighteen	sixty
forty	sixteen

Pronunciation, Exercise 8, page 11

eighty rooms	fourteen dollars
eighteen rooms	sixty miles
forty dollars	sixteen miles

Pronunciation, Exercise 9, page 11

The Four Seasons is a luxury hotel just 13 minutes from the international airport. We offer limousine service to and from the airport. We have 218 guest rooms, including 30 guest suites with balconies. All rooms come with fax and computer hook-ups and high-speed Internet access. The hotel features three fine dining restaurants and two cafés. We provide room service 24 hours a day.

For weddings and other formal occasions, choose from one of our three elegant ballrooms, for a total of 9,650 square feet of luxury dining and dancing.

For your business needs, we offer 15 conference rooms equipped with state-of-the-art audio/visual services, including simultaneous translation. After your meetings, you can relax in our sauna, swim in our Olympic-size pool, or work out in one of our three fitness centers. For your convenience, we also provide baby-sitting services and 24-hour business services.

We look forward to welcoming you to the Four Seasons.

Unit 4 Allergic reactions

Getting started, Exercise 2, page 14

a headache	d
a sore throat	c
a rash	b
a cold	e
a backache	g
a stomachache	a
an earache	f

(illnesses are repeated without answers)

Reading from page 15 for the optional Grammar Warm-up

Note: See the Reading on *Student Book* page 15 for the text of the audio.

Pronunciation, Exercise 4, page 16

relaxed	depressed	frightened
bored	annoyed	interested
excited	frustrated	embarrassed
tired	surprised	
disappointed	shocked	

Pronunciation, Exercise 5, page 16

Column 1	Column 2
relaxed	excited
bored	disappointed
tired	frustrated
depressed	interested
annoyed	
surprised	
shocked	
frightened	
embarrassed	

Review 1 Units 1–4

Unit 1, Nice to see you again, Exercise 1, page 18

A: Are you changing your diet?
B: Yes, I am. I'm not eating bread or pasta.
A: That's interesting. Thanks.

Unit 2, Why women iron, Exercise 4, page 18

A: In my opinion, men are more cooperative than women.
B: I disagree. Women are much more cooperative than men.
A: Really? Why do you think so?
B: Well, men argue and fight much more than women.

Unit 3, Living in luxury, Exercise 7, page 19

A: Could you tell me a little bit about the hotel?
B: Sure. What would you like to know?
A: Well, how many guest rooms does it have?
B: We have 78 guest rooms.
A: How much is a room?
B: A room for one night is $59.
A: I see. Do you offer a baby-sitting service?
B: Yes, and we also offer "a kids' club" for . . .

Unit 4, Allergic reactions, Exercise 11, page 19

A: OK. I move one . . . um . . . I feel annoyed when people on the train talk loudly on their cell phones.
B: That's a correct sentence. You stay on that space. Now it's my turn. I'm going to toss the coin and take my . . .

World of Music 1 Good to See You

Listening, Exercises 2 and 3, pages 20 and 21

Good to see you
Good to see you again
Good to see your face again
Good to see you

I'm the suitcase in your hallway
I'm the footsteps on your floor
When I'm looking down on you
I feel like I know what my life is for

Good to see you
Good to see you again
Good to see your face again
Good to see you

I've been down the endless highway
I've passed on the solid line
Now at last I'm home to you
I feel like making up for lost time

Good to see you
Good to see you again
Good to see your face again
It's good to see you

Unit 5 A typical day

Listening, Exercises 5 and 6, page 23

I = Interviewer   R = Ron

I: Ron, you have a very unusual job.
R: Yes—I deliver singing telegrams. You know, a singing telegram is much more memorable and original than sending a greeting card.
I: So what exactly do you do?
R: Well, I compose a song based on the occasion—a birthday, anniversary, office party, or holiday, and then I go to the person, usually while they're at work, and sing the song.
I: Is it expensive to send someone a singing telegram?
R: Not really. Each singing telegram costs about $50.00.
I: So who hires you?
R: Actually, I work for an agency called Say It with a Song.
I: So let's say I want to send a singing telegram to my wife. What do I do?
R: Just make a phone call. Call the agency and tell them you want to hire me, Ron Bates, to deliver a singing telegram. They'll ask you a few questions. Just tell them what the occasion is and what day you want the telegram delivered. Then just wait for the special day when I show up at your wife's workplace and deliver your singing telegram.
I: And who do I pay? Do I pay you or the agency?
R: The agency. Then the agency pays me.
I: I guess you don't work alone. Who helps you?
R: My wife, Mary. She buys some flowers. Then she comes with me and takes a picture as I give the person flowers and sing the song.
I: Do you get tired of your job?
R: No, not really. I love singing, and I like to make people happy. And, you know, no one forgets a singing telegram.

Pronunciation, Exercise 4, page 25

A: Who gets up first in your house?
B: Usually I do.

Pronunciation, Exercises 5 and 6, page 25

A: Who does the shopping in your house?
B: Usually my father.
A: Who does the cooking?
B: My mother does.
A: Who pays the bills?
B: My parents both do.
A: Who takes out the trash?
B: My older brother.

Unit 6 It's absolutely true!

Pronunciation, Exercise 5, page 27

hot	packed	freezing	good
awful	interesting	enormous	boiling
cold	fascinating	big	exhausted
fantastic	bad	crowded	tired

Pronunciation, Exercise 6, page 27

Column 1	Column 2	Column 3
hot	awful	fantastic
cold	freezing	enormous
packed	crowded	exhausted
bad	boiling	
big		
good		
tired		

Column 4	Column 5
interesting	fascinating

Listening, Exercises 9 and 10, page 27

A: So, where did you go on your vacation?
B: To Brazil—Rio de Janeiro.
A: Wow, sounds great!
B: Yeah, I went just in time for Carnaval and well, you know what Brazil can be like in February.
A: Very hot, I imagine.
B: Hot! It's absolutely boiling!
A: Huh.
B: Well, it was hot, but this year it was also raining—a very heavy rain—something like two feet of water an hour. It was really, really wet—in fact, the Sambadrome was totally flooded.
A: What's the Sambadrome?
B: Oh, you know, it's that enormous stadium where the incredible samba parade is held. And everyone was getting very worried that they might cancel Carnaval or something.
A: That would have been really awful.
B: Yeah. Just imagine all the thousands of people involved in Carnaval, and the 300,000 tourists or so, all waiting and then it's canceled!
A: Incredible!
B: But then the weather changed, and the rain stopped.
A: That was lucky.
B: Yeah, so the Carnaval parade started on time after all, and the schools did their Samba—it was so colorful! Did you know there are over 70,000 dancers?
A: It must have been very crowded.
B: Not just crowded—really, really packed!
A: Hmm!
B: . . . and so I stayed out and danced all night, and all the next night.
A: I guess you were tired.
B: Absolutely exhausted! But I didn't mind . . .
A: No?
B: . . . because I was in Brazil . . . and it was Carnaval.
A: Well, yeah.
B: It was fantastic! Absolutely fantastic!

Unit 7 Eating out

Getting started, Exercise 2, page 30

Type of Restaurant	Nutritional Value
casual	greasy
elegant	healthful
formal	low-fat
romantic	nutritious

Food Flavor	Service
bland	courteous
hot	indifferent
salty	polite
sour	rude
spicy	
sweet	

Pronunciation, Exercises 4 and 5, page 31

casual	healthful
nutritious	indifferent

Pronunciation, Exercises 6 and 7, page 31

polite	elegant
formal	courteous

Reading from page 31 for the optional Grammar Warm-up

Note: See the Reading on *Student Book* page 31 for the text of the audio.

Unit 8 It's a deal!

Getting started, Exercise 2, page 34

1. When people are under stress, they may lose their temper.
2. Nowadays, both men and women do the housework.
3. Before they get married, celebrities often make prenuptial agreements.
4. The way to protect your possessions is to have some kind of insurance.
5. People should be responsible and take care of their financial obligations.
6. When you marry someone, you actually sign a contract.
7. It's good to know how your spouse will react to problems.
8. At weddings, most couples exchange wedding rings.

Reading from page 35 for the optional Grammar Warm-up

Note: See the Reading on *Student Book* page 35 for the text of the audio.

Pronunciation, Exercises 4 and 5, page 37

have to
They have to see a lawyer.
He doesn't have to sign the agreement.
Do they have to have an agreement?
has to
Bruce has to do the housework.
Susan has to pay the bills.
Who has to do the cooking?

Review 2 Units 5–8

Unit 5, A typical day, Exercise 1, page 38

A: Okay, I move two squares. A telephone … Hmm … Who makes the most telephone calls in your house?
B: My daughter.
A: Who does she call?
B: Everyone!
C: OK. My turn. One square … a computer. OK.

Unit 6, It's absolutely true!, Exercise 3, page 38

A: Here's the beginning of the story we have to finish: "Barbara was walking her dog one day when suddenly it started raining. The weather was absolutely awful! She didn't know what to do, so she took an umbrella that was leaning against a car." Now, what are we going to say?
B: I know, how about this? "When she got home, she and the dog were both wet and absolutely freezing. She dried the dog, and put the umbrella in the shower so it could dry. As she was hanging it up, she saw a sticker on the handle. It said, 'Please return to M.J. Smith, 25 Walton Street.'"
A: Oh, that's good. Here's my part: "The next day she decided to take the umbrella back. As she was walking down the street, she remembered that she had a friend from high school named Mary Jane Smith. She thought, 'It will be really interesting if it's the same person!'"
C: OK, now for my sentences! "As Barbara was walking down Walton Street, she saw a woman coming toward her who looked very familiar. The woman smiled at her and said, 'Barbara? What are you doing here? And why do you have my umbrella?' Barbara answered, 'Mary Jane! It's great to see you. Let's go have a cup of coffee.'"
A: Perfect!
B: We finished it!

Unit 7, Eating out, Exercise 6, page 39

A: Where do you want to go for dinner tonight?
B: I think Alice's Restaurant is pretty good. Let's go there tonight.
A: Hmm, I don't know. The last time I went there, the food wasn't fantastic. They said my dish was spicy, but it really wasn't. Why don't we try the Blue Lantern this time?
B: The Blue Lantern is too formal for me. And it's too expensive for me right now. Alice's is a lot cheaper, and they do great hamburgers.
A: But they don't serve enough vegetarian dishes.
B: They have a lot of salads.
A: Yeah, but I like to choose from a variety of foods, you know, try something new.
B: They always have at least one vegetarian soup, and those are usually pretty interesting.
A: Hmm, OK. But when you get your next paycheck, let's go to the Blue Lantern.

Unit 8, It's a deal!, Exercise 8, page 39

J = Jim   M = Molly

J: Hi, Molly. This is Jim.
M: Oh, hi, Jim.
J: Umm, I was wondering if you'd like to go to the movies tonight.
M: I'm sorry, I can't. I have to do my laundry tonight.
J: Oh, come on. You don't have to do it tonight. You can still do it tomorrow.
M: No, I can't. All my clothes are dirty. And I also have to pay the bills. And then I have to do my homework.
J: Oh, OK. Well, maybe another time when you don't have so many things to do.
M: Yes, maybe.

Unit 9 The river

Listening, Exercises 4 and 5, page 41

M = Maria   C = Caller

M: Good morning, Riverside Tours. Maria speaking. How can I help you?

C: I have a reservation for the River Tour next week, and I have a few questions.

M: Yes, of course. What's the reference number for your tour?

C: Um . . . oh, here it is, it's 334516.

M: 334516 . . . OK . . . the River Thames, a two-day tour. How can I help you?

C: Well, first, the departure time—what time does the boat actually head out from Kingston?

M: Nine o'clock, Monday morning. But we ask you to arrive about fifteen minutes before that.

C: OK. So we leave at nine, and how long do we stay at Hampton Court?

M: About four hours—you get off the boat at Hampton Court around ten-thirty. If you like, the guide can show you around, or you can walk around on your own. Then the tour goes on to Richmond Park and Kew Gardens in the afternoon.

C: Oh, that sounds great. What about the evening?

M: There's a walking tour around the local area that starts off from the hotel. Start time is seven-thirty, and it lasts about an hour. It's optional—just tell the guide if you want to go or not.

C: I'm meeting a friend for dinner and he's putting me up for the night, so I think I'll skip the walking tour.

M: No problem. It's entirely optional.

C: What about the next day?

M: Well, on Tuesday, you head out at ten o'clock, and the tour takes you through the heart of London. You go past many famous sites: the Houses of Parliament, the Tate Modern, Shakespeare's Globe Theater . . . they're all listed on your map.

C: Just one more thing . . .

M: Yes, of course.

C: What time does the tour end on the second day? I'm going to the theater in the evening, and the show starts at eight o'clock. I already have the tickets, and I really don't want to be late.

M: You'll be fine. The tour ends at Tower Bridge, at five-thirty.

C: Great. Well, that's it. And thanks for your help.

M: You're welcome. Enjoy your trip.

Pronunciation, Exercises 4 and 5, page 42

head out
When does the boat head out?
get off
We get off at Hampton Court.
show us around
A guide will show us around.
go on
Then we go on to the park.
putting me up
A friend is putting me up.

Unit 10 On the other hand

Getting started, Exercise 2, page 44

Column 1	Column 2	Column 3
easy	OK	difficult
a piece of cake	doable	challenging
no trouble	manageable	complicated
simple		hard
straightforward		impossible
		tough

(adjectives are repeated without column numbers)

Reading from page 45 for the optional Grammar Warm-up

Note: See the Reading on *Student Book* page 45 for the text of the audio.

Listening, Exercise 6, page 45

M = Mike   J = Juliana

M: Juliana! I didn't realize you were left-handed.

J: What do you mean? Are you left-handed, too?

M: Yeah. Well, actually I'm kind of ambidextrous because I write with my left hand and I draw with my left hand, but . . .

J: Oh, yeah. I've heard a lot of artists are left-handed.

M: Yeah . . . but for sports and stuff I usually use my right hand. You know, like when I play baseball, I bat right-handed . . . .

J: Yeah, I know what you mean, because I use my right hand to play tennis, but my left for everything else.

M: Yeah, and I kick a ball with my right foot instead of my left foot. I guess that makes me right-footed! Hey! Do you want to try this test I read about? It's a kind of ability test to see if you're ambidextrous . . . I don't think it'll take long.

J: OK, sure. What do I have to do?

Listening, Exercise 7, page 45

M = Mike   J = Juliana

M: So, let's see how we did with our right hands . . . I managed to throw the ball OK. In fact, it was pretty easy with my right hand.

J: Yeah, me, too—that was a piece of cake. How about the writing, though? Huh, look at my message—I couldn't do it at all. It was really challenging for me. And it looks like a four-year-old wrote it!

M: Oh, I don't know, it looks OK to me. I found the writing hard at first, but then it actually wasn't too difficult. I bet with practice it would feel normal.

J: Yeah, yours isn't bad at all—I can read it fine. What about the scissors? I actually found I could use them better with my right hand than I could with my left. They were more manageable with my right.

M: Yeah, me too. It was more, uh, straightforward with my right hand.

J: So that leaves the drawing. Let me see yours. Oh, wow, it's really good!

M: Thanks! Yeah, it was pretty simple.

J: No, for me it was complicated. I just wasn't able to hold the pencil right. Here, look, it's pretty embarrassing.

M: Uhhh . . . is that supposed to be me?!

Pronunciation, Exercises 4 and 5, page 47

She can throw a ball with either hand.
I can't draw with my left hand.
He could play chess when he was four.
I couldn't cook until I got married.

Pronunciation, Exercise 6, page 47

1. They can dance very well.
2. She could ride a bike.
3. He can play the guitar.
4. My grandmother couldn't speak English.
5. I can't read without glasses.
6. He can write with his left hand.

Unit 11 Trading spaces

Pronunciation, Exercise 4, page 49

magazine   table   art

Pronunciation, Exercise 6, page 49

Column 1	Column 2	Column 3
magazine	table	art
cabinet	fireplace	armchair
rack	bookcase	carpet
basket	drapes	
lamp		
plants		

(furniture is repeated without column numbers)

Reading from page 49 for the optional Grammar Warm-up

Note: See the Reading on *Student Book* page 49 for the text of the audio.

Listening, Exercises 8 and 9, page 49

A = Announcer   C = Carla   P = Pedro

A: OK . . . you can open your eyes now.
C: Oh, my goodness. What a change!
P: What have they done?
A: What do you think? They've redecorated your living room.
P: Well, it's certainly . . . different.
C: Look at the floor. There's no carpet.
P: Hmm . . . They've refinished the wood floor . . . I like that!
C: Yeah, it's beautiful. I'm not sure about the red walls, though . . .
P: Yes. Well—it's certainly an interesting color. I like it . . . I think.
C: Not me. I liked it the way it was.
A: Oh dear . . .
P: But the new drapes look great. They're a real nice change.
A: Yes, Cassie and John made those. They're very proud of them.
P: And look . . . they've moved the sofa. It's under the window now. I like that. There's more light there.
C: Oh, look over there! Are those new armchairs?
A: No, but they look great, don't they? That was Cassie's idea. She hasn't bought new armchairs—just new covers and matching throw pillows.
P: Yes, but where's the bookcase?
A: It's gone, I'm afraid! The first thing they did was throw that away.
C: I don't mind. I always hated it. But where are the books?
A: They're inside that gorgeous cabinet over there. Your television is over there too—it's your new home entertainment center.
C: What a good idea!
A: So all in all, then, what's the verdict?
P: Really nice. They've done a good job. I like it a lot.
C: Me too . . . except for those red walls!!

Unit 12 A soccer fan's website

Getting started, Exercise 2, page 52

Column 1: in	Column 2: on	Column 3: at
in the evening	on Thursday	at noon
in the morning		at 6:45 P.M.

Column 4: no preposition
last Friday afternoon
yesterday morning
next Monday evening
this Thursday

Pronunciation, Exercises 4 and 5, page 52

We're leaving at ten.
We arrive at four in the afternoon.
We can walk around in the morning. There's a tour at noon on Sunday.
I think I'll go shopping on Tuesday.
Let's meet at our hotel in the evening.

Listening, Exercises 9 and 10, page 53

C = Charles   P = Peter

C: Hello.
P: Hello. Is that Charles?
C: Yes.
P: Charles, this is Peter Gibson. You know, the one organizing the Manchester United trip.
C: Oh, yes.
P: Just calling to tell you about a few possible changes.
C: Not the date, I hope. I couldn't ask my boss for any more time off work.
P: No, no. The beginning and end dates are the same. It's just that you may need to get out of bed a little earlier on Friday. We might leave at ten o'clock in the morning, not twelve o'clock.
C: Oh? So we could arrive in Kuala Lumpur in the middle of the night?
P: Yes, we may arrive in Kuala Lumpur at around four o'clock in the morning Malaysian time. Then we may take a taxi or we could take a bus to the hotel. You can go to sleep when we get there.
C: I see. Anything else?
P: Yes, a couple of things. On Sunday we might not be able to get a bus for the sightseeing tour. You could take a walking tour instead if you want to.
C: Right.
P: And on Monday, Raffles is full already, so we might have dinner at the restaurant in our hotel instead.
C: Oh, that's too bad.
P: Yes, sorry about that. But if someone cancels their reservation at Raffles, they might be able to fit us in. And the last thing is . . . since some people may not want to go sightseeing on Tuesday, we might arrange a shopping trip, too.
C: Yeah, that sounds good. I might have to buy some things for my girlfriend. She said she might even give me a list! I really can't wait to go. It'll be interesting to see if Manchester . . . .

Review 3   Units 9–12

Unit 9, The river, Exercise 1, page 56

A: I want to go shopping at Marshall Fields first, so I thought I'd get on the trolley at Marshall Fields around eleven. How does that sound?
B: Well, I was going to head out earlier. But I guess I could do some shopping first and then get on the trolley with you at 11.
A: Great. And then I thought we'd get off at the Art Institute around 11:15 and stay there an hour or so.
C: That sounds good. I thought it would be fun to take the trolley to Navy Pier. We could get something to eat there and just walk around for a while.
A: That's a good idea. So then we'd leave Navy Pier around 1:30 or so . . . that'll give us just enough time to see the water tower before we head back to the hotel.
C: Yeah, that sounds perfect.
B: Great, let's do that.

Unit 10, On the other hand, Exercise 4, page 56

A: I could only manage to wink my right eye. It's almost impossible for me to wink my left. How about you?
B: Oh, I can wink either eye with no trouble at all. It's very straightforward for me. What about wiggling your ears? I couldn't do that at all.
A: Well, I managed to do it just a little, but it was pretty hard. I had to really concentrate. Can you touch your toes without bending your knees?

Unit 11, Trading spaces, Exercise 7, page 57

A: Mom really went crazy with redecorating the kitchen, didn't she?
B: She sure did. At first I thought I was in the wrong house. Let's see . . . she's moved the stove from one end of the kitchen to the other.
A: Yes, and she's completely redone the cabinets. She's painted them all gray.
B: And the counter top? What color was that before? I don't remember . . .

Unit 12, A soccer fan's website, Exercise 10, page 57

A: What are you doing this weekend?
B: Well, I might meet some friends Saturday morning, and then in the afternoon, we could go to a museum or a movie. If we go to the movies at 3:00, we can see two movies for the price of one. After the movie, we might go to a party. Or we might not. If we're tired, we may just go home. Then, on Sunday . . .

World of Music 2 My Way

Listening, Exercises 2 and 3, page 58

And now, the end is near;
And so I face the final curtain.
My friend, I'll say it clear,
I'll state my case, of which I'm certain.

I've lived a life that's full.
I've traveled each and ev'ry highway;
But more, much more than this,
I did it my way.

Regrets, I've had a few;
But then again, too few to mention.
I did what I had to do
And saw it through without exemption.

I planned each charted course;
Each careful step along the byway,
But more, much more than this,
I did it my way.

Yes, there were times, I'm sure you knew
When I bit off more than I could chew.
But through it all, when there was doubt,
I ate it up and spit it out.
I faced it all and I stood tall;
And did it my way.

I've loved, I've laughed and cried.
I've had my fill; my share of losing.
And now, as tears subside,
I find it all so amusing.

To think I did all that;
And may I say—"Not in a shy way,"
Oh no, oh no, not me,
I did it my way.

For what is a man, what has he got?
If not himself, then he has not
to say the things he truly feels,
And not the words of one who kneels.
The record shows I took the blows—
And did it my way!

Unit 13 Green card

Getting started, Exercises 2, page 60

Going to the United States
Before you visit the United States, check to see if you need a tourist visa. Some nationalities need to have one, but others don't. If you have a valid visa but want to stay longer than 90 days, you can apply to the immigration department for an extension. If you want to work in the U.S., you need a work permit. If you want to live and work in the U.S. permanently, you need to go through a long process to get a green card. When you get it, you are considered a permanent resident of the United States. No matter what your status, it's a good idea to carry an ID card or your passport with you so that you can prove who you are.

Reading, Exercise 7, page 61

A: So how long have you been in the United States, Miss Bolton?

B: You mean *Mrs.* Bolton. Umm.... I've been in the U.S. for eight months, but I've only been in New York for five months. I was in Los Angeles before.

A: And how long have you known Mr. Bolton?

B: Uhh... I've known Rod since December, so... December, January, February, March... Er, I've known him for four months. Yes, we met four months ago.

A: And you've been married for three months?

B: Yes, I saw him at a party, and it was love at first sight.

A: Mmm. I understand. And what do you do, Mrs. Bolton?

B: I'm a dancer. I teach dance.

A: Your neighbor says she has never seen you with your husband.

B: Ah, yes, I can explain that. Umm, you see we like very different things. So we don't go out together very often.

A: Ah, I see. OK, Mrs. Bolton. That's all I need to know. Thank you. Could I use your bathroom before I go?

B: Bathroom?

A: I think in England you say toilet?

B: Ah, the loo, of course.

A: And where is it?

B: Ah, erm, erm, yes, where is it? Ermm...

A: Never mind. I have a few more questions, Mrs. Bolton....

Pronunciation, Exercises 5 and 6, page 63

A: How long have you been married?
B: We've been married for three months.
A: How long has she been in the U.S.?
B: She's been here since September.
A: Has she been to England since then?
B: No, she hasn't.
A: Yes, she has.
B: Have you known each other for a long time?
A: No, we haven't.
B: Yes, we have.
A: Your neighbor hasn't seen you together.
B: We haven't lived here very long.

Unit 14   What's that noise?

Getting started, Exercise 2, page 64

1. [sounds of people cheering]
2. [sounds of young man laughing]
3. [sounds of a person whistling]
4. [sounds of a woman crying]
5. [sounds of a woman screaming]
6. [sounds of a man shouting]
7. [sounds of an audience clapping]
8. [sounds of a woman yawning]

Listening, Exercises 4, 5, and 7, page 65

J = Jason   M = Maria   S = Steve

J: This is Jason Miller and you're listening to XRT at 96.3 FM, and it's time for our contest *What's That Job?* You'll hear someone doing their job. Guess which job it is, and you'll win two movie tickets. Let's go to Maria on line one. Hello, Maria. Are you ready to play?

M: Yes, Jason, I think so . . .

J: Then listen.

[sounds of traffic, background noise, and people walking and talking]

M: Well, the person is somewhere noisy. I hear people walking and someone shouting. The person might work in a train station or an airport. Can I hear a bit more, Jason?

J: OK.

[sound of same background traffic and crowd noise, a whistle, plus coins dropping in a fare box, doors shutting, and then traffic noise is muffled]

M: Well, I heard traffic and a whistle. The person is definitely outside somewhere. He might be in a car . . . but he can't be a taxi driver because people don't drop coins in a machine to pay a taxi driver. I think the person must be a bus driver.

J: That's right! . . . a bus driver. Excellent, Maria, you've won two tickets to the movies. Now let's go to Steve on line two. This one is a bit more difficult, Steve. Are you ready?

S: Yeah. I'm ready.

J: OK . . . Listen to this and tell me what this person's job is . . .

[sounds of a crowd of people and bursts of clapping and cheering]

S: Well, I hear cheering and clapping, so he could be a lot of things. He might be an actor in a theater. He might be a musician at a concert , or maybe a golfer. Hmm . . . He can't be a basketball player—it's noisier than that at a basketball game.

J: You're close . . . Listen some more . . .

[sounds of the crowd, but then they die down; sound of a tennis ball being hit by a racket]

S: Well, he must be playing some kind of sport. Is he a volleyball player?

J: No, sorry, Steve, time's up. Let's listen to the whole sequence . . .

[sounds of the crowd, a racket hitting the ball on a serve, then sounds of footsteps running to the ball, a few volleys, crowd sounds, and the referee calling "Out!"]

He's not a volleyball player. He's a tennis player. Sorry, no movie tickets this time, Steve. OK, We'll play more of *What's That Job?* again a little bit later, but right now it's time for the latest weather and traffic report. Remember, this is 96.3 . . .

Pronunciation, Exercises 4 and 5, page 67

He might be at an airport.
He can't be a taxi driver.
He must be a bus driver.
She might be British.
No, she can't be.
Then she must be Australian.

Speaking, Exercise 7, page 67

Listen to the clues and guess the person's job. Listen to the first clue.

[sound of writing, books opening and closing, shuffling feet]

Now listen to the second clue.

[sound of writing, books opening and closing, shuffling feet, whispering, erasing, then blowing away eraser dust]

Not sure yet? Listen to the third and final clue.

[sound of writing, books opening and closing, shuffling feet, whispering, erasing, then blowing away eraser dust, a school bell and scraping of chairs, packing up books and backpacks, talking]

I'm sure you know the person's job by now . . . That's right. This person is a teacher! You heard writing and students opening and closing books, someone erasing their paper, and then the bell and students getting ready to leave.

Speaking, Exercise 8, page 67

Listen to the clues and guess the person's job. Listen to the first clue.

[sound of a jet engine running]

Now listen to the second clue.

[sound of a jet engine running, the bell to call a flight attendant on a plane, click of fastening a seat belt, an overhead compartment door shutting]

Not sure yet? Listen to the third and final clue.

[sound of a jet engine running, the bell to call a flight attendant on a plane, click of fastening a seat belt, an overhead compartment door shutting, flaps on wings opening and closing; roar of engines as plane speeds up and takes off]

Did you guess the person's job? That's right. This person is a flight attendant. You heard the sound of the plane's engines, the button to call the flight attendant, someone fastening their seat belt, the overhead compartment closing, and the plane taking off.

Unit 15 Mumbai Soap

Reading from page 68 for the optional Grammar Warm-up

Note: See the Reading on *Student Book* page 68 for the text of the audio.

Pronunciation, Exercises 4 and 5, page 70

I'll always
I'll always love you.
you'll forget
You'll forget me.
it'll be
Do you think it'll be too late?
her heart will break
She thinks her heart will break.

Speaking, Exercise 8, page 71

A = Announcer S = Sanjay N = Nina

A: After the soccer game in Liverpool, Sanjay had a day off, and he decided to go to London to see Nina. He went straight to Nina's apartment, but he was so nervous that he couldn't ring the bell.

S: Will she really want to see me? Maybe it wasn't a good idea to come here, after all. Why didn't I stay in Liverpool with my teammates?

A: All of a sudden, the door opened, and . . . there was Nina.

N: Sanjay! What are you doing in London?

S: The soccer game. We played yesterday, in Liverpool. Don't tell me you didn't know.

N: Of course, I didn't. Why didn't you call me?

S: I was afraid you wouldn't want to see me again.

N: Of course I wanted to see you. I never stopped thinking about you. And I promise you, this time, I'll go to my parents. They'll have to understand that we belong together . . .

Unit 16 The message behind the ad

Listening, Exercises 6 and 7, page 73

I = Interviewer J = Joanna

I: For tonight's news spotlight, we're talking to advertising executive Joanna Lindsey about television ads. Good evening, Joanna. Thank you for joining us tonight.

J: Good evening, Jim. It's a pleasure to be here.

I: So, Joanna, when you're creating an ad, where do you start?

J: Well, first we think about the group of people who might want this product. Are they men or women, young or old, how much money do they have?

I: Can you give me an example?

J: Sure. In an ad for an expensive car, for example, we often use young, good-looking men or women who look like they have a lot of money. The message is: "If you're young and successful, this is the car for you."

I: And in the ad, it's usually the man who drives the car, isn't it?

J: That's often true—but not always . . .

I: And usually the man has a good-looking female next to him. So isn't the message really: "If you buy this car, you'll meet a beautiful woman"?

J: Not necessarily. Our point is: "If you try our product, you won't regret it." And we don't always use young attractive people to sell things. For example, if the product is sunscreen, we'll probably use a family. Parents worry about their children so the message here is: "Your kids won't get sunburned if you use this sunscreen."

I: OK, families for sunscreen, but what about shampoo?

J: Well, yes, often the message is that you'll meet the man or woman of your dreams if your hair is soft and shiny. Will that really happen just because you used a certain shampoo? No, of course not. The messages in ads are often exaggerated. And you know, sometimes we use humor to get the message across. People will remember an ad if it's funny.

I: For example?

J: We created an advertising campaign that shows a family getting up in complete darkness. They're bumping into each other and tripping over things. It's not until one of them takes a drink of orange juice that the sun comes up, like a big orange. The message is: "If you don't drink orange juice, the sun won't come up."

I: That's funny . . . and probably very effective. Well, I'm afraid that's all we have time for. Thanks for being with us today, Joanna.

J: Thank you.

Pronunciation, Exercises 4 and 5, page 74

If you buy this car, you'll meet a beautiful woman.
If the ad is funny, people will remember it.
If you use this sunscreen, your kids won't get sunburned.
If you try our product, you won't regret it.

Review 4 Units 13–16

Unit 13, Green card, Exercise 1, page 76

A: OK, so how long have you been living in the U.S.?
B: Umm, I've been living here for about five years.
A: And how long have you known your roommate?
B: Since last January.
A: And how long have you shared an apartment?
B: We moved in in March, so it's been almost a year . . .

Unit 14, What's that noise?, Exercise 5, page 76

A: I can hear people clapping.
B: You might be at a basketball game.
A: No, that's not the place. I can also hear people singing.
B: Oh, then you must be at a concert.
A: That's right! Two points for you.
C: OK, now it's our turn. I can hear . . .

Unit 15, Mumbai Soap, Exercise 9, page 77

A: Well, I think while they are apart, they'll both realize how much they love each other. And I think that on Wednesday, they'll call each other and get back together.
B: Oh, I don't think so. I think the radio station will call them on Wednesday and offer them a lot of money if they agree to go ahead and get married live on the radio.
A: Really! Well what do you think will happen on Friday during the final episode?
B: I think they'll both show up at the wedding. But they won't get married.
A: They won't? What do you mean?
B: Well, I think they'll pretend they're getting married, and they'll put on a great show for the radio audience. But then they'll . . .

Unit 16, The message behind the ad, Exercise 11, page 77

A: OK, here's my shampoo ad: "If you use the fabulous new V6 Shampoo, your hair will be shiny and beautiful."
B: My slogan is: "You'll meet a lot of fun people if you buy the TX5. It's more than just a car."
C: My ad is about a vitamin drink. My slogan is: "Vita-Might Tonight! If you drink Vita-Might every night, you'll never need to take vitamins."

Unit 17   Willpower

Reading from page 79 for the optional Grammar Warm-up

Note: See the Reading on *Student Book* page 79 for the text of the audio.

Pronunciation, Exercises 4 and 5, page 81

I want to lose weight.
I want to eat less.
I need to get more exercise.
I decided to stop eating chocolate.
I learned to play tennis.
I decided to go jogging every day.
But then I wanted to eat more.
And I needed to lose more weight.

Unit 18   Wave of the future

Listening, Exercise 5, page 83

B = Beth   H = Han-su

H: Hi, Beth. How are you doing?
B: Han-su! Long time no see!
H: Yeah. How's life? What are you doing these days?
B: Well, I'm working for a company called WorldWide Visions. I'm a trend spotter.
H: A trend spotter? I've never heard of that before.
B: I know. It's a new thing. Basically, we predict trends. You know, predicting the future used to be a business for fortune-tellers, but now it's serious business. Major companies actually hire people in my field to spot future trends in their area.
H: Wow! That's interesting. So, how do you predict the future? Isn't that pretty impossible to do?

Listening, Exercise 6, page 83

B = Beth   H = Han-su

B: It's not easy, but let me give you an example of what we do. A few years ago, people used to think that regular books and magazines printed on paper would disappear. People wouldn't stop talking about electronic books. Everyone used to say that they were the wave of the future. So far, that prediction has not come true.
H: That's true. I still buy and read good old-fashioned books. But, what's a trend that you spotted that actually has come true?
B: Well, everyone used to think that "going to work" meant leaving your house. We would all get up, get dressed, and go to our workplaces. But I started to notice, oh, about 20 years ago, that some of my friends would get up and go to their computer instead of going to work. I spotted this trend toward telecommuting, and now it's become very common.
H: And I guess there are many changes happening in the field of energy, right?
B: Yeah. People used to think we could use as much energy as we wanted. They would buy big cars and use a lot of electricity at home, with no concern about energy. But now almost everyone knows that we need to conserve and start using renewable resources like wind and solar power. I think there will soon be solar panels on every home and business, not to mention hybrid cars, which are becoming very popular these days.
H: Actually, solar energy is starting to be very popular in places like Germany and Japan. But I'm not sure I agree with what you said about cars. My sister, for instance, used to drive a small car, but now she drives an SUV. And it's not just my sister.
B: I think SUVs are just a trend that will go away with time.
H: Who knows? But many things are changing these days, that's for sure, especially...

Pronunciation, Exercises 5 and 6, page 85

used to
She used to drive a small car.
use to
Did you use to work in an office?
didn't use to
I didn't use to like vegetables.

Unit 19 Made in the U.S.A.

Getting started, Exercise 2, page 86

cotton	G	pewter	D
glass	B	lycra	E
gold	C	silver	A
leather	F	wood	H

(materials are repeated without answers)

Listening, Exercises 4 and 5, page 87

M = Marcela   P = Peter   S = Salesman

M: Look, Peter! This place is fantastic . . . there are so many things to buy, and they're from all over the world!
P: Yeah, but take it easy. Things are pretty expensive here.
M: Yes, but it's my birthday, and I'd love something from Fisherman's Wharf.
P: Well, what do you think of these mirrors?
M: Hmm, very unusual. I like the colors around the glass.
S: Yes, they're handmade by a small company in Holland.
M: How much are they?
S: A hundred dollars. And I can wrap them up for travel.
P: Marcela, that's too expensive. Let's go look at those boxes.
M: OK . . . mmm . . . What lovely wood. Where are they made?
S: They're made in Morocco. They're hand-painted.
M: Beautiful. How much are they?
S: That one's 50 dollars. It's sold for at least 75 dollars in the big stores.
M: What do you think, Peter?
P: I think we should look at a few more things.
M: That sounds like a good idea.
P: Marcela, look at these. What do you think of these earrings?
M: Very pretty. Where are they from?
S: Mexico. All of my silver jewelry is imported from Mexico.
M: Oh, really? How much are they?
S: Twenty-five dollars.
P: Fantastic. Marcela, I'm going to buy you these earrings.
M: Wait, Peter. They're not what I like best . . .

P: But look, they're only 25 dollars! Happy birthday! . . . Umm . . . Marcela?
M: Yes?
P: Could you lend me 10 dollars?

Pronunciation, Exercise 7, page 87

cotton	metal
wooden	sandals
didn't	candlesticks

Pronunciation, Exercises 8 and 9, page 87

They didn't buy the cotton shirt.
They didn't buy the wooden boxes.
They didn't buy the sandals.
They didn't buy the metal candlesticks.

Unit 20 At the movies

Pronunciation, Exercise 2, page 91

action movie	martial arts film
animated	musical
comedy	science fiction
drama	thriller
horror movie	western

Pronunciation, Exercise 3, page 91

Column 1	Column 2
drama	comedy
thriller	musical
western	

Column 3	Column 4
martial arts film	action movie
science fiction	animated
	horror movie

(movie types are repeated without column numbers)

Listening, Exercises 6 and 7, page 91

I = Interviewer   M = Michael

I: Our guest today is Michael Marksman, who has just written a fascinating book, *Movie Facts for Movie Fans*. You're a movie fan, Michael . . . so what's your all-time favorite movie?
M: Hmm. That's a tough question. I can't really answer it.
I: You know what? I can't answer that question, either! OK. Let me be more specific: What's your favorite action movie?
M: That's easy! The original *Star Wars* movie. I think it's one of the best action movies ever made.
I: Really? I do, too! I loved it!
M: A lot of people love that movie. But guess what the biggest moneymaking movie of all time is.
I: Was it *Star Wars*? Or maybe *E.T.*?
M: No, it was *Titanic*. It made over 600 million dollars, more than any other film.

I: Really? And what about the most expensive movie ever made?

M: *Titanic*, again . . . at least, to date. It was both the most expensive movie to make and the one that made the most money. I was really surprised.

I: Me, too! Unbelievable! Michael, one of the most fascinating parts of your book was about mistakes that are not caught before a movie is released.

M: Yeah. It's impossible to make a perfect movie. You know there's so much going on in every frame of a movie that mistakes happen. Things are left in that couldn't possibly be correct for the time or place of the movie.

I: OK, like what? Could you give us some examples?

M: Sure. Did you know that in one scene of *Lord of the Rings*, there's a car in a field in the distance?

I: You're kidding! No, I didn't know that, and neither did a lot of *Lord of the Rings* fans, I suspect. And in your book, you talk about watches—it seems a lot of actors and extras forget to take off their watches in movies.

M: Yes, that's true. In fact, the biggest mistake you'll see—if you watch very carefully—is that actors are wearing watches in scenes when they shouldn't.

I: Wow. The editors must be very upset when they see it later.

M: They're definitely upset . . . and so are the directors! In *Titanic* for example, when people were jumping onto the lifeboats, one of them was wearing a digital watch!

I: A digital watch? That's amazing! So, movie fans, do you want to hear more amazing movie facts? Well, so do I! But we have to take a break now—and when we come back, we'll continue our interview with Michael Marksman, author of the new book *Movie Facts for Movie Fans*.

Review 5   Units 17–20

Unit 17, Willpower, Exercise 1, page 94

A: OK, I can start. Um . . . Matthew enjoys playing soccer. He likes most sports, but soccer is his favorite. He gave up playing basketball because he wanted to have more time for soccer.

B: That's good. OK, you used *enjoy* and *give up*. All right, I can go next. Um . . . He learned to play when he was ten. He practiced every day. At first he wasn't very good.

A: OK, and you used *learn* and *practice*. Bob, you go next.

C: OK, he wasn't very good. All right, after a while, he stopped trying because none of his shots went into the goal. He was disappointed and frustrated . . . .

Unit 18, Wave of the future, Exercise 5, page 94

A: Did your parents use to buy records?

B: Yes, they did. They would buy at least one record a month, but now they buy CDs.

A: Do they think CDs are better?

B: Yeah, because the records would get damaged all the time.

A: And what did they do with their old records?

B: They still have them in a box at home. I don't think they'll ever use them again, but they don't want to throw them away.

Unit 19, Made in the U.S.A., Exercise 8, page 95

A: May I help you?

B: Yes, please. What are you selling today?

A: We have beautiful jewelry boxes.

C: What are they made of?

D: They're made of wood and silver.

C: Where are they made?

A: They're made in Maine by a group of artists. Aren't they beautiful?

B: Yes, they are. But what else do you have?

Unit 20, At the movies, Exercise 10, page 95

A: What did you think of *Legally Blonde*?

B: I thought it was really funny. I love comedies.

A: So do I. What did you especially like about it?

B: I especially liked her application video. That was hilarious.

A: I liked that part too. Jennifer, what did you think of *Legally Blonde*?

C: Well, I didn't think it was that funny . . .

World of Music 3   You've Got a Friend

Listening, Exercises 2 and 3, page 96

When you're down and troubled
and you need some love and care
and nothing, nothing is going right.
Close your eyes and think of me
and soon I will be there
to brighten up even your darkest night.

You just call out my name,
and you know wherever I am
I'll come running to see you again.
Winter, spring, summer, or fall,
all you have to do is call
and I'll be there.
You've got a friend.

If the sky above you
grows dark and full of clouds
and that old north wind begins to blow
Keep your head together and call my name out loud
Soon you'll hear me knocking at your door.

You just call out my name,
and you know wherever I am
I'll come running, running, yeah yeah
to see you again.
Winter, spring, summer, or fall
all you have to do is call
and I'll be there, yes, I will.

Now, ain't it good to know that you've got a friend
When people can be so cold?
They'll hurt you, yes and desert you.
And take your soul if you let them.
Ah, but don't you let them.

You just call out my name,
and you know wherever I am
I'll come running, running, yeah, yeah
to see you again.
Winter, spring, summer, or fall,
All you have to do is call.
And, I'll be there, yes, I will.
You've got a friend.
You've got a friend. Yeah, baby.
You've got a friend.
Ain't it good to know you've got a friend.
Ain't it good to know you've got a friend.
Oh, yeah now.
You've got a friend.
Oh, yeah.
You've got a friend.

Unit 21   How polite are you?

Reading, Exercise 4, page 99

[sound of a cell phone ringing]
[sound of a person whistling a tune]
[sound of music from another person's headphones]
[sound of a person banging on a piano]
[sound of a person drumming his or her fingers on a hard surface]
[sound of a person jangling coins in his or her pocket]

Reading from page 99 for the optional Grammar Warm-up

Note: See the Reading on *Student Book* page 99 for the text of the audio.

Pronunciation, Exercises 4 and 5, page 101

Would you
Would you please turn the music down?
Would you mind lowering your voice?
Could you
Could you please stop doing that?
Could you make your dog stop barking?

Unit 22   The art of crime

Getting started, Exercise 2, page 102

robbery
robber
rob (a person or place)
burglary
burglar
burglarize (a place)
mugging
mugger
mug (someone)
scam
con artist
scam (someone)
shoplifting
shoplifter
shoplift (something)
theft
thief
steal (something)

Listening, Exercises 6 and 7, page 103

The Mona Lisa was painted by Leonardo Da Vinci and is probably the world's most famous painting. You can see it in the Louvre, in Paris. But are you sure it was painted by Leonardo Da Vinci?

In 1911 the painting was stolen from the museum. Two years later it was offered to an art dealer in Florence by someone called Vincenzo Perugia for 500,000 lire. The art dealer called the police, and Perugia was arrested. It seems that the painting was in Perugia's apartment for two years. But why?

In fact, the theft was planned by a con artist called Eduardo de Valfierno. He asked Perugia to steal the Mona Lisa. Then six brilliant copies were made and sold to rich collectors. Each collector thought his copy was the original, and when the painting was found, Valfierno simply told them that it was only a copy. Valfierno was paid for the painting six times, and Perugia was never paid for his help.

So the Mona Lisa was returned to the Louvre. But are we sure that the painting in the museum is really the original, and not one of the copies?

Pronunciation, Exercises 4 and 5, page 105

How were the thieves caught?
When was the painting stolen?
Copies of the painting were made.
The copies were sold to collectors.
The original was offered to a dealer.
The painting was returned to the museum.

Unit 23   A balanced life

Listening, Exercise 5, page 107

M = Marta   I = Ian

M: Ian! Come on! It's time to go to the gym. We'll be late.
I: I'm . . . uh . . . I'm not going tonight.
M: Not going?
I: No. I've decided to take the evening off. I think I've been taking on too much recently.
M: But I thought you enjoyed exercising.
I: Well I do, it's just . . .
M: But last week you said you were really into exercising and losing weight.
I: Yeah, but now I can't stand it. In fact, I'm sick of running around the gym.
M: I don't understand.
I: I think I've been taking it too seriously—I need to take a break.

M: This is ridiculous! You'll enjoy it when you get there.
I: Look, honey, I don't mind staying in and taking it easy for a change. You go without me. I'll be OK. Honestly.
M: Hello, yes . . . . yes . . . OK. I'll tell him. Bye.
I: Who was that?
M: It was Dave.
I: Dave?
M: Yeah, he says he has the pizza, and he'll be here in about 20 minutes . . .
I: Oh, really?
M: . . . to watch the basketball game on TV with you. It's not that you can't stand working out—it's just that you love watching basketball!

Pronunciation, Exercises 4 and 5, page 108

I can't stand playing tennis but I don't mind swimming.
She hates watching sports, but she loves practicing yoga.
He likes exercising, but sometimes he needs to take a break.

Unit 24   Digital age

Pronunciation, Exercise 3, page 110

keyboard   digital camera

Pronunciation, Exercise 5, page 110

cell phone	DVD player	remote control
computer	laptop	scanner
digital TV	printer	

Reading from page 111 for the optional Grammar Warm-up

Note: See the Reading on *Student Book* page 111 for the text of the audio.

Review 6   Units 21-24

Unit 21, How polite are you? Exercise 1, page 114

A: OK. So here's how you do this math problem. Remember, A squared plus B squared equals C squared.
B: I'm sorry, I still don't understand. Could you explain it again, please?

Unit 22, The art of crime, Exercise 4, page 114

A: What was broken into?
B: A bakery was broken into.
A: What was stolen?
B: 500 donuts were stolen.
A: Who was attacked?
B: The baker and a watchdog were attacked.

Unit 23, A balanced life, Exercise 6, page 115

A: What do you do?
B: I'm a salesperson at a bookstore.
A: Do you enjoy working there?
B: Yes, most of the time I enjoy it. I'm really into books.
A: Do you like your boss?
B: Well, not much, but I don't mind working for him. He's not at the store much, so it's OK.
A: And what do you do on weekends?
B: I mostly just go out with friends. We really enjoy talking and going to movies.
A: So, would you say you have a balanced life?
B: Yes, I think so.

Unit 24, Digital age, Exercise 10, page 115

A: OK, What do you call a person who flies planes?
B: That's easy. A pilot. Umm, what's the thing that keeps pages together?
C: A paperclip . . .
B: No . . . it keeps them together better than a paper clip . . .
D: Oh, I know. A staple.
B: Yeah. OK, your turn.
D: What do you call the thing that records CDs in your computer?
A: A CD burner.

Unit 25   Arranged marriages

Pronunciation, Exercises 5 and 6, page 117

went out together
They went out together for three years.
during that time
During that time, they got to know each other well.
get upset
At times, they get upset with each other.
get on each other's nerves
Sometimes they get on each other's nerves.
get along well
But most of the time, they get along well.

Listening, Exercises 8 and 9, page 117

M = Monica   C = Carlos
M: Hi, Carlos.
C: Hi, Monica. What's up?
M: I saw a terrific movie last night—*Monsoon Wedding*. You should see it.
C: Really. Why?
M: It's all about families and marriage, and you're getting married soon, right?
C: Yes, next June.

M: Well go see it . . . it's about this young woman, Aditi—oh, it takes place in India. Well, Aditi's parents think it's time for her to get married, and they've found the perfect man for her—an Indian guy who's working in Texas.

C: Her parents are choosing her husband? A guy who lives on the other side of the world?

M: Yes. Arranged marriages are still a tradition in many parts of the world. And it's important for her to marry someone her parents like.

C: Isn't it more important to love the person you're marrying than to please your family?

M: Well, a lot of people who marry for love get divorced, so maybe it's a good idea to let your parents arrange things.

C: OK, so what happens?

M: Well, her parents find this handsome, intelligent man who works in Texas and start to plan their wedding.

C: What?? They start planning a wedding before the couple even meets? It's crazy to get married to someone you don't know.

M: Well, they know his family, and they're sure the two families will get along. In India, it's important for the families to get along, not just the married couple. That way marriages last longer.

C: I still think it's absurd to marry someone you've never even met before.

M: Well, they do meet a few days before the wedding. If the couple doesn't get along, they can always cancel the wedding. But Aditi likes this guy and agrees to have the huge wedding her parents want. There are dozens of bridesmaids and flower girls. It's really a beautiful wedding and a gorgeous movie. I think it's important for you and your fiancée to see it. She'll love it!

C: Why not? We both like romantic movies. But I still think it's a bad idea to get married . . .

Unit 26 Money matters

Reading from page 121 for the optional Grammar Warm-up

Note: See the Reading on *Student Book* page 121 for the text of the audio.

Pronunciation, Exercises 4 and 5, page 122

He sent me a bill.
They owe us money.
I can lend you some money.
We sent them a check.
I gave him a receipt.
Did you buy her a present?

Pronunciation, Exercise 6, page 122

1. I showed him the statement.
2. We owe them money.
3. I gave her a check.
4. Did you give her a receipt?
5. I sent them a bill.
6. I lent him five dollars.

Unit 27 Less is more

Getting started, Exercise 3, page 124

use paper	spend money
use time	save paper
use electricity	save time
use energy	save electricity
use money	save energy
use space	save money
use resources	save space
spend time	save resources

Listening, Exercises 7 and 8, page 125

I = Interviewer   L = Laura

I: Today we are speaking with author Laura Chang. Thank you for joining us, Laura. In your book, you seem to want less of everything!

L: In many ways, I do, yes. Take the work week, and I know this will sound strange, but I say we should work shorter hours . . .

I: That would be popular with many people.

L: Of course, everyone wants to be successful, but people who work the longest hours have more stress, so they often achieve less.

I: Your position, then, is that less is more?

L: Exactly. You know . . . balance is the real answer. People need to find more balance in their lives.

I: Balance?

L: Yes, take sleep, for example. If you don't get enough sleep, you are tired and irritable, you're not very energetic, and not very productive. On the other hand, if you spend too much time sleeping, you're wasting time, and it can actually make you more tired. In general, I think people shouldn't sleep so much.

I: I never find my time sleeping a waste.

L: Well, I find a ten-minute nap in the afternoon gives me more energy than an extra hour in bed at night. You ought to try it.

I: Yes, maybe I should. You also say that we use too much technology.

L: That's right. We shouldn't forget that technology is for saving energy, not wasting it. We should all spend less time at the computer.

I: . . . and should we eat less too?

L: Yes, research shows that monkeys are healthier when they eat half their normal diet. If it works for them, maybe we could try it too.

I: Maybe I should try that. Well, Laura, sorry to stop you . . . I'd like to talk more but we appear to have less time than I thought. Laura Chang, thank you for spending time with us . . . And now, for some more music.

Pronunciation, Exercise 5 and 6, page 127

What should I do?
You should work shorter hours.
You could take an afternoon nap.
You could spend less time at the computer.
You ought to relax more.
You ought to sleep less.

Unit 28 Celebrate

Reading from page 129 for the optional Grammar Warm-up

Note: See the Reading on *Student Book* page 129 for the text of the audio.

Pronunciation, Exercises 4 and 5, page 130

Where would it be?
If you could have a party, where would it be?
I'd have the party at a restaurant.
I wouldn't cook.
We'd have live music.
They'd play salsa.
We'd dance all night.
Everyone would have a great time.

Review 7   Units 25-28

Unit 25, Arranged marriages, Exercise 1, page 132

A: I think it's a good idea to get married to someone when you first fall in love.
B: Really? I think it's crazy to get married until you've had time to get to know each other.
A: I think it's very important for the families of the couple to get along.
B: I disagree. I think it's more important for the couple to get along.

Unit 26, Money matters, Exercise 3, page 132

A: Hi, Paul! I heard you just won a million dollars. Congratulations!
B: Umm. Thanks, umm. I have to be going now . . .
A: Not so fast . . . remember that time 20 years ago when you needed a thousand dollars?
B: Umm, . . . maybe.
A: Well, I lent that money to you, and I was happy to do it. But now, considering that you're a millionaire, I've calculated that you owe me $36,000 with all the interest on the loan. And I could use that money now.
B: Really? Umm, well, I can't . . .
C: Wait, but I need some money, too. I really *need* it for my family . . .

Unit 27, Less is more, Exercise 5, page 133

A: I can't sleep at night. What should I do?
B: Well, you could try exercising more. Then you'll be tired at night.
B: I spend too much money. What should I do?
A: You ought to throw away all your credit cards. That's what I did.

Unit 28, Celebrate, Exercise 7, page 133

A: What if you could live anywhere in the world?
B: If I could live anywhere in the world, I'd live in Hawaii.
A: Why Hawaii?
B: Because I hate cold weather.

World of Music 4   If I Could Turn Back Time

Listening, Exercises 2 and 3, page 134

If I could turn back time
If I could find a way
I'd take back those words that hurt you and you'd stay

I don't know why I did the things I did
I don't know why I said the things I said
Pride's like a knife it can cut deep inside
Words are like weapons, they wound sometimes
I didn't really mean to hurt you
I didn't wanna see you go
I know I made you cry, but baby

CHORUS:
If I could turn back time
If I could find a way,
I'd take back those words that hurt you
and you'd stay
If I could reach the stars
I'd give them all to you
then you'd love me, love me, like you used to do
if I could turn back time

My world was shattered I was torn apart
Like someone took a knife and drove it
deep in my heart
You walked out that door I swore that I didn't care
but I lost everything darling then and there
Too strong to tell you I was sorry

CHORUS

Workbook Audioscript
Based on the Student Audio CD

Unit 1

Listening, Exercises 6 and 7, page 14

Script same as *Student Book* Listening, Exercises 6 and 7, page T154

Pronunciation, Exercises 8 and 9, page 14

Script same as *Student Book* Pronunciation, Exercises 4 and 5, page T154

Unit 2

Listening, Exercises 5 and 6, page 17 (Student CD track 4)

At school, boys are usually messier and more competitive than girls; boys like to win! But girls are often better students. They're more hardworking than boys, and they do more homework. Girls may be more talkative than boys, but boys are noisier. Some doctors believe that baby girls are stronger than baby boys. But by school age, girls aren't as strong as boys. Why? Does society—our family, friends, and teachers—change us?

A lot of people believe that society teaches boys and girls to behave differently. They say that as adults we can change this. The "new man" should cook, take care of the children, and be more cooperative and less aggressive. He should be neater, more emotional, and a better listener. But are these changes possible? Can men be as emotional as women, for example?

Pronunciation, Exercises 7 and 8, page 17 (Student CD track 64)

1. Men are taller than women.
2. Girls aren't as fast as boys.
3. Boys are noisier than girls.
4. Women are more talkative than men.
5. Women are more emotional than men.
6. Men are messier than women.
7. In school, boys aren't as hardworking as girls.
8. Girls aren't as good as boys at soccer.

Unit 3

Listening, Exercises 4 and 5, page 20

Script same as *Student Book* Listening, Exercise 6, page T155

Pronunciation, Exercise 6, page 20

Script same as *Student Book* Pronunciation, Exercise 7, page T155

Pronunciation, Exercise 8, page 20 (Student CD track 9)

The Four Seasons is a luxury hotel just 13 minutes from the international airport. We have 218 guest rooms, including 30 guest suites with balconies. For weddings and other formal occasions, choose from one of our three elegant ballrooms, for a total of 9,650 square feet of luxury dining and dancing.

For your business needs, we offer 15 conference rooms equipped with state-of-the-art audio/visual services, including simultaneous translation. We look forward to welcoming you to the Four Seasons.

Unit 4

Listening, Exercises 5 and 6, page 23

Note: See the Reading, *Student Book* page 15, for the text of the audio.

Pronunciation, Exercises 7 and 8, page 23

Script same as *Student Book* Pronunciation, Exercise 4, page T155

Unit 5

Listening, Exercises 4 and 5, page 28

Script same as *Student Book* Listening, Exercises 5 and 6, page T156

Pronunciation, Exercise 6, page 28

Script same as *Student Book* Pronunciation, Exercise 4, page T157

Pronunciation, Exercise 7, page 28 (Student CD track 65)

1. And who do you have breakfast with?
2. Who uses the phone the most in your house?
3. Who do you call the most?
4. Who do you spend more time with, your mother or your father?

Unit 6

Listening, Exercises 5 and 6, page 31

Script same as *Student Book* Listening, Exercises 9 and 10, page T157

Pronunciation, Exercises 7, 8, and 9, page 31 (Student CD track 66)

fantastic	enormous
packed	crowded
interesting	boiling
fascinating	exhausted
freezing	tired

Unit 7

Listening, Exercises 5 and 6, page 34

(**Note:** See the Reading, *Student Book* page 31, for the text of the audio.)

Pronunciation, Exercises 7 and 8, page 34

Script same as *Student Book* Pronunciation, Exercises 4 and 6, page T157

Unit 8

Listening, Exercises 5 and 6, page 37 (Student CD track 20)

F = Female   M = Male   S = Susan

F: Legal Terms of Endearment

M: These days, it seems like Hollywood stars must sign a prenuptial agreement before they exchange wedding rings.

But times are changing. Prenuptial agreements aren't just for entertainers or millionaires anymore. They can help clarify financial obligations and other responsibilities in any marriage. Bruce Collins and Susan Taylor live in Dayton, Ohio. He is a math teacher, and she is a lawyer. Susan makes a lot more money than Bruce, and Bruce has more free time. So what's in their prenuptial agreement? They agreed that Bruce has to do all the housework and cook dinner. Susan has to pay the bills. And if they get divorced, Bruce can't ask Susan for any money.

S: When I first mentioned the prenuptial agreement, he refused to even talk about it. When I insisted, he even lost his temper and accused me of not trusting him. Finally, we reached an agreement because Bruce understood that we're both sensible people. And sensible people have life insurance, car insurance, and homeowner's insurance. So why shouldn't they have marriage insurance?

Pronunciation, Exercises 7 and 8, page 37 (Student CD track 67)

1. I have to see a doctor.
2. She has to come to the party.
3. They have to do the housework.
4. Who has to do the shopping?
5. He has to give her a lot of money.
6. Do we have to sign an agreement?

Unit 9

Listening, Exercises 5 and 6, page 42 (Student CD track 22)

M = Maria   C = Caller

M: Good morning, Riverside Tours. Maria speaking. How can I help you?

C: I have a reservation for the River Tour next week, and I have a few questions.

M: Yes, of course.

C: Well, first, the departure time—what time does the boat actually head out from Kingston?

M: Nine o'clock, Monday morning. But we ask you to arrive about fifteen minutes before that.

C: OK. So we leave at nine, and how long do we stay at Hampton Court?

M: About four hours—you get off the boat at Hampton Court around ten-thirty. If you like, the guide can show you around, or you can walk around on your own. Then the tour goes on to Richmond Park and Kew Gardens in the afternoon.

C: Oh, that sounds great. What about the evening?

M: There's a walking tour around the local area that starts off from the hotel. Start time is seven-thirty, and it lasts about an hour. It's optional—just tell the guide if you want to go or not.

C: I'm meeting a friend for dinner and he's putting me up for the night, so I think I'll skip the walking tour.

M: No problem. It's entirely optional.

C: What about the next day?

M: Well, on Tuesday, you head out at ten o'clock, and the tour takes you through the heart of London. You go past many famous sites: the Houses of Parliament, the Tate Modern, Shakespeare's Globe Theater . . . they're all listed on your map.

C: Just one more thing . . .

Pronunciation, Exercises 7 and 8, page 42

Script same as *Student Book* Pronunciation, Exercises 4 and 5, page T159

Unit 10

Listening, Exercises 5 and 6, page 45

Script same as *Student Book* Listening, Exercise 7, page T159

Pronunciation, Exercises 7 and 8, page 45

Script same as *Student Book* Pronunciation, Exercises 4, 5, and 6, page T160

Unit 11

Listening, Exercises 5 and 6, page 48

Script same as *Student Book* Listening, Exercises 8 and 9, page T160

Pronunciation, Exercise 7, page 48 (Student CD track 68)

armchair   lamp   table   drapes

Pronunciation, Exercises 8 and 9, page 48 (Student CD track 69)

basket   cabinet   carpet   fireplace
plants   bookcase   rack

Unit 12

Listening, Exercises 5 and 6, page 51

Script same as *Student Book* Listening, Exercises 9 and 10, page T161

Pronunciation, Exercises 7 and 8, page 51

Script same as *Student Book* Pronunciation, Exercises 4 and 5, page T161

Unit 13

Listening, Exercises 5 and 6, page 56

Script same as *Student Book* Reading, Exercise 7, page T162

Pronunciation, Exercises 7 and 8, page 56 (Student CD track 70)

1. I've told this story to many people already.
2. She's visited me several times.
3. They've lived together in this apartment.
4. I've watched her teach dancing.
5. He's played football.

Unit 14

Listening, Exercises 5 and 6, page 59 (Student CD track 33)

J = Jason   M = Maria

J: This is Jason Miller and you're listening to XRT at 96.3 FM, and it's time for our contest *What's That Job?* You will hear someone doing their job. Guess which job it is, and you'll win two movie tickets. Let's go to Maria on line one. Hello, Maria. Are you ready to play?

M: Yes, Jason, I think so . . .

J: Then listen.
[sounds of traffic, background noise, and people walking and talking]

M: Well, the person is somewhere noisy. I hear people walking and someone shouting. The person might work in a train station or an airport. Can I hear a bit more, Jason?

J: OK.
[sound of same background traffic and crowd noise, a whistle plus coins dropping in a fare box, doors shutting, and then traffic noise is muffled]

M: Well, I heard traffic and a whistle. The person is definitely outside somewhere. He might be in a car . . . but he can't be a taxi driver because people don't drop coins in a machine to pay a taxi driver. I think the person must be a bus driver.

J: That's right! . . . a bus driver. Excellent, Maria, you've won two tickets to the movies.

Pronunciation, Exercises 7, 8, and 9, page 59

Script same as *Student Book* Pronunciation, Exercises 4 and 5, page T163

Unit 15

Listening, Exercises 5 and 6, page 62

Note: See the Reading, *Student Book* pages 68 and 69, for the text of the audio.

Pronunciation, Exercises 7 and 8, page 62 (Student CD track 71)

1. I'll always love you.
2. You'll forget me.
3. I'll go to London.
4. I think they'll get married.
5. Do you think it will be too late?
6. She'll marry someone else.
7. She thinks her heart will break.

Unit 16

Listening, Exercises 5 and 6, page 65 (Student CD track 37)

I = Interviewer   J = Joanna

I: For tonight's news spotlight, we're talking to advertising executive Joanna Lindsey about television ads. Good evening, Joanna. Thank you for joining us tonight.

J: Good evening, Jim. It's a pleasure to be here.

I: So, Joanna, when you're creating an ad, where do you start?

J: Well, first we think about the group of people who might want this product. Are they men or women, young or old, how much money do they have?

I: Can you give me an example?

J: Sure. In an ad for an expensive car, we often use young, good-looking men or women who look like they have a lot of money. The message is: "If you're young and successful, this is the car for you."

I: Usually it's the man who drives the car, though, isn't it?

J: That's often true—but not always . . .

I: And usually the man has a good-looking female next to him. So isn't the message really: "If you buy this car, you'll meet a beautiful woman."

J: Not necessarily. Our point is: "if you try our product, you won't regret it." And we don't always use young attractive people to sell things. For example, if the product is sunscreen, we'll probably use a family. Parents worry about their children so the message here is: "Your kids won't get sunburned if you use this sunscreen."

I: OK, families for sunscreen, but what about shampoo?

J: Well, yes, often the message is that you will meet the man or woman of your dreams if your hair is soft and shiny. Will that really happen just because you used a certain shampoo? No, of course not. The messages in ads are often exaggerated. And you know sometimes we use humor to get the message across. People will remember an ad if it's funny.

Pronunciation, Exercises 7 and 8, page 65

Script same as *Student Book* Pronunciation, Exercises 4 and 5, page T164

Unit 17

Listening, Exercises 5 and 6, page 70

Note: See the Reading, *Student Book* page 79, for the text of the audio.

Pronunciation, Exercises 7 and 8, page 70

Script same as *Student Book* Pronunciation, Exercises 4 and 5, page T165

Unit 18

Listening, Exercises 5 and 6, page 73

Script same as *Student Book* Listening, Exercises 5 and 6, page T165

Pronunciation, Exercise 7, page 73 (Student CD track 72)

1. Did you use to work in an office?
2. I didn't use to like vegetables.
3. He didn't use to ride his bicycle to work.
4. They used to take a vacation in Italy every year.
5. Did he use to be so nervous all the time?

Unit 19

Listening, Exercises 5 and 6, page 76

Script same as *Student Book* Listening, Exercises 4 and 5, page T166

Pronunciation, Exercises 7 and 8, page 76

Script same as *Student Book* Pronunciation, Exercise 7, page T166

Pronunciation, Exercise 9, page 76

Script same as *Student Book* Pronunciation, Exercises 8 and 9, page T166

Unit 20

Listening, Exercises 5 and 6, page 79 (Student CD track 47)

I = Interviewer   M = Michael

I: Our guest today is Michael Marksman, who has just written a fascinating book, *Movie Facts for Movie Fans*. You're a movie fan, Michael . . . so what's your all-time favorite movie?

M: Hmm. That's a tough question. I can't really answer it.

I: You know what? I can't answer that question, either! OK. Let me be more specific: What's your favorite action movie?

M: That's easy! The original *Star Wars* movie. I think it's one of the best action movies ever made.

I: Really? I do, too! I loved it!

M: A lot of people love that movie. But guess what the biggest moneymaking movie of all time is.

I: Was it *Star Wars*? Or maybe *E.T.*?

M: No, it was *Titanic*. It made over 600 million dollars, more than any other film.

I: Really? And what about the most expensive movie ever made?

M: *Titanic*, again . . . at least, to date. It was both the most expensive movie to make and the one that made the most money. I was really surprised.

I: Me, too! Unbelievable! Michael, one of the most fascinating parts of your book was about mistakes.

M: Yeah. It's impossible to make a perfect movie.

I: Could you give us some examples?

M: Sure. Did you know that in one scene of *Lord of the Rings*, there's a car in a field in the distance?

I: You're kidding! No, I didn't know that, and neither did a lot of *Lord of the Rings* fans, I suspect. And in your book, you talk about watches—it seems a lot of actors and extras forget to take off their watches in movies.

M: Yes, that's true. In fact, the biggest mistake you'll see—if you watch very carefully—is that actors are wearing watches in scenes when they shouldn't.

I: Wow. The editor must be very upset when he or she sees it later.

M: They're definitely upset . . . and so are the directors! In *Titanic* for example, when people were jumping onto the lifeboats, one of them was wearing a digital watch!

I: A digital watch? That's amazing!

Pronunciation, Exercises 6 and 7, page 79

Script same as *Student Book* Pronunciation, Exercises 2 and 3, page T00

Unit 21

Listening, Exercises 5 and 6, page 84 (Student CD track 48)

A: Excuse Me…
  One
B: You're on a bus. The person next to you is playing loud music. What do you say?
C: A. Would you mind turning the music down, please?
  B. Driver! Can you tell this guy that it's illegal to play music on the bus?
  C. You're being very rude!
A: Two
B: You're on a train. The passenger is kicking your seat. What do you say?
C: A. Could you stop doing that, please? I can't concentrate.
  B. Conductor! He's kicking my chair!
  C. Stop that now!
A: Three
B: You're having a romantic dinner in a restaurant. A man near you is speaking loudly on his cell phone. What do you say?
C: A. Would you mind lowering your voice, please?
  B. Waiter! Please tell this man to go outside.
  C. We're trying to have a nice, quiet dinner, and you're disturbing us.

Pronunciation, Exercises 7 and 8, page 84

Script same as *Student Book* Pronunciation, Exercises 4 and 5, page T168

Unit 22

Listening, Exercises 6 and 7, page 87

Script same as *Student Book* Listening, Exercises 6 and 7, page T168

Pronunciation, Exercises 7 and 8, page 87

Script same as *Student Book* Pronunciation, Exercises 4 and 5, page T168

Unit 23

Listening, Exercises 5 and 6, page 90

Script same as *Student Book* Listening, Exercise 5, page T168

Pronunciation, Exercises 7 and 8, page 90

Script same as *Student Book* Pronunciation, Exercises 4 and 5, page T169

Unit 24

Listening, Exercises 5 and 6, page 93 (Student CD track 55)

A: How does digital TV work?
B: As you know, a TV studio is a place where they produce TV programs. These programs are "the information" sent from the TV studio to our homes. Traditional TV needs a lot of space to send the information. With digital systems, the information is in digital form and it can be compressed, so the system can send and receive more information.
  Additionally, digital TV systems only send the parts of the picture that change. So they send a picture of a building once, because it doesn't move. But they send a lot of pictures of people who are walking or cars that are moving around that building.
A: Do I need a special TV?
B: In areas where the service is available, you need either a special TV or a special box that can put the pictures together for your non-digital TV. Then you can watch your favorite program and even "talk" to the station.

Pronunciation, Exercises 7 and 8, page 93

Script same as *Student Book* Pronunciation Exercises 3 and 5, page T169

Unit 25

Listening, Exercises 5 and 6, page 98 (Student CD track 57)

M = Monica   C = Carlos

M: Hi, Carlos.
C: Hi, Monica. What's up?
M: I saw a terrific movie last night—*Monsoon Wedding*. You should see it. . . . it's about this young woman, Aditi—oh, it takes place in India. Well, Aditi's parents think it's time for her to get married, and they've found the perfect man for her—an Indian guy who is working in Texas.
C: Her parents are choosing her husband? A guy who lives on the other side of the world?
M: Yes. Arranged marriages are still a tradition in many parts of the world. And it's important for her to marry someone her parents like.
C: Isn't it more important to love the person you're marrying than to please your family?
M: Well, a lot of people who marry for love get divorced, so maybe it's a good idea to let your parents arrange things.

C: OK, so what happens?

M: Well, her parents find this handsome, intelligent man who works in Texas and start to plan their wedding.

C: What?? They start planning a wedding before the couple even meets? It's crazy to get married to someone you don't know.

M: Well, they know his family, and they're sure the two families will get along. In India, it's important for the families to get along, not just the married couple. That way, marriages last longer.

C: I still think it's absurd to marry someone you've never even met before.

Pronunciation Exercises 7 and 8, page 98 (Student CD track 73)

1. They went out together for three years.
2. Sometimes they get on each other's nerves.
3. They got to know each other well.
4. But most of the time, they get along well.
5. She got married in September.

Unit 26

Listening, Exercises 5 and 6, page 101 (Student CD track 58)

A: Welcome to DirBanking.

B: Tired of paying high interest rates on loans?
   Still waiting for your bank to send you a statement?
   Bored with spending your lunch break waiting in line at the bank?
   Here at DirBanking, we save you time and money. You can access your account 24 hours a day, 7 days a week.

A: We provide full banking services to you through your telephone, computer, or cell phone.
   We can lend you money at the best interest rates.
   We can give you advice on buying and selling stocks online.
   We bring financial security to you and your family.
   We offer you first-class service.
   We give you peace of mind.

B: Remember: DirBanking promises you first-class banking—direct to you, wherever you are.

Pronunciation, Exercises 7 and 8, page 101

Script same as *Student Book* Pronunciation, Exercises 4 and 5, page T170

Unit 27

Listening, Exercises 5 and 6, page 104 (Student CD track 60)

L = Laura   I = Interviewer

I: Today we are speaking with author Laura Chang. Thank you for joining us today. Laura, in your book, you seem to want less of everything!

L: In many ways, I do, yes. Take the work week, and I know this will sound strange, but I say we should work shorter hours . . .

I: That would be popular with many people.

L: Exactly. You know . . . balance is the real answer. People need to find more balance in their lives.

I: Balance?

L: Yes, take sleep, for example. If you don't get enough sleep, you are tired and irritable, you're not very energetic, and not very productive. On the other hand, if you spend too much time sleeping, you're wasting time, and it can actually make you more tired. In general, I think people shouldn't sleep so much.

I: I never find my time sleeping a waste. You also say that we use too much technology.

L: That's right. We shouldn't forget that technology is for saving energy, not wasting it. We should all spend less time at the computer.

I: . . . and should we eat less too?

L: Yes, research shows that monkeys are healthier when they eat half their normal diet. If it works for them, maybe we could try it too.

I: Maybe I should try that.

Pronunciation Exercises 7 and 8, page 104

Script same as *Student Book* Pronunciation, Exercises 5 and 6, page T171

Unit 28

Listening, Exercises 5 and 6, page 107

Note: See the Reading, *Student Book* page 129, for the text of the audio.

Pronunciation, Exercises 7 and 8, page 107

Script same as *Student Book* Pronunciation, Exercises 4 and 6, page T171

Workbook Answer Key

Unit 1

Vocabulary, Exercise 1
1. The weather has been really wonderful. D
2. That's a great scarf! C
3. I'd like you to meet my friend Nadia. B
4. This is my husband, Martin. B
5. Goodbye. E
6. That was a fun party. C
7. Hi, Doug, how's it going? A
8. See you later. E
9. Hello, Maria. How are you doing? A
10. Did you watch the show about Alaska last night? D

Vocabulary, Exercise 2
1. Do you have time for coffee?
2. Hey, that's a great tie.
3. OK, see you later.
4. I'm busy, but everything is fine.
5. Hi, Nelson, how are you doing?
6. Thanks. It was a present from my wife.
7. Sorry, but I'm late for an appointment.
8. OK, goodbye.

Vocabulary, Exercise 3
A: Hi, Nelson, how are you doing?
B: I'm busy, but everything is fine.
A: Hey, that's a great tie.
B: Thanks. It was a present from my wife.
A: Do you have time for coffee?
B: Sorry, I'm late for an appointment.
A: OK, see you later.
B: OK, goodbye.

Grammar, Exercise 4
1. live
2. work
3. grow
4. raise
5. are thinking
6. is getting
7. are waiting
8. are not thinking
9. are planning
10. are thinking
11. go
12. have

Grammar, Exercise 5
1. are you doing
2. don't have
3. 's working
4. wants
5. works
6. 's taking
7. goes
8. 's painting
9. 's helping
10. doesn't have
11. 'm beginning
12. don't have

Listening, Exercise 6
4 talk about the weather
2 compliment
5 make plans to meet later
1 greet
6 end the conversation
3 introduce

Listening, Exercise 7
1. He lives in New York.
2. He is visiting an old friend.
3. She's doing really well.
4. He's still working at Green Advertising.
5. She is working with Bernardo.
6. She's doing her master's degree in web design.

Pronunciation, Exercise 8
1. <u>How</u> are you <u>doing</u>?
2. <u>Great</u>. <u>What</u> about <u>you</u>?
3. So, <u>how</u> do you like Califo<u>rn</u>ia?
4. It's <u>great</u>. I <u>love</u> the <u>weather</u> here.
5. It was <u>good</u> to see you again.
6. <u>Why</u> don't you <u>give</u> me a <u>call</u>?

Unit 2

Vocabulary, Exercise 1
1. competitive
2. cooperative
3. messy
4. emotional
5. noisy
6. aggressive
7. talkative
8. hardworking

Vocabulary, Exercise 2
1. hardworking
2. competitive
3. aggressive
4. noisy
5. talkative
6. messy

Grammar, Exercise 3
1. Alex is more cooperative than Silvia.
2. Alex is more competitive than Silvia.
3. Alex is more hardworking than Silvia.
4. Silvia is messier than Alex.
5. Alex is more talkative than Silvia.
6. Silvia is more emotional than Alex.

Grammar, Exercise 4
1. Silvia isn't as cooperative as Alex.
2. Silvia isn't as competitive as Alex.
3. Silvia isn't as hardworking as Alex.
4. Alex isn't as messy as Silvia.
5. Silvia isn't as talkative as Alex.
6. Alex isn't as emotional as Silvia.

Listening, Exercise 5
1. Boys
2. Boys
3. Girls
4. Girls
5. Girls
6. Boys
7. Girls
8. Boys

Listening, Exercise 6
1. more cooperative
2. less aggressive
3. neater
4. more emotional
5. better listener

Pronunciation, Exercise 7
1. taller than
2. as fast as
3. noisier than
4. more talkative than
5. more emotional than
6. messier than
7. as hardworking as
8. as good as

Unit 3

Vocabulary, Exercise 1

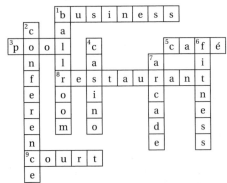

Grammar, Exercise 2

1. How many guest rooms does the hotel have?
2. How much does a single room without a balcony cost?
3. Does the hotel have a restaurant?
4. Does the hotel provide free shuttle service from the train station?
5. Does the hotel have a swimming pool or a fitness center?
6. Do the rooms come with Internet access?

Grammar, Exercise 3

1. The hotel has 45 guest rooms.
2. A single room without a balcony costs $195.
3. No, it doesn't, (but there are restaurants nearby).
4. Yes, it does.
5. No, it doesn't have a swimming pool, but it has a fitness center.
6. No, the rooms don't have Internet access, (but there is Internet access in the business center).

Listening, Exercise 4

58 hotels in over 27 countries
14,850 rooms
26,000 employees
Premier Suite—ocean view—$1,300
Deluxe double—without ocean view—$550

Listening, Exercise 5

Name: Lisa and Peter Murphy
City: Miami
Dates: Check in: May 26th
       Check out: May 28th
Room: Deluxe double
Rate: $550
Note: Guests celebrating their anniversary

Pronunciation, Exercise 6

1. eighty   eighteen
2. forty   fourteen
3. sixty   sixteen

Pronunciation, Exercise 8

1. 13   3. 30   5. 9,650
2. 218   4. 3   6. 15

Unit 4

Vocabulary, Exercise 1

```
A S L M O U H L L B
E O D A D H E S I A
A R B S S A A T E C
R E S T E N D O A S
A T S I N E A M R O
C H V T H R C M M R
H R (C O L D) H T T
E O U A C H E H C E
O A L T B A L A M O
L T (B A C K A C H E)
E I U B (R A S H) Y M
  T Y P M U S S E P L
```

Vocabulary, Exercise 2

1. earache   4. stomachache   7. sore throat
2. headache   5. rash
3. backache   6. cold

Grammar, Exercise 3

1. frustrated   5. bored   9. frightening
2. depressed   6. exciting   10. surprised
3. irritated   7. interesting
4. tired   8. annoying

Grammar, Exercise 4

I feel so ~~tiring~~ **tired** lately. Even getting up in the morning and taking a shower is tiring for me. I'm just not ~~interesting~~ **interested** in anything anymore. I don't have any energy, and the situation is getting really ~~annoyed~~ **annoying**. It's ~~frustrated~~ **frustrating** to me, and I'm starting to get depressed. I'm worried that I might lose my job. I just don't know what to do. I'm too ~~embarrassing~~ **embarrassed** to talk to anyone about this problem. Can you help me?

Listening, Exercise 5

1. Sarah—depressed   3. Fabio—annoyed
2. Silvia—embarrassed

Listening, Exercise 6

Fabio had cold symptoms because he was allergic to pollen.
Silvia had a rash because she was allergic to animals.
Sarah had headaches because she was allergic to chocolate.

Pronunciation, Exercise 7

excited   disappointed   frustrated   interested

Unit 5

Vocabulary, Exercise 1

1. a meeting   4. time   7. a meeting
2. a movie   5. a phone   8. an appointment
3. a letter   6. bills

Vocabulary, Exercise 2

1. pay   3. hire   5. take   7. take out
2. send   4. make   6. spend   8. deliver

Grammar, Exercise 3

1. Who does Jim argue with?
2. Who is never late for class?
3. Who catches the 8:40 bus?
4. Who gets up at 7:00 A.M.?
5. Who does Jim get angry with?
6. Who spends hours in the bathroom?
7. Who tells Alicia and Jim to be quiet?

Listening, Exercise 4

1. It's more memorable and original.
2. Ron composes for (choose any two) a birthday, anniversary, office party, holiday.
3. It's the agency Ron works for.
4. Ron's wife, Mary, takes pictures.
5. No one forgets a singing telegram.

Listening, Exercise 5

1. Is it expensive to send someone a singing telegram?
2. So who hires you?
3. What do I do?
4. And who do I pay?
5. Who helps you?
6. Do you get tired of your job?

Pronunciation, Exercise 6

first, I

Pronunciation, Exercise 7
1. breakfast
2. phone
3. call
4. spend, mother, father

Unit 6
Vocabulary, Exercise 1
1. big, enormous
2. tired, exhausted
3. bad, awful
4. cold, freezing
5. good, fantastic
6. crowded, packed
7. hot, boiling

Vocabulary, Exercise 2
1. really
2. absolutely
3. very, really
4. very, really
5. absolutely
6. absolutely, really
7. absolutely, really

Grammar, Exercise 3
1. were traveling
2. was snowing
3. went
4. began
5. became
6. was carrying
7. was digging
8. felt
9. stopped
10. realized
11. were shouting
12. was blowing
13. did not hear
14. began
15. heard
16. thought
17. came
18. found
19. shouted (was shouting)

Grammar, Exercise 4
1. They were traveling in Antarctica.
2. It was snowing.
3. He was carrying only one tool.
4. They were shouting and looking for him.
5. He shouted, "I'm alive! I'm alive!"

Listening, Exercise 5
absolutely fantastic

Listening, Exercise 6
1. F Sara went to Rio de Janeiro, Brazil, on her vacation.
2. F The tourists were waiting for Carnaval.
3. F Brazil is absolutely boiling in February.
4. F The Sambadrome is an enormous stadium.
5. F The rain stopped. / It stopped raining.
6. F The Carnaval parade started on time.
7. T

Pronunciation, Exercise 7
fantastic 3
packed 1
interesting 3
fascinating 4
freezing 2
enormous 3
crowded 2
boiling 2
exhausted 3
tired 1

Pronunciation, Exercise 8
fan<u>tas</u>tic
<u>packed</u>
<u>in</u>teresting
<u>fas</u>cinating
<u>free</u>zing
e<u>nor</u>mous
<u>crow</u>ded
<u>boi</u>ling
ex<u>haus</u>ted
<u>tired</u>

Unit 7
Vocabulary, Exercise 1
1. formal
2. rude
3. romantic
4. spicy
5. courteous

Vocabulary, Exercise 2
1. elegant
2. romantic
3. low-fat
4. healthful
5. casual
6. rude
7. bland
8. courteous

Grammar, Exercise 3
1. wasn't cold enough to be safe to drink
2. too spicy for the children
3. too greasy for me
4. do enough exercise
5. quiet enough for a business lunch
6. too strong for me to drink
7. not formal enough for a business dinner

Grammar, Exercise 4
We went to City Escapes tonight and didn't have a very good time. First, we had to wait for a table because the place is small. There ~~is enough room~~ **isn't enough room** between the tables, so you don't have any privacy when you speak. Then came the food. The fish was not ~~enough fresh~~ **fresh enough**, it didn't have ~~salt enough~~ **enough salt**, and it was too cooked. To make things worse, the tea wasn't ~~enough hot~~ **hot enough**. I know I shouldn't complain about prices because I didn't pay, but everything was ~~too much expensive~~ **much too expensive**. The service wasn't very good either. The restaurant doesn't have ~~waiters enough~~ **enough waiters**, and they weren't ~~enough attentive~~ **attentive enough**. The manager must not be ~~enough strict~~ **strict enough** with them. When we complained, the manager did give us free desserts, but they were too sweet!

Listening, Exercise 5
fried calamari, cheesecake, chicken, double chocolate cake, fruit salad, Mexican appetizers, stuffed mushrooms

Listening, Exercise 6
1. quiet enough
2. too complicated
3. large enough
4. too spicy
5. not enough

Pronunciation, Exercise 7
casu(a)l nutrio(us) healthf(u)l indiffer(e)nt
p(o)lite form(a)l el(e)gant courte(ou)s

Unit 8
Vocabulary, Exercise 1
1. a job
2. the bills
3. a decision
4. an agreement
5. danger
6. an agreement
7. a decision
8. problems

Vocabulary, Exercise 2
1. exchanged wedding rings
2. take care of our (the) financial obligations
3. do/take care of the housework
4. loses his temper
5. sign/have a prenuptial agreement
6. sign a contract

Grammar, Exercise 3
1. You can't buy the tickets online.
2. I have to get up at 6 A.M. every day.
3. You don't have to buy the tickets in advance.
4. What time do you have to get up in the morning?
5. If the bride signs a prenuptial agreement, the groom has to sign it, too.
6. In many countries, you can't get married before you're eighteen.
7. Not every contract has to be written by a lawyer, but it's always good advice to contact one for any legal matter.

Grammar, Exercise 4
1. You can't talk.
2. You must turn right.
3. You can't ride a bicycle.
4. You must stop.
5. You can't park here.
6. You can't fish here.
7. You can't enter.
8. You must buckle your seat belt.

Listening, Exercise 5
Do the housework, cook dinner—Bruce
Pay the bills—Susan

Listening, Exercise 6
1. F Prenuptial agreements are not only for very rich people.
2. F Susan makes more money than Bruce.
3. F Bruce is a math teacher, and Susan is a lawyer.
4. F Bruce can't ask Susan for money.
5. T
6. T

Pronunciation, Exercise 7
1. I have to
2. She has to
3. They have to
4. Who has to
5. He has to
6. Do we have to

Unit 9

Vocabulary, Exercise 1
1. broke down
2. head out
3. put us up
4. show us around
5. went on
6. started off
7. got off

Vocabulary, Exercise 2
1. head out
2. broke down
3. got off
4. show us around
5. put us up
6. went on

Grammar, Exercise 3
1. are you doing
2. am/'m going
3. are you seeing
4. starts
5. am/'m working
6. am/'m leaving
7. Are you coming
8. doesn't leave
9. are you landing
10. Is someone meeting

Grammar, Exercise 4
Guess what! ~~I go~~ **I'm going** to Seattle with my friends, Mon and Frank, on Saturday. ~~We take~~ **We're taking** a bus. It's a long trip—about 6 hours. The bus ~~is leaving~~ **leaves** at 11:00 and ~~we're arriving~~ **we arrive** in Seattle at 5:00.

In Seattle, ~~we stay~~ **we're staying** at a hotel near the Space Needle. The first morning, ~~we take~~ **we're taking** a walking tour of different neighborhoods. In the afternoon, we're going to the Pike Place Market. After that, we're having coffee at the first Starbuck's! For dinner, ~~we eat~~ **we're eating** at a great sushi bar. Then ~~we meet~~ **we're meeting** friends of Mon's in the Capitol Hill district. There are a lot of music clubs there.

The next day, ~~we visit~~ **we're visiting** the Space Needle, the Pacific Science Center, and Experience Music Project. ~~We have~~ **We're having** dinner that night at a restaurant that Mon's friends recommended. If we're not too tired, we're going out to a dance club after dinner.

Listening, Exercise 5
6 go to the theater
4 meet Raul for dinner
1 head out from Kingston
3 see Richmond Park and Kew Gardens
5 go past the Houses of Parliament, Tate Modern, and Globe Theatre
2 tour Hampton Court

Listening, Exercise 6
1. a   2. a   3. b   4. a

Pronunciation, Exercise 7
head out   show us around   me up
get off   go on

Unit 10

Vocabulary, Exercise 1
1. no trouble
2. tough
3. a piece of cake
4. complicated
5. manageable

Vocabulary, Exercise 2
1. impossible
2. complicated
3. a piece of cake
4. no trouble
5. manageable
6. no trouble
7. simple
8. tough

Grammar, Exercise 3
1. She can write with either hand.
2. My dad is able to speak five languages.
3. We haven't managed to see the baby yet.
4. The weather was bad, so I couldn't take any photos.
5. It was difficult, but I was able to do it.
6. I was able to swim when I was four.

Grammar, Exercise 4
1. Are . . . able to find
2. Are . . . able to fit
3. can help
4. couldn't climb
5. couldn't fit
6. couldn't join
7. can exercise

Listening, Exercise 5
A. 3   B. 2   C. 1   D. 4

Listening, Exercise 6
1. Throwing the ball was *easy* for Mike.
2. Writing was *challenging* for Juliana.
3. Mike thinks that using the scissors was *straightforward*.
4. Drawing was *simple* for Mike.
5. Drawing was *complicated* for Juliana.

Pronunciation, Exercise 7
1. can
2. can't
3. could
4. couldn't
5. can
6. could
7. can
8. couldn't
9. can't
10. can

Unit 11

Vocabulary, Exercise 1
1 = soFa; 2 = pictUre; 3 = aRmchair;
4 = wiNdow; 5 = fIreplace; 6 = Table;
7 = rUg; 8 = thRow pillow; 9 = bookcasE
(Caps indicate letters in gray area to spell "furniture.")

Vocabulary, Exercise 2
1. rugs
2. pictures
3. windows
4. sofa
5. Bookcases
6. table
7. armchair
8. fireplace
9. throw pillows

Grammar, Exercise 3
1. has installed, has stocked
2. have moved
3. has hung
4. has bought, has placed

Grammar, Exercise 4
1. How many feng shui consultations have you done?
2. I've done so many that I can't remember.
3. I see that you've brought four crystals into the studio today.
4. It's worked very well for me on other interviews.
5. What have scientists said about the power of crystals?
6. The scientific community hasn't given an opinion.

Listening, Exercise 5

Room change	Pedro's reaction	Carla's reaction
Floor	+	+
Walls	+	–
Drapes	+	?
Sofa	+	?
Bookcase	?	+

Listening, Exercise 6
1. They've redecorated
2. They've refinished
3. They've made
4. They've moved
5. They've bought
6. They're thrown away
7. They've put

Pronunciation, Exercise 8
bāsket   câbinet   cârpet   fireplāce
plānts   bookcāse   rāck

Unit 12

Vocabulary, Exercise 1
1. on
2. on
3. on, at
4. (no preposition), at
5. (no preposition)
6. in
7. at, (no preposition)

Vocabulary, Exercise 2
It was good to talk to you ~~on~~ last Friday, and I would like to meet again ~~in~~ on Thursday afternoon ~~on~~ at about 3 P.M. Or would it be better for you to meet ~~at~~ in the morning?

Can you call me ~~in~~ this afternoon at my office? I usually leave at 6:30 P.M. We need to talk about the next sales meeting. As you may know, our sales meetings are ~~on~~ in February, and we need to discuss some details.

I can't believe it's New Year's Day on Wednesday. I'll see ~~you~~ the next year!

Grammar, Exercise 3
1. might, might
2. could, couldn't
3. may not / might not, could, may not / might not
4. may / might, may / might
5. may / might

Grammar, Exercise 4
1. may / might
2. couldn't
3. might not
4. may / might
5. may / might, may / might

Listening, Exercise 5
departure time   sightseeing tour
arrival time   restaurant for dinner

Listening, Exercise 6
1. b   2. a   3. a   4. b   5. b   6. a

Pronunciation, Exercise 7
1. at ten
2. at four in the afternoon
3. in the morning
4. at noon on Sunday
5. on Tuesday
6. at our hotel in the evening

Unit 13

Vocabulary, Exercise 1

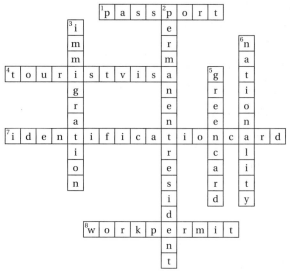

Vocabulary, Exercise 2
1. green card
2. tourist visa
3. immigration
4. identification card
5. passport
6. nationality
7. work permit
8. permanent resident

Grammar, Exercise 3
1. since   3. since   5. for, since
2. For   4. Since, for 6. For

Grammar, Exercise 4
1. Peter has lived in New York since 1998.
2. Noriko has been in the U.S. for two months.
3. Susana has had a black leather jacket for four years.
4. Victor has studied music since he was five.
5. Patricia has known Tim since 2001.
6. Lucy has had her new apartment for a week.
7. I've been a teacher since 1995.
8. Lorna and Sam have been married for a few months. / Lorna has been married for a few months.

Listening, Exercise 5
a. 4   b. 5   c. 1   d. 6   e. 2   f. 3

Listening, Exercise 6
1. Kate has been in the U.S. for eight months.
2. She has been in New York for five months.
3. She was staying in Los Angeles.
4. Kate has known Rod for four months (since December).
5. She has been in love with him since she saw him at a party.

Pronunciation, Exercise 7
1. I've told this story to many people already.
2. She's visited me several times.
3. They've lived together in this apartment.
4. I've watched her teach dancing.
5. He's played football.

Unit 14

Vocabulary, Exercise 1
1. scream   3. clap   5. laugh   7. shout
2. yawn   4. whistle   6. cheer   8. cry

Vocabulary, Exercise 2
1. cheered   3. yawned   5. clapped
2. screamed   4. cried   6. laugh

Grammar, Exercise 3
1. She can't be over 60 years old.
2. She must be Australian.
3. This might be the right stop.
4. He can't be American.
5. Jackie must be rich.
6. Chuck might be sick.

Grammar, Exercise 4
1. must   3. might   5. can't   7. must
2. might   4. must   6. must

Listening, Exercise 5
1, 2, 4, 6

Listening, Exercise 6
1. a   2. b   3. b   4. a

Pronunciation, Exercise 7
1. might   3. must   5. can't
2. can't   4. might   6. must

Pronunciation, Exercise 8
1. He migh‍t be at an airport.
2. He can'‍t be a taxi driver.
3. He mus‍t be a bus driver.
4. She migh‍t be British.
5. No, she can'‍t be.
6. Then she mus‍t be Australian.

Unit 15

Vocabulary, Exercise 1

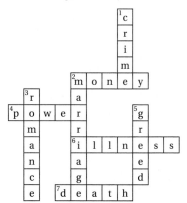

Vocabulary, Exercise 2
1. marriage   3. greed   5. illness   7. crime
2. money   4. power   6. romance

Grammar, Exercise 3
1. will move   5. will love   9. will notice
2. will be   6. will make   10. will need
3. won't have   7. won't worry
4. will fall   8. will feel

Grammar, Exercise 4
1. thinks I'll get a job in Atlanta
2. doesn't think I'll be happy in my job
3. thinks I'll quit my job and move to Paris
4. thinks I'll meet someone there and fall in love
5. thinks I'll return home alone
6. doesn't think we'll see each other for six months
7. doesn't think we'll (ever) be happy until we see each other again

Listening, Exercise 5
Nina emails Sanjay.   3
Nina's parents tell her to go to London.   2
Nina meets Sanjay at a soccer game in Mumbai.   1
Sanjay tells Nina that she should forget him.   6
Ravi asks Nina to marry him.   4
Nina gets an offer to work in a soap opera.   5

Listening, Exercise 6
1. a   2. b   3. b   4. a

Pronunciation, Exercise 7
1. I'll   3. I'll   5. it will   7. will
2. You'll   4. they'll   6. 'll

Unit 16

Vocabulary, Exercise 1
1. fast   3. fast   5. reliable
2. soft   4. healthy   6. soft

Vocabulary, Exercise 2
1. delicious   3. fresh   5. reliable
2. fast   4. shiny   6. healthy

Grammar, Exercise 3
1. What will she do if she gets sick?
   If she gets sick, she'll cancel her trip.
2. What will happen if she loses her passport?
   If she loses her passport, she'll go to the embassy.
3. If Jack is late, will you be angry?
   No, but if he doesn't call me, I won't wait for him.
4. If Nancy's car doesn't start, what will she do?
   She'll call us if that happens.
5. If Pat asks you to come to her party, will you go?
   Yes. And if I go, will you come with me?

Grammar, Exercise 4
1. don't rest, will get   5. doesn't get, will be
2. don't study, will fail   6. he'll lose weight, eats
3. won't be able, drink   7. will go away, change
4. will be, rinse   8. take, will feel

Listening, Exercise 5
car   sunscreen   shampoo

Listening, Exercise 6
1. buy, 'll meet   3. won't get, use
2. try, won't regret   4. will remember, if it's

Pronunciation, Exercise 7
1. If you buy this <u>car</u>, you'll meet a beautiful <u>woman</u>.
2. If the ad is <u>funny</u>, people will <u>remember</u> it.
3. If you use this <u>sunscreen</u>, your kids won't get <u>sunburned</u>.
4. If you try our <u>product</u>, you won't <u>regret</u> it.

Unit 17

Vocabulary, Exercise 1
1. turn
2. Cut
3. Throw
4. Take
5. Keep
6. Cut
7. Give

Vocabulary, Exercise 2
1. take up
2. cut down / cut back
3. cut back / cut down
4. gave up
5. turn down
6. throw away
7. keep on

Grammar, Exercise 3
1. reading
2. to learn
3. to visit
4. attending, being
5. to talk
6. to be, eating
7. staying, drinking

Grammar, Exercise 4
1. I want to take up yoga next year.
2. I need to cut down on the amount of coffee I drink.
3. Will you keep on taking Spanish classes?
4. Mary and John gave up watching TV.
5. If Lucy doesn't cut back on spending money, she'll be in trouble.
6. We should keep on calling her even if she never calls us back.

Listening, Exercise 5
1. have stopped eating
2. love buying
3. dislikes going
4. don't enjoy exercising; want to get

Listening, Exercise 6
1. throw away, give up
2. cut down
3. take up
4. get out of, keep on

Pronunciation, Exercise 7
1. want to
2. want to
3. need to
4. decided to
5. learned to
6. decided to
7. wanted to
8. needed to

Unit 18

Vocabulary, Exercise 1
1. c   2. e   3. b   4. f   5. d   6. a

Vocabulary, Exercise 2
1. Renewable resources
2. Instant messaging
3. Hybrid cars
4. Telecommuting
5. Genetic engineering
6. Alternative medicine

Grammar, Exercise 3
1. used to eat, would . . . start
2. used to write, would go
3. didn't use to have, would get up / used to get up
4. used to be, would dream
5. didn't use to telecommute, would drive

Grammar, Exercise 4
1. What time did you use to go to bed when you were five?
   What time would you go to bed when you were five?
2. I used to live in Brazil when I was a child.
3. Before she went on a diet, she used to eat a chocolate bar every afternoon.
   Before she went on a diet, she would eat a chocolate bar every afternoon.
4. I used to hate anchovies, but now I like them.
5. He didn't use to go out much, but now he's never at home!
6. Didn't Sara use to leave the office early every day?

Listening, Exercise 5
1. books and magazines
2. telecommuting
3. solar panels
4. hybrid car

Listening, Exercise 6
1. used to think
2. wouldn't stop
3. would
4. used to think
5. would buy

Pronunciation, Exercise 7
1. Did you use to
2. I didn't use to
3. He didn't use to
4. They used to
5. Did he use to

Unit 19

Vocabulary, Exercise 1
1. leather gloves
2. pewter tray
3. gold watch
4. glass vase
5. wood picture frame
6. cotton dress
7. lycra bicycling shorts
8. silver earrings

Vocabulary, Exercise 2
1. Pewter
2. gold
3. Lycra
4. silver
5. wood
6. leather
7. cotton
8. glass

Grammar, Exercise 3
1. is made
2. is imported
3. sell
4. is made
5. buys
6. don't sell
7. serve
8. is bought and sold

Grammar, Exercise 4
1. Harley Davidson motorcycles are made in the United States.
2. Where is most of the world's gold mined?
3. About one-third of the world's gold is mined in South Africa.
4. Brazilian coffee is sold all over the world.
5. Is a lot of chocolate made in Venezuela?
6. Some of the most reliable cars are made in Japan and Korea.
7. The World Cup trophy is made out of solid 18-carat gold.
8. Are Mexican avocados sold in California grocery stores?

Listening, Exercise 5
1. mirrors, $100   2. boxes, $50   3. earrings, $25

Listening, Exercise 6
1. The mirrors are ~~painted~~ **made** in Holland.
2. The mirrors are ~~hand painted~~ **handmade** by a small company.
3. The boxes are sold in big stores for ~~$100~~ **$75** each.
4. The boxes are made of ~~silver~~ **wood**.
5. The ~~earrings~~ **boxes** are made in Morocco.
6. All the silver jewelry is ~~exported~~ **imported** ~~to~~ **from** Mexico.

Pronunciation, Exercise 8
1. cotto̸n
2. woode̸n
3. didn't
4. meta̸l
5. sanda̸ls
6. candle̸sticks

Unit 20

Vocabulary, Exercise 1
1. action
2. martial arts
3. western
4. animated
5. thriller
6. science fiction
7. drama
8. comedy
9. horror
10. musical

Vocabulary, Exercise 2
1. thriller
2. martial arts
3. animated film
4. drama
5. science fiction
6. westerns
7. musical
8. horror
9. action
10. comedies

Grammar, Exercise 3
1. Sebastian lives in Brazil, and Silvia does too. Sebastian lives in Brazil, and so does Silvia.
2. Inez will visit New York in the winter, and so will Sebastian. Inez will visit New York in the winter, and Sebastian will, too.
3. Silvia has bought a car recently, and so has Mi-sook. Silvia has bought a car recently, and Mi-sook has, too.
4. Sebastian can speak Portuguese, and Silvia can, too. Sebastian can speak Portuguese, and so can Silvia.
5. Inez can't play any instrument, and neither can Sebastian. Inez can't play any instrument, and Sebastian can't either.
6. Mi-sook can play the violin, and so can Silvia. Mi-sook can play the violin, and Silvia can, too.

Listening, Exercise 4
The most expensive movie ever made. 3
Favorite action movie. 2
Common mistakes in movies. 4
All-time favorite movie. 1

Listening, Exercise 5
1. b   2. a   3. b   4. a

Pronunciation, Exercise 6
<u>a</u>ction movie	h<u>o</u>rror movie	thriller
<u>a</u>nimated	martial <u>a</u>rts film	western
comedy	musical	
drama	science fiction	

Unit 21

Vocabulary, Exercise 1
1. turn on the air conditioner
2. switch over to the movie channel
3. turn up the volume
4. turn off the lights
5. turn down my stereo

Vocabulary, Exercise 2
1. over   3. on   5. off   7. off
2. off   4. down 6. up

Grammar, Exercise 3
1. Could you please turn up the heat?
2. Could I switch over to the news now?
3. Would you mind turning the water on for me?
4. Could you turn off the gas?

Grammar, Exercise 4
1. Would you mind closing the window a little bit?
2. Can you speak more slowly?
3. Could you say that again?
4. Would you mind coming early tomorrow?
5. Would you mind helping me with my homework?

Listening, Exercise 5
1. c   2. b   3. a

Listening, Exercise 6
1. b   2. a   3. a

Pronunciation, Exercise 7
1. Would you   3. Could you
2. Would you   4. Could you

Unit 22

Vocabulary, Exercise 1
1. scam   3. shoplifting   5. theft
2. bank robbery   4. burglary   6. mugging

Vocabulary, Exercise 2
1. robbery   4. shoplifting   7. thief
2. robbed   5. shoplifters   8. burglar
3. robbers   6. theft   9. burglaries

Grammar, Exercise 3
1. walked   4. were stolen   7. escaped
2. stood   5. were valued   8. were caught
3. ran   6. were started   9. was raided

Grammar, Exercise 4
1. was stolen, ate
2. were given, turned, returned
3. were caught, was called
4. was given, didn't trust
5. were told, didn't have

Listening, Exercise 5
1. b   2. a   3. b

Listening, Exercise 6
1. The Mona Lisa was ~~created~~ **painted** by Leonardo da Vinci.
2. In 1911, painting was ~~taken~~ **stolen** from the museum.
3. Two years later, it was ~~sold~~ **offered** to an art dealer in Florence.
4. In fact, the theft was ~~carried out~~ **planned** by a con artist called Eduardo de Valfierno.
5. The Mona Lisa was ~~brought back~~ **returned** to the Louvre.

Pronunciation, Exercise 7
1. <u>How</u> were the <u>thieves</u> <u>caught</u>?
2. <u>When</u> was the <u>painting</u> <u>stolen</u>?
3. <u>Copies</u> of the <u>painting</u> were <u>made</u>.
4. The <u>copies</u> were <u>sold</u> to collectors.
5. The <u>original</u> was <u>offered</u> to a <u>dealer</u>.
6. The <u>painting</u> was <u>returned</u> to a museum.

Unit 23

Vocabulary, Exercise 1
1. part   3. off   5. up
2. a break   4. it easy 6. on

Vocabulary, Exercise 2
1. I love Latin music, so I'm going to take up salsa dancing.
2. My wife says I take on too many extra jobs at work, but it's really hard to say no to my boss.
3. Tomorrow Thomas and I are going to take part in a marathon to raise money for charity.
4. We don't have any plans for Saturday—we're just going to take it easy.

5. I'm going to take some time off from work so I can show my Brazilian friends around.
6. You've been working too hard lately. Why don't you stop and take a break?

Grammar, Exercise 3

1. to play / playing
2. to study / studying
3. playing
4. cooking
5. to go / going
6. to watch / watching
7. working
8. playing

Grammar, Exercise 4

Usually I don't mind ~~to do~~ **doing** my homework, but last night I was so sick of ~~do~~ **doing** homework that I decided to go out with George. He enjoys ~~to go~~ **going** to the movies, so I suggested a romantic comedy. But George said he hates to watch romantic movies and suggested an action movie instead. But I can't stand seeing so much violence, so finally we decided ~~seeing~~ **to see** that new Japanese animated film. We both really enjoyed ~~to watch~~ **watching** it, and we had a wonderful time.

Listening, Exercise 5

Decided to take the evening off
Can't stand exercising
Sick of running around the gym
Needs to take a break

Listening, Exercise 6

1. take, off
2. taking on
3. were, into
4. sick of running
5. taking it too seriously
6. take a break
7. taking it easy

Pronunciation, Exercise 7

1. stand playing, don't mind
2. hates watching sports, loves practicing
3. likes exercising, sometimes, needs, break

Unit 24

Vocabulary, Exercise 1

1. digital TV
2. scanner
3. computer
4. printer
5. DVD player
6. cell phone
7. digital camera
8. laptop computer

Vocabulary, Exercise 2

1. Digital TV
2. laptop computer
3. cell phone
4. scanner
5. digital camera
6. printers
7. DVD player
8. computer

Grammar, Exercise 3

1. that / which
2. who / that
3. where
4. that / which
5. where
6. who / that
7. that / which

Grammar, Exercise 4

I just read a book called *Technophobia*, ~~who~~ **which** was written by Dr. Linda Smith, a psychologist and computer programmer. Dr. Smith says that the word "technophobia" was first used in 1978 in Silicon Valley, California, ~~which~~ **where** many computer people work. Of course, people ~~which~~ **who/that** work with computers don't understand "technophobes," the people ~~which~~ **who/that** are afraid to use new technology.

But I understand what Dr. Smith is writing about because I have a friend **that [correct] / who** is a technophobe. She is very intelligent, but she can't deal with technology.

Dr. Smith says that technophobia is a problem ~~who~~ **that/which** affects many people. It prevents them from using technology ~~who~~ **that/which** could save them time and effort. But she also says technophobia is not hard to overcome. Dr. Smith gives many helpful tips in her book, ~~who~~ **which** can be purchased from her website.

Listening, Exercise 5

1. b
2. c

Listening, Exercise 6

1. where they produce
2. the parts of the picture that
3. of people who are, that are
4. where the service, a special box that

Pronunciation, Exercise 7

1. <u>cell</u> phone
2. com<u>pu</u>ter
3. <u>digital TV</u>
4. <u>DVD player</u>
5. <u>laptop</u>
6. <u>printer</u>
7. re<u>mote</u> con<u>trol</u>
8. <u>scanner</u>

Unit 25

Vocabulary, Exercise 1

1. g 2. i 3. d 4. b 5. h 6. a 7. f 8. c 9. e

Vocabulary, Exercise 2

1. got engaged
2. get along
3. get on each others' nerves
4. got upset
5. gotten over
6. get married
7. get divorced

Grammar, Exercise 3

1. it's a good idea for people to get married
2. It's wonderful for people to get married
3. it's a bad idea for people to make rushed decisions
4. It's crazy to think that you will get to know
5. It's wonderful to fall in love
6. it's absurd for anyone to think
7. it's not important to wait a long time

Grammar, Exercise 4

1. It's a good idea to let your parents help you choose your spouse.
2. It's wonderful that Beth and Scott are getting married!
3. It's crazy (It's a bad idea) for people to wait for "Mr. Right" or "Ms. Right" to come along.
4. It's a good idea (It's important) to know someone for at least three years before you get married.
5. It's absurd/not a good idea for couples to abandon their friends after getting married.
6. It's not important for couples to have the same hobbies and interests.

Listening, Exercise 5

wedding   get married   love   get divorced
marriage   husband   the married couple

Listening, Exercise 6

1. important for her to
2. a good idea to
3. crazy to
4. important for the families
5. absurd to

Pronunciation, Exercise 7

1. out together   3. got to   5. got married
2. get on   4. get along

Unit 26

Vocabulary, Exercise 1

1. bank statement   3. receive interest   5. borrowed
2. withdraw money   4. in the red

Vocabulary, Exercise 2

1. saving   5. interest   9. lend
2. borrowed   6. withdrawing   10. in the black
3. deposit   7. checking
4. savings   8. statement

Grammar, Exercise 3

1. The bank lent me the money.
2. They told us the news.
3. He brought me a present from Brazil.
4. Could you please show it to me?
5. The teacher explained our grammar to us.
6. You can always ask me for help.

Grammar, Exercise 4

1. The bank will pay 3 percent interest to you.
2. Please send the brochure to me.
3. I lent my sister $50.
4. He brings flowers to me every time we meet.
5. Can I get you some coffee?
6. My nephew drew me this picture.
7. He gave a great birthday present to me.
8. They offered a terrific deal to us.

Listening, Exercise 5

2, 3, 1

Listening, Exercise 6

provide, to you   offer you
lend you   give you
give you   promises you
bring, to you and your family

Pronunciation, Exercise 7

1. me   3. you   5. him
2. us   4. them   6. her

Unit 27

Vocabulary, Exercise 1

1. uses   3. waste   5. spend
2. save   4. save   6. wastes

Vocabulary, Exercise 2

1. Spend some time
2. Save your energy
3. using your time
4. wasting time
5. waste of energy, save you time

Grammar, Exercise 3

1. You should take more breaks.
2. You could try taking ten deep breaths.
3. You should not eat lunch at your desk.
4. You ought to do some exercise every day.
5. You could take a walk outdoors.
6. You should go out to dinner with a friend.
7. You could refuse to work overtime.

Grammar, Exercise 4

It sounds like you've been working way too hard. You ~~no should~~ **shouldn't** worry about being late for work—everyone is late for work sometimes. At work, you ought to ~~taking~~ **take** more breaks. You should ~~to make~~ **make** time for yourself throughout the day.

And another thing . . . maybe you ~~should~~ **shouldn't** drive your car so much. It's very nerve-wracking to commute during rush hour. Perhaps you could ~~trying~~ **try** walking to work instead.

And finally—you should never work past 7:00. You're so tired that everything takes twice as long then. Nothing is so important that it can't wait until tomorrow!

You know what? You should ~~to go~~ **go** away for the weekend. Have fun!

Listening, Exercise 5

a. 3   b. 2   c. 4   d. 1

Listening, Exercise 6

1. b   2. a   3. b   4. a   5. b

Pronunciation, Exercise 7

1. should   3. could   5. ought to
2. should   4. could   6. ought to

Unit 28

Vocabulary, Exercise 1

1. potluck dinner   3. DJ   5. live music
2. pianist   4. dinner

Vocabulary, Exercise 2

1. pianist   3. anniversary   5. graduation
2. barbecue   4. potluck dinner   6. DJ

Grammar, Exercise 3

1. If I knew his phone number, I'd call him.
2. She'd eat out tonight if she had enough money.
3. If Kim studied harder, she'd pass her exam.
4. If Jason exercised more, he'd be in better shape.
5. I'd go to the gym tonight if I weren't really tired.
6. If I had my credit card with me, I'd buy the jacket.

Grammar, Exercise 4

1. If he had three weeks off, he would take a trip to Korea.
2. If he had a sailboat, he would go sailing every weekend.
3. If he lived in the country, he would buy a horse.
4. If he got a salary increase, he would be very happy.

Listening, Exercise 5

1. They are celebrating their 100th edition.
2. You can win the party of a lifetime for someone you love.
3. The sponsors will pay for everything.

Listening, Exercise 6

1. Who would it   5. Where would you
2. When would you   6. What, would
3. What would you   7. How many, would you
4. What, would

Pronunciation, Exercise 7

1. would   3. I'd   5. We'd   7. We'd
2. would   4. wouldn't   6. They'd   8. would

PRONUNCIATION TABLE

(Adapted from the *Longman Dictionary of American English*)

VOWELS

Symbol	Key Word
i	beat, feed
ɪ	bit, did
eɪ	date, paid
ɛ	bet, bed
æ	bat, bad
ɑ	box, odd, father
ɔ	bought, dog
oʊ	boat, road
ʊ	book, good
u	boot, food, student
ʌ	but, mud, mother
ə	banana, among
ɚ	shirt, murder
aɪ	bite, cry, buy, eye
aʊ	about, how
ɔɪ	voice, boy
ɪr	beer
ɛr	bare
ɑr	bar
ɔr	door
ʊr	tour

CONSONANTS

Symbol	Key Word
p	pack, happy
b	back, rubber
t	tie
d	die
k	came, key, quick
g	game, guest
tʃ	church, nature, watch
dʒ	judge, general, major
f	fan, photograph
v	van
θ	thing, breath
ð	then, breathe
s	sip, city, psychology
z	zip, please, goes
ʃ	ship, machine, station, special, discussion
ʒ	measure, vision
h	hot, who
m	men, some
n	sun, know, pneumonia
ŋ	sung, ringing
w	wet, white
l	light, long
r	right, wrong
y	yes, use, music